GW00937869

Also by Howard Jackson

Mortal Shuffle

Innocent Mosquitoes -
From Liverpool to the backlands of Brazil

Both available early 2012

TREAT ME NICE

Elvis Presley, his music and the Frankenstein Creature

Howard Jackson

Treat Me Nice
2011

First edition - September 2011
Second edition - January 2012

Ackowledgments are at the end of the book
but a special thanks to Clive Bradley for
his support and encouragement.

Front and back cover and
artwork by Robin Castle.

Copyright © Howard Jackson 2011.

The moral right of the author has been asserted.

A CIP catalogue record for this book is
available from the British Library.

ISBN 978-1-907540-47-9

Printed and bound in Great Britain by
Anchor Print Group Limited.

Published by Anchor Print Group Limited
in association with Red Rattle Books.

www.howard-jackson.net

*Dedicated to the woman who bought
me my first rock and roll record*

My mother, Frances Jackson, 1922-2003

CONTENTS

THE TALE

Addiction

Is there anything better in American popular music than the Louis Armstrong version of 'Stardust'?

Armstrong is a suitable place to begin because he is a figure similar to Elvis, brilliant but, for a long time now, sneered at for being unfashionable. People remember the song, 'What A Wonderful World', ignore the jazz and dismiss him as too deferential and conformist. In the epic, TV documentary, 'Jazz', made by Ken Burns, there is a scene that quotes a journalist from the American South. The journalist remembered seeing Louis Armstrong for the first time and comparing what he saw to what he had been taught to believe in his Dixie home. After Louis, the journalist never saw black people in the same way again and he was never able to accept the racial superiority he had been promised as his birthright.

I am not an American. Neither was I, like the child murdered in the Frankenstein movie, sitting alone by the lake when I first heard Elvis but I was eight years old, a similar age to the victim. 'Hound Dog' was playing on a TV programme called 'The Jack Jackson Show'. The show always had a spot where a record was accompanied by lyrics on the screen and the TV audience was invited to sing along in their homes. The producers picked 'Hound Dog' because they thought it would be a clever joke to have the British population singing nonsense alongside an inarticulate creature who could only shout. I sang along and my parents shook their heads. In my bedroom, I carried on singing long enough to make myself hoarse and, the next day, I refused to go to school. Galvanised and stung, I was in no mood to face the village and I pretended I had a sore throat. Really, I needed to think about what I had heard. Like Captain Vere in 'Billy Budd', the Herman Melville story, 'I had caught him to my heart.'

After that song, like the journalist, I never thought about myself the same way again. The birthright had been redefined. The village was suddenly in a different place.

There was another Elvis occasion when I was twelve years old. I sat with my mother and watched her poke the fire.

'I have an insurance policy,' she said. 'It expires when you're sixteen. You can use it to buy a record player and treat yourself to some Elvis records.'

The gesture was appreciated but I found it inconceivable I would ever be sixteen. 'He probably won't be around by then. I might be fed up of him, then.'

My mother stared at the fire. My remarks had disappointed her. She poked the fire some more. 'Well, there will probably be somebody else, then, that you like.'

Many years later, she would remember the conversation and laugh.

When I was fourteen I read the novel, 'The Desolate Breed', by Borden Deal. This was a serious attempt to tell a story of a country music family in the American South. The book was dominated by the conflict between religion and music in that region. Towards the end of the book, the car of the family breaks down and the family is obliged to walk the highway. They meet a group of black musicians. As they play music together, the young son in the country music family responds to the music being played by his new acquaintances. The final few pages reveal that the young son becomes famous playing a different style of music. His music is heavily influenced by what he heard that day on the highway. I was amazed that someone, who was intelligent enough to write a book, could give Elvis and rock and roll any credit and understand it was a culmination of a tradition. It persuaded me, though, that what I liked had substance. The child by the lake was now loyal and committed.

The record player from my mother never did arrive. When I was sixteen I asked my mother about the insurance policy and she said the money had to be used for something else. I was a naive sixteen year old but I understood. By then, though, I was working part time and I could soon afford my own record player. I scrounged EPs and singles and bought the occasional LP and I had a collection by the time I went to University.

My career as a student unravelled badly and, just as this was happening, Elvis made his comeback. This was a difficult period and, while I floundered, Elvis and his music became a dangerous narcotic. The relationship with my father had always been complicated and I was not sure if my obsession was because Elvis represented something complex about masculinity and class which needed to be resolved, if

Elvis was actually a substitute father-figure, or if University had simply left me confused. But it may have even been more sad and desperate than any of this. Bruised and more remote from the village than before, I may have merely needed Elvis to win, to prove the superiority of people authentic and unspoilt, something to justify me, a young man narrowed by alienation, someone who envied those who could appreciate more easily what was around them.

Unfortunately, this was too much of a task for Elvis and he drifted into decline. Meanwhile, the bruised, young man recovered from the wreckage, found purpose and settled. I enjoyed listening to music that really belonged to another generation. I was criticised for not belonging to my own. Of course, despite what we tell ourselves, we all need a village. After a desperate search, I found mine in book stores and became interested in the America that existed below the Mason Dixon line. I was particularly interested in fiction about the American South and its weird, but relevant, mix of the modern and the medieval. I read everything by William Faulkner, Eudora Welty, Flannery O'Connor and Erskine Caldwell. Despite its racism, I persuaded myself that the American South included something decent that had been lost, that it had two sides. The dark side included persecution, cruelty and exploitation. The other had sweet moments of community, self-respect and innocence. I listened to a lot of American music - the blues, gospel, country, western swing and soul.

Throughout all the reading, I was obliged to absorb ideas that were new to me. Because the American South and Elvis represented certain tensions - individualism and community, Puritanism and sensuality, intolerance and compassion - I found I used Elvis as a thinking post to evaluate these ideas and others. I worried about how my thoughts so often depended on him.

Elvis worries others more than me. All the people who write passionately about Elvis are in conflict with the man, writers who resent what he denied them. Peter Guralnick is a blues purist who wanted Elvis to be a specialist, blues singer, Greil Marcus is a bohemian non-conformist who needed Elvis to exist supreme as a cultural revolutionary and humble me, who only wanted him to take his music as seriously as I did, is way behind. The frustration Elvis creates only adds to his power. If the mystery of waste creates disappointment, the puzzle is addictive especially to those who hope that solutions can compensate against their loss. I have been absorbed in the mystery of Elvis for most of my life.

In 1977, Elvis died and much more was revealed about his weakness and vulnerability. Two years later, I bought a decent road map and a book called 'Honky Tonkin' In The USA' and toured the American South, seeking out bars and various strands of American music. After a couple of weeks, I arrived at Memphis and the visits included Graceland, the famous American Sound, Sun and Stax recording studios and the infamous Lorraine Motel where Martin Luther King had been shot. At the motel, there were no visitors apart from me but the recording studios and Graceland were, of course, much different. Back then, visitors were not allowed into the house and I settled for taking photos of the graves and the music gates. Two men stood nearby. One was Sonny West, a man once employed by Elvis as helper and friend and who had appeared in Elvis documentaries. Sonny and the man next to him talked. The man next to Sonny had taken a car around Memphis to see if he liked it. The conversation irritated me. I drive but have no real interest in cars and what I hated about America most was how they relied on cars to make conversation. The English habit of using the weather is much more gracious and egalitarian. These two men talked as if they had authority, as if their pious materialism, informed by bogus technical authority, ennobled them. Not needing Elvis in the way I once had, there was no disillusionment but these friends of Elvis revealed limitations in him I knew I still side-stepped. I thought of the front of the Lorraine Motel where Martin Luther King had been shot and its empty forecourt.

I did, though, return to England with plenty of records and, inevitably, Elvis was included in these. I only visited Memphis on that one occasion and my interest in American society weakened dramatically during my fourth and last visit in 1982. By then, Ronald Reagan was in power. On TV, I watched one of his press conferences which was unedited and in full, inarticulate glory. I decided I would return only when a decent President had been elected. Although Obama makes the place more tempting, the return has yet to be arranged.

I am now quite old and books do not have the impact on me that they once did. There is no need now to use Elvis as my thinking post.

If anything, the traumas of youth helped prepare me for an uneventful existence. I often think of a scene in a casino in the classic film noir, 'Build My Gallows High.'

Robert Mitchum and Jane Greer sit next to a spinning, roulette wheel.

'That is no way to play,' says Mitchum.

'Why not?' says Greer.

'Because it isn't the way to win.'

'Is there a way to win?'

'There's a way to lose more slowly.'

My habits ensured I lost quite slowly.

One of those habits is listening to music. Apart from weekends, I listen to two or three hours of American music each evening, always diligently working through the thousand CDs from beginning to end. Such a system has its flaws because the weaker CDs of inferior artists receive the same attention as the classics by the greats. Two developments, though, occurred early. My habit is to listen to music and read at the same time. The exception is Elvis. Something always happens in his music to startle me and I am always obliged to put the book to one side. The routine progression would also be occasionally interrupted by an Elvis blitz and these blitzes of two or three evenings usually occurred after I had heard bad news about something.

He may not have been victorious in the battles that I wanted him to win but, for me, he remains different from the rest. Despite the disappointments, which at times have felt like betrayals, I enjoy his records as much as I ever did. Now, I expect his music to be there with me until the end.

Bela Lugosi understood the dependency on gratification as well as anyone and, as he said so memorably to visitors to his castle in the 1931 movie, 'Dracula', 'I bid you welcome.'

My name you already know. I am an Elvis addict.

The Tale

As early as 1840, after the novel 'Frankenstein' was transformed into a stage play, the name Frankenstein was wrongly assumed to belong to the creation rather than the creator. The plain explanation of this persistent misunderstanding is that the Creature dominates the story and no innocent man was ever likely to be called Frankenstein. The irony has significance. Shelley, who had misleadingly claimed she dreamt the name, used her novel to warn against hatred of those who were different. The audiences, who welcomed the Creature in the subsequent play and films, insisted on the opposite and demanded a monster. The fame and notoriety of her creation was supported by the prejudice Shelley thought she was undermining.

The Creature in the novel possesses curiosity, intellect and sensitivity but, for all his fine feelings and belief in his noble ambition, he is no innocent. It leaves him with extreme remorse but the need for violent vengeance exists. Readers of the novel are usually sympathetic because they discover the Creature is a talented man whose creator denies him authentic kinship and purpose. Those who know the Creature from only the Karloff movies, assume he is a monster. As Miranda Seymour explains, in her biography of Mary Shelley, 'dramatised versions had drained its life fluid while hugely increasing its fame'. If there was no more to the tale than this, it would correspond to the life and career of Elvis Presley, the creature once known as 'The Pelvis'.

The novel, 'Frankenstein', by Mary Shelley was first published in 1818. The full title is 'Frankenstein or The Modern Prometheus'. The Prometheus myth to which the title refers has the usual complicated history adored by classical scholars. Various versions exist and, within them, there are different scenarios and characters. The following account is basic but it suits the purpose of this book. Prometheus was the son of Iapitus by Clymene, one of the Oceanids. His mother was the generally well regarded goddess, Themis. Prometheus was a champion of mankind and he stole fire from Zeus by hiding it in a giant, fennel stalk.

Prometheus gave the fire to the mortals who were pleased because it had originally been stolen from them by Zeus. The god Zeus did not share the democratic sympathies of Prometheus and responded by having Prometheus chained to a rock where a great eagle attacked him and ate his liver. Each day, his liver would grow again and, each day, the eagle would return to eat his liver. Understandably, Prometheus was indignant because this is no fun. Eventually, Hercules arrived and killed the eagle with an arrow and freed Prometheus from his chains. The myth evolved further and, in the Greek Tragedy, 'Prometheus Unbound', by Aeschylus, Prometheus created life from clay and water. The introduction to the Wordsworth print of 'Frankenstein' claims, though, that this alternative myth is Roman and not Grecian. It is the version with Prometheus as the maker of mankind that inspired the Mary Shelley novel of 'Frankenstein'. Mary Shelley intended her book to be a warning against what modern man, lacking a connection to others, might do with his desire to invent, understand and control.

This is neither a book about Frankenstein nor the Prometheus myth. It is about Elvis Presley but there will be references to the novel when appropriate and this book will insist that both a curse and a complex betrayal did exist.

The Frankenstein myth, like that of Prometheus, has evolved and, within the novel and the movie adaptations, there are various elements that connect to the life of Elvis. These consist of the crude figure whose primitivism paradoxically inspires the future, the orthodox ideology that he offended, the ordinary villagers who became agitated by the myths that they created about the Creature and the mad scientist who, like Parker, failed to understand that he only brought the Creature into existence and that the Creature had independent life. The stage play added the willing assistants who failed to realise that the scientist they helped was mad rather than gifted. A century later, the 1931 movie transformed the doomed child beside the lake into someone other than the younger brother of Victor Frankenstein, someone less horrified and more trusting.

Two aspects of 'Frankenstein' and its relationship to Elvis merit immediate comment.

First, to keep the plot simple and to make him an agent of his own destruction, the Creature had to kill the child by the lake. There are different versions of this scene in the book and the movies and his culpability varies but the Creature is always capable of savage cruelty. In the Elvis story, the child by the lake not only exists but is infused with wonder at the sight of the exceptional creature. There was also more than one child and these children survived to become the fans. They constitute a separate story. Although Elvis was condemned for being uncouth by different generations in different ways and was always scorned by a large number of villagers, he, at least, had acclaim from the children by the lake. The Creature, unlike Elvis, was only hated by others.

After Elvis appeared by the lake, the children never fully understood their fabulous friend and why he could be so difficult. They defended him when they sometimes visited the village to meet those who were horrified but, unlike the other villagers, they did not want him vanquished, though, they were sometimes hurt by his indifference and destructive behaviour. Many needed an explanation of why they could be so drawn to such a difficult creature. Eventually, all these innocent children, sitting by the lake, grew and hardened. Soon, their obsession irritated the villagers who realised that these uncomprehending children had imagined an alternative creature. A more forgivable, complex and fabulous being now grew inside the spirits of the children.

Second, the Creature was severely handicapped by the crude, plastic surgery that existed in 1816. Although he had beautiful features, he was eight feet tall and his skin was stretched too tight across his face. Apart from the blind, he merely horrified. Elvis was considered handsome but the principle of maiming still exists. Early Elvis horrified with his sideburns and clothes and the later Elvis repulsed with his blown up body and white suits. There is a British TV version of 'Frankenstein', defiantly called 'The True Story', which featured a handsome actor called Michael Sarrazin as the Creature. The tale is told differently but the ending is still tragic. The unfulfilled need for authenticity and authority undermines the privilege gained by his beauty. The primitive violence of the handsome man still colludes with his destruction. Both versions, the handsome and maimed creations, apply to Elvis.

Of course, for many, the notion that Elvis was cursed is ludicrous. He became rich and famous and had a sex life that many men only dream about. Fans of soul and blues will argue he benefited disproportionately, that he was overestimated while authentic, black talents were ignored. They think of him not as the Creature but Zeus, the first to steal their fire. But, just like the handsome actor in the revisionist version of 'Frankenstein', none of this precludes him being cursed. Indeed, these beliefs once established became part of his curse. Whether the beliefs were true or not, it enabled more people to swell the already hostile crowd, to add to the number of irritated villagers waving their torches against a restless sky. Elvis was accused of being racist yet his friends insisted this was not true. As the Creature said, 'where they ought to see a feeling and kind friend they beheld only a detestable monster.'

If the early success and good fortune of Elvis distinguished him from the Creature, the story of Elvis has a similar, gloomy ending caused by neglect or a failure to nurture. Not only was Elvis cursed, he knew it and, believing that he had forfeited his opportunity for worth and grace, he wasted himself into an early death at forty two. As Mary Shelley wrote in her novel, 'But now I was finished, the beauty of the dream vanished, and breathless horror and disgust filled my heart.' In such circumstances, the notion of a curse should more than suffice for an alternative explanation of Elvis Presley, the creature we are obliged to build inside us. If there will be more than one reference to Frankenstein, the exact meaning of Prometheus can be left to the classical scholars to debate. This Elvis book has ambitions far less lofty.

Although this enquiry cannot ignore evidence entirely, it is not the work of a journalist. I am grateful for its existence but the narrative of Elvis has been exhausted. There are plenty of examples of how most of the witnesses, like the villagers who point and shout, have now become unreliable with age. The witnesses say what they want to believe or sometimes have half-heard. They too often remember what they want to make sense and not what happened. My ambition, though, remains considerable. The hope is to persuade others to think differently about Elvis, to reveal something about what makes him and his story significant for all of us and for this child by the lake, in particular.

History

The narrative of the novel, 'Frankenstein', evokes quite early the uncertainty of the destiny of the doomed creation. What would have happened if the Creature had talked longer with the blind man before his family arrived? Would the Creature have been able to agree a strategy with the sympathetic, blind man that would have integrated him successfully into his family? Perhaps, Victor Frankenstein made the tragedy inevitable when he too easily assumed that the mate the Creature wanted him to create would add to the destruction. If he had not resisted creating the mate, could they all have lived happily ever afterwards? Well, they did not. Instead, the well-read creature became a wretch and heart rending tragedy prevailed.

For many, the history of Elvis now means the Peter Guralnick books, 'Last Train To Memphis' and 'Careless Love'. Guralnick may have failed to discover what Gerard Manley Hopkins described as 'the inwardness of what happened' but he has through relentless detail provided what are regarded as the undisputed facts.

We remain, though, as uncertain as ever. There is no intention to be unkind to Guralnick. He is a fine author and 'Sweet Soul Music', his account of how black, American, soul music came to dominate popular culture, should be rated as the best book by an American, popular-music critic. What did surprise, in his book on American soul music, though, was his unqualified admiration for the sometimes squalid, sideline, entrepreneurial activities of the great, soul singer, Solomon Burke. Worship of the confident hustler appears to be a key constant in the nature of Guralnick. This personality trait inevitably leads him to overrate the manager of Elvis, a flawed Dutchman with the fake name of Thomas Parker, the mad Frankenstein in our tale.

Guralnick must have collected more information on Elvis than anyone but his overestimation of the Parker contribution is perhaps rooted in being exposed to Elvis at too tender an age. He may have been shocked by the appearance of the creature and was never able to obtain the required sympathy for the man that emerged later. The lonely individual, who possessed to paraphrase Shelley a heart fashioned to be susceptible to love and sympathy and to vice and hatred when wrenched by misery, was not the hero Guralnick wanted.

As the critic, Dave Marsh, realised, Robert Johnson is actually what Guralnick wanted Elvis to be. If Elvis had imitated the blues musician, Johnson, he would have been a pure, folk hero that appeared in Memphis in 1954 and who died in 1956 just before he signed the RCA recording contract. That way, he would have recorded only classic, roots music and would have left an unblemished legacy before dying.

Recently, Peter Gurlanick has become more open minded but he is still too quick to dismiss what he regards as inauthentic. There is an irony here. These are also my prejudices. I would have preferred Elvis from 1960 to have devoted himself to blues, gospel and jazz, spiced with the odd country tune. Not only would it have improved his recording catalogue, it might have saved jazz for commercial music and integrated it back into the popular, regional cuisine to which it belongs. Jerry Wexler, who, back in 1956, wanted to sign Elvis for Atlantic records, may have had a similar vision. He had the same ambition for Ray Charles and it worked until 1960 when Ray Charles rejected it and left Atlantic records for ABC. But Elvis was burdened with being pretty and having a tone deaf crook for a manager. Soon, he was signed to a record company that made popular music in the same way that McDonalds prepare food and exiled to a cynical Hollywood ready to exploit. The Jerry Wexler option was never likely to be realised. But what we want and what we have are always different and, as time moves on, we invariably appreciate more what we had. Now, we listen to elements within the music of Elvis we could barely tolerate when he was alive.

Why? He no longer breathes and that helps. Fans no longer listen hoping he will transform himself into their expectations. Paul Simpson says, in his 'Rough Guide To Elvis', that Guralnick makes the call too often against Elvis. Peter Guralnick insists that Parker had honourable concerns and was right to placate the anxious villagers. He forgives Parker for needing to make the creature presentable to those he made angry and is convinced that this is what the creature wanted as well. Guralnick is not persuaded by what the defenders of the creature plead.

He is not convinced by their 'eloquence and powers of expression' and believes Elvis, like the Creature, always wanted more than just the female mate and kinship that he alleged. He wanted fame and money. Well, it is complicated. We need to look at the past differently.

To the relief of some but the disappointment of others, Elvis died on August 16 1977. August 16 is the date he left for Hollywood in 1956 and it can be argued that his destruction is defined by these two coincidental dates, the beginning of the end and the result.

In the final years, his behaviour was increasingly erratic and unpredictable but, after his death, the career continued. Once his ex-wife, Priscilla, had control of his estate, his material was finally organised sensibly. Three box sets were released to represent the three decades his career covered. The collections made apparent that Elvis Presley produced music in each decade that was beyond him in each of the other decades. He did decline but bluesman BB King was right. Elvis grew as well. The despair and raw emotion of his music in the seventies may not be as appealing as the energy and optimism in his early music but all periods are essential and the differences that do exist between the decades actually extend his achievements. Because his music exists as proof of an extraordinary talent. What made the creature disturbing, made him great.

Posthumous box sets were also produced of his gospel material and his live performances in Las Vegas. Young rock critics who had assumed that Elvis had been buried in cabaret throughout the seventies were astounded by the quality of the material. The reviews in the music magazines of the 'Live In Las Vegas' box set were all five star. Around the turn of the century, Elvis with the aid of technology reunited with his band, back up singers and orchestra leader. The show made worldwide appearances. The millionth ticket for these concerts was sold some time ago. The scientists had discovered a formula which allowed the broken creature to be galvanised into action whenever needed.

Although his Frankenstein had now died alone, discredited and miserable, the creature lived again. Despite this success and adjusted acclaim, the critical fraternity was still divided. Many critics were uncomfortable with a performer who they thought could only be regarded as an entertainer, the man who refused to provide comment on his community or society. Today, he is a figure of fun for many. Now they are safe, the horror in the village has turned into laughter.

Elvis became an icon in the years, 1956-1958. In these two years, Elvis made four movies, dominated the record charts in a way never previously known and became an international star. He made a lot of money. He also created many classic records but his output was enhanced because he already had a two year old back catalogue from his time at Sun and this was cleverly integrated into the impressive collection of records he produced for RCA. This helped an astonishing talent to become bewilderingly marvellous.

This confusion may have contributed to people assuming he was a revolutionary. The way he absorbed both black music and culture and acted uninhibitedly on stage was not considered becoming. He belched, spat his chewing gum into the audience and told crude jokes. In his stage act, he used his body as a woman, seductively. This was described as outrageous sex but it was worse because he confused gender. Although white musicians in the South had always adapted or stolen black music, they had been careful to emphasise their country roots. At this time, there was a saying in country music, 'If you want to sound like a nigger, you wear a cowboy hat.' Rather than wear a cowboy hat, Elvis dressed flamboyantly and he bought his clothes from Lanskys in Beale Street. Because of the previous tradition in American music, his unusual wardrobe and appearance had for some people significance equal to the music. Not everybody was impressed and his sideburns were condemned.

Within the South, black and white musicians had always exchanged ideas. In the twenties, some hillbilly tunes were indistinguishable from the black music of the time. In the forties, country musicians, like Bob Wills, borrowed heavily from jazz and blues and created a whole genre called Western Swing. There had also been a clear link between American pop and rhythm and blues which could be heard in the music of Hoagy Carmichael, Peggy Lee, Frank Sinatra and others. Although the records by Elvis had a distinct sound, they did not smooth out the blues roots. Instead, he often increased the tempo and added unrestrained, vocal inflections. This was very different from how Peggy Lee and Frank Sinatra performed the odd, regional rhythm and blues hit that they borrowed or stole for the national market.

He had no requirement for others to be like him. To quote the Creature, 'I saw and heard of none like me.'

Two years before scandalising America, Elvis had appeared at Sun recording studios in 1954. He was dressed oddly and wore colourful clothes and had hair unusually long. He was apart from others but gave his exclusion a specific meaning by adopting the clothes of the most obvious group of outsiders in town, the black community. Despite this challenging action, he was at ease with the neighbours that excluded him. He appeared to have no need to confront in other ways his community. He was behaving differently rather than rebelling.

When he discussed with Sam Phillips at Sun what he wanted to record Elvis suggested gospel music and ballads. He presented himself as a singer-songwriter and had several songs that he had written himself. (This information was revealed by Sam in the TV, pop documentary, 'All My Loving'.) Sam was not impressed with the written material but Sam was not especially keen to record gospel tunes. He teamed Elvis with guitarist, Scotty Moore, and bassist, Bill Black. They recorded 'That's All Right' and Elvis became a regional hit in the South. The material he recorded in the next two years was exceptional but there was already a hint of unevenness, one or two mawkish ballads appeared and his up-tempo versions of 'Just Because' and 'I Don't Care If The Sun Don't Shine', although remarkable, were not as fluent as the other Sun classics. Elvis was unusual because he made his first hit record before he appeared professionally on stage. His initial appearances were brief; in his first professional, stage performance, Elvis sang two songs and repeated the second as an encore. The appearances provoked reaction but it was only when he had developed his half-hour act that people realised he was a natural and exceptional stage performer. Thomas Parker appeared and Elvis signed a contract for the galvaniser to be his manager. Sam Phillips sold the recording contract to RCA. Atlantic Records could not match their bid. One of the great mysteries of American music is what would have happened if Elvis had signed for Atlantic. Critics and fans have asked would he have made better music, would he have been as famous and, even, would America now be a different place.

In 1958, Elvis was drafted into the Army. He was now a national celebrity but widely criticised and scorned. He returned in two years.

The early signs were good. The dazzling recording session, on his return, delivered some great singles and a marvellous album, 'Elvis Is Back'. Eight years later, he was in trouble and needed to rescue his career.

The TV comeback in 1968 revealed an Elvis determined to show his worth. This was followed by two recording sessions in Memphis, a triumphant return to live performance and a marathon, recording session in Nashville. He was again brilliant but he was unable to deliver the consistency he managed when younger. But, in this brief period from 1969 to 1970, Elvis recorded enough material for two classic albums and two very good albums. Unfortunately, his record company, RCA, mishandled the material and, instead of editing the records responsibly, they produced undistinguished albums to complement the classic albums, 'From Elvis In Memphis' and 'Elvis Country'. In 1971, Elvis was featured in the documentary, 'That's The Way It Is'. This was based on his performances in Las Vegas in 1970. Elvis looked and sounded good and his stage show was original and had impressive highlights.

Despite his efforts, his talent and his success, it was also clear that the movies had taken too big a toll on his career. Many critics and music fans found it impossible to forgive what had happened. The music scene had also changed. He improved his record sales and was able to fill stadia with his concerts but he was now far from modern or dominant. As he did in the fifties, Elvis revealed a split in American society but his past association with Hollywood, his roots in the American South and his unfashionable but loyal, white, working class audience meant that this time he was identified with the conservative of America.

This social split in America and the drift away from American tradition were revealed well in another movie documentary. The film, 'Elvis On Tour', shows Elvis in performance in April 1972. This time, he was not in Las Vegas but in the heartland of a complicated, uncertain America. The movie won awards because of the subtle social points it made about a changing society. Elvis, though, no longer looked and sounded as good as he did in 1970 in the earlier documentary. The decline had been sudden and significant. His breath control had deteriorated and he was also in the grip of an eating disorder and was unable to control his weight. What went wrong? Perhaps he brooded on his memories.

After his return from the Army, the early films were mixed and not totally reprehensible but the music in the movies was much smoother than his normal music. Elvis delivered initially with panache the musical froth that these movies contained. In the next three years, he returned to the recording studio several times to make some non-movie music and he recorded some decent material and some classics but he was not as brilliant, as daring or as consistent as he had been in that first recording session after his return from the Army. It also became clear that there was pressure from his management and recording company to record material that would have wider appeal, music which would be more consistent with the songs in his movie soundtracks which were proving to be more popular than his studio albums. Elvis willingly responded to this pressure. Initially, the change of style did not cause his career to suffer and the tamer Elvis won over critics who had been previously hostile. After the success of the film, 'Blue Hawaii', the formula became established and the musicals followed each other, appearing three times a year. Meanwhile, Parker, his manager, had established song-writing deals to maximise publishing royalties. Unfortunately, the movies deteriorated as fast as their budgets were reduced. People complained that the movie songs were poor but it was obvious to anyone interested that Elvis was not making the effort he had done previously. The decline within Elvis was most apparent after 1962. His performances, from this point, were often inferior and, though the movie material was now frequently inadequate, he often, but not always, wasted the decent material that did exist.

What had previously been a sensible formula, or a sensible response from a management team only interested in making money, now appeared self-destructive and stubborn. The studio album that he recorded in 1963, his fourth since leaving the Army, was poorer than the previous studio albums but better than his movie material. It was never released because his manager wanted the movie soundtracks to dominate. The songs from the unreleased album were used to provide bonus selections for the movie albums. Between 1964 and 1968, his visits to the studios to record non-movie material were sparse but in this period he made an attempt to record authentic and personal material. In 1966, in the middle of these brief visits to the recording studios, he recorded a superb, gospel album, 'How Great Thou Art'. When the record was released it was somehow both acclaimed and ignored. Despite the infrequent visits, he produced enough records to warrant an additional, excellent, fifteen track album that would have qualified as one of his best. Again, this album was never released and, once more, the songs were used as filler for movie albums.

His memories of these events may or may not have precipitated the sudden deterioration exposed in the 1971 movie, 'Elvis On Tour'. In 1973, he performed in a show from Hawaii that was broadcast worldwide. He delivered an efficient rather than an inspired show but he was having difficulties with his physical and mental health and his prescription-drug dependency. Again, his appearances in the studio had become infrequent and he was often prepared to settle for performances and material that were for him below standard. The development of the singer-songwriter in popular music, and the insistence of his manager on the previous publishing deals, meant that the material available was often awful. The songs he recorded changed significantly to include many bleak ballads about romantic failure. The voice had deteriorated. But not all the songs were awful and, although he was slipshod in his approach, he, at least, made the effort he withheld from the movie material. There were many individual records which could be enjoyed. Unfortunately, his record company had no editing skills and failed to organise the output of an obviously struggling individual to provide one decent album a year. This could have been achieved in the more difficult years by utilising his concert material. Instead, true to the spirit of McDonalds, they released everything and ensured that all his albums from 1971 were mediocre.

In the novel, 'Frankenstein', the Creature was unable to establish any intimacy with the De Lacy family in the forest. Although Elvis was more fortunate and enjoyed fame and wealth, his glory had only been intermittent. He had been unable to sustain intimacy with a creative family for long enough to achieve real fulfilment.

Before any of this tragedy happened, Elvis had been born in 1935 to poor parents in Mississippi. They lived in a one room cabin built by his father after he had secured a $180 loan. The cabin had no electricity and an outside toilet. Early photographs of Elvis at school were revealing because he was dressed in a boiler suit. He was the only child to wear such clothing and it was not because he was being a fashion icon. The boiler suit belonged to earlier times. If he was not the poorest in the class, he looked it. In his early teens, Elvis delivered groceries for black, truck driver, John Allen Cooke, who later, said 'The Presleys always liked the blacks and were always on our side.' A white neighbour confirmed, 'They'd better have been. They would have starved without them.' Elvis had found his equivalent to the De Lacy family in 'Frankenstein' and, like the Creature, he learnt his ways by observing them.

Recently, his ex-wife and daughter sold the estate. The behaviour of the new owning company was less than impressive. They have been keen to recycle the romantic ballads which they think have wide appeal. But Elvis continues to entertain and, for the curious and resolute, the full catalogue still exists to enthral, to provide both pleasure and irritation. The fans, though, remember how he was pulled away from the people who were capable of providing sustained nurture. They know what did and can happen. Although, now, nothing exists but memories they continue to fret.

Of course, another day and another draft and something different would have emerged, different details would have been revealed and some of the points made above would have been ignored. For instance, this brief history uses the word respond to describe the participation of Elvis in his change of direction in the early sixties. Change this word to cooperate and a different scenario emerges. Elvis suddenly becomes much more complicit in the developments but there is hardly any difference between the two words

Because it focuses on the career, there is no reference to the death of his mother and whether this really did weaken him and his faith in his destiny. It also avoids details that may or may not have significance. His hairdresser, Larry Geller, implies that the final decline of Elvis began in 1967 when Parker asserted increased control over the personal life of Elvis. If this is the case, the famous comeback and brief renaissance actually masked the uninterrupted deterioration that had begun earlier. Not mentioned is that neither Parker nor his management team appeared especially concerned about the decline in his performances in the sixties and seventies. Neither, does it make clear how Elvis reacted to diminished powers. Even in this abridged account, the mystery requires a partial investigation.

The recent explanation by Guralnick is that Elvis was plagued by doubt and depression after his mother died and he was only able to overcome these emotional handicaps when inspired by exceptional circumstances like his return from the Army or when he needed to make a comeback. Put crudely, and Guralnick is never this explicit, Elvis let his career slide twice, from 1961 to 1968 and from 1971 to 1977. The first time this happened, he was offered an escape route which consisted of the 'TV Special' and the Memphis recordings sessions with Chips Moman. The second time, the slide was much more dramatic and self-destructive and, this time, Elvis exhausted his options, his talent, and, finally, himself. The manager, like Frankenstein or the more sympathetic Frankenstein that emerged in the second 1831 version of the novel by Shelley, had good intentions and did his best in difficult circumstances. Even during those long periods when he lacked interest, Elvis always earned a lot of money. In fact, he generated more income in the seventies decade than he managed in the others. The manager negotiated decent deals and he kept at bay a record company that was increasingly dissatisfied with a reluctant performer. Parker did this by supplementing studio material with live concerts and by ensuring that record producer, Felton Jarvis, mopped up whatever studio vocals he could and delivered them to the record company as completed takes. Not only does this version exonerate the manager, it avoids criticism of the record label.

Undoubtedly, Elvis was strange and flawed and fame and events in his personal life weakened him. He was culpable which is important because it was his talent and he had the greatest responsibility of all. Whichever way we want to interpret the novel by Shelley, the alienated Creature killed people. But that tale and this requires careful evaluation to understand not only the responsibility of the various participants but the factors behind the doubt, destructiveness and depression that infected Elvis and the Creature. For Elvis, it has been too easily assumed that mother dies and, later, wife departs and, bang, there goes another gifted man. Perhaps, Elvis and his mother were mutually devoted but, according to P J Proby, Elvis hated beer drinking. Proby assumed Elvis was reacting to his father but it was Gladys who was the beer drinker and the son neither approved of the drinking nor her habit of keeping the bottle in the brown bag while she sipped. Equally, it is assumed Gladys collapsed because the fame of Elvis took him away from her. But, when

Elvis became famous, Gladys was left with problems in her marriage. She was fat whilst her husband Vernon was now rich, still handsome and in a position to indulge his eye for other women.

Jerry Schilling was another paid employee of Elvis. Of the group known as the Memphis Mafia, he is one of the most thoughtful. His view is that a great, creative talent was destroyed by short-sighted management. More likely, is that the depression was probably double headed, the result of both personal and professional disappointments.

Inevitably, chance or as Shelley described it, 'the angel of destruction', dominates throughout the life of Elvis as it does with the Creature. At Sun Records, Elvis found his equivalent to the blind man and the family in the forest. This family could have been replaced easily by Jerry Wexler at Atlantic, a creator who was not repulsed by the appearance of the creature. Wexler may not have prevented the final self-destruction, which on this occasion did not occur on a self-built, funeral pyre in the icy, Northern wastes, but he would not have accepted the desire of the creature to spend so much of his short existence in hiding. Wexler was a mature individual, the equal of the father of Frankenstein, a man who gave 'indefatigable attention to public business.' When the father says to Frankenstein, 'excessive sorrow prevents improvement or even the discharge of daily usefulness', he is forbidding extended introspection. Surely, Wexler would have done the same.

Elvis let himself down but others did fail him, especially, the ones he could not shake away. Today, Elvis is owned by two companies. One takes profits from the image and marketing and the other from the music. In an odd way, little has changed. The choice of Parker, the decision to sign with RCA, the deals with Hollywood and Vegas, the premature death of the mother and the change in fashion and what was happening elsewhere in the village, all contributed to a tragedy that may have been avoided. How much of Elvis was either created or destroyed by others and, in particular, his own Frankenstein will be examined later.

An alternative history - The Lost Episode Of Space Fleet 35C

The American Nazis stand outside the huge entrance to Madison Square Garden. There are no more than a dozen but they have trampled away a large patch of snow. Everywhere else is white. All the Nazis are dressed in uniform, all wear hats and all carry huge flags with Nazi insignia. They distribute leaflets that consist of crude headlines that always include somewhere the word white. The leaflets have smudged photographs of an idealised, pastoral America. The Nazis shout at the people walking into the Garden and the police remind them to be quiet. The police threaten the Nazis with their truncheons and, occasionally, the police dogs bark but nobody is touched. Above them, a huge sign advertises the appearance at Madison Square Garden of Senator Martin Luther King.

Space Fleet Admiral Jim Word and his Rubiad engineer, Etag, have been in New York for the last two weeks. All that time, the thick snow has been permanent and Admiral Jim Word has lost some of his flab because of the cold. Etag has bemoaned constantly the crude technology available and has used this as an excuse to make brief, return trips to the waiting Space Fleet 35C. This has caused friction between the two men. Both men wear woollen hats pulled down over their ears and they look older than they do in the spaceship. Admiral Jim Word and Etag follow three well-dressed men towards the entrance.

The three men they follow are Stephen Sondheim, Leonard Bernstein and Elvis Presley. Bernstein grins at others in the crowd and sometimes waves. Sondheim laughs and giggles. His bemused eyes welcome the flattery and hint he may begin a conversation with one of the adoring strangers. Elvis occasionally and sheepishly smiles at a face that catches his eyes.

Elvis talks to Sondheim. 'You don't think I was out of my depth?'

'No,' says Sondheim. 'Sweeney Todd is a perfect part for you. My God, you make it all sound so musical. Why do you think everybody has acclaimed you?'

'I don't understand all the dark motivation.'

Sondheim brushes the face of Elvis with the tip of his finger. Elvis does not pull away but he does not respond to the platonic gesture. He is married to the actress, Tuesday Weld, has two daughters and, for the five years of his marriage, he has usually been faithful. Since he arrived in New York ten years earlier, he has had one sexual encounter with a gay friend. It happened before he met his wife when he was poor and convinced he would fail. The gay encounter was both physically and emotionally painful. The gay friend made unforgiving and cruel remarks and Elvis resolved at that point to restrict himself to the female form.

'Well, I did my best,' says Sondheim. 'The motivation in 'Sweeney Todd' is not as developed as it could have been. I am not a kidder, Elvis. I know my limitations and I know the weaknesses of others. You have modest acting ability but you can convey innocence and naive integrity. You are also convincingly violent. That is all the part needs.'

'You mean I can play stupid.'

'No, I do not. But stupid did Marlon no harm.' Sondheim puts a hand up to stop Elvis interrupting. 'No, I don't think you're ready for Stanley Kowalski. I will say to you what my agent said to me after my first effort. You have enough and you will improve.'

The three men stop by the Nazis who all look sour and arrogant. Admiral Jim Word and Etag draw close to the three men.

With a glance of his eyes, Sondheim refuses a leaflet.

'Hell,' says Elvis, 'this is worse than the Klan.'

Bernstein takes a leaflet and says, 'Six million and still no regrets.'

'No, sir,' says one of the Nazis. The others flash the salute.

Bernstein raises a fist and Elvis stands as if ready. The policemen nudge the three men forward. While Bernstein shakes his head and mutters loudly, Elvis bites his lip.

The three men walk past the Nazis and wait in the crowded foyer of Madison Square Garden. Inside, the people smile and acknowledge the famous trio. Stephen Sondheim sees someone he knows.

Sondheim says to Elvis and Bernstein. 'Oh, look, my favourite critic. I have to say hello or he will carry a grudge until the next encounter.'

Elvis and Bernstein watch Sondheim on the other side of the foyer pump hands with the critic. Admiral Jim Word and Etag move up close to listen to Elvis and Bernstein.

'The Nazis are doing King a favour,' says Bernstein. 'Even the self-serving have to accept he has right on his side.'

'Not every racist is a Nazi,' says Elvis. 'I grew up with all kinds of racists, the gentle and the nasty. You wouldn't believe.' He pauses and grins. 'But I still miss Memphis.'

'New York has been good for you, Elvis.'

'I know that, Mr Bernstein.'

'I told you we'd make a sophisticate of you.'

'You've been everything.'

'Not just me. Working in the theatre was what you needed. Intense rehearsals every day are what keep you alert. '

'I hear insights when we rehearse and, it's weird, some of them are my own. That's what I like most.

'I said it would transform you. Has your mother settled in New York?'

'It's taken time. Tuesday is attentive and patient. But Mom loves the opera here. I take her when I can. In the beginning, the opera and attending my rehearsals was what she lived for. But, these days, she never watches me working.'

Etag raises a quizzical eyebrow at Admiral Jim Word who shrugs. They continue to listen.

'Your father?' says Bernstein.

'I haven't seen him for some time.' Elvis looks away. 'He has a young wife and a big home. He has what he needs.'

'Did you take your mother to see 'Peter Grimes'?

'Mm,' says Elvis. 'I asked her if she liked it. She said only once in a while and grinned. I think that stuff is way beyond me. 'Sweeney Todd' is my limit.'

'If it is, it's only for the moment, Elvis. I have some news we will discuss properly later. I spoke to Stephen and we think I should adapt my next musical for you.' Bernstein nods his head before Elvis can interrupt. 'It is about a Southern preacher who loses his temper and kills a man with his fist. He serves a short time in prison and, when he is released, he forms a small church. Because he is notorious, he only attracts eccentrics but his small church represents a unity between black and white. I will use some familiar, gospel tunes plus some of my own. If it suits you, I will ask Stephen to help with the lyrics. It would be irresponsible for us not to respond to what is happening with King. I know it is not your kind of music but you are a Memphis boy.'

Elvis grins and, behind his shoulder, Admiral Jim Word frowns. Etag checks the Rubiad receiver on his wrist for any news about his latest demands for equipment.

Elvis says, 'Mr Bernstein, see that man between Sam Cooke and Ray Charles.'

'I see a stout man in a large hat, a man smoking a cigar?'

'He calls himself Colonel Parker. I never told anyone in New York but I made a couple of records in Memphis. They never did get played. Sam Phillips, my record producer, said his cousin, Dewey, would launch them but Dewey was knifed and killed on Beale Street the day before my first record was released. Parker came and saw my third show and said. 'Boy, I don't know if you can sing or not but what I do know is that you don't have a hit and that this country is not the same since Senator King. Black music by black people is what America wants to hear and, if I am right, King will make President and I will become a millionaire.' Afterwards, I spoke to Sam Phillips and he agreed with Parker. 'You have to do something serious with those octaves, Elvis,' he said. So, I came to New York.'

'Just like that?' says Bernstein.

'I was never going to be a country singer. I arrived in New York and gave myself three months of auditioning. I was lucky. I thought musicals would let me act. If I could do a little of both, I might get by.'

'You've done more than that, Elvis.'

'My dreams have come true.'

'You don't wish you were singing rhythm and blues and worshipped by all like Ray Charles and Sam Cooke?'

'No, I like stage musicals. I wouldn't want to just have to sing all the time like those guys.'

'They make more money.'

'I make plenty of money. More than I ever imagined.'

'Would you be comfortable singing Southern material in my musical? Be honest with me.'

'Hell, Mr Bernstein,' says Elvis. 'I was singing that shit when I was six years old.'

The two men laugh and walk into the auditorium.

Space Admiral Jim Word and Etag stand still and exchange puzzled looks.

'I am confused,' says Word. 'This is not what I read in the history books.'

Etag chews his lips a second. He has become weary of these repeated explanations to his Admiral of the paradise of infinity and parallel universes.

'This is New York, Jim, but not as we know it. In this America, Martin Luther King has appeared earlier and the Civil Rights movement has dominated popular music before Elvis could make his reputation.'

'The death of Dewey Phillips is significant. Didn't he play the first record of Elvis all night?'

'Exactly, Jim, if Elvis had had that regional hit when he met Parker, then Parker may have not been seduced by the commercial potential of black music. Is Elvis in New York because of the influence of a great man, Martin Luther King, or the intervention of a low life assassin?'

'You mean the random individual who determines history?'

'That is not quite what I mean,' says Etag. He hides his grin.

'Do you think King will make President in this world?' says Word.

'I hope we are not here long enough to find out.' Etag shivers and his ears wiggle under his woollen hat. 'Why not? Elvis is sophisticated and content here. Anything is possible in the paradise of infinity.'

THE TALENT AND
THE TALENTED

THE TALENT AND THE TALENTED

The limitations of Elvis Presley

Ultimately, we are obliged to disapprove of the Creature. Four deaths, like twenty nine movies, two Christmas albums and the worst ballads, dissipate sympathy. Nobody, though, should deny the sadness of that final scene in the novel when the Creature 'to seek the most northern extremity of the globe' mounts his ice-raft and 'is soon borne away by the waves and lost in darkness and distance.' Elvis and the Creature became immortal because they were something other than monsters. They had unused potential and they had been refused simple aspirations, worth and respect. At the end of the novel, the Creature claims, 'I shall ascend my funeral pile triumphantly.' Despite the darkness and distance, we have no doubts that this will happen. Elvis died on the toilet but this is an irrelevant detail. Both creatures ended their lives as poignant and undermined giants. The Creature was strong and defiant at the tip of the planet and Elvis was mourned by those who had never recovered from being dazzled at the edge of the lake. Their limitations, though, cannot be denied.

It is 1976. Sonny West holds his hand open in front of an over-excited, press conference. He is there to publicise the book, 'What Happened'. The book is a tell-all revelation of the dark side of Elvis. The press conference has become an attempt by the three authors to justify their betrayal of their ex-boss. Sonny West keeps his open palm in the air.

'He had it all.' He stares at his hand as if he is holding something important in his palm. 'He had it all. He had everything.'

Prior to this press conference, the writer Greil Marcus had, in his book, 'Mystery Train', imagined Elvis on stage singing the Bob Dylan song, 'I Threw It All Away.'

Both men in their different ways assumed a talent without limits. The uncomplicated West thinks he was friends with Superman whilst the intellectual Marcus is bewildered by a musician who has insisted on the wrong choices. Today, their beliefs appear flawed. Revelations have proved Elvis was no Superman. We now understand Elvis had an emotional vulnerability that precluded maturity and we are aware what happened to his health from 1971. It is also clear that some of the musical choices Elvis made were driven by expediency and not the indifferent perversity Marcus imagined. Although he sometimes pretended differently, Elvis was not omnipotent.

The weaknesses in his musical talent

This belief in infinite talent amongst his supporters contrasts with his opponents who think he has none. The opponents think only of his failures and are willing to stereotype him as the Elvis monster that appeared in his movies or grew fat. The fans are different, they remember the glorious arrival at the lake or they have belatedly acquired a full, record collection so they now know the glories. Exposed to his triumphs, they are willing to blame others for the failures.

The highlights are exceptional. Elvis was not only extremely gifted but charismatic and capable of connecting with his audience and the individuals within that audience, the weak and the strong. Elvis could do everything very well which always gave him an edge. His rivals were not able to challenge his diversity. Nor could they match him in what he could do well, rockabilly for example, or what made him special, his ability to take his music into unencumbered space. Other singers, though, also had their own independent identity and they could do better than Elvis what made them special. Jackie Wilson and Roy Hamilton achieved a plasticity in their vocals that was beyond Elvis. The voice of Elvis suited the mono production for fifties, vinyl records. The treble edge on these recordings emphasised the startling swoops and complex shading in his singing. When stereo arrived in the sixties it did expose the absence of plasticity. It may be that Elvis is making a choice between feeling and control but the absence is noticeable.

Elvis could not match the power of the great, baritone singers, for example, the black, baritone singers like Bobby Bland. Neither, does he possess the force of female singers like Mahalia Jackson and Aretha Franklin. Comparing Elvis to black performers, raises the issue of the growl. 'Jailhouse Rock' and 'Santa Claus Is Back In Town' are marvellous examples of his own growl but it does not exist as a context for him as it does with Ray Charles and other black singers. It is something he uses occasionally and it is not as sustaining for Elvis as it is for many black, soul singers. This became important after the mid-sixties when soul music emerged with its emphasis on gospel roots. For some listeners, it marginalised him and, despite the success of the soul styled album, 'From Elvis In Memphis', Elvis may have felt marginalised himself.

His range was an advantage and essential if he was to dominate but it prevented him from delivering the vocal perfection that appears always available to certain singers. As his diversity obliged him to distance himself from his roots, it meant he sometimes suffered in comparison with the specialists. Bobby Bland and George Jones may be narrower men but their narrowness enables them to focus on the strengths of their genres and retain the intensity of the roots of blues and country.

Elvis did absorb the music around him but the tradition he inherited was not as rich as that available to black performers like Aretha Franklin and Ray Charles. This meant he was distanced from jazz although he had unused potential in this area which could have been easily developed by a talented producer like Jerry Wexler. The problem had two aspects. It restricted not only his choice of material but also how he arranged his own records. It was inevitable that Elvis had to mellow and, although he did this interestingly as he aged, knowledge of jazz would have improved his taste and helped him to avoid some of his mistakes.

Elvis has been compared often to Frank Sinatra and, sometimes, unfavourably. Such comparisons ignore that Elvis had diversity, energy, rhythm, invention and a voice that could simply be beautiful. But the talent of Sinatra needs to be treated with respect. Sinatra had many attributes but the two that are important in this comparison are breath control and confidence. Elvis injects drama, tension, mystery and feeling into his great ballads. He rarely, though, sings a ballad with the aloof confidence of Sinatra. The psychology behind the ballad may be more complex with Elvis but the technique is less obvious with Sinatra. The confidence of Sinatra is crucial to his phrasing and his arrogant refusal to be hurried. At his peak, Sinatra makes the pauses musical and he often uses his voice to suggest pauses where none exist. A great example of this is his version of 'All The Way.'

Elvis is a fabulous, blues singer and it is not too much of a claim to say the greatest, white, blues singer. The fine, white, Texas, rhythm and blues man, Delbert McClinton, must rue the day when he decided to cover the Elvis classic, 'A Mess Of Blues.' Other white people cannot be compared to Elvis singing the blues. He makes even the best of them sound like amateurs. The blues, though, is a black tradition and, whilst Elvis improved many of the blues songs he covered, there are black, blues singers who have more grit, anger and power. Muddy Waters and Howling Wolf are the two obvious examples although Elvis does a fine version of 'Got My Mojo Working' and both Waters and Wolf are Elvis admirers.

These are his musical weaknesses but they have to be put in context. If the above musicians remind us of his limitations, he also exposed them as narrow specialists. Elvis reminds me of the Lake District in the north of England, one of the few places in which Victor Frankenstein on his travels found relief from his guilt. Other places may have taller mountains but the combination of various elements in the Lakes creates a unique and perfect landscape. Perhaps Elvis was not the master of the Universe he pretended but he is the only man on the planet who can deliver both the raucous 'One Night' and the exquisitely beautiful 'This Is My Heaven.' The other great, American singers, though, are important. We need to know more than Elvis.

Apart from his vocal limitations, he did not write songs and he did not develop his ability as a piano player so that it could regularly complement his performance although it can on some occasions be heard on his records. This is an accident of history. If Elvis had been born later and had needed these skills, they would have been added to his armoury. In a musical context, it is not important because what are being considered are the limits to how he defined himself as a singer. In the development of his career, though, it was very important because it made him dependent on songwriters. Unfortunately, for him, after 1966 they increasingly used their material to advance their own careers as performers.

His inability to cope with his career

He is far from explicit in his two books but Peter Guralnick has hinted elsewhere that Elvis suffered from depression as early as 1962 and that doubt existed in him before then. Although there are phases within phases after he returned from the Army, it is apparent that the Elvis who returned to civilian life was a much more passive figure than the assertive Elvis that existed from 1954 to 1958. He continued to make great and good records after 1960 but something had changed. The insipid, lethargic compliance of Elvis for most of the sixties suggests a man who wants to 'seek happiness in tranquillity and avoid ambition'. The overwhelming playfulness, impudence and gaiety evident in the fifties disappeared from his performances. Elvis was not supported by a creative management team and this restricted him but the post-Army Elvis could have made more of the opportunities that were available to him. It required confrontation but not much. It is true that he was constricted by song-writing deals but his efforts would have found their way on to vinyl if he had recorded what he wanted.

Two events have been identified as contributing to his inability to cope, the death of his mother and the failure of his relationship with his wife. The Creature wanted his mate to be created by Frankenstein and believed that such a creature, maimed like him, would end his unbearable loneliness and exclusion. Elvis was also quite specific about his ideal woman but the details were a little different. Both, though, were denied the female companion they believed would make them happy. Those who support a Freudian explanation of the tragedy, require a fragile Elvis always heavily dependent on maternal love and familial security. Elaine Dundy, in her excellent book, 'Elvis And Gladys', describes an extended Presley family but it is one that includes a promiscuous, dissolute and overbearing grandfather, a neurotic mother and an indolent father. He had complicated roots and the death of his twin at birth must have produced stubborn guilt. Alanna Nash, in her book, 'Baby Let's Play House', claims the loss of his twin created an inadequate family. In her opinion, Elvis believed his existence was a consequence of the death of his twin. The subsequent fame could only have exaggerated the guilt. An exaggerated dependency on a sibling is not unique to Elvis. Admittedly, they are fictional but

Victor Frankenstein and Robert Walton, the sea captain, who is attempting to penetrate the North Pole and whom Frankenstein encounters, are two ambitious men who both imagine fulfilment through a sibling.

Alanna Nash, in 'Baby Let's Play House', argues that, as the twin-less twin, Elvis would have needed a control figure, Parker, whilst simultaneously wanting a group he could control, the Memphis Mafia. She argues his personality was damaged and, when his mother died, he was condemned to torment and depression. Whatever the cause, it is obvious he was trapped in adolescence. There is a photograph of Elvis enjoying a rollercoaster ride in Memphis. The people with him laugh like adults, he grins like a child. The Creature called the family in the forest his protectors although they were unaware of his existence. Elvis addressed his parents in his letters as 'babies' yet they were the adults responsible for him. Perhaps, both characters believed in a companion who would make them transcend their existence because they had an ability to create connections that did not exist.

More sinister is the possibility that the death of his twin meant the ambition of Elvis was confined to confident cynicism rather than aspiration. He believed he was destined to prevail but understood the dark circumstances of triumph, the sacrifice of the twin or others. Although an innocent, he may have always been bereft of idealism and optimism. Fame may produce an arrogant indifference to others but, maybe, there was in Elvis alongside the innocence a cynical crack that fame opened easily. His early innocence was crucial to his initial triumph, so its loss would have been debilitating.

His capacity to waste himself

If Elvis was basically indolent, it would easily explain what many consider to be his overall underachievement. Linda Thompson, his girlfriend, said that at Graceland he relaxed a lot but that he took more pills to help him perform when he was in Vegas. This implies Elvis was more inert than his defenders think. When accused of incompetence by the Presley estate his manager, Parker, insisted that he was misunderstood. Presley was not easy to manage and he was lazy and difficult to motivate, claimed Parker.

There are, though, conflicting views and accounts. Parker describes a client indifferent to his career but this description differs from those offered by Leiber and Stoller and Chips Moman. They describe an enthusiast of limitless energy who was always ready to do another take in the studio. Presumably, Elvis was a man able to drift for long periods of inactivity but able to work like a demon when the situation was desperate. He was a man who responded to challenges but he was also a man who without them could easily drift. Challenges inspired him but demands drained his freedom loving spirit. The challenges that inspired him usually offered hope of change and relief which is why he responded. Their denial and his begrudged acquiescence with the alternative routine of demands were fatal for him.

In the novel by Mary Shelley, the Creature had exceptional powers, 'he contravened the seas of ice, and inhabit (sic) caves and dens where no man would venture to intrude'. He also had days when he would hide in the forest, sad and purposeless. After he had been denied his wish for a mate by Frankenstein, only vengeance gave the Creature a purpose. After Elvis had been denied a career, perhaps, his only ambition was to frustrate others. Tired of being Elvis but terrified of being anyone else, he drifted into the creative waste his fans feared more than anything.

Elvis was inspired by music and the Creature by literature and music, 'gentle manners and melody', but what inspired them prepared neither for the hostile world. Both lost ambition when they understood they would be thwarted. Feeling an absence in themselves, this made them obsessed with what they thought would make them complete. The Creature wanted his maimed mate and Elvis wanted a perfect woman to replace his mother. Most of us require belief to be truly motivated. Somewhere in his career, Elvis lost that belief. Initially, the movies, recording studio and stage offered hope and functioned as a retreat where he found solace. In the end, though, all of these retreats became centres of dread that he wanted to avoid and, at various times, he used them all cynically. The Creature avoided humans and Elvis ignored his career. The Creature was supposedly ugly and repulsed others whilst Elvis attracted people but had to cope with the demands of sustaining glory. Both became reclusive and, when that was not adequate, they destroyed themselves. The Creature, anticipating death, promised to 'exult in the anger of torturing flames.'

Before the Army, Elvis was not lazy but then he had both a career and a private existence defined by his family that he could still believe in. After the career changed and his mother died, he failed to sustain either of these fundamental beliefs for himself. His failure on both counts has to be held against him but failure in one often invokes failure in the other. This inability to fashion new, supporting beliefs is why, I believe, he failed to cope with fame, the world and others. The beliefs essential to the survival of an innocent either perished or were sacrificed and were never replaced. In the end, Elvis talked as if he was in a prison.

'I am so tired of being Elvis Presley,' he said to his first drummer, D J Fontana, when they met in the seventies.

His loss inspired compulsive religious enquiry and the search for a renewed mandate. His torment reflected the experience of his fans. The disappointment in his reduced efforts left his fans with a corresponding mystery and need for explanation.

His narcissism

Parker was neither qualified to manage a creative talent nor care for a sensitive innocent. It is no surprise, he never mentioned to Elvis that all of us need to beware the mirror. This was a pity because few could argue the claim that Elvis was a narcissist. His obsession with his hair, clothes and appearance provide sufficient evidence. Admittedly, the narcissism was mixed with aggression and insecurity but these traits merely intensified his vanity.

Despite the Victorian austerity, the pleasure of narcissism is not denied by Shelley in her novel. The Creature is anguished particularly by the first sight of his appearance which occurs when, just like Narcissus, he sees himself reflected in a small pool. He asks Frankenstein to create a mate for him because he knows she will resemble him. This can be interpreted in various ways but the three main characters in the novel - the Creature, Frankenstein and Robert Walton - all imagine love with a sibling. Walton writes earnestly to his sister, Margaret, Victor Frankenstein marries his adopted sister and the Creature wants his 'father' to create a woman for him, a woman who will be his lover and companion but who, also, will, of course, be his 'sister'. No wonder, the narcissistic Elvis resented being denied his own twin.

From the very beginning, Elvis was in competition with himself. If a journalist overheard a fan whisper, 'Have you ever heard anything that good?', it is more than likely Elvis was soon told the same. Somebody coined the term, 'King of Rock n Roll', and, whether justified or not, it was confirmed by the media. This is not like the British Royal Family. This title makes demands. Elvis had a talent based on raw material which consisted of the power and expression in his voice, his appearance and his energy. From day one, the raw material was weakening. This is the problem for the young, gifted narcissist. He will never be that great again. The initial, fabulous flame sustains a decent fire after weakening but, whatever you do afterwards, everybody, including the performer, remembers the first, fabulous flame. One day, you conquer and, the next, you provide interest and entertainment. This is what Elvis had in common with Orson Welles, the great film director whose career also deteriorated. For the gifted narcissist, avoidance of responsibility is tempting because it prevents revealing evidence of weakening and because work, no matter what new skills have been acquired, is not enhancing but reducing. Without narcissism, it is possible to be philosophical and consolidate the original triumph with solid progress. The merely talented work assiduously, adding to their achievements. Nobody expects the original glory to be replicated because it was never that glorious.

There is a moment in the documentary, 'That's The Way It Is', when Elvis is walking across the stage and warbling. His voice is strong, his body under control and his hair thick. The audience sit and adore. His comeback has been successful and he has reinvented himself to establish his superiority and talent. It is easy to imagine him thinking, 'what more can I want?' He turns around at the end of the stage and, for an instant, the smile disappears and his face hardens. Perhaps he thinks, 'what more can I do?'

In the film called 'The Chase', Marlon Brando plays a sheriff obliged to protect his prisoner and stand against the corrupt. Brando is brilliant because he plays the sheriff as a narcissist, a man not prepared for his personal glory to be tainted by ambition and compromise. This is why he agreed to be an underachieving and isolated sheriff. When he leaves the town at the end of the movie, knowing the town is an inadequate reflection of his talent and purpose, it is clear he is escaping the world for a simpler life. He is bruised and battered from a savage beating but also cleansed and he does have Angie Dickinson which is worth, at least, the loss of several teeth and a few cracked ribs. Bleeding badly, this narcissist has ironically retained his virginity and will avoid whoredom. Although 'The Chase' has a screenplay by the left-wing writer, Lillian Hellman, its tone is misanthropic and the escape of cool Brando and beautiful Angie implies that only flawed and plain people are obliged to be merchandise for the powerful and greedy. The price for the sheriff, despite his superior entitlements, is oblivion. This can be compared with the Creature whose decline was defined by key moments. Significant within them, is his shock at his reflection in the pool and his response is the same as Brando. He retreats into quiet hiding.

Elvis was at his best when his career came easily - the music of Memphis, Sam Phillips, a hands-off RCA and no Parker with movie contracts and ideas for Christmas albums. When it became difficult Elvis, perhaps, should have done what Brando did in 'The Chase', retreated to where he had control. But that would have meant oblivion and this is not acceptable to the creative temperament. Instead, he hung around and made records and appeared on the movie sets, waiting like an innocent who believes better days and nicer people will eventually appear. In an interview in 1961 he said, 'you're just better off sticking with it, till time itself just changes things.'

The commitment he made to the careerists around him was formal and contractual, like that of the whore who refuses to smile, and this lack of commitment soon spread to how he performed for his audience. In this way, he survived the worst parts of the sixties. Withdrawn and only capable of sly innuendo, he released poorly sung, soundtrack albums to confirm he was disillusioned. Later, in the seventies, he again attempted to withhold commitment but he was now older and less impressive. The narcissist suddenly had a much weaker voice and a body already revealing its incapacity to age well. Worse, he was now dependent on public appearances on stage. These appearances before fans required the whore to smile constantly.

'I feel like an old stripper.' Elvis said this on stage as early as 1970.

He also lost his Angie Dickinson. Told this way, the narcissist had no alternative but to self-destruct.

His ability to draw 'ridicule'

The term ridicule was first used by Greil Marcus. He was the first of those, who wrote about Elvis, to quote from the novel, 'Moby Dick', and to think of the singer as the American Leviathan. Is it the similarity to the whale that invites ridicule? Philip Hoare, in his book on whales, 'Leviathan', states, 'It doesn't seem right that something that big thinks the world is only water.' Many think, because Elvis was talented, he needed to know more of the world, know it was more than water or Tennessee. What is important in our relationship with the Leviathan is our own need to either claim or destroy. There is either the fan that has to buy every record or the others who sneer at the whale because they do not want to be reduced to a stare.

The documentary, 'This Is Elvis', includes an outtake from 'Elvis On Tour'. Elvis walks into the dressing room before a concert and talks about the sex he had the night before. Someone hints that the woman was unattractive and the Memphis Mafia laugh at the expense of Elvis.

Watching the scene, it is easy to forget that the man they patronise is their employer and it is his superior appeal which provides the women whom they also feel obliged to ridicule. The brief dialogue demonstrates easily how inferior men can patronise the talented and it shows how they hunt in groups, just like the villagers with their torches. Such men create a world that prohibits innocence because knowledge, experience and the ability to be included are what the talentless cursed with exceptional egos value most.

Elvis was an innocent with an unconventional talent. He was raw meat to those who want to ridicule. It is tempting to talk about class when discussing how Elvis was patronised and how his talent was unrecognised for so long. Clearly, class played a part in the antipathy.

'He needs to get rid of those sideburns,' said by Bing Crosby.

'Those dreadful clothes he wears,' said by virtually everyone.

These days, after rock and roll has been subsequently repossessed by Bob Dylan and English bands for the middle classes, the cultured prefer to remember the aspects of his early rage that did not accuse them. The outrage Elvis caused is usually assumed to be a consequence of a claim for sexual freedom. Invariably, they ignore the nihilistic anger of the dispossessed that defines both 'Hound Dog' and 'Blue Suede Shoes'.

But there are always buts with Elvis. Elvis also divided the working class and plenty of working class males were not only cold to his talent but felt this need to demean.

In the sixties, Jack Good produced a TV show called 'Around The Beatles.' The singer, P J Proby, made his British debut and sang a couple of songs. On the song, 'I Believe', he sounded very much like Elvis. The next day, it was the talking point in the school break. P J Proby was brilliant because he could imitate Elvis accurately. The excited, young men making this point were not Elvis fans. They were people desperate to enjoy the talent but unable to acknowledge the original man. Many of the people who watch modern, awful Elvis impersonators will tell you they do not like Elvis.

Why this resistance to the original man so that the talent can only be acknowledged in inferior imitators? For many, his looks and the nature of his talent only signify good fortune. They consider him a man to be unworthy of the talent and this makes them resentful. They need somebody who can articulate that talent and someone who can reveal that it took effort to develop.

The film, 'Amadeus', implies Mozart was not accepted by his rivals because of his scatological humour and boorishness. Perhaps, Mozart simply repelled others because of his innocence, the boy genius who was not required to become a man, someone not obliged to acquire the knowledge, experience and company of others. Elvis was not a man who succeeded. He was a boy who became famous and an innocent boy at that. The 'TV Special', when it appeared in 1968, was received warmly by critics, especially male critics. Everyone is agreed; it worked because he confirmed the talent. But was this the sole reason for its appeal? Or was this the moment when Elvis had to demonstrate he was no longer the boy and was it his willingness on this occasion to cope with maturity and masculinity that finally won him the withheld, critical approval from other men?

Maybe I am stretching a point. All that needs to be said is that for some people the man Elvis is off limits and that they enjoy it that way. This emotional hostility from large sections of the population clearly must have affected Elvis as it did the Creature who, much earlier than Elvis, soon abandoned hope of progress.

His lack of taste

Fans dispute whether Elvis deserves to be condemned for what is conceived as poor taste. It has been exaggerated and misunderstood and he would be less of a performer if he merely satisfied good taste and ignored his complex roots. His taste and judgement, as they did for the Creature, do, though, exist as weaknesses. Elvis was too loyal to Parker and too compliant with his wishes. He never had an alternative to replacing him although he was well disillusioned before the 'TV Special'. Elaine Dundy, in 'Elvis and Gladys', claims that, as early as 1957, Elvis wanted to restrict Parker to managing his concert tours. The research for this claim is not well defined but various quotes from the Memphis Mafia and Steve Binder support the view that he was disillusioned with Parker. It is dangerous to rely on quotes because Elvis would say different things to different people. But the success of the TV special, alone, must have convinced him that Parker was useless. If his manager had good judgement, why did he need to make a comeback? Elvis stayed with Parker until the end. This was poor judgement because he overestimated Parker and underestimated himself.

With only a little more consideration, he could have achieved so much more and it was when his energy levels dropped that he needed taste and judgement most as did the Creature when his circumstances became difficult. When the Creature says, 'the whole village was roused; some fled, some attacked me, until, grievously bruised by stones and many other kinds of missiles I escaped to open country and fearfully took refuge in a low hovel', we sympathise but we also want him to think of a possible strategy for integration. The Creature disappoints because he never rebels merely destroys. He never did understand his admittedly difficult options and neither did Elvis but, of course, both were also caught in destructive conflict with their creators.

Good taste could have disguised the physical decline of Elvis as it does with other performers. The vocal tricks that captivated when he was young, the hiccups and sighs, merely sound melodramatic after his voice had weakened. Elvis did change his style because of age but Guralnick was right when in his review of the 'Elvis Country' album he said that Elvis failed to distinguish between his strengths and weaknesses. He used power ballads as a bombastic substitute for the rock and roll he could no longer perform when he should have concentrated on his ability to impart feeling into a song and create grooves closer to his roots. The 'Elvis In Concert' CD contains performances from his last shows when the man is seriously ill. But there are three songs that are revealing. These are, 'I Really Don't Want To Know', 'That's All Right' and 'Little Sister'. All three should be a challenge that is beyond him but he sings the first two as if his powers are hardly affected. He manages this because he remembers the feel and the groove of these songs and he is able to replicate them through his memory and instinct which, for these songs, are just as important as his voice. He can do this material easily because it is part of him. The powerful 'Little Sister' is a rock and roll classic that in its original form was beyond him in 1977 but he performs it as a gentle, swing number and he gives it a new identity. He relies on his feeling and rhythm and it suffices. Not that long ago, Candi Staton appeared at the Liverpool Philharmonic Hall. She had turned sixty and, in her performance, she sidestepped all the difficult notes, smiling sweetly as she did so and implying that a lady of her age had a right. She was still brilliant and this was because she has a feeling for the blues and this alone was enough to captivate the audience. Elvis would often do the opposite on stage and mumble his way through a song to ensure he hit the high, dramatic note at the end. This approach was an error.

The other weaknesses in taste have been well documented, his suits on stage and his taste for sentimental ballads. These weaknesses have a context and should be viewed sympathetically as is done later but, considering he wanted to be commercially successful, he was insensitive in his persistence with both.

Later, I argue that the taste of Elvis was consistent with his background but this assumption, though valid, avoids a key point. Elvis spent ten years making movies. He worked with talented and creative musicians. He met the sophisticated frequently and would have received advice. His response to the limiting prescriptions of Parker was passive and accepting but, in creating his musical identity, he also felt empowered to resist informed advice. His response was to be stubbornly assertive. If he was compliant with Parker, he had an inability to evaluate criticism and suggestion. These two characteristics are not contradictory. Both are rooted in paranoia and both depend on fatalism.

His fatalism

His fatalism was that of the excluded and the ridiculed and anybody, who doubts that this fatalism was not part of his character, should listen to the brilliant 'Is It So Strange' This neglected masterpiece reveals the early flourishing of not just fatalism but a martyr complex. When, in the song, Elvis asks about his feelings, 'Is It So Strange' he is asking am I so strange and both his tone and the mood of the song make it clear. He knows he is definitely peculiar and he realises it prohibits contentment.

Greil Marcus on a BBC radio programme asked us to consider being Elvis. 'Imagine walking down a street and half the people you see think you are a God and the other half think you are the lowest, weirdest trash imaginable.'

'How would he cope with that?' asked the impeccably polite, BBC interviewer.

'He couldn't,' said Marcus. 'How could anyone?'

When half the world refuses to acknowledge you and wants to ridicule you become obsessively loyal to whatever led to the early success. For Elvis, these were his roots, his manager, the fans who demonstrated uncritical loyalty and his own defiance. Integrity is strength but Elvis was too complicated for that. His innocence did not exist alone; it was always darkened by inarticulate scorn. He was thus able to submit to Parker and to deny help and support from others. Elvis and the Creature have in common their decisive reaction to the jeers. Both were self-taught and reacted to the jeers and horror by becoming insular. Both spent long periods in hiding or avoiding their own narrative. For much of his career, Elvis appeared to have no regard to what was happening around him and willingly accepted the anachronistic absurdities that Parker foisted upon him. The Creature pledged himself to violent retribution and Elvis became resigned. Violence and resignation are the two sides of the same fatalistic coin. These were two figures maligned by people who thought they were the creators. After their wishes were treated with contempt, both Elvis and the Creature were obliged to become remote and make secret plans with their self-destruction as the climax.

Ultimately, Elvis was luckier than the Creature because his limitations did not prevent the existence of people who responded enthusiastically to his talent. Sensibly, he did not destroy the child by the lake although he did lose many because of his waywardness. But, like the Creature, he suffered because of his limitations. Both figures inspired gossip rather than accuracy. Once, Elvis was suspected of being maimed, of being seriously uncouth, the villagers soon became hostile. The villagers never troubled to imagine how the strength of the Creature might be utilised. Similarly, too many rock music critics were unwilling to recognise talent in what they considered to be another maimed creature.

The attributes of Elvis Presley

Many have already speculated as to who or what the Creature is supposed to represent and most interpretations make sense at the first reading. The book is best and normally understood as a radical masterpiece that warns against condemning those who are different, those we normally oppress. It also exists as a criticism of the scientific faith in technical mastery, especially, when it is pursued by ignoring others, by refuting 'the domestic connection'. This, though, is the conscious agenda. Other ideas and emotions will have contributed to the ideas of Shelley. Forget the violence and the repulsive appearance of the Creature and merely remember his strengths - his intelligence, his precise understanding of his situation, his critical acumen, his literary and musical sensitivity and his positive response to the life within nature. Some have suggested that the identity behind the Creature may be her husband Percy or her idol Byron but the powerful being is also remarkably similar to another famous figure from the period, William Wordsworth, minus the poems, odes and ballads. Wordsworth climbed Helvellyn in the dark when he was seventy and the Creature scaled the overhanging sides of Mont Saleve. Whoever we pick, the Creature exists as a Romantic hero but one denied tutoring and the cultural nourishment of fellow beings. Modern criticism has insisted correctly that Shelley used the Creature as a symbol of those who are oppressed and scorned but, perhaps, she was also pleading forgiveness for the creative talent who is flawed and has the mixture of dedicated inspiration and chaotic personality that she experienced with her husband, Percy Bysshe Shelley. In her biography of Mary Shelley, Miranda Seymour quotes these comments from Shelley about her fellow passengers on the Rhine. 'Twere easier for God to make entirely new men than attempt to purify such monsters as these ---- loathsome creepers'. Clearly, Shelley was in a troubled mood but these comments are consistent with the novel if not all of her writing. Shelley forgives the Creature for his actions because she understands he is misunderstood and thwarted. The same sympathy is never extended to the poverty stricken villagers. Mary Shelley was a radical. She was vehemently opposed to slavery and could speak persuasively about the merits of the poor but she was also a product of the British class system. She had her blind spots.

The flaws in the person who has the creative talent may be symbolised by the appearance of the Creature, beautiful features but skin stretched too tight. The daring idea within the novel is how a gifted man with sensitivity would have reacted if he was ugly and terrifying to others. Would a less gifted man than the Creature have survived the travails and perhaps sloped off to join a circus? Shelley makes clear that the desire of her hero to learn was rooted in a violent temper. The thwarted talent produces the anger which, unfortunately, the Creature can too easily express with destructive violence. The tragedy of the talent is that it is misplaced in a repellent freak and, therefore, according to the well groomed, non-existent.

Elvis did not require to be galvanised by Parker, TV and Hollywood to understand he had talent. The doubts about his talent only existed within him after the galvanisation.

Carl Perkins was once asked in a BBC radio programme if he resented the success Elvis had with his song, 'Blue Suede Shoes'.

'No, sir,' said Carl. 'Elvis was always the one to make it. He had the talent, the looks and the style.'

He could have added the attitude and the background. We must not forget the name, either. Now the words, Elvis Presley, are burned into our consciousness but I remember, as a child, discovering that his name was real and being pleased. I had suspected he really was unique and it had been confirmed. The oddness was always fascinating and inspiring, even to Carl Perkins. But it is not just about being unique.

In 1969, Elvis recruited his core band for his return to live performances. After all the movies, Elvis had a low critical reputation and each musician has recalled in subsequent interviews how, despite the tempting remuneration, they had doubts about working with Elvis. After the first day of rehearsals, the musicians turned up for work the next day as expected but all of them had brought their doubting spouses to witness the brilliance of their new boss. These musicians were, as Jon Landau said, in his review of a 1971 Boston concert, 'the best that money can buy.' They had already worked with the best themselves but they wanted to share what was special.

James Burton, the lead guitarist, appears to be a serious and phlegmatic man. He does much to support young, aspiring guitarists. Recently, he was interviewed on a Channel 4 programme that was supposed to determine the most important rock musician or something. In the programme, Burton was asked what made Elvis important. Fans, watching, expected and hoped for a technical answer.

James Burton looked at the interviewer and said, 'He was the best. He could do it better than anyone else.'

James Burton had worked with Elvis for nine years and, in the process, had seen him self-destruct and show total disregard for professional standards. He spoke like a man possessed perhaps by the dark magic he experienced on that first day of rehearsals.

In 1977, the weekend after Elvis died, 'The Observer' newspaper was obliged to respond with an article. The responsibility was given to their jazz critic, Dave Gelly, because, back then, the paper did not employ any rock journalists. The man had never listened to an Elvis album in his life but they gave him a copy of the most recent album by Elvis, 'Moody Blue'. Gelly, a jazz purist, was surprised by the talent on display and remarked how the first track, a live version of 'Unchained Melody', evoked Mahalia Jackson. Gelly said something like, 'From the evidence on this album he was not a spent force.' Gelly was wrong. The recordings were made when Elvis was close to death and wrecked. 'Moody Blue' is his weakest studio album. Unfortunately, Gelly had missed too much to ever realise the true potential and achievements of Elvis but, for a few moments, Gelly had been exposed and, although it was to a weakened Elvis, his purist opinion had been shaken. Similarly, the actor, Kenneth Moore, who knew only the icon Elvis, could not abide the performer. In 1964, as a guest on the programme, 'Juke Box Jury', he had to review the Elvis single, 'Such A Night'. He was astonished by the record and admitted that, despite his dislike of the singer, the record was brilliant. An exposure, lasting less than three minutes, had defeated his assumptions. It may not be comparable but their reactions make me think of the scene near the end of the 'Frankenstein' novel when Robert Walton watches the Creature grieve over the dead Frankenstein. He immediately realises and understands the sympathy and potential that exists within the monster.

In the Elvis movie, 'The Trouble With Girls', there is a song called 'Clean Up Your Own Backyard'. The song is an edgy, preachy, Delta styled, white blues not normally attempted by Elvis and it features a prominent Dobro played brilliantly by Mort Marker. The Dobro makes a very effective but distinct, metallic sound and most people would assume it is not suited to the voice of Elvis. The singer and guitarist, Bonnie Raitt, has built a reasonably successful career making this kind of smoother, Delta edged music. She has critical approval. Elvis recorded this material because he had no choice although it is clear he likes the song. He mastered the song well within an afternoon, altering his voice slightly to suit the Dobro, before moving on to something completely different. The record required not just technical skill but a feel and understanding of the genre. He needed to assimilate quickly something that has preoccupied Bonnie Raitt for most of her life. The gifted do easily what the talented find difficult. But is it all about musical mastery? Elvis had to be different in order to become important, to become something other than a musician. Photographs are important and we have plenty.

There is a photograph of Elvis from 1969. He is at the American Sound Studios in Memphis with his hero, Roy Hamilton. Compared to Elvis, Roy looks normal like a man who will go home and read the newspaper. Even the other musicians, who are probably already experimenting with dope, look conventional and ordinary, less than the talent we hear on the records. We notice Elvis, first, in these photographs because he is famous but also because he always appears different to those around him. Prettier and flashier, he is softer and stranger than the other men. He is like a visitor who has arrived from another world that is tinted by fantasy.

There are photographs of Elvis with his wife and child where he is also overdressed. He looks remote, a man who has other concerns. In these photographs with his wife and daughter, he carries a cane and, draped by a glamorous assistant and her dependant, he resembles a mysterious magician from the nineteenth century. This is a man who knows that in the future unknown possibilities wait. His strange presence contains warnings about the vulnerability of tradition but also hints that the future will never explain his secrets. So it has proved.

An earlier photograph exists of Elvis being drafted into the Army. He stands between his mother and father. His mother is distraught and the dark, smudged mascara indicates she has been weeping. The photograph is interesting because it offers comparison between the father and the son. Neither is tastefully dressed. Both wear loud sports jackets that could have been worn to greater effect with different shirts and trousers. They look what they are; two Southern, working class men in casual but slightly flash gear. The clothes do not look expensive which is odd because the family has been rich for the last two years and this is an important appearance in public for all of them. His father looks like someone ready to flop in a coffee house or bar, sit down with other men and watch the world go by. His clothes are not inappropriate for defeat. Elvis is different. He is not ready to flop down with anyone. He still looks cool and the normal, sartorial rules do not undermine him like they do his father. He has not yet acquired the power that is apparent in the photograph where he resembles the strange magician. In this photograph, he is dressed like other people. But he is still strange and remote.

The best photograph of Elvis shows a very young Elvis standing in a car park. He is wearing a white shirt, a narrow tie and pants with a thin, white stripe down the side. At his side, he holds his cased guitar. He is waiting perhaps to go on stage with the rest of the band. He leans backward against the bumper of a car. He is skinny rather than slim, unvarnished and untarnished. His hair is not especially long. He smiles at the camera, wide eyed. A young, Hillbilly singer, innocent and vulnerable but loaded with confidence and expectation. Already, he is like no one else. Even all these years later, it is possible to look at the photograph and be inspired with hope for something that cannot be, the total fulfilment of a unique talent. It is like when we remember events and imagine different endings.

But they are only photographs. They only help explain the appeal of the personality which is only part of his gift. Many of the images of Elvis are misleading, they only reveal the creature after he was galvanised and propelled towards success. These images of the galvanised Elvis are not as connected to the music as people think. The movie images of the Creature are also a stage removed from what Mary Shelley created. The Hollywood representations of the Creature undermine the novel.

Too often in rock music, we assume that the musical talent is only a means for special individuals to communicate a unique purpose and existence. The music becomes submerged under dubious, existential status. Robert Matthew Walker, in his book, 'Heartbreak Hotel', argues that Elvis did not become a great singer because he was different. He became different because he was a great singer. The gift compelled him forward. The personality could only hope to cope with the gift. Sometimes it did and sometimes it did not.

Elvis had a voice but he was surrounded by a culture that contained music rich in feeling and expression and, whether it was a consequence of his talent or not, he had a powerful personality. He also had daring.

The voice

It is necessary to collate important quotes. Henry Pleasants, in 'The Great American Popular Singers', said, 'The voice covers two octaves and a third, from the baritone low G to the tenor high B with an upward extension in falsetto to at least a D flat. Presley's best octave is in the middle, D flat to C flat. Call him a high baritone.' There is a website, 'Get A Lyric', where a fan identifies the high and low notes that Elvis achieves and the fan even provides a brief video with the examples. Such scrutiny can, though, soon become very technical and you need to be near a piano or to be familiar with a piano for it to be properly understood. Also, one high or low note in a particular performance does not vindicate a talent.

What is important is that he had a more than decent octave range. Equally significant to the impact of the voice is the centre of gravity. This is where the voice is strong and natural. Elvis had a wide centre of gravity. Gregory Sandows, Music Professor at Columbia, said, 'I suppose you'd call him a lyric baritone, although with exceptional high notes and unexpectedly rich low notes. Elvis was all at once a tenor, a baritone and bass, the most unusual voice I've ever heard.' And, presumably, he has heard a few. Lindsay Waters, in 'Come Softly, Darling, Hear What I Say', comments on the third and final constituent part of the voice, volume. His voice, she writes, needs to be measured in decibels but she adds, 'even that misses the problem of how to measure delicate whispers that are hardly audible at all.'

Elvis also has technique. Not only did he know how to open the vowels to sustain high notes, he also had an emotional range and enough imagination to communicate that range. Lindsay Waters mentions, 'tender whispers to sighs down to shouts, grunts, grumbles and sheer gruffness that could move the listener from calmness and surrender to fear.' To borrow from Elaine Dundy in 'Elvis And Gladys', he had musical aptitude, a sense of pitch, timing, harmony, rhythm, tonal memory, internal and chord discrimination.

All these elements help explain his range and command of material but only to an extent. Fortunately, Elvis had another advantage. He benefitted from his centre of gravity starting in the high baritone. This meant he could combine both the 'masculine' and 'feminine' in his singing in a way that Jackie Wilson and Roy Hamilton for all their technical control cannot. It also meant that, when he delivered rock, he could avoid the tinny shriek that sometimes afflicts singers with a capacity for high notes, for example, someone like Roy Orbison. But Elvis has so much skill, he can also deliver classic rock from the high range. His records at Sun, recorded when he was young and his voice was high, are magnificent. There are baritone singers who have a much more powerful centre of gravity than Elvis but the price they pay is an absence of range. Bobby Bland is an obvious and marvellous example of a masculine, baritone singer but he does not have the range of Elvis and he cannot combine the 'masculine' and 'feminine'. This is important because this mix was important to the musical identity of Elvis and because it also complemented his androgynous appeal to fans.

But Bobby Bland is not just a voice and neither is Elvis. They sang with feeling and they understood the blues.

The surrounding culture

Jerry Wexler, record producer at Atlantic, said, 'Presley's registration, the breadth of his tone, listening to some of his records, you'd think you were listening to an opera singer. But it's an opera singer with a deep connection to the blues.' Elvis could also be described as a blues singer with a connection to opera. The connections are easily explained.

As a child, Elvis listened to the Metropolitan Opera on the radio with his mother. Classical music was popular with radio station owners and probably featured more than the audience ratings justified. In Memphis and Mississippi, he also heard the blues, sometimes on the streets but, more often, on WDIA, the black, radio station that featured BB King as a disc jockey. Elvis assimilated musical styles easily which is why he could combine them effectively into original records. His good fortune consisted of so many musical styles being available to him as a child and a teenager. Southern music was dominated by two cities, Memphis and New Orleans, and one state, Mississippi. (Nashville was a location that became a commercial centre for country music and not a birthplace of a regional style.) Elvis was a child in Mississippi and a teenager in Memphis. He made his debut after a golden period in Southern music when the races had borrowed and influenced each other to create different stands in the gospel, blues and boogie woogie traditions. His ability to assimilate genres is dismissed by Albert Goldman, in his book, 'Elvis', as mimicry but Elvis also sounded unique which means his voice is immediately recognisable. If his gift was no more than mimicry combined with a voice of unique character, it was a gift that had incredible potential. It enabled him to leave his unique presence on anything and everything. Of course, the gift for mimicry may itself be an indicator of the depth of his talent, his ability to learn and adapt quickly. But the label of mimicry minimises his achievement. At his best, he integrated rather than copied musical mannerisms. For example, the way he uses gospel techniques to sustain notes on his early Sun, blues recordings. The 'Elvis Country' album, which inevitably and blatantly defies the genre, repeatedly integrates musical styles.

The powerful personality

Important in this personality was vitality or energy. Now we have access to outtakes from his recording sessions in the fifties, we realise he could deliver take after take without faltering. The tireless energy and the instant access he has to his rhythm test belief in the listener. We are listening to a man 'possessed by furies.' It is in this context that Elvis sought his limits; the power of 'Jailhouse Rock', the grit of 'One Night' and the sensitivity of 'Are You Lonesome Tonight'.

This vitality played a key part in how he absorbed other genres and cultures. He wanted what other people had and wanted others to have what he had. This is what makes him the great American democrat admired by Greil Marcus in 'Mystery Train'. Albert Goldman, always keen to underestimate Elvis, assumed he was a high functioning schizophrenic. The exact quantity of the individual ingredients in his personality will never be known but contradictions existed and they facilitated exceptional success and ultimate failure. How we describe it depends on our needs and prejudices. His talent enabled a complex personality to connect with the music around him and furnish an alternative, unusual identity that would be important to others. If this vitality sparked gaiety and drama in his music, it was also essential to his appetites, so it is no surprise that disillusionment malformed it later into gluttony.

When he was young, though, he had real food - vibrant cultures which clashed but influenced each other. Elvis, the quiet but neglected and hungry romantic who was later patronised for being sentimental, was the perfect outsider to absorb the complexities of these cultures. This he did but not in a way that was merely historical. Elvis was not a social documentarian and, because of that, he may have missed some of the detail and exotica of the South that is important to some critics. Instead, like the movie maker, John Ford, he was a myth maker and, rather than dig into the roots, he blurred blues, gospel and country. He made the music make sense to him. This was essential for him because he needed a reinforced identity to manage a hostile world. We have to remember the photograph of Elvis in the blue overalls in Milam School where, because of the placement policy in Memphis, Elvis, from the wrong side of the tracks, was obliged to mix with the more affluent. Later, the rich kids, when they were asked to remember him, said they could not. They talked about him as if he had been invisible which, to them, this poor boy would have been. This early invisibility gave him an experience known by the oppressed. As a child, Elvis, unlike the Creature, may not have produced horror in other humans but they did exclude him.

The music became his special powers because he required them to avoid invisibility. He used them to add grandeur to what he had to reveal. For all his insecurity about his worth, he used his gift to transform himself into the hero he had been unable to be as a child. Transformation was always important to Elvis which was why he was always so interested in make-up. The Creature was either denied these opportunities or failed to understand the potential of transformation. He does not ask Frankenstein to change him but merely find a damaged mate that resembles him. Mary Shelley, though, was a nineteenth century Englishwoman and not a twentieth century American. It is only recently that the British, like the Americans, have become less resigned to their physical inheritance. Elvis became flamboyant because, for him, it was better than being poor and normal. Unlike the Victorians, he expected solutions to his limitations. This talented man, who was obliged to think of himself as someone strange but with special powers, eventually dressed himself in capes, cloaks and extravagant suits because his insecurity came from a long-standing alienation and he had something to conceal. The costumes not only denied invisibility, they also provided a mask for the stitches he shared with the Creature.

This need for grandeur did not always make him popular with those people who like to take music seriously on its own terms. They described some of his effects as show-business but to them Elvis would probably say what he once said to a reporter, 'I 'spec you never been poor.'

These critics neither understand his needs nor the needs of his audience. Jake Hess, the gospel singer, described Elvis as a communicator. Although the ability to communicate is important, the word is inadequate. The belief that Elvis had in his special powers enabled him to make promises which his audiences found irresistible. On stage, this connection is evident but it can also be heard on his records and it is why, at his best, his up-tempo material sounds like a cry for freedom and his slow songs reveal human vulnerability and limitations that can be cherished. His despair reminds us that even sadness, because it affirms our existence and capacity, contains its own exaltation, its own triumph. This is how he connects and it is part of his psychology. As movie star, Cher, said, 'I felt he was expressing who I was.' This vulnerability and need for compensating grandeur may have been a flaw but, if he had been a perfect person, he would have only been a great musician. Temperamental strength would not only have excluded many of those he included, it would have offered far less mystery and ambition.

Outside the forces that shaped his success are two key strengths that are important to the listener, his sense of rhythm and his capacity to inject feeling into a song, his energy and his despair. The former is evident on his great rockers. In the seventies, the outtakes reveal a less committed musician and a man who is reduced, rather than expanded, by his success but, when a take follows the dull chat, we are suddenly listening to an emotional complexity and force not revealed in the earlier conversation. It can be argued that the rhythm is timing and Elvis once suggested to an interviewer that even the feeling is achieved by technique. Timing and technique do play a part but the many outtakes available suggest that these two strengths are independent gifts to his voice and musicality. Put crudely, there is something in him that gives him rhythm and intensity. Also inside him, but just as important, is his innocence.

Elaine Dundy asserts, in her book, 'Elvis and Gladys', that he has innocence unique to him. A trait that allows him to be exceptional without ever realising he may be different. Unique is a strong word but he was definitely unusual and innocence is a key not only to his singularity but to his openness and diversity. It features often in his music, in particular, the music he recorded before he went into the Army. His early performances have a sense of a life guiltlessly exploding into expression, fulfilment and potential. This intense delight of discovery and potency is constant and even overspills into the pauses in the music which are somehow suggestive breaths. His songs are not always memorable and he is hammy at times but he brings his music to life when he invites us to share in his talent and allows us to glory at the revelation of his power. His fifties records would have been much less impressive without the delight and the shock available to the innocent discovering pleasure. It is this innocence that allows him to oscillate between surreptitious grin and triumph and he is shamelessly happy for us to admire him.

Elvis lost his innocence after the death of his mother and his two years in the Army. The decline of the Creature was more complicated but happened more quickly. His innocence was lost after he saw himself in the pool and he realised the world was different to what he had read in books. The violent attack by the father whose daughter the Creature saved and the hysterical reaction of Felix, who discovered him in the cottage with the blind man, convinced the Creature he was destined to be misunderstood.

After his return from the Army, Elvis could still impress but not quite captivate as he had done because he was only at his best when expressing the two sides of innocence, its sense of freedom and its vulnerability to pain. He was still a marvellous talent but the independent cultural force no longer. Perhaps, at some point he had his own revealing reflection in the pool. This could be his tragedy, what happened was no more than the initial triumph of innocence followed by the exploitation of a strange, paradoxical, self-aware naivety. Elvis may have been a man who realised he had something more complicated than seductive talent, something which meant he would be destined to be misunderstood. In popular music, the tragedy is not unique to him but few have the ability to captivate the world with their innocence and shock it into something new. Other rock stars have come along and appealed and had influence but they did it without the shining light of his innocence. The world has changed and it is difficult to imagine it happening again.

His daring

Other singers have had a wider range of octaves and stronger centres of gravity. Mahalia Jackson and Aretha Franklin are marvellous examples of huge voices and are singers who understood their genres and made great records.

As Myrna Smith said, 'Aretha could sing rings around Elvis.' She should know because she sang with them both. She went on, though, to add that Elvis on stage created something unique and exciting. 'He went for it,' she said.

Elvis tested his voice to the limit and this willingness gave him feeling and intensity beyond his vocal talent. We respond, simply, because he is taking risks. This willingness to take risks is also fundamental to the novel by Shelley. She realises both the glory and danger of excess ambition. Victor Frankenstein is an obsessed scientist and an ambitious walker who strides across glaciers. Ultimately, he is willing to chase the Creature to the North Pole where the remote and virginal tempts both towards destruction. On the way, they meet Robert Walton who has been trapped at the North Pole in the ice for several weeks. The purpose of his voyage is no less than to locate the 'wondrous power of the needle --- the secret of the magnet' or the source of electricity. If the Creature is a suitable metaphor for Elvis, we have to remember that the Creature and Frankenstein also exist as doubles as does Elvis with Parker. The galvanised is also a galvaniser. Elvis at his best had daring and a taste for danger which is perhaps why fans and critics have frustrations with his weaker performances; his earlier daring denies him the alternative of being only interesting. The successful risk taking provides the great moments that inspire devotion and loyalty but they also produce the added burden of subsequent comparison and disappointment. The composer, Stravinsky, once said, 'It seems that once the violent has become accepted, the amiable in turn is no longer tolerable.' During his lifetime, Elvis was never forgiven for wanting to become amiable which is presumably why he envied the relaxed Dean Martin.

If Mahalia and Aretha use their talent to support their ambition, Elvis is obliged to use his ambition to support the talent. All three deal in grandeur but Elvis relies much more on himself and his will and charisma. His daring takes him further in other ways. He not only risks material others will not but he is prepared to do so much more with his voice. His music may be simple but the invention in his fifties records, when vocal tricks follow one another relentlessly, is unprecedented. Confidence allows him to be inventive but this is complemented by daring as can be heard on records like 'Blue Christmas' and 'Any Way You Want Me' which grip because of their weirdness. Disappointingly, this daring is confined to moments within his music. It did not give him the confidence to assert himself with his manager but it was a daring influenced by his earlier oppression and poverty. The desire is for freedom not struggle. This is why Elvis is at his most persuasive when he believes the music represents freedom and it is why such music encourages him to be daring. In these instances, he sings as if something other than music is at stake. His daring may be about ambition and identity but it is not the ambition of the dedicated craftsman. It is about escape and is contained within the moment or the song.

His critics conclude that the daring was not sustained throughout his recording career and argue that it should have been. His defenders claim that he was too versatile and he was obliged to express all moods and, in any case, his daring was always being resisted by the vested interests around him. The truth is that the critics will ask for too much and the defenders will excuse too easily.

His capabilities

Inevitably and invisibly, the gifts lead to capabilities and it is these that enabled him to deliver his achievements and posthumously overcome the Army, movies, Vegas, interference in the recording studio and self-destruction. The capabilities can be best explained by dividing popular music into four broad categories – rock, swing, power ballads and gentle lyricism. Rock requires a beat and relies on drum and bass and the singer to be effective requires force and timing. Swing is more subtle and the music is meant to bounce independently with the beat adding support. Force is still important because swing can include not only the gentler numbers of Frank Sinatra but Ray Charles and hardcore rhythm and blues. The power ballad is sometimes described as a torch song and usually involves full throated performances and a climax. Gentle lyricism relies on sensitivity and depends on a restrained vocal and avoids climaxes.

This is, of course, a crude categorisation, some ballads often have a beat, but it is not too crude to confirm that the full four are beyond normal singers. For example, Jackie Wilson and Ray Charles are rightly revered for their versatility but Jackie Wilson is not a master of gentle lyricism and Ray Charles does not sing rock music although he swings so powerfully few of us care. The passion and beat of soul music enables us to understand easily the limitations of white singers but it should not be assumed that every black, soul singer has within themselves the ability to deliver dance music. Their weaknesses are sometimes cleverly disguised. A heavy bass and a driving riff for the horns will carry rock and roll and soul records if the singer has no natural strength and these additions are used skilfully by record producers. A great example is 'Nowhere To Run' by Martha and the Vandellas. Some soul singers disguise their limitations with a growl, Bobby Bland and Bobby Womack, singers who relax more easily with a ballad, are good examples. The growl, though, has much in its favour and it is the preferred option for some critics. I am quite a growl fan myself but the point still needs to be made. The four categories exist.

When we divide music into these four categories Elvis stands in extremely rare company as one capable of delivering all four. Elvis also had the gift of being able to alter his voice so that he sounded like he was many singers but this ability weakened as his voice aged. Because it contains diversity, his talent is always impressive at any point in his career but his voice changed throughout his life and, even if it weakened, this development flattered his ability further to give him an unmatchable range and output.

All of this, I think, makes him stand alone. Versatility alone, though, is not necessarily enough. The first Elvis, gospel album, 'His Hand In Mine', featured on the cover a photograph of Elvis playing a piano. The record critic in 'Time' magazine wrote that the guitar was not the only instrument he played badly. What is important is whether he made good music in those categories and on how many occasions did he produce exceptional records. Elvis is like Howard Hawks who made classics in every popular, cinematic genre. His great records stretch across the divisions within the American music that existed in his lifetime - blues, country, rockabilly, rock and roll, pop, doo wop, soul and gospel. The more critical might suggest Michael Curtiz, who is more sentimental than Hawks, but Elvis went into left field too often for him to be compared with Curtiz.

In the late sixties, Phil Spector attempted to place Elvis in terms of importance in each of the genres. He rated him highly in them all. He was wrong to suggest Elvis was the greatest country singer because both George Jones and Jerry Lee Lewis were more able in this field. But Elvis was the best white, blues singer, the originator and master of rockabilly, a still great, country singer, a performer capable of delivering tough rock and roll and the greatest doo wop singer. His soul and gospel music may not respect the roots enough for purists but his efforts are still evidence of exceptional talent. 'Suspicious Minds' and 'How Great Thou Art' are supreme, soul and gospel classics. The only people who exceeded him in an individual genre were those who specialised. Even in those genres where he is less successful, the numbers of superiors are few and, whatever the genre, like Howard Hawks he produced classics.

The curse within the talent

The talent, therefore, is comprehensive and many of its elements are complementary. It should have been sufficient for the man and Elvis can be imagined as someone who, in other circumstances, would have been sufficient for himself. Shelley ascribes to her hero, and the Creature is the hero of the novel, an inadequate sufficiency. He is curious, talented and versatile but, like Elvis, there was more than one personality in the Creature. The first is a tender and generous spirit who, in the forest, not only makes rapid, intellectual progress but collects firewood and performs anonymous, domestic tasks for the De Lacey family. He is in the forest for two years, the same period Elvis spent at Sun records. The second, aware of his appearance and no longer innocent, is an angry figure but with no sense of inferiority. In her novel, 'The Last Man', Shelley describes her character, Lionel Verney, 'The sentiment of the worth of my nature supported me when others would have been oppressed.' For Elvis and the Creature, the sentiment of the worth also existed but it produced different results to Verney. The Creature had the physical prowess to seek vengeance before his escape to self-destruction at the North Pole, a destiny beyond those who hated him. Elvis had similar prowess. He had enough talent to seduce and engage the world but, later, he was able to use the same talent to treat the world and his fans with contempt. With little effort, he made more money and became more famous than those who sneered.

Both figures, despite being gifted, were cursed by being able to make damaging choices denied others. Those who forgive Elvis and the Creature do so because they understand the potential of the two figures. They realise how they suffered when they lost their innocence. Not all, though, need to forgive. Some are not interested in the talent and, with naivety they assume to be superiority, merely acknowledge that something made the two figures exceptional. These sophisticates act like Robert Walton who, after witnessing the death of Frankenstein, had to turn his ship away from 'the wondrous power of the needle.' No taste for tragedy or folly, the critics retreat easily.

THE TALENT AND THE TALENTED

The talent applied (1) – the demo discs

Two ambiguous scenes in nineteenth century, English Literature are the rape of Tess in 'Tess Of The D'Urbervilles' and the murder of the child in 'Frankenstein'. In the seduction scene in 'Tess', the author, Thomas Hardy, makes it clear that Alec d'Urberville has committed a dreadful offence and that Alec is not the first man to do whatever he did. It is the act of a selfish man and selfish man. Hardy never explains the offence other than saying Alec D'Urberville took advantage. He and others, like him, are unconcerned about the consequences for the women they seduce. The culpability or desire of Tess is never described and, consequently, Hardy implies a woman can be overpowered by something non-violent but still reprehensible. The murder of the small child in 'Frankenstein' is also confusing. Some readers have concluded the murder was an accident and that the Creature was merely trying to stop the child from screaming but Shelley makes it clear that the Creature wants vengeance against Victor Frankenstein and is prepared to use the child to satisfy his need. 'Frankenstein! You belong then to my enemy – to him towards whom I have sworn eternal revenge, you shall be my first victim.' The reason for the ambiguity in both scenes is simple, censorship in nineteenth century literature. Hardy was unable to describe the sexual act and Shelley refrained from showing the full horror of a small child being strangled by a monster. She merely mentions the Creature putting a hand to the throat of the child. Because a full description of the sex is omitted, we remain unclear about Tess and why she did have sex with Alec d'Urbervilles. Oddly, the same need for self-censorship in Shelley suggests more about the Creature. His coy narration indicates an ability to excuse too easily, a moral failure and a need for vengeance. Despite what the Creature describes, the death of a child by the lake is not an accident that he did not intend.

A highlight of the 1931 movie, 'The Curse Of Frankenstein', is the recreation of the murder of the child by the lake. It is very different to the scene in the novel. The child, who drowns, is a girl not a boy and she is the daughter of a peasant. She is not a fledgling aristocrat. The scene was originally edited to be less explicit but it has been fully restored and, without 1930s censorship, we can now see Karloff hurl the child in the water. Karloff is perfect as he holds his hand out for the child to grasp and David Thomson, the film critic, is accurate when he describes Karloff offering horror and promise, a description that could apply equally to sexual seduction or the appearance of Elvis in 1956. The child in the scene is also strange. She has no friends and apart from her naive father she has no family. It is this loneliness that makes her so susceptible to the promise of the strange Creature and, like Tess in her fateful moment, makes the child disregard the horror. Who knows why some of us are compelled by promise whilst others only respond to the horror?

'Writing For The King' is the title of a book by author Ken Sharp. The book is important because it addresses the most important issue in the discussion of Elvis, just how creative was the singer. Common sense insists that his achievements cannot always be ascribed to others because this invites the unanswerable question, why did the others not achieve similar results.

Common sense, though, is not enough. When faith is based on a promise and a wilful acceptance of horror it needs to be reaffirmed regularly. For that, we need proof or, at least, the occasional revelation. When I was a young man I made the pledge to take Elvis seriously and to credit him with talent and responsibility. Ultimately, the pledge needs to be vindicated with evidence and the book by Sharp has more evidence than most.

The book is a beautifully produced monument to persistent obsession and is valuable alone for its unexpected photograph of Freddie Bienstock with Stephen Sondheim. Freddie looks like an over-groomed, wimpy vampire who might have already lost a few teeth and Sondheim has unbelievably, like Elvis, a curled lip which surely is deliberate.

'Writing For The King' consists of two elements, a book and two CDs. The first CD is a live compilation and, although of good quality, it is difficult to see how it relates to the book. The second CD contains a selection of demo records submitted by the songwriters to Elvis. This second CD makes 'Writing For The King' unique.

In the book, all the songwriters make contributions that are first hand accounts. They do vary considerably but, amidst them, are tales of how they wrote the songs and what they thought of the contribution of Elvis. Not all these memories may be based on interviews with the author because, surely, some of the songwriters must have been dead when he wrote the book but, perhaps, he really did meet everyone. If not, the mix of the interview and research material is cleverly done and the book gives a seamless history of their contributions.

The author, Ken Sharp, does not address the actual contribution of Elvis. He simply lets the song writers share their memories. He describes himself as 'always being a song man' which I am not. I do, though, identify with him.

The first sentence lets us know that he has to thank his mother. I know the feeling. My mother did not convert me to Elvis but her interest in blues and jazz did make me familiar with American music and she talked about Elvis before he appeared so I was already primed when he roared on 'The Jack Jackson Show' in 1956. On the same page as the first sentence, there is a photograph of Ken when he was six years old. He is sitting in a small armchair, the kind that indulgent parents often buy their children. In his arms, he holds a copy of the album, 'Elvis Golden Records Volume One'. The young boy has a Beatles hair cut but he is only six years old and it is more than compensated by the Elvis record and the wide grin on his innocent face. Holding a favourite possession and blessed with parental approval, the child is secure in the warm company of his family. It is a photograph of a small boy happily being photographed by affectionate parents. The anchors are in place and their son is springing to life in a way that no doubt delights them. It is easy to believe this blissful scene - security and growth, potential promised and circumscribed without any threat. A child who knows that, because of the shared interest in Elvis, his family will always be ready to listen to what he says. Like all writers, he will grow into a person who will expect to be heard.

The first album I bought was 'Golden Records Volume One'. It became a bible for me in the same way Ken Sharp describes it was for him. Occasionally, I play it back to back with 'Blonde On Blonde' by Dylan or 'Songs In The Key Of Life' by Stevie Wonder and I still think it is a match for what followed. It exists as a reminder of what had once enticed the world, the mix of his early headstrong RCA hits and the raw revolution at Sun. More than once, I have sneaked a look at this photograph of the author, at the small child with the wide smile and the woollen pullover. The young boy has an album in his hand that has already redefined his life and the boy believes, as the grin makes obvious, that the world is now complete. I remember the belief. As a child surrounded by giants, I was easily dazzled by what I thought waited in the future. I was too ready to succumb to rock and roll stars. Only later, as a tempered adult, did I suspect that what inspired and defined me may have been the consequence of my own, innate flaws.

When Mary Shelley wrote 'Frankenstein' she utilised a formula that was irresistible, the self-taught innocent who makes progress by anonymously observing strangers but, after being betrayed by his powerful creator, becomes a vengeful murderer. If she is coy about the detail, the circumstances are not withheld from the reader. But, although everything is revealed, the characters and story are compelled to mystery. This is the legacy of chance or fate. The information released since his death has revealed as much about him as any other man, yet, the mysteries also endure about Elvis. Why he was both inspirational and dull is only one of many but it is the one that preoccupies this Elvis fan. I am no different from other fans and have become convinced that one more outtake or book will enable me to finally understand the aloof and always remote creature. This is what happens when the child by the lake survives. I read what I can and buy CDs I should not but, like Frankenstein chasing the Creature across Russia, an inconclusive glimpse of a turned shoulder between the bare trees always compels me forward.

I bought 'Writing For The King' hoping that the chase may be finally over, that it would make clear how creative Elvis was in the studio. At first, I was disappointed but I soon accepted this as inevitable because even the people, who worked with him in the studio, had different opinions about his contributions and talent although all acknowledge he had a special gift.

The book, 'Writing For The King', has been criticised. The £70 price does not help because it increases expectations; it promises to be the conclusion of our lonely chase through wintry forests. When foiled, like Frankenstein, we lose our tempers and curse and damn the powers of concealment that the creature possesses. A reviewer on Amazon complained that the songwriters had little to say, that the demo compilation was a poor choice and that the live CD was irrelevant. The book deserves some sympathy. For all the problems the author encountered in obtaining revealing demos, his book is worthwhile although the songwriters are usually uninspired conversationalists. Those who romanticise the craft of song-writing are rebuked by the comments of these songwriters. The most cerebral by far are the gifted Doc Pomus and Mort Shuman and the highly rated Mike Leiber and Jerry Stoller. The others struggle to articulate what Elvis added to their songs or what made him or their songs special. The ideas that they claim inspired the songs are usually quite banal but this should not be interpreted as a criticism. They were men and sometimes women obliged to find an idea that would kick start the song and grab listeners, nothing more.

One critic complained that too many of the demos had arrangements that Elvis did not change significantly. He suggested other examples should have been included instead of the selected songs. We know from outtakes on songs such as 'I Beg Of You', 'Little Sister' and 'True Love Travels On A Gravel Road' that Elvis definitely did on occasion alter the arrangements. We also know from his covers of songs by other people how he could change a song dramatically. 'I'll Hold You In My Heart', 'Reconsider Baby' and 'Faded Love' are songs transformed by Elvis. None of these originals are included for comparison. Presumably, the selection of demos would have been determined by what was available. Of the twenty demos, thirteen of them are film songs and these undermine the sample because the movies rarely encouraged or inspired Elvis to be creative. But, whatever the problems, a picture does emerge of Elvis at work if we add it to what we already know.

The songwriters in their accounts are often as self-serving as salesmen which, of course, were what they had to be. Their demo discs are nowhere near as accomplished as the songwriters like to pretend. This is the first surprise in the book or package. The demos that Elvis listened to before recording his versions were quite rough. There are exceptions. The demo version of 'Don't Ask Me Why' by Jimmy Breedlove is unusual because it could have been released as a commercial record and it could have even been a hit. Jimmy Breedlove, the talented demo singer who came to fame with the vocal group, The Cues, may have felt his ability was being wasted on demo records but, in 1963, he recorded 'Jealous Fool' in which he imitated Elvis quite well and without any hint of resentment. The version of 'Don't Ask Me Why' by Elvis is looser and more fluent. Somehow, Elvis offers romance and promise whereas Jimmy is always earnest. The horns and Jordanaires also help establish a different feel. It swings in a way that is beyond Jimmy Breedlove but it does not overshadow the original. Some of the later demos are also of a good standard. The demos of 'Raised On Rock' and 'Way Down' are catchy and interesting. These songs have an interesting, modern-rock feel but Elvis either ignores or fails to grasp it. They suggest that seventies, American rock with its swampy edge and emerging quirky, Louisiana ethnicity was beyond Memphis Elvis or, at least, the wasted Elvis who recorded them. The words of 'Raised' are a bit naff but the demo has a good feel as does the original of 'Way Down'. These two songs had potential beyond what Elvis realised and they exist as evidence that it was not just his temperament but his reduced powers that pushed him towards ballads at the end of his career.

Stan Gebler is unique amongst the songwriters because he claims that Elvis did an inferior version to the demo vocal on his song, 'My Desert Serenade'. He is correct because this was a poor, soundtrack song and Elvis treated it with contempt. This song was featured in the awful movie, 'Harum Scarum', and, by the time that was being completed, Elvis was making records as inept as any demo track. Elvis adds nothing to this song which was what he probably intended.

The songwriters do claim on occasions that Elvis merely copied the arrangement but there are examples where their claims are clearly contradicted. In referring to 'An American Trilogy', Mickey Newbury states that Elvis 'did the exact arrangement of my record and played it live.' This is a problem for me. If he did the exact arrangement, Newbury needs to explain what he did with the top As that Elvis sings because none exist in the original arrangement. And how did the backing singers and orchestra suddenly appear? We also know that Elvis repeated the middle section at the end of the song so it became a four verse alternative to the three verse original that Newbury recorded. This hardly constitutes exact. Not quoted in the book, but relevant, is what Paul Simon said about the version Elvis recorded of 'Bridge Over

Troubled Water'. He said something like, 'They just copied the bass line. I thought it was a bit melodramatic but how in the hell do you compete with that.' One is obliged to ask how the melodrama was created without altering the approach.

The clue is in the reference to the bass line. This is seen as the key to the arrangement. In quartet, gospel music, for example, the bass singer rather than the piano defines the arrangement. Most songwriters will claim that if the bass line is left intact then the arrangement has been unaltered. If the logic in this is self-serving and minimises the contribution of the other musicians, we do have plenty of examples of bass lines being amended. When The Beatles visited Elvis in the sixties they encountered Elvis on his sofa watching TV with the sound turned down while he was listening to a record of 'Mohair Sam' by Charlie Rich. Elvis was playing a bass guitar. He never did record a version of 'Mohair Sam', probably, because he never found the alternative bass line he was searching for that night but he found one for 'Memphis Tennessee'. This, I guess, was his substitute for 'Mohair Sam'. But an arrangement is more than a bass line, otherwise we would not have extra verses, additional instruments and singers, higher notes or changes in tempo, all of which Elvis used as a way of giving a song different feel and identity. And, if that was not enough, then he would change the bass line but, usually, he did not feel obliged to make this change because, on so many occasions, he could change a record in other ways.

We have to be wary of the claims of songwriters. Many songwriters have exposed their ambitions by claiming that Elvis copied the vocalist but this goes way too far as these demos reveal. In fact, what makes the demos amusing is how the demo vocalists try to anticipate how Elvis might sing the song and, invariably, he spites them with an alternative approach. The demo of 'Teddy Bear' is tailored for Elvis but he gives it a completely different identity to the lumbering and inarticulate demo. Elvis camps his vocal with a slurred, deep, breathy voice that is far removed from the heavy original and, suddenly, the song is full of humour and a slyness that has been missing from the imagination of the songwriter. It feels radically different. It also includes a very low note that does not exist in the demo.

In her book, 'Baby Let's Play House', Alanna Nash claims that Elvis rarely altered the arrangement but that he was the master of the studio and worked with his musicians to create a different feel and identity for the songs. This is fair. In the main, but not always, he left bass lines intact but, at his best, he would work and create a fresh approach and feel. Sometimes, it would involve musical changes but, sometimes, it could be achieved merely by the force of his musical personality. There are very good examples of this on the demo collection. 'No More' and 'Pocketful Of Rainbows' are uncomplicated ballads for the movies and it is clear from the sweet demos that the songwriters intended them to be no more than that. Elvis adjusts a couple of the bridges in 'Rainbows' and alters the tempo slightly but the changes are modest. 'No More' he sings without alteration or straight. Both songs are transformed into something clearer and purer because he is musical and can sing. It is like he has carried the songs into the clouds. The records achieve lift off in a way that nobody would predict from listening to the demos.

On 'Hard Headed Woman', he goes further. The song is converted from hard core rockabilly to something that is a mix of broader rock and roll and New Orleans rhythm and blues. The addition of a horn section obviously helps but Elvis is fundamental to its very different feel. The difference is substantial enough for it to cross genres but how this is achieved is difficult to determine precisely. It appears to be more the consequence of his personality, mood and enthusiasm than the extra instruments. The famous 'Trouble' is included and this is radically altered from the demo. The songwriters, Leiber and Stoller, were present in the studio and this might help explain how the song developed into something much different.

A major surprise in the demos is the willingness of Elvis to eschew the carefully placed hooks of the songwriters and he either makes the song plainer or he substitutes alternative hooks elsewhere. His versions of 'I've Lost You' and 'Mary In The Morning' are good examples. The demo of 'Lost You' has an arrangement that sounds like fake Vaughan Williams but he flattens out the Vaughan Williams and avoids the ornate climax. Similarly, he resists the folk chirpiness of 'Mary' and, to introduce a romance out of reach, he substitutes a smoother, gloomier approach. To the insensitive, this may be no more than interpretation but it is interpretation at the highest level although these are not his finest records. The repetitive

John Fogerty style, guitar hooks on the very decent demo of 'Burning Love' are also ignored presumably to produce something different to Creedence Clearwater and more personal to him. His version is more carefree and he obliterates the challenges rather than responds to them.

The other demos are equally fascinating. 'T-R-O-U-B-L-E' does not compare with the best of his rockers. The demo is pure country but a weakened, seventies Elvis can still cross genres and the final result is tough rock and roll. The demo of 'His Latest Flame' is especially heavy-handed although it is clearly recognisable as the source. We know from the outtakes that Elvis and the band worked hard to add to the catchy tune a tighter, more compelling hook which is what they achieved brilliantly. (This record was re-mastered for the collection, 'Elvis 30 No 1 Hits', and it really benefits from the added punch.) The demo of 'Wearing That Loved On Look' is the first to lean to a swamp sound but that is rejected by Elvis and Chips Moman and they pull the song succesfully to more traditional gospel. If it is not one of his great rockers, 'Devil In Disguise' is always worth a listen. The demo is lighter than the version by Elvis and lacks the accusatory edge although, for obvious reasons, the complicated arrangement is adhered to quite closely by Elvis. In its original form, it has a modern Western feel and the demo resembles slightly the songs Frankie Laine used to record with Chips Miller. Elvis loses this and improves the material. It is impressive how he manages to give it a firmer rock edge but establish himself as the more fragile victim. A similar, Western feel exists on the original of 'Viva Las Vegas' and the demo is presented as macho material with a tough, conquering male living in the confident, masculine world of gambling. Elvis abandons both the personality and feel and, in his version, we have a more neurotic character gripped by compulsion. The world is controlling him and not the other way round. He does the reverse on 'Good Luck Charm' and abandons the fey vocal of the demo singer for something stronger and more masculine. Similarly, he adds grit and a degree of anger to the pop tune, 'Wear My Ring Around Your Neck', so it becomes rock and roll. The demo of 'Heartbreak Hotel' is a surprise because the demo vocal prematurely anticipates Elvis as a parody. Although he follows the arrangement closely, his version has additional drama and intensity. He can sing and, after hearing the inept demo, he unleashes his talent with confidence.

These last three songs are not Elvis at his most original but they all have a different groove to the demos and this is what the book and CD continually demonstrate. Elvis, leading a band, will always create a feel that is unique to him. Constantly, the songs appear to explode into freedom and move to a higher level where they have space to roam powerfully and where he can invent a vocal identity. This is his talent and it is considerable.

So, the book and demos are informative and, when listened to in conjunction with the outtakes on the expanded albums on the 'Follow That Dream' label, we understand more the creative process. We hear how a mere singer often added through effort and instinct more than his unique and complex vocal identity although that alone always made a difference. This is why his records qualify as a musical tradition.

Despite many movie songs being included, the CD confirms the talent. If it fails to reveal all, it is still an important glimpse. The confirmation is necessary and benefits from being repeated. Without one more look, we doubt ourselves, so it is more than curiosity that itches. Most Elvis fans will approach this book with their memories of horror and promise intact. They remember not only 'Elvis Golden Records Volume 1' but 'Paradise Hawaiian Style'.

To finish this section, I looked at the book again, fortunately, no longer terrified of being disillusioned. In the opening pages, the author admits he found it easier to relate to the music of the seventies than some critics. His parents divorced some time after the photograph was taken and he feels the event and its consequences helped him recognise the despair Elvis was trying to communicate in those bleak ballads. Presumably, the smile in the photograph became tears and, for a while, the author was not the prize to his parents he had been earlier. Well, the six year old lost his innocence and became a fine detective. If the connection between lost innocence and compulsive enquiry exists for Ken Sharp, he is not alone in that because so many of the children by the lake who survive become detectives later.

In the book, the songwriter Doc Pomus explains the talent of Elvis as well as anyone. 'And like I have always told people, the one thing about getting Elvis Presley (to) record (one of my songs), that always meant you were gonna hear your song plus, because he always put something in your song that maybe you never heard. You know what I'm saying? He always put himself in them and he was always the song plus. So I always wildly anticipated the Presley record because you get something in that song you never dreamed of.'

Imagine how Pomus must have felt when he heard for the first time Elvis sing 'His Latest Flame'. Is it too fanciful to borrow from Pomus and say Elvis gave us all music we had never heard and also something we never dreamed?

As always, enquiry does not reveal all and, though, it does confirm the talent, we always want more evidence and self-justification. Meanwhile, we should be thankful for the book. The children by the lake can now hold the hand of their creature with more confidence.

———————

The talent applied (2) – classic albums

After his movies and the self-destruction, many no longer want to understand. Without either liking Elvis or knowing his full catalogue, they feel obliged to praise but, only, because he is famous and has an historical importance that cannot be ignored. Their escape route is simple. He was a significant icon and launched a social revolution but his music is poor or not as important as that made by others. People prefer the Frankenstein movies to the novel. The complicated career of Elvis is avoided. They want monsters and heroes and not someone who is both. From their limited perspective, the condemnation of Elvis is justified. They know the singles and recognise their decline in quality and they have heard the embarrassments. The truth is more complicated and more flattering. Dave Marsh, in his liner notes to the seventies box set, 'Walk A Mile In My Shoes', compares Elvis to Picasso. He distinguishes between the perfectionists who wait for inspiration and the labourers who persist and sometimes produce great results. I recently attended an exhibition of the political work by Picasso and was impressed by a painting where he had ignored the paint that had dripped to the bottom of the canvas. Other painters would have painted over what was no more than a stain. Picasso must have thought, 'Sod it. The message and the talent can still be seen.' Elvis, because of his taste and personality, was always likely to be the inconsistent labourer rather than the perfectionist but the impact of others clearly made the situation worse. But we do not criticise Picasso because not all of his paintings match the exceptional 'Guernica' or 'Les Demoiselles d'Avignon' and Elvis should not be condemned for making rubbish although he can be criticised for its quantity.

Elvis did make many inferior records and, because of the bad guys and his own failings, we now understand why but, for all the disappointments, Elvis left behind a wealth of enjoyable material. Applying what could be regarded as a deliberately harsh standard, Elvis recorded around fifty classics. In addition to this, there are nearly three hundred more that have some merit. These range from great and almost classic but marred by a slight flaw followed by the very good but it is still not Elvis at his peak and, finally, records that are just okay, perhaps, because the song is weak or Elvis is alright but uninspired. The rest are either duff songs or feature an Elvis who is either badly off form or not interested. There are plenty in this final category and these include his own errors but, more often, they were forced upon him, either because of movie contracts or song publishing deals.

It is not necessary to examine in detail the absolute rubbish because it is obvious from his career and what happened that they do not give an account of the man. And little can be said about songs like 'There's No Room To Rumba In A Sports Car' other than that they are awful and are sung by a singer who hates them as much as the listener. To think about his merits, it is only necessary to examine his positive achievements, especially, in this day of the iPod when none of us have any compunction about redefining a performer to suit our personal playlists. The priest in the sequel, 'Frankenstein's Monster', advised correctly, 'think of what the Creature did well.'

The other criticism made often is that Elvis was a shallow, singles man. He never made any great albums. True, Elvis was a performer who emerged in the fifties when albums were conceived as something that would play in the background of comfortable homes. He wanted hit singles more than anything. It would, though, be untrue to say he never recorded any great albums.

Elvis made nine classic albums and, if these appear pitifully few in a twenty three year career, it has to be remembered much of his time was devoted to movies or spent in decline awaiting a premature death. There are also other albums that may not be classic but still have merit. More important is the scandal of RCA and Parker failing to release potentially great albums. RCA also wasted his live material and, with great delicacy, avoided releasing a fabulous, live album. In their defence, they did eventually master what was required but it needed the invention of the CD and, by then, Elvis was not producing his best live performances because he was dead.

So, tolerance is required because there would have been many more if his management had been blessed with common sense.

The great albums are these and are listed in order of merit as perceived by me.

- *'How Great Thou Art'*
- *'From Elvis In Memphis'*
- *'Elvis Presley'*
- *'Elvis Is Back'*
- *'Elvis Rock And Roll No 2'*
- *'Elvis Country'*
- *'His Hand In Mine'*
- *'Elvis TV Special'*
- *'King Creole'*

Within that list, are two gospel albums, the recording from the 'TV Special' and, from the movies, a less than authentic soundtrack. Without them, the list would only be five. Either way, it is not many but there are reasons. There are only three albums from the fifties and no one, who knows the music of Elvis Presley, believes that his fifties material amounts to little more than three great albums or thirty six songs. The UK editions of the singles albums, 'Golden Records Volume 1 and 2', collected thirty classic tracks and, in the fifties, these existed for his fans as the ultimate confirmation of his worth. Two additional, great albums could have been issued with material to spare and these existing, marvellous, singles collections of alternative material kept intact. Some of this other material was actually used to create the collections issued while he was in the Army - 'Elvis' and 'A Date With Elvis'. These are great albums but not included in the list because, although released before 1960, they exist as retrospective collections. Using different definitions, it can be claimed seven great albums were issued in the fifties alone. The list would have been much longer if his output had been organised with the objective of producing memorable albums.

'How Great Thou Art'

Obviously, any selection is subjective and younger fans may insist that other albums such as 'That's The Way It Is' should be included. Well, I acquired a long time ago a taste for the music of the American poor. If Elvis has finally persuaded me of the merits of the alternatives, I still have my preferences. So, his gospel material appeals because it is close to his roots and those roots have value. Women critics say something similar about 'Mathilda' and the feminist writing of Shelley.

'How Great Thou Art' should not be called a concept album but it is richly thematic and, because of that, there is no hesitation in focussing on the messages within the music rather than giving attention to the musical detail. I am an atheist but the themes within the album are also what echo in my insubstantial heart. They are human fragility and isolation, the need for spiritual support and the dissipating presence of guilt and death. This is music with substance.

Elvis ensures that the album illuminates these themes without ever demonstrating that he understands the intellectual concerns behind any of these issues and this is to his credit. Too often, intellectuals assume that it is only the educated that are capable of being haunted. The album is to Elvis what 'The Magnificent Ambersons' would have been to Orson Welles if RKO had left the original ending intact. His movie, 'Citizen Kane', is brilliant and enhanced by virtuosity but 'Ambersons' is from the heart. Similarly, 'How Great Thou Art' is a personal and profound statement from a unique talent. The music on the album identifies human isolation and insists on the need for metaphysical contact and support.

I first bought 'How Great Thou Art' in 1971 for £1 in a Glasgow record shop. Up till then, I had avoided the gospel material. It had been bad enough dealing with the movies but the record was only a quid and I took a chance. That afternoon, I visited my soon to be wife, later divorced. We talked and listened to the album. Soon, and without warning, she confessed about a previous relationship that she had ended badly. The incident, like the relationship, was inconsequential but, that afternoon, she was prepared to accept a moral responsibility and guilt previously considered trivial.

'I don't know why I am suddenly telling you this,' she said.

I looked at the record player. 'It's the music,' I said.

We listened to the rest of the album without speaking.

Some days later, I returned to my home in Merseyside. I played the album, now my surprising treasure, for my parents.

'What do you think?' I said.

'By the hell,' said my father.

My mother nodded and smiled.

'How Great Thou Art' cannot be listened to endlessly. In the same way, we cannot exist for too long with the sensitivity that the death of someone close inspires. The music is too intense and we need to resume living. But, for half an hour, the album mixes self-hatred, aspiration and hope with a piety, sympathy and self-awareness that cannot be ignored. He gives a voice to the powerless because he still understands that life is a struggle for the ordinary and he has just enough religious conviction for him to insist that there is neither escape nor reward without a conscience. The album is also about Elvis and it is clearly the music of a man who has lost self-respect and is desperate to know if it is indeed possible to regain. None of this is made explicit. It is what I feel when I listen to the album. Greil Marcus, in 'Mystery Train', said the album is good enough to want to make you convert. Not necessarily but it does persuade that true tolerance requires both understanding and piety and, perhaps, when the two do combine, which is rare, we witness what is best about religious faith.

Guralnick, in 'Careless Love', has described the recording sessions as highly productive, music made by people who inspired each other. Other than the movie filler before 'How Great Thou Art', Elvis had not visited a studio for two years and, then, he had only recorded three songs. The album was recorded in 1966. Although the sixties are usually dismissed as the movie period, the years from 1960 to 1968 can be divided into three phases. The first two triumphant years, the next two years when Elvis indicated disillusionment and the final four years when his movie efforts become even worse but he made an attempt to improve his non-movie studio material.

Felton Jarvis began working with Elvis in 1966 at the beginning of the third sixties phase and, after the soulless producer, Chet Atkins, he provided initial relief. He was an Elvis fan and he soon established a rapport and friendship. The last studio session before the arrival of Jarvis produced 'Memphis Tennessee', 'Ask Me' and 'It Hurts Me'. They are all fine records and a huge improvement on the studio recordings that had preceded them in the previous two years. The consensus is that Elvis was focused and enthusiastic. They hint that a renaissance may have been possible earlier and it could have occurred without Jarvis. Supposedly, Elvis did not visit the studio for another two years because he was not interested. These three records do not support the claim but, in his lecture to the Country Music Hall Of Fame, Peter Gurlanick stated that Parker wanted Elvis in the studio making hits. This, though, is not consistent with Parker in this phase using most of the songs Elvis recorded in the studio as bonus tracks for soundtrack albums or with Parker from the early sixties insisting that Elvis only record the minimum amount of non-film material required by RCA.

More through intuition than any evidence, I will concede that Guralnick is half right. Elvis, supposedly, was already suffering from depression and was a man who now needed support to visit the studio, support that was beyond the management style of Parker and RCA. Undoubtedly, Parker would have liked a few hit singles and would have even settled for rock and roll but his obsession with movies and their contract fulfilment meant the organisation of studio sessions was beyond him. Equally, the possibility that Elvis resisted appearing in the studios out of simple spite cannot be dismissed. Whatever caused the impasse, it was resolved by Parker or RCA tempting Elvis back into the studio to record a gospel album.

For once, the album was made on his terms although the sessions did not work to an exact blueprint. Inevitably, some songs were suddenly added or switched. Elvis had originally wanted Jimmy Jones, the black, bass singer, who was not available. Jimmy Jones is a loss because it is easy to imagine how his lilting, almost hesitant but fine, bass voice would have fitted into the measured feel of the album. Albert Goldman also noticed how the demands of Elvis were accepted on these sessions. He believes that the album is a failure but this view is only sustained by a stereotypical view of gospel music. Goldman assumes it has to be fervent hand clapping, heart rending bellows and obvious virtuosity. The much more restrained 'How Great Thou Art' he condemns as crooning as he probably would Jimmy Jones.

Goldman misses the point. Less is sometimes more. This is not music for you to admire. Elvis is not interested in the cheap effects of galvanisation. It is music for you to feel. If you do, you will become human again and experience the exaltation of despair. It is why my father said, 'By the hell' and why my fiancée reacted the way she did. It touches nerves dulled by the modern world.

Musicologists, whenever possible, are keen to point out the similarity of arrangements in his gospel music to the originals but, inevitably, Elvis moves beyond white gospel because of his always insistent, vocal identity. His own style is somewhere between white and black and, compared to Elvis, traditional, white, gospel music sounds a little stiff necked although there are some fabulous exceptions. The nearest example to Elvis singing white gospel is the beautiful 'A Satisfied Mind' by Mahalia Jackson which has a six-eight time and sounds like a western tune. She sings it similar to how Elvis sings much of his gospel music. Nothing is hurried but notes are emphasised with a slow burn. In particular, her singing on the phrase, 'a satisfied mind', sounds like Elvis. So, Elvis alone makes a difference but the album also has Elvis singing extended leads with eight male and four female singers in support. The piano is supplemented by an instrumental group. White gospel is essentially four men and a piano and the vocal solos are usually quite brief. It all sounds different because it is different.

Elvis had originally wanted his voice turned low so that it would merge into all the other voices. RCA did not entirely acquiesce to his wishes and turned up his voice a little in the final master but not to normal levels. This is a hint that Elvis wanted to make music that we would feel rather than admire and it shows an understanding on his part that, if his fame was not to be an obstacle, his presence needed to be controlled. Of course, this may be pure supposition and it may have been no more than his specific taste in harmony. He may have also been playing games with RCA and Parker who, he knew, would turn up his voice anyway. We do, though, have an idea of what the records may have sounded like if he had been obeyed completely. 'Down In The Alley', a raunchy rhythm and blues recorded on the first day of the sessions, has his voice quite low in the mix yet it still rocks. 'Beyond The Reef', recorded the day after 'Down In The Alley', was only released after his death. Again, his voice is very quiet. The song is nothing special but the harmonies are beautiful. His fifties recording of the Cole Porter song, 'True Love', is an earlier, similar example that has Elvis merely harmonising with the Jordanaires. The result is a delight.

Possibly, the qualities I ascribe to 'How Great Thou Art' underestimate what can be found in all gospel music. In other words, gospel music is spiritual and much of it is profound. These are not pop tunes. I have a reasonable collection of American, gospel music and, indeed, some gospel music, in particular, black, gospel music, has qualities that 'How Great Thou Art' lacks. Elvis is not the gospel equivalent of Mahalia Jackson and no gospel record by anyone compares to her triumph, 'In The Upper Room'. But black, gospel music, like the best, black, American music, is about an oppressed race using their talent to break free of their shackles. This is why African-American music is relentlessly innovative. The shackles are still there and virtuosity and defiance remain important for racial pride. The gospel music of Elvis is different. The album, 'How Great Thou Art', is personal to him and it reflects not just his memory of the inspiring conscience in the powerless but also the spiritual loss that comfort and success have brought him. His life has become disappointing and this is why a God, imagined or real, is necessary. He pleads not only for himself but the others he left behind and the triumph is that his music is perfectly suited to his ambition. Some may perceive this achievement as not especially ambitious but it is significant for him and that makes it meaningful.

In such circumstances, it is dangerous to highlight individual tracks. There are no bad recordings on 'How Great Thou Art' although the hand clapping, revivalist numbers, though fine, are the weakest. Some critics feel Elvis sacrifices an opportunity to demonstrate his vocal strength but it would have reduced the album if he had completely embraced exhilaration. Instead, he remembers the ultimate ambition and calls it correctly. 'Run On' is the highlight of the jubilee numbers and it contains enough of a threat to make it exciting. It is also humorous but the fast talking humour, as it should not, offers no relief, only warnings. The vocal backing, which includes Jake Hess, is superb and full of interesting detail. More than one voice makes a distinct contribution so there is both progress and comparison as the song proceeds. Elvis avoids aggression and, more importantly, knowing smugness but, despite his restraint, he is still able to chew down on the words and it is enough to make it swing wonderfully.

The slower numbers are perfect and everyone will have individual favourites but mine is 'Stand By Me'. Despite a need to maintain hesitancy and fear, the beautifully clear vocal dominates and thrills and Elvis ensures the tension never weakens. The lines, 'When I do the best I can and all my friends misunderstan'', are as poignant as anything I have ever heard. Elvis extends the word 'do' so we understand he really does try but his treble lets us know why his efforts are inadequate and his unusual phrasing on 'misunderstan'' defines brilliantly his consequent confusion. Besides this, we have the justly recognised, 'How Great Thou Art' which Elvis performs like a bass singer from a Russian choir or a Portuguese Fado singer. He summons up his all talent and strength to make an offering worthy of the superior power. The virtuosity and power impress but behind it is the contrasting echo of humility and deference. Elvis is aware of the metaphysical irony that dominates his triumph.

In the same way Sister Rosetta Tharpe in her brilliant 'That's All' condemns intellectuals who do not believe in God, Elvis throughout the album insists it is his ignorance before mystery that makes him worthwhile. The weird mix of dread and optimism that form the emotional pulse of the songs are drenched with humility and the elements complement one another beautifully. All the ballads are achingly slow and soulful, often slower than the originals, and all have fine, female accompaniment. They have a magic beyond criticism and understanding, they simply groove on a higher plane. 'Somebody Bigger Than You And I' swings charmingly and has just a hint of the blues. Mahalia Jackson has also recorded a version of 'Somebody' and, because of her unique voice, it inevitably has moments of virtuosity beyond Elvis but he more than holds his own against this great, gospel singer. His interpretation has a profundity that is not in the version by Mahalia.

The 'How Great Thou Art' album is Elvis performing the music he understands and, within his own milieu, he reveals he can be a man of taste. When he sings he reaches out into temporal mystery, armed with the faith that his Maker is palpable and will ultimately provide for him what he is worth.

'How Great Thou Art' is album number one although his technical virtuosity is less obvious here than on other albums. Instead, he uses his talent modestly in the service of another ambition, to acknowledge himself and to honour his roots and his God. Although it does not exist alone, this album alone would have ensured his life was not wasted.

'From Elvis In Memphis'

Soon after this album was released, a group of British fans visited America to see Elvis in concert. They recalled their dismay when they met young, white, American fans from Memphis who condemned the album for being too much like black, soul music. Elvis, of course, saw it somewhat differently as he made clear when he recruited the black, female, vocal group - the Sweet Inspirations - to back him on stage.

Although Chips Moman successfully did his job as producer and made it all sound contemporary, the album exists as a claim by Elvis on his inheritance and that inheritance includes the American music he enjoys, black and white, old and modern. He also insists that these alternative forms of music can be combined and not only the album but individual tracks stand as a testament to his belief in musical integration which, of course, was also informed by his belief in racial integration. This does not mean that 'From Elvis In Memphis' is thematic although I doubt myself because it can also be interpreted as an expression of the romantic fatalism that clouded his life.

Interestingly, the history of the album evokes controversy. Every fan knows the story that the RCA executives did not want Elvis to record 'Suspicious Minds' because it was not subject to the song writing deals that guaranteed them a high percentage on royalties. Chips said, that he believed in the song and, if he could not record it, he would close the session and let RCA have the tapes already recorded for free. His firm stand ensured he kept control and strong material could be available.

Pardon the odd doubt.

An argument definitely took place but it is rarely mentioned that Elvis had already recorded eighteen tracks prior to the debate about 'Suspicious Minds' which was the last song of the first sessions in January.

The majority of the thirty one tracks from American Sound were completed before the argument over 'Suspicious Minds'. The material does improve after 'Suspicious Minds' but not to the extent that is often assumed. The last, three songs of the second sessions are actually quite poor. Also included in the additional thirteen is 'Power Of My Love' which, although great, has to be an overspill, movie song. 'Stranger In My Own Home Town' is also fabulous but it is Elvis jamming with the band and it would not have been a song that Moman wanted to record. Because the songs that follow 'Suspicious Minds' are all recorded in the later sessions in February, Elvis is now familiar with his surroundings. According to Peter Guralnick, Elvis after his return was much more confident and his behaviour bordered on the arrogant. The success of the second session was rooted in a freer and more assured Elvis rather than improved material.

Moman could have reasonably said that they would be using what he regarded as unacceptable material if they relied on existing sources in the next session. But eighteen tracks had already been recorded and this number was probably consistent with the contract offered to Moman, an album plus some singles. The notion that Moman would have honoured his contract for eighteen songs and then waived his fee is ludicrous. There was an argument and it did have an impact on the sessions but it came late. Relevant to how we interpret the events at American Sound Studios is the subsequent statement by Moman that he never intended to have released from the sessions more than one album and three double sided singles. Not only does this correspond to what we would assume to be a normal contract, it strengthens the claim that Moman would never have surrendered eighteen tracks without a fee. Perhaps Moman wanted extra tracks to strengthen his selection of the final eighteen and the argument about 'Suspicious Minds' became confused with the need to debate if continuing was possible. All thirty two tracks from the two sessions were released and, as thirty were actually released within a year, it could be argued that, if Chips Moman intended to improve the choice available for the ultimate eighteen tracks, he lost the argument. The whole tale becomes murky because it is clear that the sessions merit more than a mere eighteen for release although Moman is right to say not all the thirty two tracks should have been made available to the public.

The lack of quality control is offered as a reason why Chips never worked with Elvis again. Marty Lacker, a friend of both Elvis and Moman, maintains that the working relationship between the two men was okay but claims that after the sessions Elvis was fed lies about Moman and responded by refusing to return to American Sound Studios. I did actually visit the studios in 1979 and met the ex-Vice President and his daughter. I explored these issues with them but unsuccessfully.

The ex-Vice President looked at me and grinned. 'You guys from England always know more than we remember. We just made the records and parcelled them off.'

We certainly know what Elvis did with his tonsils. The unresolved question is what did Chips contribute? Most of what fans regard as the highlights did not necessarily appeal to Moman. Elvis brought to the sessions old songs that he liked such as 'After Loving You' and 'I'll Hold You In My Heart.' If Elvis wanted to combine the authentic and the plastic, Moman was not always as convinced about the benefits of the authentic. Both Elvis and Chips contributed to the success of the sessions and both undermined each other. Elvis introduced material that Chips considered dated, songs that were important to Elvis because it would allow him to indulge his extravagant vocals. Chips always attempted to leave the mark of his studio, sometimes on material that should have been merely recognised for its passion and strength. In other words, neither man agreed on the identity for the album but the unique, album identity that eventually emerged is to the credit of both men. 'From Elvis In Memphis' exists as an example of two talented but different men meeting in a middle place and without enfeebling compromise.

The album, though, contains the successes. Elsewhere, there are failures and, perhaps, Moman would argue that is inevitable which is why a producer should have the freedom to throw away what does not succeed. If failures are inevitable, there are also examples that indicate destructive forces occasionally existed. The song, 'Do You Know Who I Am', is not exceptional but the bluesy interpretation by Elvis is perfect and it would now be regarded as a deep soul classic if it had not been drowned by strings and girls. This is a serious error by Moman that should have been revisited. Against this, it is obvious that Moman knows how to produce. His arrangements lift the voice brilliantly. Elvis is a fabulous singer but Moman knows how to make him sound even better.

Moman did not want to make a great, Elvis album and Elvis did not want to make a great, Moman album but Moman was fortunate Elvis was committed to the project and the early outtakes reveal astonishing ambition in his vocals. Moman, though, plays his part and it is easy to notice in the outtakes a patient and confident man who understands the potential of the musicians and his singer, even, when they initially flounder. The argument over 'Suspicious Minds' may have been exaggerated but the various accounts describe Moman as a strong man, confident enough to manage his talented ensemble in order that they deliver only what he insists will be acceptable. Listening to the outtakes, it is clear that Moman will be obliged to indulge his headstrong vocalist but it is also obvious that he knew how to inspire Elvis further. The track, 'Any Day Now', is a good example. In the early take, Elvis is awful but, with encouragement, he persisted and the final record is one of his greatest achievements. This would not have happened without the strong presence, self-belief and determination of Moman.

As with 'How Great Thou Art', all the individual tracks on this album are fine. As Peter Guralnick wrote in his original review, 'If it were made only of its weaker moments it would still be a good record and one that would fulfil in many ways all the expectations we might have had of Elvis.' Indeed, the album could have been used to provide six singles with the weaker tracks used as highly welcome 'B' sides.

Included in the weaker elements identified by Guralnick are 'Only The Strong Survive' and the already mentioned 'Any Day Now'. They are are actually brilliant. Guralnick appears to have revised his early opinion of 'Only' and his Elvis biography, 'Careless Love', now describes it as a major achievement which it is. To appreciate its strengths, listen to the inferior original by Jerry Butler which was good enough to be a big hit. After a spoken introduction, which merits being included somewhere in a major movie, Elvis establishes his authority immediately by how he sings the word 'boy'. He adds at least two extra syllables and inserts the letter A to produce a pronunciation quite unique. The vocal is a marvellous mix of dependency and arrogant confidence and the record is precious because these qualities define Elvis well.

Perhaps, Peter Guralnick initially reacted to 'Any Day Now' being written by Burt Bacharach but it was previously recorded by soul singer, Chuck Jackson, so that should have persuaded him. Greil Marcus identifies it as a highlight and he is correct. It has a beat and it soon transcends what Bacharach intended. The arrangement is fine and the strings are used inventively with more reliance on soloists than normal. These are complemented perfectly by a punchy, horn arrangement. Elvis is at his peak although it is significant that he found the song initially challenging. Clearly, the conquering of the song inspires him and he finally sings it with freedom and a mastery that delights him. This time, his virtuosity is fully revealed. Near the end, he sings, 'don't fly away my beautiful bird'. The way he renders 'bird' with a passionate trill is unforgettable and I impatiently wait for it each time I hear the record.

If 'From Elvis In Memphis' had not included its two greatest achievements, it would have been a fabulous, ten track album but, of course, it had twelve tracks and this leads us to 'I'll Hold You In My Heart' and 'Long Black Limousine.'

Much has been written about these tracks already. Both are glorious but in different ways. 'Hold' reveals what Elvis can achieve with just a half remembered song and, although he repeats the one verse for four and a half minutes, his emotional intensity and free wanderings prevent it from being dull. It grips and challenges and he makes the simple, country song echo with blues, soul and gospel. It stands as a testament not only to his brilliance but to the power and potential of unpretentious music. The listener is involved and stretched without ever thinking about the song. Instead, we relish the performance.

'Limousine' is the cheesiest song on the album, a tearjerker about a man watching his old lover being driven to a funeral. Elvis sings it with such intensity, and the arrangement is so dramatic and insistent, it becomes a soulful classic. Somehow, the corny lines are transformed into images of small town life and we believe that we are listening to a complicated drama involving real people. This community is fractured with envy and waste and we can imagine this because Elvis does more than simply sing the song. He achieves what the song without him cannot. He brings the narrator to believable life and the Elvis we know suddenly disappears to reveal a singer with an identity and history relevant to the song. Despite his loyalty to the South, this Elvis is as wary of the village as the Creature.

The inclusion of 'Hold You In My Heart' and 'Long Black Limousine' takes the album to the highest level. It can be compared to 'I Never Loved A Man' by Aretha Franklin and 'Two Steps From The Blues' by Bobby Bland. These are mentioned because they are the two best, soul albums ever.

As Peter Guralnick wrote in his review, this is Elvis making a special effort. When he does he is a match for anyone. Every track has its fabulous moments and all contain surprises, the advantage of having two great, creative talents in the studio, Presley and Moman.

'Elvis Presley'

This was the first album released by RCA in 1956. The album inspired The Clash to imitate the cover for their debut album. Many critics consider this to be the finest Elvis album ever made but, too often, they value it more as a sociological relic than a musical achievement. To them, this is 'good Elvis' because he is being subversive and this is what many rock critics believe is the ultimate responsibility of rock musicians. It is a fine album and its freshness and historical impact should be given some significance which is why it is placed above 'Elvis Is Back' although I listen to the latter more.

But, if we ignore retrospective compilations, it also happens to be the finest rockabilly album ever recorded by anyone although other rockabilly performers have recorded classic singles superior to the rockers on this album. Jerry Lee Lewis and 'Great Balls Of Fire' is an obvious example.

The album mixes songs he recorded at Sun with some of his first recordings at RCA. The inclusion of Sun material complements well the early, RCA efforts and its success inspired RCA to add Sun material to RCA albums throughout the two years before he joined the Army. This flattered his achievements but it meant this two year period was impossible to replicate afterwards. This may, or may not have, persuaded Elvis to become reticent later. Because the Sun material stands alone and many believe it has an authentic purity that was dissipated and eventually lost at RCA, I will take the opportunity to mention Sam Phillips, the finest mentor Elvis ever had.

Sam Phillips exists as an alternative hero for those who acknowledge

Elvis made some great records but who are still appalled by the commercial icon. Such critics believe this was the man who understood the common ground between black and white Americans and the creative worth and potential of the oppressed of the South. He was a man who stayed loyal to his vision throughout his career and demonstrated integrity beyond the materialistic ambitions of Elvis.

This is not history, of course. It is romance. Elaine Dundy, in 'Elvis And Gladys', discovered a man who was cautious and haunted by indecision. It is this, she argues, that delayed the release of so many of his records and kept him rooted in Memphis living on past glories. Dundy does not regard Phillips as the egalitarian champion claimed by his fans. To her, he is the patronising Southern master who graciously indulges the irresistible charms of his authentic inferiors. Sam did provide work for musicians not welcomed by others but he also refused to pay union rates to his musicians. This evokes the famous line that Joseph Cotton throws at Orson Welles in 'Citizen Kane.'

'Your precious working man you care so much about. Your working man will soon be organised labour and you won't like that one bit.'

The most important claim on his behalf is that Phillips created rockabilly. Dundy feels that the emergence of a rockabilly record from Elvis on the spur of the moment is a myth. Elvis had been working on a ballad that night but Dundy makes the point that the trio had played together for several months and had had ample opportunity to explore the music they liked. She quotes neighbours who say that they had heard Elvis and Scotty playing their version of rhythm and blues well before 'That's All Right' was recorded. Elvis was clearly a fan of Arthur Crudup and he not only recorded Crudup songs after he moved to RCA but paid for a recording session by the neglected, blues singer. Later, Elvis made disparaging remarks about his own Sun records. These are quoted as evidence that Elvis was not an authentic, rockabilly hero but merely a puppet of Sam. Certainly, Elvis referred critically to their excess echo. For all we know, he may have been unhappy with the amplified sound that appeared on the Sun records processed by RCA. On stage in the seventies, Elvis speeded up his rock and roll, RCA hits but, apart from 'That's All Right' which he used briefly to open the show, he did not do this with the rockabilly. He performed respectful versions of his Sun hits until the end of his career. Rockabilly existed in his soul and it remained there to the end but so did his taste for sentimental ballads which is why the less complicated romance about Phillips is so attractive to some.

The credit needs to be given to Elvis, Scotty and Bill. They were playing their instruments the moment rockabilly was created and Sam Phillips admits that what they produced caught him by surprise. Certainly, there is nothing in the Sun catalogue prior to Elvis that prepares us for what the trio produced that night. Elvis, though, was lucky because he had an open minded and talented producer who had spent the previous five years producing rhythm and blues.

If Sam Phillips made many great, rockabilly records after Elvis, he only expanded on his achievements in terms of quantity and variety. Jerry Lee Lewis, Carl Perkins and Johnny Cash are great musicians and this is evident in their music. Sam Phillips produces their records well but the effects that please us are identifiable. The records by Elvis are much more mysterious. After him, there are no additional breakthroughs at Sun. Indeed, some of the later rockabilly records by lesser artists, although exciting, are crude in comparison to the earlier records by Elvis. But this may be how Sam operated, he let the musicians find their level and what made them effective. Inevitably, no one else found the level available to Elvis. An example of the Phillips approach that works spectacularly well is 'Ain't Got A Thing' by Sonny Burgess. The musicians sound unpractised but their unsophisticated enthusiasm is undeniably infectious.

There is further evidence that Elvis was not radically altered by the coaching of Sam Phillips. This is the acetate of 'My Happiness' which Elvis privately recorded before he met Sam Phillips. Elvis made this when he was just eighteen years old but the unique style already exists, his willingness to do more with his voice than other singers, the weird combination of a lyrical baritone to carry the tune and a piercing treble for intensity and drama. He used the same combination on his version of 'Tomorrow Night', a fine, blues ballad by the great Lonnie Johnson. The later record is supervised by Sam Phillips but the two recordings demonstrate consistency rather than subsequent discovery.

No doubt, most record producers would have recognised Elvis as a special talent. Few, though, would have indulged him like Sam Phillips who teased out the creative potential of Elvis and caught the result on record so spectacularly. He both permitted and encouraged Elvis to be revolutionary. He may have been mean with money but he also appeared to be a fair man. His sense of fairness, and his consequent desire to scrutinise, may well have been the key to his taste and verbosity. He told the tale that when he first heard 'Don't Be Cruel' he pulled the car over to listen to it in admiration. His belief that it was superior to what he recorded with Elvis at Sun may be flawed but his acknowledgement of what he regards as an achievement beyond him is impressive.

Sam Phillips cannot be left without, though, a mention of Marion Keisker, as steadfast a female as the idealised creatures, Justine and Elizabeth, that Mary Shelley created in 'Frankenstein'. Marion is the Sun employee who passed on the acetate of 'My Happiness' to Sam Phillips and reminded Phillips to take a look at the young singer. Sam had to be reminded more than once because that is what happens to undiscovered talent. Elvis was always appreciative of her efforts. She could also have been forgiven for wanting to avoid the strange looking and unsophisticated, young man who introduced himself that day. She did not and, whilst it did not require hard work or real creativity on her part, she did have faith. It was her decision to promote him with Sam that changed so many lives.

The strength of 'Elvis Presley' is its independent identity and its commitment to hard core rockabilly. If the twelve tracks were not the best available to RCA in 1956, it does all hang together extremely well. Strangely, a more accomplished album may have served less well as a symbol of rebellion and not been as important. Although Elvis dominates the album and provides the highlights, it is not just about him. We are able to enjoy the pleasure of listening to a rockabilly group driving the music forward as they would on stage. Elvis is the exceptional talent but he is also a loyal artisan working with other talented artisans. Aspiration is rejected; there is no desire to please his superiors or his elders. This is Elvis at his most class conscious which, no doubt, is why it was popular with British, punk bands.

Even the coy ballad, 'I Love You Because', is stained with rockabilly attitude so it sounds as if it is less about dedicated love and more about the harshness of being anonymous and poor. The woman does love him but there is no pleasure to share, only misery. It is how Hank Williams would sound if he could sing like Elvis. Indeed, the original by Leon Payne echoes Hank Williams.

The album has two other ballads but because of the solid, rockabilly identity in this album and the naked emotion in the songs they fit in neatly. 'I'll Never Let You Go' is extravagant and its drama contains a threat. Elvis sounds like a possible psychopath, in his sweeter moments, of course, but still dangerous and the surprise ending exposes the danger clearly. There is also the delightfully weird 'Blue Moon'. Elvis not only takes the Rodgers and Hart song towards Hank Williams but goes beyond to somewhere bleaker again so he evokes a defeated, rural, blues singer grasping a disillusioned breath away from the crowd. Okay, it does not sound like Lonnie Johnson but he would have approved and, if he had heard this version, he would have probably bought it for one of his many girlfriends. The great Lonnie may have been an inspiration. We are left with the image of a lost soul weighed down by his failure and by the humid weight of impervious human beings. The record is eerie and intense and only Elvis could have succeeded with a Rodgers and Hart song on a rockabilly album.

'Trying To Get To You' is slow but has too much power to be regarded as a ballad. Elvis sings it with such intensity, the verses throb as he drives his way through the words. When his voice wails the formidable challenges he is willing to conquer the chorus explodes into a harsh blues. He never hesitates as he reaches for both notes and effects and we can easily imagine him battling mountains to reach his love or possibly his next victim. It anticipates the masterful 'One Night' but it is more subtle and has within it more elements to thrill. The guitar accompaniment by Scotty Moore is also fine and, as he adds some jazz effects, he gives an early indication of the range and potential of rockabilly.

The rest are rockers. The best of them is 'Money Honey'. It has an interesting arrangement which substitutes the catchy swing of the Drifters original with a more direct, rockabilly beat and relies on good contributions from Scotty Moore and Floyd Cramer. They allow each to take a break and they ensure the record has plenty of fine moments. Elvis sings with intensity and panache and, without ever taking the cynical lyrics too seriously, he still works his way to a triumph that may, or may not be, based on his new, jaundiced realism.

All the rockers are full of energy and power but none represent Elvis at his absolute best. If his performances have plenty of invention, he does not deliver the higher groove found on classics like 'Mystery Train' or 'Jailhouse Rock'. But this is what gives the album its strength and its substance. This is the voice of somebody ordinary, but independent, warning his supposed superiors of the dangers the ordinary, like him, have within their potential. This album for many was an introduction to the young singer and we meet Elvis as rock and roll hero. As Robert Matthew Walker wrote in his book, 'Heartbreak Hotel', 'This is real rock and roll'. It is great music because rockabilly is a magic formula that, when done well, never fails to excite. It is why the album is popular with critics and it explains why they felt so betrayed later when Elvis explored his talent in ways that were important to him or when he no longer wanted to belong with the ordinary. 'Elvis Presley' may be short on classic grooves but it does have that rockabilly beat. Although his own, rockabilly classics reside in alternative locations to this album, here, Elvis still demonstrates he is its greatest exponent.

'Elvis Is Back'

This album was taken from the sessions that were recorded after Elvis returned from the Army. The sessions produced the two hit singles, 'It's Now Or Never' and 'Are You Lonesome Tonight'. Both of these singles became massive sellers and their success has led to a simple explanation of his career. Critics have mistakenly assumed that the sessions marked the moment when Elvis became middle of the road or adjusted his appeal to adults. There were adjustments but it was a little more complicated than is normally understood. The big hits, 'Now Or Never' and 'Lonesome Tonight', were not typical of the sessions. Eighteen songs were recorded over two long, eleven hour shifts and they covered a wide range of American music. Elvis re-defined himself and his music but, apart from the extreme examples of 'Never' and 'Lonesome', he remained true to his roots. Since he had entered the Army, his voice had become deeper and richer and he was able to extend his range and this, no doubt, also influenced his choice of material. It was as if he tried to imagine himself as the Frank Sinatra of rock and roll, a performer willing to make popular music but determined to maintain links with the less commercial.

Sinatra mixed the commercial with jazz. In these sessions, Elvis mixed the commercial with blues and gospel styled ballads and integrated it all into his new style. The album was produced by Chet Atkins. Elvis recorded with Atkins from 1956 to 1964 but Steve Sholes was credited as the producer until as late as May 1963. In interviews, Ernst Jorgensen has stated that Sholes was not a producer but more the man who arranged the sessions, a producer in the movie sense. From that, we have to assume Atkins was other than Elvis the main influence inside the studio.

Even without Sholes to consider, it is not easy to define the influence of Atkins. Elvis recorded at night and, supposedly, on more than one occasion in the middle of a session Elvis would stop work and walk over to a slumped Atkins and scream in his face, 'Wake up, you mother fucker!'

The music Atkins played and promoted had many qualities but he always sounded like a man without passion. Atkins has played country, jazz and classical guitar and other guitarists sit and listen with wonder. His technical gifts make them feel inadequate. He introduced a picking style based on the thumb and two fingers. His guitar playing on his record, 'Boogie Man Boogie', is adept and a joy. His music, though, lacks what is essential to Elvis and what is always present when Elvis is great, guts. Bland is what Elvis does least well.

Chet Atkins liked instead a hummable tune that confirmed what was right with the world and existence and, to be fair, was sometimes explorative. When Elvis became famous and privileged he alternated between self-destruction and a search for spiritual meaning. Chet Atkins used the same opportunities of freedom to play golf. If he had regrets about watering down country music for the newly affluent of a post-war United States, he never admitted to them. I imagine an uncomplicated man carried forward by the future to success but, unlike Victor Frankenstein, not able to anticipate and understand what makes the future different. Atkins did not belong with the cursed creature from Memphis who would have offended his idealism of gentility.

It is difficult to credit that the well paid but non-participant Atkins steered Elvis away from his own rock and roll to the smoother sound of Studio A, Nashville but that journey happened. No doubt, Elvis agreed to mellow the sound. He was persuaded that he needed to extend his appeal to the older record buyers and he also wanted to extend his voice and range. But Atkins was more than willing to help and he deserves criticism if only for his eagerness to take a performer in his prime away from his natural strengths. The album, 'Elvis Is Back', proved that the ambition of Elvis to extend his range could be achieved without a loss of quality but Atkins dealt in units shipped and the first attempt did not produce the commercial success wanted. This original and honourable attempt was compromised further each time Elvis went into the studio with Atkins. Defenders of Atkins would argue that he was only supporting the commercial ambitions of Elvis. But the sessions from 1961 to 1963 reveal an Elvis who is increasingly less committed. If Elvis had intended to make music similar to that of Jim Reeves and Eddy Arnold, pals of Atkins, why did Elvis in this period become so unenthusiastic?

One has to conclude that Atkins worked to his own objectives and to an employer other than Elvis. This is the underlying tragedy of Elvis, of course. He was surrounded by people but, ultimately, nobody apart from his stage musicians worked for him. They all worked for someone else, people who needed Elvis to serve them rather than express himself.

We will never know what happened in the conversations between Atkins and Elvis. It is possible both men had to respond to demands by Parker who, himself, may have had to listen to the demands of movie producers who wanted the Elvis outside the movies to be consistent with the one inside. We do, though, have evidence of how Atkins kept Elvis within what he thought was acceptable. The various outtakes confirm for the listener an Atkins keen to take the sting and bite out of the music. It begins on the 'Something For Everybody' album. The song, 'Put The Blame On Me', in the early takes reveals Elvis attempting a Little Willie John styled blues but, as soon as Elvis struggles with the pitch of the song, Atkins intervenes to steer it into something safer. What should have been gained is lost. The comparison with the patient Moman is unflattering to Atkins. We know now that Elvis conceived of a new style for the up-tempo material included on the 'Pot Luck' album. This consisted of two drums and a heavy, rhythm section to support him introducing lighter vocals. Elvis may have thought that this approach would please both his rock and roll and movie fans. Personally, I think this was poorly conceived but it was soon abandoned and what replaced it was worse, light vocals and inappropriate, light accompaniment. It would be wrong to argue that there is great, unrealised grit in the mid-sixties material but the sly nudging from Atkins to insipid pop exists and it neither helps Elvis nor the material.

Nothing, though, defines Chet Atkins and his work for Elvis better than what he did to the already mentioned 'Tomorrow Night'. When, in the early sixties, Chet Atkins remixed the Sun recording he sweetened everything to make it an inoffensive, smooth ballad. The consequence is that even the voice of Elvis, though no different, sounds mild and tame. The re-mixed record poses two questions. Did Atkins set up an environment that inhibited Elvis from being as soulful as he could be and did Atkins filter out some of the soul that, despite everything, existed in the records? The answer has to be yes. The only issue is to what extent.

This was the man Elvis worked with from 1956 to 1958 and from 1960 to 1964. We can conclude that in the first period Elvis definitely prevailed because the music he made is far different from anything Atkins ever recorded elsewhere. Although it was a different Elvis in the second period and he had changed requirements, the outtakes and the work Atkins did with Reeves and Arnold support the argument of Elvis being subdued by others.

The defenders of Atkins can argue that he was the consummate professional. 'Elvis Is Back' was well engineered and Atkins did participate in the classic rock and roll made by Elvis. Atkins also acknowledges that Elvis was a great talent. But the two men were not complimentary characters and, if that can sometimes create a productive tension, their relationship was one that only sustained decline. Chet Atkins was an unfortunate choice as producer. There are no comparisons to be made with any of the characters in the novel, 'Frankenstein'. He is too grey for the imagination of Shelley. Elvis needed men and women who could help realise his need for ecstasy and share his nightmares. Relaxed men, he only confused and these invariably served him poorly. But in 1960, fresh out of the Army, Elvis was purposeful and Atkins was unable to either confuse or contain him.

Consequently, the album is fabulous. Elvis was in stunning form and some mundane material becomes memorable, simply, because of his performances. It could have been better because not all the highlights of the sessions were included. The complete sessions are actually more of a triumph than the album. All of the tracks on the album, though, are essential listening. In one bold move, Elvis had devised a new approach which should have ensured he would be dominant for the rest of his life. Just like Sinatra, in fact.

It did not happen. Despite a favourable critical reception and the approval of fans, the album was not one of his most popular. Even now after it has had time to add additional sales, it is still supposedly outsold by the 'Frankie And Johnnie' soundtrack album, a collection of junk sung by a performer showing obvious distaste for his material. 'Elvis Is Back' initially sold 200, 000 copies and it is interesting and sad that this was perceived as a commercial disappointment. It indicates the pressure the management team put on Elvis and themselves. This perceived commercial failure, the disappointing attendances for his two serious films made soon after the album and the success of the froth of 'G I Blues' convinced Parker that Elvis had to be steered away from his previous ambitions. Elvis became cynical and despondent and Parker became cynical and triumphant. Thought of in this way, it becomes apparent that the subsequent problems were a consequence of the weaknesses of two men. This was a dysfunctional relationship and, as happens in such relationships, the partners not only betrayed each other but themselves, compounding destruction in a way that probably neither man could have anticipated. Imitating Frankenstein and his Creature, the two men from this point led one another to their doom and, just like their predecessors on their ice sledges, the two men did not always know who was chasing who.

'Elvis Is Back' exists as a record of what Elvis achieved in only his first attempt in a new identity and it should be regarded as the stepping stone to what might have been rather than the summit of his achievements. Perhaps 'From Elvis In Memphis' would have arrived earlier and that would have led to even greater albums. We have what we have. If 'Elvis Is Back' does not have the integrity of 'Elvis Presley', everything is invigorated with his marvellous singing and confidence. The material on the album has been compared with what Charlie Rich recorded at Smash and the argument is valid but Elvis has the edge because he can deliver more surprises and more voices. The talented, jazz singer, Sarah Vaughan, also made some pop mid-career and the tracks are on a level with her commercial classics, 'Broken Hearted Melody' and 'Smooth Operator.' Technically, he is that good and has that much control.

All the tracks on 'Elvis Is Back' have merit but the highlights are the equal of anything else he ever did. Previously, 'Such A Night' was recorded by Clyde McPhatter and covered by Johnnie Ray. Interestingly, the song, like the majority of the tracks on the second side of the album, conveys a belief in promiscuity which means the message of the album is at odds with the image of a reformed Elvis. Elvis did exactly what he wanted with 'Such A Night' as his flat out chorus indicates. The way he suddenly launches into a cool, Mel Torme jazz style in the final verse, aloof and unflappable, is a real surprise. The call and response routine at the climax is even better. If he had still had his sideburns, his lascivious 'yeaaah' at the end would have been banned.

'Like A Baby' is a cover of a record written by Jesse Stone. The original by Vikki Nelson is obscure so it is difficult to know how the version of Elvis compares. Vikki Nelson did make a fine record called 'Bright Side' in which she does a fair imitation of Etta James, so presumably she would not have hesitated belting out the original. In his anthology, 'A Life In Music, The Complete Recording Sessions', Ernst Jorgenson states that an important version had come from Toni Arden. This beggars belief because Toni Arden was a singer of Italian descent who sang conventional, fifties, Mitch Miller style ballads but if Ernst says so it must be true. Maybe, secretly, she was a female Dion. It is difficult to imagine either Vikki or Toni would have been a match for Elvis. What we do know is that this is a fine record and, although Elvis ranges from bass to tenor with the odd, husky phrase in between, there is no straining for effect. Elvis is bluesy and soulful and his mournful sounds are not only backed impressively by the wails of Boots Randolph on saxophone but, also, by The Jordanaires. This is probably their finest moment with Elvis.

The ultimate, exceptional track is 'Reconsider Baby'. Is this his greatest record ever? Elvis made too many classics and was too versatile for meaningful comparisons but this would be the one if I had to pick a favourite. It is the best, blues record by the best, white, blues singer and, after hearing it, one is tempted to say the only white, blues singer. It is simply on another level and what makes it so great will never be properly explained. It just is. Elvis himself realises this when halfway through the instrumental break he says, 'yeah, yeah'. It defines his pleasure and satisfaction and echoes our own. Elvis leads with real mastery, a dominant, aggressive force in total control. The musicians are all perfect and they play at their best. I once saw the saxophone player, Boots Randolph, in his nightclub in Nashville. He was making a living and his playing had become ordinary and predictable. On 'Reconsider Baby', Boots and everyone else play like men who are staking a flag in the ground, as if it is the night when they will prove their worth. This is what they did. Elvis transforms the original by Lowell Fulsom into something much darker and threatening but, ultimately, it succeeds because he has devised, and performs to perfection, an original groove that grips and inspires from beginning to end.

The album demonstrated to those who listened that Elvis at that time was ahead of his rivals, a man who could mix the earthy with the pure and the primitive with the sophisticated. 'Elvis Is Back' may not be quite the equal of 'From Elvis In Memphis' but it is a close contest. It is not what introduced me to his music but it did make me a believer.

'Elvis Rock And Roll No 2'

For a long time, this was a source of disappointment to me. Circumstances did not help. I first listened to it in the house of a friend and was particularly impressed by the track, 'So Glad You're Mine'. At the time, it convinced me, immediately, that The Beatles, who were emerging as the favourites of everyone, were not genuine alternatives and I retreated into an American cocoon. I did not actually buy the album until much later and I had the misfortune to buy something mangled into reprocessed stereo. Later again, I finally bought a mono copy and I was still not impressed. The album suffered from not being the definitive, rebellious, rock and roll statement I was expecting and probably needed. I was also unhappy with the inclusion of three Little Richard covers. Although all the tracks have merit, 'Elvis Rock And Roll No 2' mixes rock and roll, melodrama and sentimentality. It does not hide his excesses nor does it reveal a young man who was as independent as I had hoped when I originally bought the album.

Later, no longer quite so young, I heard 'The Way I Am' by Merle Haggard. I liked its pleasant feel and the way the musicians inhabited the music without showing off. The BB King CD, 'Blues On The Bayou', is successful for the same reasons, BB playing familiar tunes with a talented band who know one another well. The three Ernest Tubb covers on the Haggard album did not offend me because I enjoyed sharing the pleasure of the musicians playing their favourites and it was clear that the songs were a response to the relaxed groove that had emerged that day.

When I read in the liner notes to the fifties box set, 'The King Of Rock 'N' Roll', that the sessions for 'Rock And Roll No 2' had caught the feeling of the early Sun recordings I thought of Merle Haggard, marvellous without ever being showy.

There are now two detailed accounts of the sessions. The first is by Peter Guralnick and is in 'Last Train To Memphis' and the second, by Ernst Jorgenson, is in 'A Life In Music, The Complete Recording Sessions'. Guralnick describes a successful two days whilst Jorgenson puts more emphasis on the difficulties with certain tracks and the overall anxiety created by a shortage of material. So, my initial reason for listening to it differently may or may not be valid. It may not bear any comparison with 'The Way I Am'. And I will never know if Merle and his band were relaxed that day. The musicians may have been irritated and faking it but that is not important. For me, the 'Way I Am' album has an inner life, one that suggests survival exists as sweet compensation for regret. This may be fanciful but the fancies of the listener are important. Elvis, for this listener, is entitled to be gentle and 'Rock And Roll No 2' (called 'Elvis' in the States) is no more than gentle rock and roll. There is no subversive message and, if anything, it celebrates his roots. In contrast to the Little Richard covers, there are also country songs that show the traditional rspect for fate.

'Rock And Roll No 2' is significant for being his first attempt at an album which is probably why the material feels more relaxed than his other fifties material. The piano playing is also shared between Gordon Stoker of The Jordanaires and Elvis so we hear more of him as the musician than normal. Amazingly, nobody remembered to obtain a piano player for the hottest sensation in rock and roll. Chet Atkins was present to supposedly produce. The absence of a piano player defines his engagement in the project quite well.

The best track is 'So Glad You're Mine'. The song was actually recorded at an earlier session. It is the only song in the set that was not recorded in the two days in September 1956. If 'So Glad' was the song that argued Elvis was more important than regional loyalties to The Beatles, the actual inspiration was even more specific than the song. In the chorus, he quotes his satisfied girl friend who cries, 'Oowee.' I was fifteen years old when I heard that 'Oowee' for the first time. In an instant, the listener was pointed in a direction away from The Beatles and he has never been tempted to alter his path since then. It proclaimed an American entitlement that consisted of authenticity and the triumph of simple pleasures, in this case, sexual. Musically, the note is significant because it and the overall performance take the song away from the rural sound of Crudup. It is like Elvis has added a vocal horn to complete the band. The honky piano, presumably by Stoker, is also worthwhile and is a force throughout, adding to the guitar solo by Scotty. If, in retrospect, it is probably the weakest of his three Arthur Crudup covers, it is still iconic.

'Old Shep' is mentioned elsewhere. This was originally recorded by Red Foley, a deservedly popular singer whose up tempo records indicated a path from country towards rockabilly. Compared to Elvis, his version of 'Old Shep' is inferior; it lacks the pathos and the sense of capricious doom that haunts the Elvis performance. Red is accompanied by guitar, probably the great Grady Martin, whilst Elvis accompanies himself on the piano with some feeling. Sophisticates may find this material objectionable but nobody can deny the record by Elvis has an inner spirit. I used to hate it but now find it compelling. The line, 'gone where the good doggies go', was originally featured in an English, folk song called 'Bellum'. This is available on a compilation CD by the very talented, Yorkshire, folk family, The Watersons.

'How's The World Treating You' is one of his classic ballads. This time, Scotty manages more than the odd note and his scales in reply to the piano are lovely. The bass is prominent and effective. The piano playing by Elvis is simple and perhaps heavy handed but atmospheric and soulful. We can only imagine how different his career would have been if he had made this talent an integral part of his performances and development. The words in the song are melodramatic but inconsequential because what dominates is Elvis and he captures what it is like to be in the middle of a heart-break, the suspicion it will be endless.

Half the songs concentrate on his interests in rhythm and blues which results in the album being even handed in its concerns. The vocal on 'Any Place Is Paradise' resembles Billy Eckstein although it is anything but a straight impression. It was a trick he never repeated again, possibly, because the song took him twenty two takes although it may have been the band who found it difficult to produce a swing blues in a rockabilly setting. The result, though, is fine and the sparse setting makes it more bluesy and raunchy than a Billy Eckstein blues with a big band.

'Rock And Roll No 2' serves effectively as homage to the roots of Elvis but within his explorations are persistent warnings of an originality that will, despite the affection, ultimately undermine those roots. For that reason, this effort survives as an important testament to his unique talent and complicated destiny.

'Elvis Country – I Was Born 10,000 Years Ago'

Most of 'Elvis Country' was recorded in June 1970 in Nashville; twelve months after Elvis had worked with Chips Moman in Memphis. Two of the songs on the album were recorded later in September, again, in Nashville. The music has been described as organic which is an alternative term to rough. The outtakes reveal an approach that is instinctive rather than prepared and, at times, Elvis sounds like someone rehearsing a band for a stage show. This approach may be a legacy from his return to live appearances. Despite the approach, the finished result actually sounds quite sophisticated because, although there are mistakes, Elvis and the band are in top form and spark each other into life frequently.

The 1970 session that produced an unbelievable thirty four songs was produced by Felton Jarvis who should be given credit for providing first class musicians and for allowing Elvis to follow his instincts. Although some of the weaker songs should have been rejected, there was enough material for one great album, 'Elvis Country', and another that would have been impressive. This second album was squandered to support two alternatives which were a documentary soundtrack and a studio collection. The latter should never have been released.

Now he has been mentioned, we need to examine the role of Jarvis.

Everybody is agreed that Felton Jarvis is a decent man. He was as cheerful as Fitz, the assistant to Frankenstein in the 1931 movie, and, like Fitz did with Frankenstein, he spent too much of his life skipping around Elvis. Of course, Jarvis was superior to Fitz because, like Professor Waldeman at the University of Geneva, he meant well. Waldeman may have been misguided but he was also a generous paternalist and a university requires them but, lacking the imagination to be suspicious, he failed to arrest the dark obsession of Victor Frankenstein. Similarly, Jarvis was too amiable to be wary and worry properly. He neither challenged RCA nor Elvis adequately when, after these 1970 sessions, Elvis went into self-destructive decline and, from that point, Felton Jarvis did no more than pick up the pieces. His patience must have been tested on many occasions. Alanna Nash records in her book on Parker that one day after they had been recording songs Jarvis had been asked by telephone how the previous, evening session had progressed.

'Not well,' said Jarvis.

It is not difficult to imagine and sympathise with the weariness in his voice. Not well is a euphemism that means I am now working with a man who is away with the mixer. For those who want evidence of how mad Elvis became, there is a photograph on the internet of Elvis visiting a hospital. He is attending a sick child to try his faith healing powers. He is wearing a turban with an embossed ruby and dangling scarf. Another child of about eight looks on with the firm conviction that this strange man should be kept off the streets. In these circumstances, Jarvis dependent on a singer who had messianic fantasies the equal of Little Richard, it was inevitable that the quality of the records would decline.

Felton Jarvis had the most difficult of roles; he was the man in the middle. The job of the middle man required him to be tough with both RCA and Elvis and poor Felton Jarvis was neither. Like Fitz, he was too forgiving of the madness around him. Jarvis may have needed the comfort that Fitz found in the remote tower and Waldeman enjoyed in the University. All three were too happy being devoted servants. It could not have been easy working with Elvis after 1970 but the uncritical demeanour of Jarvis made the situation worse. The outtakes from the brief session that took place in September 1970 reveal an Elvis who is rude and obnoxious but clearly troubled. Jarvis had a responsibility to the other musicians to forbid this behaviour as Moman would have done. If Jarvis had protested, it may have made a difference to what followed. As Professor M. Waldeman discovered, the quizzical eyebrow and frown is not always enough.

Oddly, the sessions in Memphis, which were successful in themselves, actually left Elvis cursed. Prior to Moman, Elvis knew what was being submitted to RCA. Admittedly, RCA or Parker would turn down the volume on the backing instruments but that was all they could do, play with the volume controls. The Memphis sessions introduced the dubbing of horns, strings and female voices. From that point on, Elvis was only able to deliver his own vocal and inspire the musicians around him to respond. Unfortunately, this approach meant that after 1969 Elvis had less control and Jarvis through no effort on his part had more. To what extent, Jarvis was involved in dubbing extra instruments is not clear but, whether it was him or RCA alone, the results that were produced after Memphis were disappointing. Admittedly, the seventies were a difficult period because studio equipment had suddenly become more sophisticated and everybody was now determined to use extra channels and dubbing facilities. It produced an aesthetic that affected the work of many performers and, forty years later, much appears flawed. The better producers coped. Jarvis was not their equal. He was also unlucky. The decline of Elvis coincided with Jarvis experiencing health problems of his own. Perhaps, if he had stayed healthy, he would have been more assertive and successful.

But Jarvis, like his mentor Chet Atkins, sidestepped challenges too quickly. Once a take exposed the need for careful effort, the cry he made was to avoid the challenge. This is very different from Sam Phillips and Chips Moman who were gifted enough to recognise that the difficulties, when worked out, would produce the brilliant and memorable, especially, when the talent is Elvis. Evidence for this charge against Jarvis is in his decisions regarding the songs, 'Amazing Grace' and 'I'll Be Home On Christmas Day'. Elvis attempted bluesy versions which, even though rejected, are superior to what Jarvis released. Because the early versions were not perfect, Jarvis pushed Elvis into something safer and more comfortable.

He was probably sidestepping challenges when he agreed to include the ambitions from RCA and Parker for no less than three albums - gospel, Christmas and secular - in the May 1971 sessions at Nashville.

As producer, Jarvis should have insisted on one project at a time. Elvis also had a responsibility and needs to be criticised but he was thinking about turbans and faith healing. Jarvis was the producer and organiser and he had persuasive arguments to resist RCA such as the recent, mental and physical decline in Elvis which Jarvis had witnessed in late 1970. When Elvis began to behave oddly the consequences needed to be debated urgently with the record company and Elvis. No evidence exists to suggest Jarvis did this.

Examining his contribution now, it is possible to define the man in two responses.

'I'll see what I can do.'

'See what you can do.'

The first would have been his response to RCA and the second would have been what he said to Elvis. Not everybody will condemn the paternal Professor Waldeman when they read the novel, 'Frankenstein'. They will conclude that he was misled by events and people he knew only in certain circumstances. I am not so forgiving.

But in 1970, Elvis was not quite so crazy and Jarvis coped. The results from these Nashville sessions were good overall but, somewhere in the middle of the marathon session, Elvis rushed into recording more traditional material. More interested in recording songs to suit himself, and possibly remembering the attitude of Chips Moman in Memphis, Elvis was willing or able to pick material not owned by the preferred, publishing companies. Eight of the songs on 'Elvis Country' are within this category. Many of the songs were chosen on the spur of the moment and the musicians have recalled their astonishment at how, once Elvis found his mood, he could instantly create great and original music. Like the Memphis sessions, these Nashville sessions produced enough material for one tremendous album, one good album which was not realised or released by his record company and some junk.

Unfortunately, one example of the latter is used as the introduction. 'Snowbird' has no redeeming features. It is the kind of song one associates with the wispy, clingy introverts best avoided at parties. Presumably, Elvis or someone thought it contemporary and it would widen his appeal or, maybe, Elvis thought it a pretty tune. The outtake without the strings is better but it should be avoided completely. The song was recorded at the later session in September when Elvis was behaving strangely, so, possibly, it exists as early evidence of the imminent decline. Why it should have been included on an album that emphasises his retrospective interests is a puzzle. The discarded, Lester Flatt song, '100 Years From Now', would have been an excellent choice. 'Elvis Country' is splendid but it can be improved even further if 'Snowbird' is replaced with the bluegrass alternative.

Despite the traditional emphasis, the album is remarkable for its radicalism and the bold way old, country classics are redefined. Ernest Tubb sings the original version of 'Tomorrow Never Comes' well but it is pitched at the one level to suit his voice. Elvis gives the song an ascending arrangement so that it climaxes in a spectacular chorus. Done this way, the song sounds like a march. The drumming emphasises this aspect. Ultimately, it succeeds because Elvis sings it so dramatically and fearlessly. It is obvious from the early notes that the vocal challenges will soon appear and, when they do, he handles them easily. The passion increases until the glorious end when one is tempted to cheer. If it had been performed in a concert, it would have had everyone on their feet, crude, definitely, but irresistible.

His version of 'Faded Love' takes the heresy even further. Not surprisingly, the album was condemned on release by some country purists. The original by Bob Wills had been a big hit in the forties and was popular with American servicemen whose wartime experience made them sensitive to the appeal of a simple, cowboy song. The version by Elvis features a tough and prominent guitar by James Burton and bluesy harmonica by Charlie McCoy with support from saxophone. Elvis provides a tough rather than a rocking vocal but it comes to dynamic life in the chorus. Independent and assertive, his singing provides an effective link between the original song and the modern, rock and roll played by the band. All together, it makes a highly original and valuable rocker.

Equally radical are 'I Washed My Hands In Muddy Water' and 'I Really Don't Want To Know.' Peter Guralnick compares the version by Elvis of 'Muddy Water' to that by Charlie Rich. Both versions are fast and excellent but there are differences. The version by Charlie Rich rolls like a blues whilst Elvis is more frenetic and closer to rockabilly. Again, the band is allowed full freedom and all provide highlights, in particular,

David Briggs on piano who demonstrates why Elvis always rated him highly. Elvis and the band capture the nature of the lead character and his predicament and it is easy to visualise the escaped convict rushing across Georgia, no more than an urgent breath away from the 'bloodhounds on his trail' mentioned in the lyrics, uncatchable because of his brilliance and the support of an incomparable band. There is a moment when Elvis asks himself, 'what you do?' and he replies, 'I washed my hands'. The tension in this brief reply alone makes the record special and confirms, like the 'Oowee' in 'So Glad You're Mine', his fabulous talent.

'I Really Don't Want To Know' is a bluesy version of a Don Robertson song originally recorded by Eddy Arnold. The Elvis version is closer to that made by the legendary Solomon Burke. Both records are marvellous and exceptional but the arrangement on the Elvis record is preferable because the waltz tempo is less prominent and because the arrangement behind Solomon is a strange mixture of the inspired and the obvious. Solomon, though, provides a perfect, soulful vocal. Elvis pushes himself harder and the bluesy arrangement has no compromises. It feels more consequential and Elvis convinces us it is impossible to avoid the torment indicated by the song. Solomon sounds rueful and knowing whilst Elvis is a victim in pain. Both, though, are great records and both are essential.

When Peter Guralnick wrote an excellent review of 'Elvis Country' for 'Rolling Stone' he stated it was the finest music from Elvis since his Sun recordings. Since then, he has leaned back to the Memphis sessions. It is possible he suspects that the album was a lucky accident and it flatters the ambition Elvis had in 1970. Such judgements are probably irrelevant. Elvis provides a set of stunning vocals and manages an unusual take on all the songs in what is one of the more interesting song selections. He is also supported by a cracking band inspired by his great talent and obvious authority and they all must have had real pride in what they achieved.

'His Hand In Mine'

Elvis recorded his first gospel album, in 1960 just after he returned from his service in the Army. Now, one suspects something Machiavellian in Parker agreeing to something less commercial than normal. Possibly,

Parker always hoped that 'Elvis Is Back', the two 'serious' movies Elvis made for Twentieth Century Fox and this gospel project would, because of their limited success, give him enough ammunition to insist upon his programme of continual, mechanical galvanisation. Or, maybe, there was no sinister plan; he just overreacted to what was disappointing but actually credible, commercial appeal.

'His Hand In Mine' provides a marvellous companion piece to 'How Great Thou Art'. As mentioned earlier, I think somewhat pretentiously of the two albums as the Elvis equivalent to 'Citizen Kane' and 'The Magnificent Ambersons', the movies by Orson Welles. 'Citizen Kane' leaves its audiences spellbound with its ambition and reveals, for the first time, a cinematic virtuoso. 'Ambersons' has less obvious ambition but is rich with feeling and sadness and, although the ending was later ruined by interfering executives, it is not impossible to be moved by the knowledge within the film that fate excuses all but only after it steals everything we have. 'His Hand In Mine' does not have the spiritual depth of 'How Great Thou Art' but it reveals virtuosity as Elvis audaciously uses various voices to recreate the music he loves. I was tempted to put it higher up the list but it lacks the spontaneous invention of what is above. In this instance, Elvis is too deferential to his roots. Albert Goldman insists that the gospel music of Elvis is sentimental. This is a worthless generalisation but, on 'His Hand In Mine', there is a conformist piety and parochial pride that prevents the emotional breakthrough that makes 'How Great Thou Art' so impressive.

It is still a classic album. Despite his loyalty, his versions of these gospel favourites have their own identity. His voice alone makes them different but he is also recording with a band and that and his own, unique feel ensures he usually makes some modest adjustments.

Important to the album are 'Mansion Over The Hilltop' and 'In My Father's House'. Both use a mansion as a metaphor for heaven. The metaphor is telling because heaven is imagined as a place that offers a relief from poverty. This is the strength of this material because it captures the modest hopes of the poor. His Sun records have the innocent conviction of the deprived, that fun and excitement are rewards enough. Similarly, the gospel music on 'His Hand In Mine' is not capable of imagining fulfilment and transcendence. The ambition is merely material relief, to walk on streets amidst wealth. This narrow perspective which matches the early, simple hopes of the Creature in 'Frankenstein' is what makes these two tracks have such intensity. Although not political in their intent, their obsession with escape and relief do have a political consequence. Elvis sings sincerely and conveys perfectly the innocent trust of the dispossessed and anxious. The original version of 'Mansion' sounds like an old cowboy tune and, somehow, Elvis makes the song sound more gospel yet a little sweeter but, here, the sweetness is appropriate because it implies respect for the suffering. For the track, 'In My Father's House', Elvis uses his full range from tenor to baritone but never forfeits the gentle sincerity. The third verse is given to Ray Walker, the bass singer in the Jordanaires. This adds to the sense of 'My Father's House' being an inclusive home, welcoming those who have worshipped God.

'Working On The Building' also uses the house as metaphor but this revival number assumes the building is here on earth while the reward in heaven will be something different. Elvis accompanies the Jordanaires rather than they accompany him and it anticipates his later ambition for 'How Great Thou Art'. He actually drops his voice so the Jordanaires can dominate the climax. It is a bold move and it makes memorable what are interesting performances. 'I'm Gonna Walk Dem Golden Stairs' also needs to be mentioned because, of course, the stairs provide a link between the unfinished building and the comfortable mansions in the sky.

But, houses apart and metaphors in the distance, the very best track is 'He Knows Just What I Need'. The piano concentrates on a simple, two part beat which allows Elvis to dominate. The music ebbs and swells yet, apart from one chorus by the backing singers, this is all achieved by Elvis. He makes the verse atmospheric with a smoky vocal and the chorus thrilling with his high tenor. Dragging the rhythm until it grabs, he also fills the notes so there is added tension within the phrases. It is a perfect performance and it obviously requires effort because we hear Elvis quietly gulp breath at one point.

'His Hand In Mine' is not as memorable as 'How Great Thou Art' because it fails to embrace despair. But his voice is marvellous and the technique wide ranging. The album has significance. He not only demonstrates his own brilliance but acknowledges the valid hopes and ambitions of those not honoured by gifts or rewards. He pays his respects to his community and remembers their privations.

'Elvis TV Special'

The arguments against including this on a list of classics are substantial. Most of the songs had been recorded before and the TV show is now available on DVD which is probably how most people experience the 'Special'. The original album and TV show even miss the two raunchiest performances, 'Tiger Man' and 'Let Yourself Go'. There is, though, something about listening to it without the TV visuals. It allows the listener to concentrate on what is happening and appreciate the solid impact of the force of his music and talent. Popular music is dominated by the audio recording and it is fitting that such an important event is committed to record. It also suits the album format as it contains a varied collection of live shows, informal jams and mini-operas that still surprise when you listen. The original release lasts forty eight minutes which makes it longer than normal and this contributes to the weight and achievement. When the CD has finished I always sit back surprised that I have listened to so much music.

Although Steve Binder shocked the Deep South in America by letting Harry Belafonte on TV touch Petula Clark on her arm, he is now more famous for creating the 'Elvis TV Special' and opposing the wishes of Parker. Dave Marsh, in 'ELVIS', believes that the contribution of Binder has been much exaggerated and that the triumph belongs to Elvis alone. Those who agree with Marsh, point to the creative failures of Binder within the 'TV Special', the over choreographed, gospel and movie segments and the hammy, showbiz orchestra. If the creative hand of Binder is not always expert, we are talking about a man developed by American TV. In himself, Binder was a bold, young man who was prepared to take risks and he already had a decent record behind him before he met Elvis. He had produced 'Hullabaloo' and the exceptional, concert film, 'The T.A.M.I. Show'.

It has been forgotten that the comeback was not quite the commercial breakthrough often assumed. Elvis was limited by a history that made him unacceptable to many. Nor were the more mature critics approving of the 'TV Special'. I remember reading a review of the show in the 'Evening Standard' the night after it was first shown in America. It mentioned that the singer was nervous and that the event was not a success. The article was brief and patronising. I was eating a meal alone at the time and I put the paper to one side with mild disappointment but no real surprise. It only confirmed what I had learnt to accept. Elvis was finished. The reputation of the show was almost immediately restored by the newly influential, rock critics of 'Rolling Stone' which, at the time, was beginning to be to rock and roll what 'Cahiers Du Cinema' was to movies. Other music magazines followed suit. A week later, the music papers of England had picture spreads of the show and ecstatic prose. Elvis had sideburns again and the world offered hope to his fans once more.

Did Binder actually rebel against the plans of Parker and, if he did, what caused the stubborn rebellion? Reading the various interviews by Binder, it is apparent what was important to him. Elvis had to deliver something fresh and urgent or they would both have missed huge, career opportunities. Binder also understood that Elvis would only succeed if he himself challenged what he had become and reclaimed not only his authenticity but coped with the modern. Binder is close to what Victor Frankenstein is in his rare, best moments when he has hope and courage and understands what the Creature needs for a decent destiny. During these moments, the Creature forgets his need for vengeance but Frankenstein soon weakens and, as he forgets his purpose, he dooms the Creature. Elvis and the Creature behaved well when they thought, to quote my grandmother in different circumstances, 'they were on a promise'. Denied the promise, they both soon became destructive.

The novel by Shelley condemns the ambition of those who only want to be omnipotent. Shelley argues that virtue only exists when we connect with others. In an odd way, the TV show insists upon the same. The 'TV Special' can be viewed as a representation of the difference between what Elvis had been, a remote, dazzling icon, and what he should become, a worthwhile, relevant musician. Binder argued that alternatives existed to the all conquering fame promised by Parker, the desire for omnipotence that pulled Parker to wealth and Robert Walton to the North Pole and 'the wondrous power of the needle.'

Watching the show, we remember what had always made Elvis great, the belief that, as a Southern young man who remembered his roots, he could have both the authentic and the plastic. The reactionary element within the show is summed up in a re-written verse for 'Guitar Man'.

'I'll never be more than what I am, a swinging little guitar man.'

The first thing Binder needed was Elvis to be serious. He had to set Elvis free from his defensiveness and reveal himself. The purpose of Binder becomes obvious in the outtakes from the 'TV Special'. We hear Binder insist that Elvis talks to his audience. He will not hide or be remote this time. There is the famous tale of when Binder took Elvis out on to the street so the singer could understand his decline and what was at stake. Binder claims that Elvis walked the street unrecognised and, though this has been dismissed as nonsense by some of the Memphis Mafia, the tale can be given credence. Binder also had conversations with Elvis to establish if the singer was aware of others and committed to the modern. In retrospect, these appear fraught with danger because Binder chose, as his symbol of modernism, the song, 'MacArthur Park.' Binder asked Elvis if he would be prepared to record the song. Elvis said he would although he could have easily said that the song was awful and overblown and, if that was modern, Binder could keep it. Fortunately, this time, Elvis did the right thing. He did not record the song and he lied to Binder. The two men also discussed the assassination of Robert Kennedy and this may have had more significance. Greil Marcus states, in 'Invisible Republic', that after the slaughter of Robert Kennedy the country had split in half. The conversation between Binder and Elvis, who was appalled by the killings of Kennedy and Martin Luther King, confirmed that the two men were in the liberal half. This may sound odd to people who remember Elvis posing with Nixon at the White House but, for all his Southern loyalties and reservations about hippies, Elvis never quite belonged in the reactionary half of America.

Binder not only needed to waylay the past mistakes of Elvis and help him realise his talent fully but show that Elvis was still capable of what was in the air at the end of the decade, defiance and rebellion. This was the understanding that Binder established with Elvis and, to the surprise of virtually everyone, Elvis delivered. The romantics believe that Elvis Presley was set free with one introductory conversation. The more suspicious argue that Binder would have needed to be persistent. Binder has admitted in later inquests that he actually told Elvis that after the 'TV Special' Elvis would eventually falter and be unable to resist the demands of his management team. This belief was based on a simple fact. Elvis may have been a co-conspirator with Binder but he never once opposed Parker face to face when the show was being discussed. The Creature had a similar character because, for all his willpower and capacity for vengeance, he failed to stand his ground to explain himself with those who found him repulsive. Unlike the timid Elvis, he did, though, make demands of his galvaniser.

Although his judgement was not flawless, Binder did have some good ideas. Binder decided to let Elvis sing with a small group of musicians in the round, he included a gospel medley and, for the live, stand up segment before an audience, he put Elvis in a small, boxing ring shaped square. The show also began with 'Trouble' which Elvis sang magnificently. He produced a version much better than the original in 'King Creole'. Binder also made mistakes. The gospel medley was lip synched when it should have been live and the dance sequences before the movie and gospel segments are too long. These two dance numbers are the only interruptions. The rest is exclusively Elvis and this had never been done before. There were no guest stars. The orchestra does not add to the music but its contribution reflected how American TV operated then.

Binder did establish his independence but he did have backing from NBC executive, Bob Finkel, who played a key part by diverting Parker with flattery. Though Binder has been given much credit for opposing the wishes of Parker for a Christmas special full of carols, the nature of the confrontation on this issue has been overplayed. It is far from clear whether Parker wanted a show packed with Christmas songs although he did originally send NBC a tape of a radio show made the year before that featured songs from the 'Christmas' album. The music publishers, though, had also sent the televison company a list of Elvis songs that they thought could be suitable. This included Christmas songs but also blues like 'Reconsider Baby' and 'Down In The Alley'. Parker may have even accepted that Elvis needed to adjust to a changing world and remind everyone of his own, rebellious past. According to Alanna Nash, the manager was thinking of what to do after the movie contracts would expire and he wanted a dynamic show to drag the punters to the Vegas seasons he was negotiating. Although Parker made key decisions that ruined the final part of the career of Elvis - the long term contract for Vegas, no tours overseas and retention of the crippling, song writing deals - these were business decisions. He exercised no creative control after the movies ended in ruin. Much of the antics of Parker during the making of the 'TV Special' can be interpreted as the bluster of an unpleasant man who is determined to maintain status above someone more influential. Alanna Nash has dug deeper than anyone on Parker and she reveals only marginal pressure from Parker on Binder. Originally, Parker wanted the show to be concluded with a Christmas song. It was instead replaced by 'If I Can Dream', a song that Elvis initially thought was too Broadway. Parker conceded the point but was not defeated because the show actually featured a Christmas song in the informal segment. This was when Elvis was supposed to be at his most relaxed and authentic. Binder may have considered this a sensible compromise because it gave Parker what he wanted, something to enable the show to be shown each Christmas. Of course, the Christmas repeats never happened. What Elvis and Binder created was much more important than what Parker could imagine. The concession actually weakened the 'TV Special' because 'Blue Christmas' replaced the fabulous show stopper, 'Tiger Man'. Parker, as always, left a mark that undermined the achievements of his client.

Elvis made the 'Special' when rebellion was in the air and this contributed to the appeal and success of the show. Binder and Elvis embraced the mood which was why it was important for Binder to establish that Elvis had a social conscience. The emerging culture, though, was not expressed with the profundity Binder sometimes claims. Leiber and Stoller would have produced something smarter and avoided the trendy superficiality of Binder but he did deliver which is why he has survived as a producer. Binder held his nerve and this makes him a good guy.

The contribution of Elvis, though, is important. He not only sang with real passion, he produced a special, husky voice for the occasion. If it was the result of a creative decision taken by Elvis, it has never been explained adequately. Albert Goldman suggests Elvis based it on James Brown. Elvis was a fan of Brown and once said that nobody 'gets down' like The Godfather Of Soul. It is possible that he decided this was the way he would make an impact and reclaim his audience. When Elvis met James Brown and shared a table at a Jackie Wilson show it was Elvis who sought and approached Brown. The Creature also had a husky voice but this was a handicap because it made him sound inarticulate and brutal. The Creature hated the brutal tones he had inherited, Elvis delighted in them.

Although the DVD is enjoyable, the physical performer and icon can distract. Elvis is impressive on stage but I am not as big a fan of Elvis the visual performer as I am of the music maker. On record, it is easier to appreciate that Elvis is not only performing at full tilt but actually being inventive. The medley, 'Trouble/Guitar Man', is a good example of that. The lines of 'Trouble', he finishes with a subtle, rising intonation that combines irony, threat and confidence. He ends 'Guitar Man' with startling, rapid phrases and, though the performance is not as good as the original, he changes the meaning. Here, there is no wry irony in the reference to starving to death in Memphis, only anger and a desire for recompense. In this version, as he does in other songs, he reminds us that his aggression is important to him, just as the vengeful will of the Creature always complemented the sensitivity. The defiance persists throughout and, even, the grunts in the instrumental breaks are special. When he wails 'aah' at the end of 'All Shook Up' his contempt and delight reminds us all of why rock and roll has universal appeal. The jam sessions are intense and raucous and 'Lawdy Miss Clawdy', 'One Night' and 'Baby What You Want Me To Do' become compelling blues that are hammered home with pride and belief. For most of the jam sessions, Elvis plays electric lead. It is definitely crude and simple but he knows how to drive the songs and add urgency. He is the main man on his records and we now understand why. The ballads are few but they help to confirm Elvis as a crucial being, just like the Creature, violent when energised but lyrical and assured when offered peace.

The show has two mini operas, one that focuses on three gospel songs and the other that deals supposedly ironically with the movie mistakes. His gospel performances are closer to rock than the music Elvis made on his more heartfelt, gospel records. The approach makes sense because the segment is meant to entertain rather than convince. It finishes with the tongue in cheek 'Saved'. Elvis delivers it with supreme confidence but he is also self-conscious and calculating. Amazingly, it still bounces. All the gospel music sounds alive and it has energy that, no doubt, some critics would have preferred to have heard on his gospel albums. Although it may not be the equal of the version on 'How Great Thou Art', it is good to hear a more harsh and bluesy alternative of 'Where Could I Go But To The Lord.'

The movie opera is also fine. His version of 'Big Boss Man' is obvious but energetic and powerful and 'Little Egypt' is improved with the additional grit. The stand up segment features his hits and it would have been easy for these performances to suffer in comparison. Instead, they are all breathtaking. The show reaches its climax with 'If I Can Dream', the moment when Broadway meets James Brown. Musically dodgy, the song perhaps sums up the 'TV Special'. A crude orchestra flirts dangerously with being out of tune and Elvis is not too interested in the nuances of phrasing but all of it is made irrelevant by passion. There is an ambition to make a statement, to remember pride and reject the contempt of others. The 'TV Special' is when Elvis made it clear to those who listened that his success was not a fluke. He was as good as the emerging rivals and he decided it was best demonstrated by punching home rock and roll that would frighten his wilder competitors. The album captures Elvis not only enjoying the grooves behind his music, 'the gospel and rhythm and blues', he mentions, but also lets us hear why he enjoys those grooves which is why the grunts and asides are so important. It is the ultimate bootleg, a record where the integrated outtakes become the summit of its achievement. 'Elvis TV Special' will not have the same impact on younger listeners who listen to their music in massive, I Pod chunks. They are reluctant to compare albums in the way my generation did. But this one feels like a lot more than its substantial forty eight minutes. Listen to it and you feel you have understood his singularity and ambition and have been led across a continent by the force of his original will. Frankenstein must have felt something similar as he chased the Creature across the snowy wastes around the North Pole.

'King Creole'

I had not originally intended to include 'King Creole'. The damned thing only lasts for just over twenty minutes and it includes fake material written to order. Like the soundtrack from 'Loving You', it reveals the difference between the rock and roll that emerged from American, working class communities and the contrived alternatives created by corporate professionals. But, once the context is understood, then credit has to be given to what Elvis achieves.

In this instance, the series of four CDs called 'ELVIS AS HE WAS MEANT TO BE HEARD' should be mentioned. These are a response to recent re-mastering and contain his fifties and early sixties material. Reproduced from vinyl, the CDs reveal how the songs sounded on the original singles and albums. RCA borrowed this sound from the Columbia style of mastering fifties records. This process added life to vocals and there is no doubt that in its original form 'King Creole' is more powerful. When the vocals are heard in their fifties mono glory and come alive with sharp treble and reverberation it is easy to understand how, despite its lack of authenticity, rock and roll fans still rate and regard it as the last great album Elvis made. Without the Columbia sound, when the vocals do not dominate in the same way, the weakness in the material is more obvious.

Even then, 'King Creole' is fine but in its original state, mastered like everything else in that period, it becomes great. If the songs are often fake alternatives to the genres they are supposed to represent, Elvis really is in superb form. His mood is odd considering he will soon be joining the Army but, perhaps, he is simply determined to enjoy himself, to celebrate his talent and avoid other preoccupations. Relaxed, he reveals a show off at his most charming. He is also well supported by a Hollywood orchestra with some fine, Dixieland style, horn accompaniment. Having Leiber and Stoller in the studio also helps because their presence ensures that most of the songs qualify as commercial rhythm and blues.

The songwriters, Jerry Leiber and Mike Stoller, featured briefly from 1957 to 1958. Elvis recorded Leiber and Stoller songs after that but they were covers of songs already recorded by other performers. Between 1957 and 1958, they not only submitted songs not recorded by anyone else but they actually worked with Elvis in the studio on the production of his records. Parker decided after this brief twelve month period that they would no longer be given access to Elvis. His defenders would say the manager had his reasons and that the songwriters broke a code that was important to Parker. What we do know is that Elvis wanted them in the studio. If he was critical of any elements in a song, they would refine it for a later attempt. He liked their songs but he also liked the way they worked because it was the way he liked to work. The ideas were improvised and the gaps between formal takes would be filled with informal exploration and enjoyment of other music. Leiber describes it as getting high on music and then seeing what happens. In the Shelley novel, Henry Clerval was so inspired by the heroes of Greek mythology he defied his father to go to university. If he had befriended the Creature and not Frankenstein, he might have formed a relationship not unlike Elvis had with Leiber and Stoller, a successful, creative partnership. Clerval and the Creature would have become high on books. Instead, the Creature was burdened with the self-obsessed Frankenstein and, like Elvis did later, led his galvaniser to self-destruction and defeat. Most managers would have considered the encounter with Leiber and Stoller to be a lucky break and would have flattered the two men to ensure they stayed to contribute, especially, as they had already been extremely successful with other artists. Parker was too coarse and arrogant for that. All of which inspires the question, how influential were Leiber and Stoller.

Before he went in the Army in 1958, Elvis recorded thirteen songs by the songwriters. He worked on nine of their songs in the studio with them present and they were involved in the sessions that produced the 'Christmas' and 'King Creole' albums. If one compares their four songs he recorded before meeting them, there is little evidence to suggest a creative breakthrough caused by their presence. Leiber and Stoller were absent when the ballad, 'Loving You', was recorded and present when the comparable 'Don't' was completed. The results and instrumentation are very similar although the latter is superior. Elvis uses the same techniques to sell the songs. They would have submitted the demos but this would not be a factor. In this period, Elvis defined his material with his musical identity. If the 'Trouble' demo by Leiber and Stoller is typical, the demos submitted by them would have been basic, no more than rough sketches.

In the early eighties, an album was released of all the twenty Leiber and Stoller songs that Elvis had recorded in his career. It is well worth the price but it surprised people who were expecting a collection of Elvis classics. Elvis made fine records with Leiber and Stoller, for example, 'Treat Me Nice' and 'Baby I Don't Care', but only 'Jailhouse Rock', 'Santa Claus Is Back In Town' and 'Don't' should be included amongst his greatest.

This does not mean their contribution was not important. They had the ability to solve problems quickly, either by producing songs on demand, 'Santa Claus Is Back In Town', or by simplifying arrangements,

'King Creole'. This helped but they were more than this. The two men were sophisticated and, outside music, had a broader sensibility. Mike Stoller wrote the existential, Peggy Lee hit, 'Is That All There Is', after reading Thomas Mann. It may not quite summarise 'The Magic Mountain' in the way Mann admirers would want but it does exist as evidence that they were unusual in fifties pop music.

When Elvis met Leiber and Stoller he was already in the second phase of his career. World famous but now required to deliver big hits, he had to achieve something not previously contemplated, plentiful, commercial rock and roll which needed to be fresh. Elvis had made successful records but their appeal for many was based on his audacity as much as their merit. This was no longer sufficient. Elvis needed to understand how to utilise his love of music and cope with the demands of money men (and himself) for hits, how to avoid disabling compromise. He had to successfully combine the indigenous with modern plastic. Leiber and Stoller had been successful in taking rhythm and blues and adding commercial appeal. For a while, Leiber and Stoller helped Elvis understand the new world around him and how it could not only be satisfied but also enjoyed rather than endured.

1957, when Leiber and Stoller joined Elvis, is actually the weakest of the pre-Army years and it provides a decent explanation of the subsequent contradictions that followed. Elvis produces rock and roll classics but, already, he is obliged to produce a soundtrack album and a Christmas album. Elvis also indulges himself with the occasional ballad. The result is classic rock and roll, product for the crass money men plus examples of dubious judgement on the part of Elvis. Leiber and Stoller missed the 'Loving You' soundtrack album but they participated in other disappointments. It can, though, be claimed that, because of them, he survived the 'Christmas' album and the later, soundtrack album, 'King Creole'. They helped Elvis turn the encroachments and crass vision of his management into something worthwhile. Leiber and Stoller provided growth and fulfilment. They viewed the commercial world as something that offered opportunities rather than threats but they also provided the support and the hope a creative talent needs. Elvis survived in 1957 what could have been his first disaster. Leiber and Stoller were dismissed when Elvis was twenty three years old. The close relationship with Elvis ended after he had recorded their thirteenth song. After that, Elvis was allowed to meet songwriters for only brief courtesies. The irony is that Parker dismissed the two men best suited to integrating his commercial vision with the authentic potential of Elvis. In a similar manner, Victor Frankenstein abandoned the Creature at its conception, at the moment he had the greatest opportunity for influence. Only thinking of himself, Frankenstein ran off to wail self-pityingly into the night.

After the departure of Leiber and Stoller, an unhappy Elvis initially floundered. In the final recording session before he joined the Army, Elvis recovered his form but he did it through aggression and anger although some of that emotion would have also been the result of his induction into the Army. It led to some of his finest rock and roll.

Much of the music that Elvis and Leiber and Stoller made together was quite light but it is finessed with such skill that it never occurs to the listener that the performer is being compromised. If they are not the very best Elvis records, they are irresistible and smart. They contain enough promise for anyone to wonder what would have happened if a tone deaf bully had not interfered. At least, we have the amazing 'Jailhouse Rock'. There is also the 'King Creole' album.

The only song that carries serious emotion within the set is the ballad, 'As Long As I Have You'. This is a corny song that promises only fulfilment but Elvis ignores the corn and sings it like someone who has recognised the chilling prophecy delivered by Peggy Lee in 'The Folks Who Live On The Hill'. He makes the record extremely bleak and haunting and his performance emphasises what awaits the powerless. He denies the words so now they stand merely as a desperate delusion.

The rest of 'King Creole' is very different. He sings everything with a huge smile on his face and he delights in his talent and sidesteps the material to relish his own glory. For example, the song, 'Young Dreams', is pretend Doo Wop but it does not matter because Elvis soars way above his material and his singing is peppered with swoops, tricks, gasps and surprises. Melodramatic and absurd it may be but the pleasure is in being perpetually surprised by the next note and his total disregard for the lyrics. The record exists simply to demonstrate his talent and success and he is aware of how winning carries its own distinct charm. He toys with the listener throughout and he delights in being allowed to share his supremacy and good fortune with his audience.

The song, 'Crawfish', is considered to be a classic and appeals to virtually everyone. This is no small achievement because the song is mediocre, Hollywood swill. The dependency of his movies on exotic locations has meant that Elvis has on more than one occasion on his soundtracks sung about fish. If you need to have defined the difference between an inspired, creative Elvis and the sleepwalker of the later movies, listen to 'Crawfish' and the 'Girls Girls Girls' soundtrack in 1962. There were songs in that later movie that also referred to fish but those recordings only confirmed his subsequent alienation. 'Crawfish', though, is brilliant. It has a great, bass line and superb, backing vocals from Kitty White which would be enough, except Elvis produces a vocal full of drama and tension. He pulls in the listener with a magnet he has found in his throat. The same magnet appears on the track, 'Lover Doll', which is also inconsequential pop but succeeds because he is extremely playful and seductive and, not short of tricks, he again gives the song plenty of hooks. This is a long way from the heavy and sometimes plodding material he recorded in the seventies when he may have feeling but not the same capacity for invention. 'Lover Doll' and the whole album are full of originality.

'Trouble' is pastiche Muddy Waters. It is not great blues but that is not important because so much of the album is sung with a sly grin. When he sings the verses we do not believe in Elvis as all conquering, machismo warrior but, in the chorus, he reminds us how he can conquer in other ways. There is bravura and impudence that is unique to him and that is sufficient. 'Dixieland Rock' and 'Hard Headed Woman' are both good songs and all Elvis needs to do is bring them to life. This he does without pausing. He delivers them full on. There is less vocal embroidery than on the other tracks but the two songs do not need it. He still inhabits them completely and stamps his musical identity on the rock and roll. The horn section is great throughout the album but it is probably on these two tracks that it is heard at its best. The musicians sound as if they are enjoying every moment.

The 'King Creole' album is a compromise and rockabilly and blues purists may consider it to have dated. It was not considered a betrayal at the time when we all responded to the knowing humour of Leiber and Stoller and the elan of Elvis. The album was received gratefully by record buyers as a further example of what could be achieved by a great talent. It also exists as a sly truth, a hint of what Elvis might have done with Hollywood if he had stayed motivated or if his manager had not revealed his greed and cynicism prematurely.

These are the nine classic albums that were released in his lifetime. Alone they amount to a remarkable contribution to American popular music and they should have assured critical respect. Indeed, it is certain he would have had approval if these had existed without anything else. There would have been no disturbing fall to contemplate. But, fine as they are, they minimise his achievements. The fifties collections above only include the Sun rejects. Imagine an additional, twelve track album of his Sun singles plus a fifties album that included classics like 'Is It So Strange', 'My Baby Left Me' and 'Lawdy Miss Clawdy'.

Similar opportunities were missed later in his career when quality material was squandered on inferior compilations or scattered around soundtrack albums. The first 'missing' album could have defined what he produced in Nashville from 1966 to 1968, the second could have enlarged upon the achievements with Chips Moman in Memphis in 1969 and the third could have given a much improved 1970 all studio alternative to 'That's The Way It Is' and this, itself, may have also generated a proper, definitive, live album from Las Vegas. There are also the albums that do not deserve classic status but have fine moments. 'Something For Everybody' is not the equal of 'Elvis Is Back' but it is much improved when the best recording from the session, 'I Feel So Bad', is included and the songs are arranged in a sensible order,. Similarly, 'Pot Luck' has three marvellous ballads that represent a musical breakthrough for Elvis and is listenable even when weak. It would have been significantly superior if Parker had not been allowed to include movie tracks and prohibit the inclusion of singles. It is doubtful if any of the albums from 1971 -1977 could have been edited to become classics but they could have been organised so they, at least, were worth what they cost to buy. There is also a huge amount of live material including an exceptional number of songs that were never recorded in the studio and which exist as alternative music. If the frequency of essential recordings diminished as his career progressed, they still stubbornly appeared until the end.

Ultimately, we need the triumphs but also the reduced Elvis to not only appeal to our various moods but to help us distinguish achievement from failure, right from wrong and to realise that both contain contradictions. The Creature always had remorse and Satan or, at least, the fallen angel in 'Paradise Lost' who was admired by Shelley and the Romantics, never completely lost his charm. Satan, the Creature and Elvis Presley were all restless and persuasive. Shelley makes clear in 'Frankenstein' what is the tragedy of her abandoned 'Adam'. It consists of the the failure by the Creature to fulfil his original potential and the prolonged but avoidable misunderstanding between Frankenstein and his creation which resulted in violence and harm. Okay, Elvis had more opportunities and moments than the Creature but all this applies to Elvis. The achievements were exceptional and required initial fortune but, ultimately, the potential was maliciously thwarted and he was damned.

Both the Creature and Elvis had willingness and a curiosity but Frankenstein and Parker refused to recognise merit in someone whom they regarded as inferior and flawed. They considered only the importance of their own authority. Both men died believing they were blameless. It is the tragic waste of individuals and not the symbolism that haunts the reader of 'Frankenstein'. It is what haunts me about Elvis, the knowledge that his great records could have led to something even greater. For some, this disappointment meant he had to be abandoned and the riches he created denied. These people, who soon swelled the hostile village, do not realise it is the failure and his contradictory legacy that has kept his fans loyal for so long.

The talented rivals

The horror characters that have been created in fiction and the movies may now number as many as a thousand. Even a narrow genre such as cannibalism creates numerous alternatives and its heroes range from the pie making Titus Andronicus, in the not so well-regarded play by Shakespeare, to the more fastidious Hannibal Lecter. Not all of these can be considered as rivals to the Creature because they often belong to another age or have narrower concerns. The modern, horror figures either have chainsaws or worry about which sauce should compliment which human body part. His true rivals exist in the Gothic horror of the literature of the 18th and the 19th Century. Gothic horror and what terrifies us today are very different and can be compared to the unamplified music to which Elvis listened and the music that followed the innovations of the late 1960s. For many, the music of Elvis has been left behind by modern technology and the need for lyrical significance or explicitness. Something similar happened to the Hammer horror movies. Amidst the many alternatives that exist in Gothic horror, the only serious rivals for the Creature are Dracula, Dr Jekyll and Mr Hyde and the Wolf Man who is basically a movie alternative to Jekyll and Hyde. The character was merely given a wet nose and fur. Dracula had the same understanding of his unrequited hunger as the Creature and Jekyll and the Wolf Man were as tortured. None had the burden of his permanent disfigurement and, when they became monsters, none was as articulate as the Creature. They may have had alternative, charming, daytime identities but all lacked his potential for virtue. Among the horror creations, only the Creature was capable of challenging and facilitating the modern world. Elvis, innovative but also conservative, did the same in rock and roll.

In 1979, the then Prime Minister, James Callaghan, appeared in Liverpool. His speech, which was in the middle of a General Election campaign, was aimed at the TV news that night and he included a couple of quotes that he knew would make the broadcast. Later, the long speech only produced a small, news item. Callaghan, no doubt, understood what would happen which is why he had his special quotes prepared. I cannot remember the TV quotes but, at the time, I knew immediately they would be on the TV from the way he delivered them. They were like the top As in the performance of a singer. Apart from reassuring a TV audience, he also had to keep red toothed, Scouse Marxists at bay and he made two brief references as to why Socialism was still important to him. The impact on the audience was electric and, no matter their ideological hostility to the man, they launched into enthusiastic applause. When his speech had finished Callaghan was bundled into a limousine and the media crowd left quickly and efficiently. The rest of the meeting consisted of local, Party leaders committing themselves to Clause 4 and radical politics. Despite the purity and appeal of these thoughts, the audience merely clapped politely.

Some years later, a BB King concert was shown late at night on Channel 4. BB was appearing in a blues festival and, before he appeared, journeymen, blues guitarists opened the show. These blues guitarists who appeared before BB King reminded me of the Liverpool Marxists. Their integrity was too easy and, after a couple of blues riffs, they, like the Marxists, soon became inconsequential. Callaghan had to deal with power and compromise, the dictate of the floating vote and the fight to be top dog. Through it all, he never forgot his left wing roots. They had to take their place but they were there and, when he revealed them in their compromised fashion, they actually had more impact because they were not wrapped in integrity. Callaghan, though, was not comparable to BB King because BB was not fighting to be top dog and he never had a floating vote to concern him. No, those electric moments from Callaghan were like Elvis in Vegas when, after all that has happened, he reminds you that he still likes the blues. His diversity is not everything that makes Elvis appealing but, when combined with his success, it might be what makes him unique. He was, like Callaghan, obliged to work compromises on a scale comparable to no one else. When he reveals he is still one of us it is more important and rewarding than when we hear a dedicated, genre specialist merely play what we want to hear.

His rivals, then, required comparable talent but, equally important, they needed similar opportunities and the increased challenges that accompanied those opportunities. Without them, they lack comparable consequence. Their importance is not simply about musical ability and their talent may not even dominate how we regard them. But all the rivals had merit that needs to be shown appropriate respect. In music, a lot of talent often achieves little, the ability to entertain a large crowd for an hour and, when faced with the increased demands of a recording studio, deliver a range that can justify one interesting CD, either an album or a compilation. Most popular performers are not capable of more than this but this alone requires a gift that makes them admirable.

The following comparisons concentrate on those people whom I like. There is no such a thing as objective criticism because we like what we need and we are all different. This is why the selection can be regarded as eccentric. Bob Dylan and The Beatles, though, are included because of their importance and because they follow Elvis in terms of how they influenced pop and achieved iconic status. It is also dangerous to leap too many generations which is why what followed The Beatles and Dylan has been avoided and why Tobe Hooper should never be allowed to direct a Frankenstein movie.

Elvis exists as a great performer of American music and his range is most sympathetic to the music of the American South. This consists of not just what the people of the American South produced but also what they would listen to on their radios. Elvis is important not because he embraced most of the music made in the American South but also because he had the audacity to include everything they imported.

The only comparable performer with this ability and, equally important, similar interest and ambition is Ray Charles. Although I will always lean to Elvis because he is the man who shaped me, I would not insist on my arguments with a Ray Charles fan. Obviously, they believe their man is the most important and the difference between the performers is too close for any of us to be truly objective. What surprises, though, is that, amongst the great, soul and blues performers of the fifties and sixties, it is Ray Charles who is the least appreciative of Elvis although, surprisingly, he did visit Graceland. Maybe he mellowed with time or, like the rest of us, he finally latched on to one record that turned his head. The antipathy exists probably because they are genuine peers. Ray resented this white guy who, just like him, had the confidence to sing everything.

Ray Charles has done it all and, in the beginning when he struggled for material, he even wrote some worthy songs. But, he never enjoyed writing and he soon settled for re-defining the songs of others. He has made many iconic records and, unlike Elvis, his fierce ambition and insistence upon control ensured that he maintained consistency throughout his career. He also made appealing, riff laden, jazz albums. The scope of his music has not persuaded all the critics. Some would have preferred him to be far less versatile and to have been restricted to the successful, gospel based rhythm and blues that he pioneered in the fifties. When he suddenly switched to country music in the sixties and, then, began to make albums of American standards they were aghast. This willingness to defy critics makes him similar to Elvis and, though both men were flawed in different ways, it may be because of this independence of thought that history will eventually consider them both heroic. So, when people say Elvis is great, because nobody else can sing everything, they need to be challenged. So can Ray Charles. His versatility meant inevitably that some of his albums were unfocussed and not entirely successful but his albums are all important. In all of them, there will be sublime moments that will take the listener to another level where, suddenly, life feels good again. His fans argue that his experience as a black American gives his records an authenticity and soul that Elvis lacks. He communicates suffering and agony beyond Elvis. I am not so sure. Perhaps they just sound different. Both men understand the exaltation of despair and the ecstasy of freedom and release but, clearly, the experience of a blind Charles in an oppressed minority gives him a different perspective. The two men are complex personalities and both suffered a loss of sibling and idolised their mother. Similar emotional needs can be heard in their music. Both men were identified originally as being violent but, like the Creature, the two men yearned for a familial kinship to soothe their hearts.

If I have to argue Elvis has an edge, and I am not sure it is important that I do, I would say that, although both men can handle the same range of material, Elvis has a voice that is the more complex instrument or it sounds that way. Ray Charles has the one voice and he uses it brilliantly to shape a broad range of material in his image. Elvis, though, has many voices and he uses his material to reveal many images of himself. Ray Charles is more musical and is a gifted arranger but Elvis has inspired instincts. Ultimately, no one should care. Both should be remembered as giants because of the range and quality of their legacy. Equally significant, they blurred genres and re-defined American music. They refused to settle for what was supposed to be their racial inheritance. I have every record plus some outtakes by Elvis but I have also bought everything by Ray Charles, also including some outtakes, and merely looking at his box sets can produce pathetic moments of pleasure. I also own every record plus outtakes made by Aretha Franklin and Jerry Lee Lewis which is why they are considered next. (I know, the medical problem is worse than previously indicated.)

Aretha Franklin is the great voice in American music. She can hit more notes than anyone else and sustain them for longer. She has a powerhouse style that can also be remarkably subtle. The voice never reveals any hint of strain and is always musical. Her records utilise her roots in rich, black music. Blues, jazz, gospel and rhythm and blues give her records an added substance that the music of Elvis, because of its roots in less complex, country tunes, often lacks. She also worked in an excellent environment at Atlantic and with producers who believed that more, rather than less, ambition was important to the quality of the records. Her ballads are filled with feeling, her dance numbers swing with fierce energy and she uses her gifts to seek out original grooves to lift the material. Can Elvis hope to compete? Many fans and critics of black music think not. Certainly, he is the inferior performer if one assumes that music begins and ends with American soul and blues. This could be why Elvis never stayed loyal to the rhythm and blues he so clearly enjoyed performing. Not only did he have his own complicated roots to explore but he believed that the genre already had its own masters. It is worth repeating what Myrna Smith said. Myrna Smith, who, as a member of the Sweet Inspirations, backed both Elvis and Aretha, said this about his stage show, 'His was the most exciting show I've ever worked in …... He just put so much into it. Aretha could sing rings around Elvis if you're talking about vocal prowess but as far as wanting to be on stage you just got drawn into it.' Another way of expressing this is Aretha had the voice but Elvis had daring. She understood music while he understood our dreams. Aretha also had taste and selected material that suited her considerable strengths. Elvis was undisciplined, often picking songs that failed to reveal his ability. But, for all his self-destructive indolence, there was an enthusiast in Elvis which encouraged him to take risks. Unfortunately, the enthusiast only responded to challenges because he had sensitivity that distinguished easily between challenges and demands. His response to challenges could sometimes be heroic but he became pathetic when faced with routine demands. This means his music lacked the consistency of Aretha but it did have the diversions that make him continually interesting.

Aretha was truly great when she worked with a talented producer but could be disappointing with others. Although sometimes undermined by producers, Elvis and Ray Charles give the listener the sense that the performer dominates everything. Aretha surrendered probably too often to the vision of the producer. Her early work on Columbia is distinguished by a fabulous voice but refuses to sparkle. The eventual surrender in the eighties to producers and drum machines reveals a modesty and malleability as disheartening as the careless indolence of Elvis. It is also odd how such a marvellous singer can occasionally make inferior versions of songs. There are many marvellous exceptions, of course, 'You're All I Need To Get By', 'The Tracks Of My Tears' and 'The Weight' are just three where she exceeds the quality of brilliant originals But 'Son Of A Preacher Man' by Dusty Springfield, 'Baby I Love You' by Irma Thomas and, even, 'I've Got The Music In Me' by Kiki Dee are records by singers much inferior to Aretha but whose versions are all an improvement on the covers by Aretha. Of course, she is a serious musician and her versions always have a distinct arrangement. If they do not always succeed, and often they do, there is the voice and that is always inspirational. But, although we are all agreed she is indeed the Queen of Soul and essential to any CD collection, she does not dominate the turntable of this admirer as much as Elvis and Ray Charles, possibly, because she avoided the leap into the dark that Elvis and Ray Charles so often made. Despite that, Aretha is an exceptional talent and ground should be conceded to her loyalists but that same ground can also be claimed by Elvis fans. She is so good and so important, there is no comparative, female figure in American, soul music and this is not because there are not other, considerable talents. Etta James and Irma Thomas are also marvellous and responsible for many classic records and they have plenty of female singers in support like Candi Staton and Betty Swann. Aretha, though, is where her early

Atlantic treasures promised she would be, at the very top and required to be acknowledged on her own terms.

Jerry Lee Lewis has many admirers and they are like their hero in that they concede second place to no one. Jerry Lee confined his output to rock and roll, country, rhythm and blues and some gospel. He rarely dabbled in pop and had contempt for crooners; he was never likely to be waylaid by the need for kinship like the Creature. His lifestyle asserted an egotistic entitlement to freedom and pleasure that matched the promise of rock and roll perfectly. He sustained his career until the late eighties by singing country material but he never forgot the rock and roll entirely. His larger than life personality, cynicism and confidence ensured that the sentimental moments of country would never be more than ironical. He has, in fact, the personality and record catalogue that early fans expected from Elvis. He is the monster without pity that many fans have always craved. His relentlessness makes him the rock and roll equivalent of Freddie from 'Friday The Thirteenth'. He can also play a piano and, like Freddie, has a dynamic stage presence. The Jerry Lee fans that do have records by Elvis will usually have nothing that was recorded by Elvis after 1958 and these records are usually kept a respectful distance from those of their hero. Jerry Lee is a marvellous performer and his achievements, like those of Aretha Franklin and Ray Charles, cannot be restricted to a single, greatest hits CD.

But, if Jerry Lee is the man rock and rollers wanted Elvis to be, he is not an equal talent. He has made great records, his two big hits, 'Great Balls Of Fire' and 'Whole Lotta Shaking Going On', are equalled by the great rocker, 'High School Confidential', and a marvellous interpretation of the Hank Williams song, 'You Win Again'. He is more than willing, though, to repeat himself and his music, though still marvellous, is not ageing as well as was once expected. Like Ray Charles, he fashions a wide range of material in his strident image. But he lacks the soul of Ray Charles or the emotional complexity of Elvis. For those who only want to see their idealised, rebellious selves in a performer, he is perfect. He is consistent but his records have been dominated by two great producers, Sam Phillips and Jerry Kennedy, so they should be. If he avoids mistakes, the peaks are few when compared to Elvis. His best records are impressive, and most of the rest have merit, but his top fifty records are not the equivalent of the best fifty made by Elvis. Purists will argue that his catalogue on Sun is classic rock and roll. It is very good but, at times, it sounds a little thin and formulaic. Though confined to fewer tracks, the rockabilly of Elvis exists on a higher level. Jerry Lee is also an unconvincing blues and gospel singer, the latter sounding no different to his other music. He is, though, a great, country performer and, because he subverts the genre, he is more interesting in this field than Elvis. He does maintain a formula which means there are periods when his country music is predictable but it is fabulous overall. Jerry Lee has avoided the recorded embarrassments that plagued Elvis. But, if we compiled best of, four CD, box sets, one for Elvis and one for Jerry Lee, the collection by Elvis would be much superior. Believe me, I have done it and can quote from experience.

The other white, American performers of the generation of Elvis are too narrow in their abilities to be compared. Charlie Rich is great and has made some classics. The best of his music on Smash makes a fine, double album and his record, 'Tears A Go Go', describes an irresistible, dystopian fantasy about an exclusive nightclub where the bouncers bar anyone who does not have a broken heart. It is one of the best songs in American music. 'Who Will The Next Fool Be', which was recorded at Sun, is equally magnificent. Elvis, though, has the edge and superior range. Buddy Holly has his fans and was gifted but he died very early and we will have to wonder what he could have achieved. The Callaghan moments were not intended for him. Johnny Cash attracts loyalty and is a singular talent and man but is to be admired more for his left wing, populist attitudes and larger than life personality than his actual, musical ability. Others have made rockabilly with a better beat and country music with more melody than Cash. He can fill a stage but his records are too often about the props, his messages and his integrity rather than the actual music. His fans will disagree violently with this claim and will insist his great songs make him important. He remained successful in the late sixties as a bridge between country music and Dylan and it can be claimed his mix of country and folk protest anticipated Dylan. Amongst the male, country performers, George Jones is easily the finest vocalist. He performs everything with passion and feeling and his vibrato is second to none when a hook is needed. But, again, he is narrow and the great records he has made resemble one another too closely for him to be compared to Elvis.

This can also be said for the other great talents that have dominated country music. As important as they are, and people like Merle Haggard and Hank Williams are very important, they exist as a reminder of how bold Elvis was when he defined his unique role for himself. Bob Wills probably needs a special mention because he dominated Western Swing in the forties and, like Elvis, he merged country music with the blues and jazz he was hearing in the South and on the radio but the two men are too far apart in history to be compared meaningfully. Wills was a musician who constructed a dazzling ensemble while Elvis was an individual who focussed on his own talent. The versatility of the talented and underrated Bobby Darin cannot be ignored but he is not an original stylist and he lacks independent authority. But many now have seen the movie, 'Beyond The Sea', and the director, Kevin Spacey, clearly disagrees. 'Roy Orbison deserves a mention if only because Elvis was a keen admirer and he rated him as an equal. Elvis underestimated himself. The Big O is a great ballad singer and is responsible for a handful of immortal singles. His cover of 'Mean Woman Blues' apart, he is no rocker. Orbison exists as a reminder that being distinct and effective requires acclaim. But, in his music and in his personality, Elvis always had the ability to claim vantage from the middle. What made Elvis unusual was that he did this by visiting the extremes. Roy Orbison, although very good, was too narrow for that.'

Inevitably, rhythm and blues and soul, which has been a continual source of innovation, contains more great talents and rivals than the country alternative. Two performers need to be mentioned again. They are important because they have superior, technical ability and because Elvis was a keen admirer. Roy Hamilton predated Elvis by half a decade and, although an influence, he is a very different kind of singer. They share an interest in melodrama but Elvis is much more about raw emotion while Roy Hamilton is controlled and calculating. His records exert a hold because of the appeal of his voice and the perfect execution. He is better at ballads but, without being really convincing, he has made excellent rock and roll, soul and dance music. His breath control is superior to Elvis and his voice suggests that his throat is a kind of trumpet with a volume control. Ultimately, though, he is not as inventive as Elvis, either within a song or across the range of his interests. But he is an influence. The seventies stage shows of Elvis with their set piece, dramatic ballads and top A finishes stand as a tribute to Roy Hamilton.

Another spirit present in those shows is Jackie Wilson. Like Roy Hamilton, he is classically trained and has the breath control of an opera singer. (As Alex Ross reveals in 'The Rest Is Noise', another reason African American, popular music is superior to that of its white equivalent is the presence of classically trained musicians. Unable to obtain a career in classical music because of discrimination, they added their virtuosity to the popular.) Jackie Wilson has often been compared to Elvis and has by some been described as the black Elvis although others would prefer to describe Elvis as the white Jackie Wilson. There are similarities. Both men were charismatic performers and both were extremely versatile. When he sings on stage and, even, in the movies Elvis can resemble Jackie Wilson. There are grins and gestures that are very similar. The record, 'Return To Sender', echoes Jackie Wilson and the performance of the song by Elvis in the film, 'Girls, Girls, Girls', is a sly tribute. The admiration between the two men was mutual and it is not unreasonable to say that the two men influenced each other. Although he had a premature end to his life, Jackie Wilson finished his career well as a contemporary, soul performer. For all his talent, Jackie Wilson cannot be considered as seriously as Elvis. Wilson has elements in common with Elvis but the people who insist upon equality are limiting Elvis to his stereotype, the flirtatious and hip swivelling performer and the big ballads. Elvis could be more subtle and has two big advantages. Although technically inferior, his voice is more pleasant to the ear and, because he is emotionally complex, he is more interesting. He trumps the others with the number of his different, musical personalities. Elvis is like Ray Charles because he has his demons and agonies. Although neither really explains what haunts and baffles them, their complexities broaden and dramatise their music. This is what puts them ahead of singers like Jackie Wilson.

A singer who is as listenable as Elvis is Solomon Burke. He belongs to the select few that can perform ballads and dance numbers equally well. Given the right song, he is second to no one but he is less impressive with average material. This is why he has made great singles but his albums have been less successful. He rarely transcends his material in the way Elvis or Ray can but he is equally adept at soul and country. He has a beautiful voice and he knows, as well as anyone, how to squeeze the groove out of the song. He has not had the opportunities he should have had but, for a while, he was championed by fans and critics. He was christened the 'King Of Rock And Soul' and it should not be begrudged but his emotional interests were narrower than either those of Elvis or Ray. Like Jackie Wilson, he was a cheerful, confident man who precipitated grins in others. This may make him likeable but perhaps it has restricted his influence. Nevertheless, his records deserve to be bought and they can all be easily found in record stores and online.

Bobby Bland is somebody who could never be described as cheerful. If his records are to be believed, he has been betrayed by more women than any other man on earth. His performances are so heartfelt that we believe him. He is an amazing vocalist. Although his style varies little, it is unique to him and it combines brilliantly his gospel, blues and soul roots. We may hear the same singer every time but what a singer, especially as his phrasing is the equal of Sinatra. His performances are controlled and measured but, like Sinatra, each line has its moments of drama and, usually, he will pick a note to extend and fill with despair and sometimes honour with a growl that is musical and challenging. Bobby Bland can growl his way through octaves. If this was the extent of his talent, it would be enough but each song floats on his soulful mood and the blues is always present in his attitude. His voice has hardly deteriorated with age and all the different phases of his career have been successful although he did not sustain himself as a crossover artist. This speaks volumes about the absence of taste in the rock audience. I have seen him on stage three times and was privileged to see him perform in Texas in front of a mainly black and appreciative audience which was an unforgettable experience because, that night, Bobby and the audience were in the mood. In the novel, 'Frankenstein', the Creature was musical; he enjoyed listening to the blind man play the guitar. Obviously, he had no iPod to listen to when he drove his ice sledge across the icy waste to the North Pole but, if he had, the Creature, as he spat out his curses at his wolves, would have listened to Bobby Bland.

In the film, 'Mystery Train', by Jim Jarmusch, Elvis is compared unfavourably to Bobby Bland. Elvis is described as a white, less competent and more pop alternative. This is unfair. Bobby Bland is great and a supreme, soulful, ballad singer but his up tempo material is not as successful. He has produced up tempo classics, like 'Turn On Your Lovelight' and 'Who's Fooling Who', but they usually depend more on the arrangements than Bland for their impact. Bobby is a man who has fun but only because it is relief from his despair and isolation. His dance records swing but the mystery and transcendence of ecstasy is beyond him. And so it should be. He has been betrayed too many times for that which may be why his album, 'Two Steps From The Blues', remains unsurpassed.

It occurs to me that I could write another book about comparable, black talents because there are so many. Of course, it is what writers have done elsewhere so many times. And this book is primarily concerned with rescuing the reputation of one singer. I will restrict myself to a few more examples.

The obvious, rock and roll rival is Little Richard. He made the most powerful records in the fifties and they benefitted from being made at Speciality who used either the Columbia sound, or their version of it, to give his performances extra punch. When I was young I was a major fan of Little Richard but something must have happened to my ears over the years because, now, I find his rock and roll classics unlistenable. This is not quite true. I can listen to Little Richard but no more than a song in a night. It is as if he defined brilliantly himself in one record and then repeats the formula. This is an irony because he is actually quite versatile with an amazing voice. Somehow he was never able to exploit the versatility properly and his career faded badly. There are, though, after his rock and roll phase some marvellous exceptions, dance floor hits and great, soul ballads. Nowadays, I listen to these more than the rock and roll. His gospel music, which can be downloaded from Amazon, exposes the wonder of his voice brilliantly and is essential. He has his devotees who will explain patiently his importance in shaping rock and roll.

Larry Williams is not a rival but he deserves a mention because he is interesting and, alongside Elvis and Little Richard, he made a very persuasive case for primitivism. His triumphs are few but they are special. 'Baby's Crazy' and 'Slow Down', with their irresistible hooks and 'Dizzy Miss Lizzy', full of obsessive nonsense, challenge those who believe music should be something other than merely entertaining. These records capture the appeal of great rock and roll and they disturb because they convincingly condemn aspiration as phony. Obviously, life is more complicated than what they insisted upon but, for the duration of the records, his argument is persuasive. Unlike the rock and roll of Little Richard, his music remains appealing. Williams had a short life because he was murdered. His main income was not derived from music but prostitution and hard drugs. It should be no surprise that he understood perfectly the nihilistic appeal of early rock and roll.

The music of Muddy Waters is unique and represents a breakthrough in the blues. He was a gritty, powerful vocalist and, like Stevie Wonder after him, he was successful in using technology to expand genres. He is great but he lacked the capacity to re-invent himself when needed which is why his music peaks early even though his vocal power lasts well beyond his decline. Of course, if he had reinvented himself, he would have been of accused of lacking integrity. This way, he represents his culture and people and it is why he is regarded as a hero. Howling Wolf is a comparable figure although his music is narrower than that made by Waters. Sam Phillips once said, his most important discovery was Howling Wolf and not Elvis but then Sam does like to talk and, on another day, he would contradict himself. Presumably, Sam meant that Wolf after working with Sam at Sun was able to go to Chess in Chicago where he invented a no compromise, electric blues that insisted primitivism would prevail in modern rock and roll. Wolf and Waters are important. Their music is in the consciousness of my generation and it did raise the stakes. But, if modern rock and roll is not just about Elvis, it is not just about Wolf and Waters either. Wolf is a truly powerful bluesman and he was described by those who knew him as an impressive human being which is what one would expect from listening to the ferocity in his vocals. Waters and Wolf had personalities never short of consequence and their music was consistent with their stature.

BB King is a bluesman who has dominated the blues for most of his career. He is not the preferred choice of the critics. Muddy Waters and Howling Wolf are usually viewed as the more vibrant performers and other blues guitarists are rated more highly. But, if his guitar playing is simple, it is full of feeling and very attractive. The tone is unique to him. He is smart and knows how to make one note ring with emotion. He is also an underrated singer and actually sings the blues with an operatic technique. True, he does not sound like an opera singer because he is too hoarse but he uses the same trick of bringing his voice up from his diaphragm. He vomits out the words. BB King is different from other blues performers because he has redefined his music and extended himself to stay interesting to people other than purists. He has stayed loyal to the blues but made albums with commercial appeal. His album, 'Love Me Tender', mixes country and mellow blues. No wonder the critics are hostile. He has also managed his career effectively. He is almost to the blues what Elvis is to rock music and he has been capable of surprises. His career, in fact, could have been the model for Elvis because it showed how Elvis might have avoided the embarrassments and still made money. Unfortunately, Elvis was distracted by movies, tone deaf managers and his own lack of industry. Although BB has made many fine records and is incredibly admirable, he does not have the unique gifts of some of the characters above. But wit and persistence and a fair amount of talent have produced a legacy of which he can be proud.

Not everybody would identify Bobby Womack as one of the great rivals and, to be honest, I am not sure how great he is either. His albums are variable and, although his songs can be memorable, his list of classic singles is not long. But I like him and, once, he put on a show in Manchester to a half filled Apollo that was heart stopping. He has been self-destructive and this has produced gaps in his career. His voice is great but not as great as the black singers mentioned above. He has performed a range of material and has an effective growl but he is less successful on the up tempo numbers which he fakes, albeit effectively. Like Elvis, he requires indulgence with some material which can be too sentimental or self-conscious but he is never less than interesting. His albums always spring surprises. He is also never dominated by a record producer although he came perilously close to surrendering his identity to Van McCoy on the album, 'Safety Zone'. His music of the seventies and eighties suffers, like most of the music of those decades, through having too much happening in the studio. Something, though, in his open, curious spirit always prevails and one of his albums always makes this listener feel the experience has been worthwhile. As he makes his strange and imaginative journey through his musical inheritance, his progress makes you warm to the man.

There are, of course, many other great black performers in rhythm and blues and soul. James Brown and Sam Cooke are obvious figures and those who champion their cause may wish them to be considered alongside Ray Charles, Aretha and Elvis. James Brown was a fabulous stage performer and very innovative. He has influenced subsequent generations but, possibly, because they were looking for a role model they could easily imitate. This is the problem with the conceptualists. They multiply at a faster rate than other performers. I do listen to him but have to restrict the dosage. He has serious, vocal limitations and, as I am not one who listens to hear cleverness, I eventually became weary of his harsh singing. But he has made some great records and some of have been overlooked despite his high profile. 'How Do You Stop' is a wise sermon with a firm beat that belongs in any record collection. His early rhythm and blues is also something of a surprise and it complements the later funk very well.

Sam Cooke has a marvellous voice and is a unique stylist. He also made at least half a dozen peerless records. He has his devoted fans and he has been extremely influential on gifted singers such as Bobby Womack. Personally, I would prefer a little more grit occasionally. Like Elvis, he was burdened with RCA for a record company and, if anything, they sweetened him more than Elvis. Admittedly, he had no movie horrors but, after his more impressive, gospel years, the influence of RCA applied to almost everything. At least, Elvis was schizophrenic and left alternatives. Okay, so did Sam but they are very few in number. It is, of course, a matter of taste. I can appreciate his great records that utilise worthwhile songs but I am less enthusiastic with him singing either average or more familiar material. His voice, as great as it is, does not seduce me. Elvis has vulnerability and this makes the listener feel like an equal. Sam is drenched in self-adoration and, on too many occasions, this can be a real barrier. Nevertheless, there are still those half a dozen iconic records. These include 'A Change Is Gonna Come', 'I'll Come Running Back To You' and 'Bring It On Home To Me' and these alone make him important and make you wonder what he might have achieved if he had not signed for RCA or if he had stayed at another motel the night he was shot.

Some people will say Stevie Wonder and Marvin Gaye need to be considered but it is doubtful that, without technology, Wonder would be the giant he sometimes appears although he is uniquely talented and has his own, special rhthym and soul. He was also bold at the right times. Marvin Gaye was interesting and his early period contains incomparable, Motown classics like 'Can I Get A Witness' but, later, he was not always quite as captivating as he thought. I also saw him give one of the most cliché, soul shows imaginable which probably makes me prejudiced. One is obliged to note their seminal albums, 'Songs In The Key Of Life' and 'What's Going On', but, despite these historical achievements and classic singles such as 'I Was Made To Love Her' and 'I Heard It Through The Grapevine' they are not on a par with Aretha and Ray and even people anti-Elvis would admit that. Where they would disagree with me is that I consider Elvis to be at least an equal with Aretha and Ray. As said previously, another book could be written about black singers and, as this has already been done, I will leave it there but with a reminder that there are many more fabulous talents in soul, gospel and rhythm and blues. I have not mentioned Otis Redding because, although I think he is talented, my ears only respond to odd tracks rather than albums. What I have done, because it may have interest, is list from those genres the great talents whom I rate. This is to ensure that a reader can leave even a book on Elvis with a respect for a culture that for a long time was not exposed or appreciated in the way it should have been.

Once we delve into modern pop and rock, we meet an aesthetic which is very different to that preached by Elvis. When David Bowie revealed his favourites on his iPod he mentioned avant garde pieces by John Adams. Not only would Elvis not do this, he stands opposed to the avant garde. Comparisons are not really valid but we would not be this far if we were not curious. Although he is becoming passé with age, one figure dominates the others in this alternative aesthetic. I was never, though, destined to be a Bob Dylan fan. My ex-wife actually met him in a bus stop in Glasgow when he was taking the air before his concert. Dylan asked her if she was a Scottish colleen. She told him he was in the wrong country and colleens were Irish. He offered her a couple of tickets for his show that night but she refused. Back then, she was a Tamla fan and she thought he was too skinny and smelled. Well, he was a heavy smoker. Dylan and his friends moved on to another bus stop. After I divorced, I met my partner. The relationship began when I visited her in what should have been a suburban retreat. I discovered she was living next door to two heroin addicts who, when high, would stay up all night listening to 'Blonde On Blonde'. That first visit to her home happened over twenty years ago. The heroin addicts died a couple of years after that visit. They discovered their bodies were not quite as partial to heroin as they were. My partner has never listened to Dylan since and it has to be on the headphones if I do. He is not part of my normal, listening habits and, as the little I do involves a betrayal, I am not objective.

I accept that Bob Dylan, because of his bohemian and intellectual roots, is everything that Elvis is not. His lyrics are ambitious, he is politically and intellectually aware, he applies himself diligently and he introduced themes into his music that were previously not the concern of pop music. 'Not Dark Yet', for example, may not be Proust but it is a reasonable account of ageing and the threat of death although the cliché about Gay Paree clangs badly. 'Desolation Row' lasts for ten minutes but the record actually passes quickly because the tune is hypnotic and the lyrics never flag. This is way beyond Elvis. But, of course, Dylan is not Elvis either. Both men have talent beyond the other. The vocals of Dylan do not have the quality his fans are desperate to imagine. Although his songs, because of their complex lyrics, do not often require great performances, he mars too many with his croak. On 'Forever Young', which is a beautiful song, he is not only flat but loses the tune and even drifts into an alternative melody. It is true his material can benefit from his personal involvement and this is evident on his great records. 'It Ain't Me, Babe' and 'It's All Over Now, Baby Blue' are fine examples and both draw strength from his real disillusionment. But there is no glorious voice and no ability to transform material through performance alone. Yet, if Dylan cannot sing like Elvis, he can carry the odd tune when it is needed and he has a decent feeling for the blues. For example, his record, 'Leopard Skin Pillbox Hat', is a good attempt at risqué rhythm and blues, even, if its simple beat appears to be beyond his musicians.

Nick Tosches, the country music critic, is famous for saying, 'There was more mystery, more power, in Elvis, singer of 'Danny Boy' than in Bob Dylan, utterer of hermetic ironies.' Tosches is, of course, referring deliberately to questionable material performed by an over-weight Elvis, a singer near the end of his life and with reduced powers. This forces the question, is it a fair statement? Probably not but Tosches should be admired for saying it. Both Dylan and Elvis have taken pop music to another level but in very different ways and there are people who are fans of both. I am not one of them although some of the records of Dylan appeal. 'It Takes A Lot To Laugh, It Takes A Train To Cry' is a magnificent effort and there are plenty of others. I suppose I have always had respect for Dylan and am even interested in his music but, for some reason, I am not dazzled like some. Dylan captivated and intoxicated my generation. Unfortunately, my generation never appealed to me and, like his generation, Dylan proclaimed his righteousness and the need to indulge himself and he did it as if the latter confirmed the first.

I will always prefer the innocent to the sophisticated because their emotional commitments are more desperate and the burden of their persistent bafflement needs to be acknowledged. 'Like A Rolling Stone' is a fabulous record but the scornful, superior narrator alienates me well before it is finished. What is odd about this record is that the contempt in the vocal and the chorus mask a Scott Fitzgerald type tale about a naive, privileged girl that is actually quite poignant. It is as if Dylan describes a human situation but is too filled with hatred to understand what his talent had produced. Dylan actually mentions Fitzgerald in 'Ballad Of A Thin Man'. This is also a major record but, if there is an argument against myopic, parched dilettantism, 'Ballad Of A Thin Man' for all its brilliance does not understand the debate properly. I am not an expert on his music but it appears to me that Dylan rarely examines himself in his critical analysis. His disappointment is usually with something or someone other than him. These comments may appear to be hyper-critical, especially, from someone who listens to Elvis and responds to rock and roll gibberish. Elvis, though, is no intellectual nor pretends to be and primitive rock and roll delights in its intellectual irresponsibility. Neither man could be contained within basic, rock music. Elvis refused to hide his heart and Dylan, with references to Pound and Eliot and song titles like 'Temporary Like Achilles' is intent on revealing his intelligence. The two men make us critical because they have a talent that insists they operate at a higher level. Elvis needs to feel his music and Dylan needs to be perceptive. When these qualities are missing they fail.

Thinking of Dylan and Elvis always reminds me of the two movies, 'To Have And Have Not' directed by Howard Hawks and 'Build My Gallows High' directed by Jacques Tourneur. The latter is sometimes known as 'Out Of The Past'. Before Sky wrecked the schedules, most people used to watch them on late night TV. The former movie is escapist glamour with a romanticised view of the Humphrey Bogart character. 'Build My Gallows High' is a dark tale with complex characterisation and knowing existentialism. On TV, it has the edge because it is more thoughtful. I once saw the two movies back to back in an art house cinema. 'Gallows' was a surprise disappointment. The big screen failed to bring it to life in the way it did 'To Have'. Both are great films but it was the Bogart film that was more cinematic. What is cinematic? It is difficult to explain but it is recognisable in the cinema because the cinematic film has an irresistible sweep and finesse that carries along the viewer. Of course, there are many movies that engage in other ways, the dry, intense efforts of the ascetic, Christian moralist, Carl Dreyer, or the cerebral but gloomy Bergman. But, for all their qualities, they are not cinematic like Howard Hawks.

Dylan is musical with a good ear for what makes American music special but his music would not have dominated without his ability to engage lyrically and to be serious and humorous. His music is rich with the folk tradition. Folk music has its verbal and independent strengths but it also has its baggage and, when folk is added to rock and roll, the result can sometimes be like an anthem or even sing along smugness. His rock and roll may have attitude and his music does embrace many rich, American forms and is always interesting but, often, it lacks the ultimate, musical authority and force. Too many of his records are like Woody Allen films and feel unfinished, a take away from true greatness. But, if Elvis sweeps you along, Dylan amuses and he is always interesting, often musically. Robbie Robertson, the guitarist from The Band, once admitted to watching the Tom Jones show regularly on television. 'It is only by watching Jones you understand what makes Elvis great.' He was talking about what made Elvis superior. The same could be said of Bruce Springsteen and Dylan. Obviously, there is room for both Elvis and Dylan and I need to be consistent because I am a fan of both Howard Hawks and Carl Dreyer. I do, though, like the quote from Nick Tosches.

If Dylan requires a mention, so do The Beatles. No doubt, many people find them inspirational. I live on Merseyside and regularly visit the city centre of Liverpool. It is easy to spot the visiting, Beatle fans. Wearing large headphones under long hair, and dressed in T shirts imprinted with the covers of Beatles albums, they wander around the city wide eyed, believing their own romance, much like I did when I visited Memphis many years ago. The Beatles wrote catchy tunes and, even, when there lyrics were simple, they sounded different to others. People who are not Beatles fans but, like me, acknowledge their importance, believe that they peaked with their album, 'Rubber Soul', and that they lost the knack of simple but great songs after that. The fans see or hear it differently and worship 'Revolver' and what followed because it embraces modernism. Undoubtedly, these albums represent growth and application. Elvis, in the seventies, is a form of growth but neither late Beatles nor late Elvis is an adequate substitute for inspiration and conquering, carefree confidence. It is not the perception but their recording career was actually quite short. Their last, serious effort was the overrated 'Abbey Road' which appeared six years after their debut on British TV. If we compare their total six years with the first six years of Elvis, their triumph is not the obvious eclipse of their predecessor that many believe. Because they were local, I grew up liking The Beatles but I always thought Elvis had the edge. They were, though, popular. Their music was pleasant and it was a temptation for a teenager. Being an Elvis fan was a much more lonely business in the sixties on Merseyside than shaking heads to 'Can't Buy Me Love.' McCartney and Lennon are exceptionally talented. Ultimately, though, it was easy to stay loyal. The guttural cries of Elvis always convinced me there was something more important than appealing tunes and knowingness.

As time moved on, American music, and those emotion baring elements that often alienated others, became more important to me. Dan Penn, the famous songwriter and demo singer from Stax records in Memphis, once said, 'I never did like The Beatles. All they ever did was release a whole load of damn guitar players.' Penn admires singers because he understands that, as talented as the pickers are, they are not different enough to other mortals. As Elvis discovered with dismay, great singers become something other than human, they, like the Creature, stumble into lonely, mythical territory. Like Dylan, The Beatles have been hugely influential and it is the combined aesthetic of the two plus the latest innovations from black performers and their inevitable, white imitators that dominate modern, popular music. All embrace modernism but none have been able to shake off the reactionary impulse that Elvis set in motion in the fifties. This is an irony that appears to escape most of their fans.

Jim Dickinson, a Memphis musician, coined the term, 'primitive modernism', to describe modern rock and roll and Greil Marcus, in 'Invisible Republic', accepts it as a rallying cry for the future of rock and roll. I am not convinced the two elements are compatible. Both undermine each other and the champions of the modern should listen to the records of Larry Williams which will never be matched for their energy and sweep and which benefited from his immoral contempt for his betters. It is the contradictory traits of aspiration and sensation that undermine modern, popular music. Whilst both need to exist, there is a question of balance and the rock stars of today with their verbose self-regard too often take the energy out of rock and roll. These are the cries of men and women who are desperate to overcome the traditionalist roots they are obliged to embrace. This is not a defence of Elvis who made his own mistakes and also failed to find the right balance between aspiration and sensation.

There are many others who have had impact but selection is subjective. Chuck Berry is a great songwriter and his songs are amusing and rhyme fabulously without any strain but rock and roll records need rhythm that sounds spontaneous and he is less successful at that. It does not elude him totally and the successful occurrences such as 'Bye Bye Johnny', 'Let It Rock' and 'You Never Can Tell' have made him rightly famous but, unbelievably, his genuine classics are only enough to fill a single CD. This is a harsh perspective because he is unique and fabulous which is why there are plenty of good records just short of classic status with fine lyrics. In his defence, his rock and roll could have been given better musical support at Chess. Bo Diddley was a great original but narrow and it takes a strange kind of devotee to listen to one of his box sets. Again, though, he gave an unforgettable performance in Liverpool when the guitar appeared to be part of him and a simple chord could proclaim something earth connected and profound. That night, he performed in a blues club but now I can only picture the scene as if it happened in a living room. The experience was that powerful and intimate. Jimi Hendrix has plenty of fans capable of devotion and worship and, for those who like guitar players, he is without equal. He is another great original but, for all his deference to the blues, his attempts at the genre are not convincing, mainly because he is a driven individualist, a unique talent obliged to be elitist. He is at his best outside the genres when he is searching for something original inside his own head. Roots and community are not the essence of Jimi Hendrix which is why he, like Dylan, should not be compared with Elvis. The list from rock music could go on and we are all different. Not everybody shares my passion for singers and each generation requires something new. The few mentioned here is not to make a conclusive point but to present Elvis in a comparative context.

The Sons Of The Pioneers are not rivals and history distances them, as it does Bob Wills, but they are important to anyone who wants to understand Elvis Presley. The group was formed in 1933 by Roy Rogers who progressed from the group and became a Hollywood cowboy. He actually was both self-mocking and accomplished in the Bob Hope comedy western, 'Son Of Paleface'. Clearly a pragmatic man, he allowed his four legged friend, Trigger, to upstage him on more than one occasion and I was eight years old and one of many witnesses when he did it at the Liverpool Empire in 1956. I still remember my intake of breath as the horse appeared and swished his famous, white tail. John Ford liked The Pioneers and they can be heard providing traditional and beautiful harmonies in several of his westerns. Their repeated appearances on the soundtracks almost make 'Rio Grande' and 'Wagonmaster' musicals. Despite the fame of Rogers and the involvement of the Pioneers in Hollywood movies, they had only one hit outside the American country chart and that was no more than a top thirty hit. What makes the Pioneers comparable to Elvis is that they represent a long-standing tradition within musicians from the Deep South, musicians who play what appeals to them but who will also play anything that might appeal to an audience. Their music ranges through ragtime, folk, jazz, blues, cowboy tunes and gospel to sentimental 'tin pan alley' although they are more sentimental about animals, the prairie and the open trail than women. The Pioneers were also prepared to indulge an audience; they played a tune for only as long as it kept the record buyers interested. Many of their songs are under two minutes long. Understandably, not all of it is wonderful but the fine moments are interesting because they are so different. Their harmonies have already been mentioned but their music also has lively, fiddle solos and, even, jazz, guitar breaks that resemble Django Rhinehart. The Pioneers have that Callaghan dimension of knowing and compromise that began this chapter. They may have been willing to be hokey but they refused to be defined by others. Elvis heard it all as a child and, like all the music he heard, it must have influenced him. Supposedly, his decision to record 'How Great Thou Art' was determined by him hearing the version by the Pioneers. Their influence can also be heard in his 'Blue Hawaii' soundtrack where he mixes the lilt of Hawaiian music with the gentle swing of a Pioneers cowboy tune, best heard on the empty but still pretty 'Moonlight Swim'. Elvis and friends in what they thought was a private moment did a very good impression of The Pioneers singing 'Tumbling Tumbleweeds' but the influence of this group was more than musical. Nobody ever condemned the Pioneers for their lack of independent taste. They were viewed as willing musicians always available to play what pleased the people. Because they were successful, they were role models to aspiring musicians. Their open-minded tolerance and passivity may explain why Elvis was prepared to make the compromises he did.

The difference between Elvis and the Pioneers is that the latter performed in a musical environment that supported their approach throughout their career. Ten years after Elvis had his first hit record, a new generation of musical performers claimed popular music for social and personal rebellion and the avant-garde. Elvis had encouraged and facilitated this stance but his own attitude was much more complex. Rock and roll continued to be for the young and non-conformist and for those who pretended they were but it also sustained itself and became the music of parents. Songwriters emerged proclaiming integrity and independence. The Pioneers career model was in tatters and neither Elvis nor his manager responded quickly enough to these developments. Certainly, performers like the Pioneers would have been unable to advise Elvis.

In a strange way, this leads to the next comparable figure, the previously mentioned film director, Orson Welles. They are connected because both Elvis and Orson were victims of history. Orson Welles came to fame as an innovative, theatre director in New York. He also made controversial but popular, radio programmes. He is most famous for his first movie, 'Citizen Kane', which he produced and directed when he was a mere twenty six years old. The film is an achievement that is as unprecedented and as baffling as the debut single by Elvis, 'That's All Right', recorded when Elvis was only nineteen years old. Orson Welles never equalled 'Citizen Kane' and, like many of the albums recorded by Elvis after 1961, his later films mix the sublime with the appalling. For the credulous, there is a simple explanation for Elvis. He was a shy, naive and uneducated country boy. Orson Welles could not have been more different. A hugely confident, child prodigy from affluent and cultured parents, he dominated people easily with his charm and wit. Not quite as handsome as Elvis, he was, though, physically charismatic when young. As David Thomson, the film critic, wrote, 'He inhaled legend and changed the air we breathe.'

'Citizen Kane' is a great film and it can be viewed repeatedly because of its style, rich themes and character studies but, when it is first seen, it impresses particularly because its revolutionary use of techniques anticipates the future and defines instantly a modern aesthetic. This, of course, is what Welles had done on the stage and radio prior to Hollywood. Elvis did something similar with the double A sided single, 'Hound Dog' and 'Don't Be Cruel', not the invention of rock and roll but the creation of a modern aesthetic. What followed 'Kane' was difficult for Welles. His next film was butchered by Hollywood in a way that could have inspired Parker and Chet Atkins. The work on the Brazilian documentary, 'Its All True', which followed, ended in good time chaos and was never released. Welles had intended to catch the Samba on film but, instead, it caught him. After that, Welles, like Elvis later, was obliged to play catch up and he never quite managed to re-establish himself at the top. Soon, there was an alternative modernism that was rooted in working class reality and authenticity and Welles with his classical interests in Shakespeare and Cervantes struggled to adapt. His film, 'Touch Of Evil', exists as a brilliant but flawed exception. After Marlon Brando, the modern artefact of 'Kane' was still impressive but it was no longer modern. There is an interview with the older Welles in which he admits he would have liked to have played the Brando role in 'The Godfather'. The notion, of course, is ridiculous and it exists as evidence of how the world reorganised itself to exclude Welles. Dylan did the same to Elvis.

It became clear that the man behind 'Kane', like Elvis, was not even a modernist. Admittedly, he had liberal sympathies and he was a virtuoso and technician who would always be obliged to innovate but his heart was in the past. He used his fame and wealth to escape to traditional communities. Welles retreated to the rural world of Ronda in Spain. Elvis holed himself up in Graceland with his working class friends. The later movies of Welles ignore the modern world and are more interested in the traditional mysteries of life and death. He defined his movies as an examination of his belief that 'there are no happy endings.' Dead right (forgive the pun) but try telling it to the next generation.

Both Elvis and Orson Welles were supremely talented and both compromised themselves badly, either through cheap, Hollywood musicals or TV chat-shows. They were men too aware of the past to fulfil themselves as perpetual rebels and their later work inevitably disappointed those who only wanted their radical sensibilities to be re-tuned continually. Although in their youth their talent indicated that they, more than anyone, would master their fates, they were never in control. To his friends and admirers, Elvis could be the coolest man on the planet but, with the truly arrogant who understood power, he was easily intimidated. Welles was similar. With those who valued talent and creativity, he was a fabulous inspiration but his marvellous personality and charm was less effective with the dry souls who only knew financial accounts. Welles realised it which is why he avoided conflict with them. Defeated or disillusioned or possibly both, the two men put on weight and became caricatures. Elvis wore extravagant, white suits on stage and, in his spare time, even wilder outfits. Orson Welles wore wide fedoras and flowing capes and was as obsessed with the colour black as Elvis was with white. His cigars matched those of Castro and were soon attached to him permanently. Elvis used sunglasses in the same way.

It is impossible to remember either man and not think of defeat and unfulfilled potential. Except, both men, alhough their brilliance was only intermittent later, did enough. Until the end of their lives, either working or relaxing, they reminded us of their legend and nagged us to be careful about the air we breathed.

The comparison is given an added dimension because, at certain angles, the singer Mario Lanza resembles Welles. As a personality, Lanza was more like Elvis than Welles. Reared in a poor, working class district of Philadelphia, Lanza had immense confidence in his talent but he had no confidence in himself as a human being. The film director, Gene Nelson, said the same of Elvis. As a performer, Lanza experienced idolatry but, for him, it produced self-hatred and self-destruction. His first love was opera and he talked constantly about switching his career to the music he loved but Hollywood had him. On the rare occasions when he became serious about this demanding ambition, there was usually another well paid deal to tempt him back into the world that destroyed him and a beautiful, fame seduced woman who allowed him to forget his inadequacy. Remind you of anyone? The three men had more in common than is usually understood - talent, immediate success and the capacity to inspire others. Three handsome men prone to fat, even their bodies betrayed them.

Although vampire movies and books are more fashionable than ever, Dracula has had to concede his leading position to young men with better hair and young women with shapelier legs. The Creature enjoyed peak popularity just after the novel was published and, later, when James Whale stole him to create an alternative, fashion icon. Nobody conquers time and revisionists are always ready to pounce on our inadequate memories of glory and distil it into something acceptable to their aloof detachment. The Creature will make periodic returns but it will depend on the moment. Elvis will be the same and, because both figures are special, each generation will always produce a hardcore but diminishing group of eccentric devotees.

The above comparisons are not meant to prove that Elvis exceeds everyone. He cannot because he is not comparable to all. The all conquering title that Elvis acquired is crass and was even refuted by him. If he has talent beyond the heroes of others, we have to acknowledge that they have talent beyond him. When expressed that way the comparisons convince me that his importance and gifts are substantial. He is a major figure who belongs with all the other heroes of rock and roll except his contradictions ensure he is more again. Like the Creature, he also was interested in beauty and ordinary decency, something to complement the challenges generated by his ego and need for conquering dominance. The ambition of the Creature was denied because others found him horrifying. The villagers thought they knew how to define him and, after he responded with anger, they refused to believe he was capable of anything other than violence. Elvis was assumed to be fit for nothing other than rock and roll and, when he had the nerve to insist he was capable of more, too many villagers banded together to proclaim he was not even capable of that.

THE FAILURE
TO NURTURE

Nurture and goodness

In Gothic horror entertainments, we usually have a central figure that is either evil or reduced in such a way that destruction exists within him despite his original nature. The Creature, Mr Hyde and The Wolfman are interesting because their afflictions ensure that they blur the difference between good and bad. The novel, 'Dracula' is different because it provides a clear distinction. The good are usually loyal women and relatives. The bad are demanding, repellent individuals or those who belong amongst the unsophisticated, the mob which loses its way when influenced by others. Although Mary Shelley blurred the notions of good and bad by creating an afflicted Creature, she did use this distinction to support a major theme within the novel. She argued that the responsibility to nurture can only be done if we behave like the good, if we make a 'domestic connection' with others. Victor Frankenstein, because he is obsessed with galvanisation and his own will to power and fame, neglects this responsibility with horrifying consequences. He behaves badly.

Elvis is different to the Creature because he became famous and divided opinion. The failure to nurture was not as damaging to him as it was to the wholly excluded Creature and, of course, the damage always co-existed with the adoration of his fans. For Elvis, the communications of the modern world ensured the failure to nurture existed in two ways. Those who had power and opportunity, and who believed too much in their own galvanising skills, restricted his opportunities and failed to nurture his talent. Those who persuaded others that their voices were important, influenced the hostile villagers. These persuaders failed to nurture his memory.

The failure to nurture the talent

Freddie the Vampire

Freddie Bienstock lived a long and prosperous life. He died when he was eighty six years old. If anything, he belongs in a vampire movie. His full head of grey hair, the sly grin and sartorial elegance would make him a white haired, more than adequate substitute for Bela Lugosi. Nobody can match the claims of Parker to be Frankenstein but, after Parker, Freddie was the keenest to exploit Elvis. Once he tasted blood, Freddie could not help himself and he drained Elvis with one bad song after another. He shared with Parker the same myopia rooted in financial lust. Bienstock is the match for the blinkered, sea captain, Robert Walton, who finds Victor Frankenstein in the desolate, icy waste of the North Pole. Walton is seeking a passage way to glory through the North Pole but the phallic thrusts of his ship have been halted by a beautiful, white landscape whose virginity is not quite as submissive as his masculine arrogance and will to power had assumed. Inspired to tell the details to his sister, he explains in his letters how he identifies with the wounded Frankenstein and soon talks of his love for the man, two people who can provide for each other the purpose and contemplation they find lacking in others. Two men so self-absorbed that their curiosity in women is limited to the sister and step-sister they worship. After witnessing the decline of Frankenstein, he concedes to his crew his folly and turns the ship south and to home. The weight of the albatross of ambitious faith in discovery has been lifted. Unfortunately, Freddie lacked the wit and basic decency of Walton who, despite his flaws, could spot the obvious and was ultimately moved by the damage he was doing to his crew. Freddie just continued to suck blood.

Freddie Bienstock supplied the songs for the recording sessions and the movies. He was the man who insisted that only songs from songwriters prepared to waive a portion of their royalties would be considered suitable. This was the unsavoury job he did on behalf of Parker and the music publishers, Hill and Range. Elvis is rumoured to have called him, 'Freddie the Freeloader.'

As always, Alanna Nash provides details. Jerry Leiber recalls Freddie demanding a song. 'Get it to me tomorrow morning. I don't care how good it is.'

Freddie Bienstock even admits to resubmitting material that Elvis had previously rejected. He told the tale of one song that Elvis had dismissed after hearing the first eight bars. Nine months later he submitted the song again. Nine months had passed and Elvis had only heard eight bars so Freddie thought he stood a chance.

'I did not like it the first time and I do not like it now,' said Elvis.

Good for Elvis but Freddie had quantity and, more important, was shameless. He beat Elvis in the end and he did not turn the ship south. The rubbish just kept coming which is why Elvis not only made some of the greatest records in American popular music but also some of the worst. Freddie has his excuses, of course. The movies required a lot of material quickly and, from the late sixties, the dominance of the singer-songwriter restricted original material. This is only half-true. If he had been allowed, Elvis was more than capable of taking the songs from his own record collection and creating a memorable album of covers of other songs. This is what he did on 'Elvis Country'. Obviously, the policy of Freddie was destructive. It not only destroyed the credibility and ability of a great musician, it actually meant declining revenue. It is apparent that Freddie did not have a conscience but it is less obvious why a man would support a policy that meant inferior commercial success.

It is best to think of car salesmen. There are two types. Those who want to sell cars and those who only want to make the good deal. Invariably, the garages who only want to make the good deal make less money than the garages whose owners realise how many cars they sell is also important. The events in the career of Elvis, like those in the story of Frankenstein, produced doubles at will - RCA and Hollywood, Jarvis and Chet Atkins, Phillips and Moman and others. Freddie, like his double Parker, only ever wanted to make the good deal.

Possibly, Freddie was simply guilty of being insensitive to the destruction of a great talent and he did his best in demanding circumstances. But this is enough to condemn him. The crime, though, was worse than this. It is far from clear that Elvis benefited financially from the special, publishing deals, 'the Elvis tax' as more than one songwriter described them. Occasionally, the publishers and Freddie would lean on a desperate songwriter to insist on Elvis being given a song writing credit. The name Elvis Presley featured on thirty three titles. Alanna Nash has revealed that Hill and Range never registered Elvis as a songwriter, so he received not one penny in extra royalty from this source. Put simply, they used his name to line their pockets. Presumably, the publishing companies, 'Elvis Presley Music' and 'Gladys Music', would have generated Elvis money but one should be hesitant before assuming these contracts would have been dealt with honour.

The generous or argumentative will assume that Freddie did his best but this ignores him always looking for a cheaper song. He may have taken songs from inferior English songwriters because he had no choice but it is just as likely that after his cousin passed on to him his British holdings he could not resist exploiting the material that he inherited. Ultimately, did he exceed Dracula and begin to feed upon himself? The songs he brought to Elvis were often truly awful.

In August 1972, Bienstock and Parker established a new publishing company to control the songs. The same destructive principles remained and, although hardly possible, the songs became worse. One musician recalled Elvis destroying the demo discs with his hands in frustration. Remember, we have only heard what he felt obliged to record. Imagine what was rejected by Elvis. This nightmare could have been avoided if Elvis had at least been allowed to pick his own covers. His encyclopaedic knowledge was more than adequate to sustain a career. But, always, it was the deal that was important.

Freddie used to wear a monocle on a cord. Picture him sharp suited, eating his expensive meal in an exclusive restaurant, occasionally putting his ridiculous monocle to his eye and chortling over the latest deal that has secured him an unmerited advantage. Freddie is only at the dinner table because his career was secured through nepotism. He joined his cousins, Jean and Julia Aberbach, in their music publishing company in the mid-fifties. No doubt, he eats without remembering his good fortune.

Of course, another analysis could present a more sympathetic case but this is the man who submitted 'Heart Of Rome', 'This Is Our Dance' and 'Sylvia' and, equally important, watched them being recorded. The Creature understood how the cruelty of others had made him a wretch and Elvis must have understood his own wretchedness when he was compromised this way. This, plus the trash that must have been rejected, damns Freddie. The problem with the really greedy is that they cannot resist using their need for money to demean others. Often, this is part of the attraction of the deal. Once they have mastered the trick, they are compelled, because of their need for advantage, to repeat it continually. Walton was the same with his crew, continually denying the demands of his increasingly abused men until, finally, the regret and remorse of Frankenstein helped him understand the vanity of his ambition and how he neglected his responsibility to others.

Compared to the ambition and vanity of Bienstock and his silent witness to the exploitation and perversion of an authentic talent, the desperate car salesman is an innocent and Walton is honourable. If Bienstock had been managing a garage, he would have let it go out of business in the same way he watched Elvis destroy himself. This metaphor of the ruinous garage also defines what surrounded Elvis, a malfunctioning operation manned by greedy hustlers who thought they were smart, merely, because they were callous. Such garages do not emerge haphazardly. They usually require an insensitive will and a winner take all philosophy. In the case of Elvis, this was supplied by the biggest and most dangerous villain of them all, the unredeemable Frankenstein at the heart of our tale.

Frankenstein and Fitz

Although Frankenstein pursued the Creature, he was unable to imagine responsibilities to anything other than the refined world he knew, the comfortably glamorous he was inclined to overestimate. Parker was only obliged to make money, 'the vagabond pursuit of dreadful safety', a phrase that Shelley uses in an apocalyptic context but will do here. Frankenstein thought the world would settle when the Creature was dead and Parker imagined money being made more easily after the death of Elvis.

'This changes nothing,' he said, when told Elvis had died.

Mr Thomas Parker or, for those who prefer authenticity, Andreas van Kujik.

First, his good points because, although not as virtuous or as idealistic as the young Frankenstein, he did have some. He was kind to animals, he kept his word and was loyal to people who had honoured his deals, he took risks in establishing himself in the United States, he was faithful to his wife, he negotiated well paid contracts for Elvis and he promoted Elvis diligently. Oh, and he learnt to speak English. Presumably, it is this list that seduces his apologists.

But the career of Elvis Presley, for all its achievements, marvellous moments and continuing longevity, is a tragedy of unfulfilled potential, wasted opportunities and embarrassing baggage. The choice is simple for critics. Parker was a decent man with flaws that were badly exposed by a talent he failed to appreciate or he is a monster of a man, someone obsessed with money and deals who ruthlessly sacrificed the gifts of a performer. Peter Guralnick now appears to suggest that even the former opinion with its reference to forgivable flaws underestimates the calibre of Parker. Although it is too easy for fans, like me, to imagine fashioning a more powerful career for Elvis and to ignore that Elvis would have also had something to say about our grand schemes, the second more critical opinion is still persuasive. Without understanding the ignorant wilfulness of Parker, we will neither understand the scale of the tragedy nor the extent of the talent that was mismanaged.

Parker lived originally in The Netherlands, in Breda, a garrison town where Rene Descartes, as a soldier, became interested in maths. No evidence exists to indicate Parker was ever inspired by this or any other example of intellectual curiosity. He entered the United States as an illegal immigrant. Somehow, he passed himself off as a citizen and entered the Army and, with cynical contempt, became a deserter. Although he had no direct, financial dependants, he did have a family in The Netherlands. He felt no responsibility to his Dutch relatives and he never shared any of his wealth with them. Once successful, he would invite people to his apartment and then pass a bowl around for money to buy food for his fridge. The same cheapskate, according to Alanna Nash, never paid for any office space for his staff. Invariably, it had to be provided as part of a deal negotiated on Elvis, the man he referred to as merchandise. Nash also states that Parker was always willing to refer to his weak heart and use the threat of a heart attack to make Elvis capitulate to his plans.

Parker, like Elvis, was a sleepwalker but, unlike Elvis, he had a professional, psychiatric diagnosis. His psychological flaws were such that they helped him avoid punishment for being an Army deserter. This improved self-awareness would have made most men modest and cautious and acknowledge others but, like Victor Frankenstein, he only ever listened to himself. His ego was too great to let a critical, psychiatric report deny him his appetites for success and status. Neither Parker nor Frankenstein thought they had need for advice and both lived a life that began and ended with their own deliberations. Despite major errors in his early life, Parker, like Frankenstein, was an unreliable narrator who misinterpreted everything. In his view, talent did not exist, only gimmicks. Victor Frankenstein usurped woman by creating life whilst Parker with the same faith in galvanisation believed effect and empty spectacle could be a substitute for creativity and human connection. Like many men obsessed with money, Parker had a need to humiliate others. Prior to Elvis, Parker managed country singers, Gene Austin and Eddy Arnold, and was dismissed by both. Arnold stated he found the boorish behaviour of Parker intolerable. The tales of his outlandish behaviour indicate a cruel show off who needed to be the centre of attention. Frankenstein had higher motives but he wanted his scientific prowess to win him the esteem of others.

The family of Parker had an aristocratic role in the Middle Ages and this may or may not have been a factor in his ambition. The aristocratic tradition may have fed the ego of both men, the Baron and the fake Colonel. Alanna Nash states that Parker, according to screenwriter, Hal Kanter, wanted Paul Newman to play Parker in a film of his life. When Kanter suggested for the role somebody more like W C Fields the face of Parker turned puce. The psychiatrists did say he was crazy.

Before we look at his quite disastrous decision making, we need first to establish his achievements because, maybe, Parker was like Elvis and had both good and bad periods. Parker signed Elvis in 1955, a performer who had had only one number one, country hit before he recorded at RCA in early 1956. Obtaining a contract for Elvis from RCA would not have been especially challenging for Parker as both Atlantic and RCA were rivals to exploit his potential. There was also a third bid from Mitch Miller which Sam Phillips refused before Parker was involved. (Miller was a record producer who coarsened and trivialised everything he touched. He would have made a perfect partner for Parker. There is a consolation in knowing that the ultimate tragedy was avoided.)

The great achievement of Parker was that Elvis was signed to appear on national TV before his first RCA single, 'Heartbreak Hotel', had even been recorded and that the movie contract was signed before the next single was released. This was extraordinary hustling although it should be noted that movie producer, Hal Wallis, contacted Parker after his assistant, Joseph Hazen, had seen Elvis on TV. But we cannot forget the initial TV appearance. This was the moment of galvanisation when the creature was brought to life by the electric tube. Frankenstein fled from the Creature when he came to life while Parker stayed within reach. Both men, though, failed at the moment of galvanisation to see within their creation the emotion and heart that was at risk. Frankenstein reacted by wailing in self-pity against the night, resentful of the albatross he now possessed. When he returned to his home and laboratory the Creature had disappeared. His relief and joy were overwhelming and he had no curiosity as to what might happen to his creation. Parker had the same lack of concern over the consequences for his creature and his absence of pity continued beyond the waste of the innocent he had galvanised.

'This changes nothing,' he said, when Elvis died.

Like Frankenstein, Parker had complicated feelings for what he had created. Perhaps what repulsed the two men was not the creation but the independent being that was the price of galvanised life. There are parallels here with the Hitchcock movie, 'Vertigo', and the conflicted male who wants to recreate the woman he desires as the perfect female but is horrified to discover she is human.

Echoing the theme of the double in the novel, the behaviour of Elvis mirrored that of Parker. Subject to the control of a Dutch Frankenstein, Elvis attempted to be his own Frankenstein with the women in his life. Shelley was a keen advocate of female emancipation and her novel fits the feminist interpretation of the inability of men to share power with women because they are unable to accept the different sides of the female personality. She would have not only disapproved of the lack of scholarship of Parker and Elvis but recognised the parallell will to power in both men and noted how it was subservient to a malevolent force. For Parker, that force was money and for Elvis it was Parker. Shelley may have concluded they deserved each other although, as a rebel and home builder, she would have had more sympathy for Elvis than Parker.

How did Parker manage to convince the TV company to provide the enormous charge of electricity required for the galvanisation? Firstly, American TV was not averse to the odd, brief spot for country performers. Even in the fifties, there was some national interest in the music of the South. Not only were rhythm and blues songs borrowed by pop singers but it also happened with country material. Rosemary Clooney recorded a version of 'Half As Much' by Hank Williams. Secondly, Parker could claim exceptional interest in Elvis in the Southern States and he had, as leverage, the profile and power of RCA, his new record company. He also had good contacts in the TV industry from when he worked with Eddy Arnold.

The TV appearance launched Elvis Presley nationally in the United States and it was done both brilliantly and with astonishing speed. Despite the favourable circumstances, it remains an exceptional achievement by Parker. Today, there are millions of people who are only Elvis fans because of this event and what followed. No doubt, I am one of them. Admittedly, it required Elvis to be sensational and, more important, to be the sensation that the youth of the fifties craved. As Elvis once said in his 'TV Special', albeit in a different context, 'Okay, it sprang from that.' But I think he was sensational because I am a fan. Was he sensational or was what impressed people the actual process of galvanisation? Maybe the event excited the audience simply because it witnessed a normally anonymous, powerless and inarticulate creature brought to life. The charge from the 1956 event was so powerful it galvanised the other strange, rock and roll creatures, those who had been previously invisible. Parker, like Frankenstein, had no doubts he was responsible. He probably thought it was not the musical talents that emerged who created rock and roll but him. Without the media charge to galvanise, there would have been no life.

Before the first TV show in 1956, Elvis killed time in a wintry New York by visiting a record shop. He was lonely and unrecognised. I suspect Elvis understood this achievement of Parker as well as anyone and this understanding and his memory of that cold night on the streets of New York kept Elvis loyal through the rubbish that followed. Perhaps Elvis never stopped believing that without Parker he would be alone and penniless again. If Elvis, like many other poor Southerners, had a mix of contempt and excessive respect for the rich, he would have believed that without help from somebody 'smart' like Parker he would be unable to match them. Elvis eventually realised Parker stopped him from fulfilling his potential but he remained superstitious. He feared his luck would disappear if Parker left.

The cold, lonely night in a record shop in New York persisted as a memory but that was 1956 and Parker was rarely that good again. Equally, we cannot assume Parker was perfect in the fifties. As early as 1955, he wanted to dump the musical accompaniment of Scotty and Bill to save money and he totally misread the 82.6% viewing figures for the appearance of Elvis on the Ed Sullivan show. He concluded the show might consolidate the appeal of Elvis to adults when it actually did the opposite. The youth phenomenon passed Parker by and he always undersold Elvis, small theatres in the 1950s, cheap movies, Vegas in 1969, a stage appearance in New York delayed until 1972 and no world tour. Critics, attempting to explain their disappointment with Elvis, not unreasonably focus on what happened after Elvis returned from the Army. The second volume of the Guralnick biography which begins in 1960 has the sub-title 'The Unmaking Of Elvis Presley'. The unmaking actually began in 1957. As already stated, it is in 1957 that the three elements in the paradox of Elvis Presley are revealed, a marvellous rhythmic talent, a less than precise critical acuity in Presley and an overbearing and cynical manager. Elvis only survived 1957 and its injuries because his talent was young and vibrant. Somehow, with the help of Leiber and Stoller, he managed to make everything qualify as rock and roll.

Unlike Victor Frankenstein, Parker had no chateau in which he could adore himself and his family. He did, though, love Christmas and he used to dress up as Father Christmas even when it was out of season. This was how Parker liked to demonstrate his largesse and assume the role of superior patron. Elvis eventually recorded two Christmas albums despite wanting to do neither. It is no coincidence that two of the toughest blues recordings of Elvis, 'Santa Claus Is Back In Town' and 'Merry Christmas Baby', emerged from these Christmas sessions. They are evidence of his protest as is the fierce, sarcastic and incongruous, bluesy ending of 'Winter Wonderland'.

It is true, Elvis wanted to be in movies but he had no ambition to make musicals. In his last stage show in 1970, he did announce that 'he loved the man' but Elvis had just done a three hour show and was high on his performance. The Creature was similarly affected when he saw the dead Frankenstein. It was also in that Vegas season that Parker for once had supported Elvis in his dispute with the hotel management over the sound system. On other occasions, Elvis was extremely critical of Parker who was compelled, like Frankenstein with the Creature, to deny Elvis what he needed, recognition and love. Not only was Parker unable to respond like the virtuous mother that Elvis needed, he was not even a fan.

Elvis grew up in the United States of the thirties. This meant his life and his culture were a mix of what the poor created for themselves and what they absorbed through others and because of technology. If he had not combined the two, he would neither have been true to himself nor culturally representative of anything. It is why earnest, folk singers with their anachronistic definition of the authentic usually strike working class people as phoney. Parker, though, only understood plastic. He believed that the suckers would buy anything which is why he was able to tolerate those periods when Elvis either lacked commitment or indulged in self-destructive protest. It also probably appealed to his ego. If Elvis made inferior product, which Parker could sell, it proved it was the galvaniser that was the man responsible for all the success.

Of course, few of us will ever agree what is the honourable combination of authentic and plastic and Parker never promised a creative contribution, only to make Elvis rich and famous which he did. A more sophisticated man would have been tempted to develop Elvis before his first TV appearance but, to his credit, Parker let Elvis appear on TV as himself, not even with extra grooming. His raw appearance helped make Elvis the sensation. Only later, did Parker have misgivings and was concerned about what he thought he had brought to life, a creature that shocked people. Frankenstein had found beautiful features for his Creature but was repelled by 'the skin (that) stretched so tight it barely covered his face.' Parker had found a talent with beauty but soon realised that adults repelled by rock and roll only noticed the vulgarity, 'the tight skin.'

It may have been a brilliant move but Elvis was not initially groomed because Parker was superficial. Nothing demonstrates this better than the sale of future royalties to RCA by Parker in 1973. Before concluding the deal, he consulted Vernon Presley for advice. Vernon was not the brightest and the scene can easily be pictured, two overachieving, unqualified dopes monosyllabically agreeing the most stupid deal in music. Parker later denied his responsibility, insisted that he was reluctant to interfere but this is an absurd claim because it was always his ambition that prevailed. Parker wanted movie contracts, soundtrack albums, publishing deals, the satellite show, avoidance of other countries for touring, long Vegas contracts and Elvis singing music that appealed to Mrs Parker. All of which, demonstrates his appalling judgement and his need to cripple his creation, to avoid hearing the words which so disturbed Victor Frankenstein, 'Thou hast made me more powerful than thyself.'

One can half understand his desire to negotiate a long term, movie contract because what Parker achieved initially in Hollywood in 1956 was anything but secure. The fee for each film was dependent on the success of the previous film. Unfortunately, he was so obsessed with maximising any deal, he always ignored how it would fit into a long term strategy. He could not help being the small hustler. His plans were never more than a compulsive habit, to milk an idea until death and, then, think of something else because he had that small time faith which assumes you can always start again in another town. The tame corpse and the stupid punters could always take one more electric shock. With this blinkered attitude of the mediocre hustler, he constantly ignored any possible consequences and was unable to foresee, like Frankenstein, that the self-destructive will of his creature would lead both to an icy waste.

Elaine Dundy, in 'Elvis And Gladys', states that Twentieth Century Fox were unhappy with the number of Elvis appearances on TV in 1956 because they believed it would affect sales of tickets for their movie, 'Love Me Tender'. Elvis had only been lent to the company for one movie and, even, they made significant demands. Imagine what was insisted upon by the Hollywood companies who had the long term contracts. No wonder, Elvis was prevented from making personal appearances between 1960 and 1969. The loyalists of Parker claim he did try and arrange a forty three city tour for 1964 and, only, when RCA refused to provide the $1,000,000 to fund the tour and offered instead $500,000 to fund an eleven city tour did it fail to happen. Surely, Parker was bluffing. The tour because of the movies was never possible. His suggestion of a tour was intended to stall the conflicting demands of the record company and the movie producers. The proposal was designed not to succeed, not being on stage was the price of Elvis being in hock with Hollywood. In this context, it is likely that Hollywood influenced the mellowing of Elvis in the recording studio. They would have wanted him to make records consistent with the Elvis of their wholesome, escapist movies.

If the long term, movie contracts had once appeared a good idea, it became obvious, when Elvis drifted into lethargy and the record sales dipped, that they needed to change direction. This could have been renegotiated with Hollywood who themselves were seeing declining profits from their plans. None of it happened and it persisted until the appalling end of the original contracts. The Beatles movie, 'Hard Day's Night', delivered a brutal shock that sent virtually everyone in pop music in different directions. The response from Parker was to arrange the worst and cheapest Elvis movie ever, 'Harum Scarum'. What damns Parker is that Elvis made another twelve movies after 'Hard Day's Night' appeared. This inability to respond to events and change direction demonstrates how Parker was incapable of managing anyone beyond the short term.

We all make mistakes, of course, but, as soon as Elvis returned to the stage in 1969, Parker repeated the error by signing Elvis the night after his debut to another long term contract with the International Hotel in Vegas. When it was established that Elvis could fill large concert halls in the United States the ritual of cross country tours was again continued without any thought of a long term strategy.

Recently, I saw 'Elvis The Concert' in a packed 02 Arena in London, watched his image on screen while his original band and singers accompanied him on stage. Thirty three years after the death of Elvis, I sat with my daughters high in the fourth tier and we all looked down over the huge, capacity crowd of 23,000 European fans.

The daughter nearest to me turned and said, 'This is something else Parker got wrong.'

Much has been said about why Parker did not let Elvis tour abroad in the seventies. Frankenstein refused to make the Creature a wife.

Few, other than Frankenstein, would have risked the vengeance of the Creature and no manager other than Parker would have restricted Elvis to the States. The explanation is that Parker was either afraid of leaving the United States or was unwilling to let Elvis be abroad out of his control. None of this is believable. He was simply being true to his primitive, business principles. Any idea had to be pursued to disaster and why not he might argue. Without the disaster, the hard as nails hustler and galvaniser would not be able to launch the romantic recovery his ego and conceit required. Nothing can be more pathetic than the revelation by Alanna Nash that Parker had in May 1977 contacted Peter Grant, the manager of Led Zeppelin, with the idea of finally arranging a European tour. Elvis was dead three months after Parker contacted Peter Grant. This time the brinkmanship of which he was so proud really did blow up in his face, just like sticky chewing gum. It is so typical of Parker, always too late to respond, and is comparable to the hapless Frankenstein who is unable to form a plan which will prevent the Creature killing his wife. Indeed, only, when Elizabeth screams in the room next to him does Frankenstein realise that she, and not him, was the intended victim on his wedding night. Parker is similar, assumes he is at the centre of everything which is why he felt the death of Elvis changed nothing. Once satisfied by his galvanising of an unsophisticated innocent, he was now ready to face the challenge he craved, the galvanisation of a corpse.

'This changes nothing,' said Parker.

But it did because he failed to realise how his errors had been obscured by the appeal of his client. Elvis continued whilst Parker perished. The above is mere strategy. It is the details that are truly repellent, that reveal this 'unfeeling, heartless creature'. In 1966, after he had transformed Elvis into a laughing stock and observed the record sales reduce by 40%, Parker felt that this perverse achievement needed to be recognised. From this point, he would take 50% of the money Elvis made. When Parker signed Elvis for Las Vegas it meant that almost immediately Elvis lost many of the potential fans he had tempted back after the 'TV Special'. The contract for Elvis to return to the stage in Vegas was signed a mere twelve days after the TV appearance. The long term contract that followed was for Elvis to receive $125,000 a week less the cut for Parker. The house receipts were $840,000 a week and they improved with inflation. The salary for Elvis did not and was tied for five years. The deal making after the 'TV Special' was too rushed and his plan for what followed Hollywood was just as crass as his plan for the movies. After the success of the 'TV Special', he should have realised that his client still had potential as a rock performer and Vegas was not a desirable option.

Admittedly, much of what went wrong with the career of Elvis can be attributed to the record company, RCA, and to Elvis being self-destructive. Alanna Nash states, though, that Parker in time held himself above everyone, certainly the powers at RCA. The abysmal albums, 'Elvis Sings For Children' which collects the most cloying garbage from his movies and 'Burning Love And Hits From The Movies' which does the same, are the products of the warped thinking of Parker. Ernst Jorgensen quotes the latter album as a particularly disgraceful example of Parker acting immediately to undermine the prospects offered by the success of the single, 'Burning Love'. Jorgenson is baffled by the action of Parker but it makes sense if we remember the scientist who is frightened of the independent Creature inside his creation. The album is especially offensive because, of course, 'Burning Love' was never recorded for a movie. No doubt, the implied lie in the title satisfied the contempt Parker had for the Elvis audience, people he regarded as suckers. This is best revealed by the album, 'Having Fun With Elvis On Stage.' This album consisted only of clips of Elvis introducing songs and making the occasional joke. Parker released it on his 'Boxcar' record label. None of the material was original because it already existed between the songs on his live albums. We can only guess how many people wasted money on this trash and, like those who bought 'Burning Love And Hits From The Movies', vowed never to buy another Elvis record. This process of Parker taking action to lose Elvis his fans becomes a constant theme. Parker must have looked at those trashy, album covers and said something like Colin Clive in the 1931 movie when he stroked the arm of a sleeping Boris Karloff, 'Look, no blood, no decay, just a few stitches.'

His interference was always destructive. It was Parker who insisted on only one duet with Ann-Margret in the movie, 'Viva Las Vegas'. As a result of his meddling, one of the better songs in the movie, 'You're The Boss', was removed. When Eisenstein showed Stalin his film, 'Ivan The Terrible', Stalin said, 'You can show he was cruel but you must show why he needs to be cruel.' True, his remarks supported a not entirely honourable agenda but, as dramatic criticism, this was not unreasonable. If only Elvis had had to endure the artistic compromises insisted upon by Stalin.

In the seventies, Elvis was clearly a man struggling to cope but he delivered enough material to create adequate albums. Not classics but adequate. List 12 in the attached appendices identifies four twelve track albums plus a gospel album. RCA had a contract for three albums a year which was probably intended to maintain the revenue previously generated by soundtrack albums. Once the weakened Elvis emerged in 1971, this contract should have been re-negotiated to ensure a degree of quality but, because Parker had no concept of quality, the scraps were piled up in thoughtless packages to produce the second embarrassing phase of the career of his client, 'just a few stitches.' Inevitably, more fans and revenue were lost. In the nineties, when Ernst Jorgensen suggested producing a fifties box set he was told by the marketing men of the record company that Elvis only sold to the poor and his albums had to be retailed at $8 dollars or less. This prejudice is the legacy of Parker. Those words could be his. Despite the marketing men, the box set was produced. I bought mine for £45. It sold half a million copies and I only bought one. This is a telling statistic and it condemns both Parker and RCA. Parker even undermined the stage performances of his client by insisting failed, unfunny comics had to open the shows.

The weakened Elvis was a consequence of his own temperament and drug and diet abuse and, although his own taste was not perfect, creative disappointment. All singers perform the occasional mistake but Elvis must be exceptional in being obliged to record so much rubbish that he thought was rubbish. His temperamental weaknesses may have been deep rooted but they could have been mitigated. The existence of Parker only made them worse. Parker never arranged for any psychiatric support and failed to provide adequate treatment for the drug habit. Maybe this is expecting too much and, perhaps, Parker cannot be condemned for not being alert to these issues but more than one, Lamar Fike and Jerry Schilling for example, recommended to Parker that he take action. He ignored them. There really was a failure to nurture and Mary Shelley was right to warn us about the consequences of such failure.

Parker was also the man who blocked off creative talent from Elvis and preferred him to be surrounded by the adolescent Memphis Mafia. The excellent BBC documentary, 'Elvis In Las Vegas', included an interview with Joe Esposito, foreman of the Memphis Mafia and main lackey for Parker.

With total blindness, Esposito said, 'The Vegas years were fun. We partied every night.'

We now know that Elvis thought those years to be anything but fun and the words of Myopic Joe contrast somewhat with Elvis blurting out on stage, 'I fucking hate Vegas.'

Sap Joe must have missed that one. His job was to ensure a safe environment for the man who earned all the income. Unfortunately, the earner had a drug problem and this was managed by Sensitive Joe by having parties every night. This is for a man who, for half his time in Vegas, was addicted to liquid cocaine and heroine substitutes. Note that it is all done with the approval of Parker. Okay, Elvis wasted his talent and died prematurely but, at least, Party Joe had fun. It is the same Joe Esposito who claimed Elvis kept his 'beautiful voice until the end.' No, he did not. His voice, though still good, had deteriorated badly before he died. Myopic Joe appears to be a little deaf as well. I should not, though, use these cheap nicknames for Joe Esposito because there is only one alternative name that is appropriate. This is Fitz, the enthusiastic and loyal helper from the original stage play and 1931 movie. Fitz is damned with inadequate, moral competence and fails to see the chaos around him and Frankenstein. Imagine Esposito, a twisted smile on his face, walking around the morning after what he considers another successful party, a contented, chuckling man stepping over bare backsides to pick up the empty beer bottles, cigarette packets and amphetamine strips.

Although Fitz and Joe are the first we mock, they were only mentally challenged assistants. Parker had the responsibility and the important question is, could Parker have been more stupid. Considering he used a fully committed hedonist to manage the relaxation of his drug dependent client, it is doubtful. Perhaps Elvis would have always self-destructed but few managers would have permitted it to happen so quickly and done so little about the consequences. A man with such inadequate understanding, inevitably, had to rely on incompetent cronies for the personal support of his performer. The same weakness is present in the Frankenstein played by Colin Clive in the 1931 movie, the Frankenstein who was blind to damaged Fitz. Not surprisingly, Duke Bardwell, bassist on stage with Elvis in the mid-seventies, felt that Parker let Elvis die.

But let us give Parker a break for the moment. In his defence, he does not deserve to be criticised for refusing to let Elvis appear in 'A Star Is Born' with Barbra Streisand. This project, inspired by a quite likeable egomaniac and her over promoted hairdresser, was always likely to be a disaster and, for once, Parker called it right although one is always suspicious about his motives. What was not honourable was Parker on TV denying that Elvis ever wanted to do the film. A letter written by Parker to Roger Davis, a William Morris lawyer, states the opposite. Immediately, we have returned to examples of his flaws.

Alanna Nash quotes examples of how Parker preferred some fees to be paid in cash to him. There is no evidence to show that these cash payments were ever shared with Elvis. When Parker set up his Boxcar Company to market his commercial interests Parker awarded himself 40% control. Elvis had just 8%. Parker paid himself $27,650 a year. Elvis, whose name would have been on every item of merchandise, received $2,750 a year. Alanna Nash believes that Parker ensured Elvis paid his taxes in full because he did not want Elvis to be exposed to an intelligent accountant capable of informed criticism of Parker. Interestingly, according to Nash, Elvis was the highest tax payer in the USA. Odd, that right wing Elvis becomes a record tax payer whilst those popular egalitarians and street fighting revolutionaries, The Rolling Stones, have since 1972 paid a mere £4m in taxes. When Elvis died he owed Parker over $1m. Whether Parker was actually entitled to the money is doubtful.

He was a man made unstable by 'the intoxicating draught of ambition and dominion'. If Parker had been merely a crass glutton, it might have been possible that his interests could have coincided with his client but he was also an unbalanced incompetent with a psychiatric report in his attic. A man who, having no idea what to do with all the money he chiselled from his victims, gambled his fortune away in Vegas. He was happy to lose millions because he needed to be told he was a big shot. Once Parker became old, he was desperate to wallow in the gaze of spectators.

Elsewhere, the final judgements about Parker have been harsh although Guralnick does have the odd, inevitable revisionist for company.

Apart from Peter Guralnick, the most positive view is that held by music journalist, Michael Streissguth. He argues that Parker preserved the career of Elvis by keeping him in the movies. Parker helped Elvis to avoid the rejection of audiences with changing tastes that other musicians had to endure. He does not, though, believe that this was the product of intelligence but nothing more than 'dumb luck'. Streissguth feels it was this preservation in celluloid mothballs that facilitated Elvis making great music in the late sixties and early seventies. These are thoughtful remarks but there are valid objections. An Elvis obliged to focus mainly on music would have remained dominant and maintained his career without too much difficulty. If Elvis had stayed involved with his music, the times would have changed differently and, probably, in a way more sympathetic to him. Soul music would have happened and prevailed but vital, American rock and roll led by Elvis would have resisted the embarrassingly second rate, English invasion. If this is too fanciful, we can think more modestly. Jerry Lee Lewis survived the changing times and also made great music in the late sixties and early seventies. Not everybody agrees but I think Elvis had more talent than The Killer. Elvis had also avoided the career sapping scandal of the Lewis marriage. The movies did not preserve the career of Elvis. They lost him fans and made him unacceptable to many in the new audience. Like the plays based on 'Frankenstein', they introduced the mute idiot.

Dr Beecher Smith, one of the Presley Estate's Memphis attorneys, acknowledges what Parker did to launch Elvis but also says, 'There were villainous elements - . His greatest weakness was not being savvy about the state of the industry during the last five or ten years of his life.'

In a recent interview, Alanna Nash agreed Parker was a lousy manager but a great promoter. She may be correct but, from a European distance, this view appears to be informed by an American or, in her case, Canadian insularity. If he was such a great promoter, why was Elvis actually more successful outside the States? Probably because the promotion within the States was invariably cynical and crass and that it alienated as many people as it attracted. Only Parker knew what he hoped to achieve carrying Elvis balloons and walking around in coats plastered with Elvis stickers. His tasteless boorishness must have had a similar, counterproductive effect in his deal making. Many backers with interesting proposals must have lost interest in Elvis because it was simply not worth dealing with the phony and bully who represented him. Ernest Tubb, the shrewd, country singer, understood the personality of Parker and would never use him on a long term basis.

He said, 'He'd constantly try to put one over on you, that was the life he led as a carny.'

This probably explains why Parker opened up Graceland to the press after the death of Gladys and why we now have in the public domain the appalling photograph of Elvis in desolate grief with his father, a private moment that should have stayed that way. This betrayal alone is enough for the conscience of any man.

The best summary of his limitations is provided by rock writer, Dave Marsh. 'Parker was the most overrated person in the history of show business. The Colonel went to his grave believing he had pulled off some carny trick, when what he had actually done was sell genius short for twenty three years.' Marsh adds, 'To stand that close to the centre of such a phenomenon and miss altogether its most important, long-lasting qualities, requires a genius that is truly rare.'

Horace Logan from the Louisiana Hayride expresses himself more crudely. 'The son of a bitch ought to be hung up by his balls. He practically destroyed one of the greatest talents that ever lived.'

I do not want to be unkind but I am certain that for all his tough guy fantasies the testicles of Parker would never have supported all that weight. Maybe it is not such a bad idea from Horace after all. It should not be thought that this criticism is made with the benefit of hindsight. There were rumblings and discontent amongst Elvis fans from as early as 1962 and it had already hardened into disappointment and anger by 1964.

Parker should not be criticised for not anticipating the emerging dominance of rock and roll. When Elvis returned from the Army the conservative attitude of Parker left him two choices. He could base the future career of Elvis on either Frank Sinatra or Bing Crosby. The former option would have been proved by hindsight to be an error but it would have given Elvis recovery space and some credibility. The latter option was what he chose. This error, pursued relentlessly with no interest in quality until it became a crime, happened because he failed to appreciate the capability of his client and because he overestimated himself. He lost not only huge chunks of the potential and actual audience but his client. Elvis was no self-reliant hero but it is interesting that Parker probably lost his performer before the audience. Guralnick, in 'Careless Love', writes that a disillusioned Elvis on the set of 'Blue Hawaii' shared his self-disgust with Marion Keisker, the lady who discovered him at Sun.

Even without hindsight, it is obvious that the business plan for Elvis (the word business is chosen carefully) should have been four singles, one studio album and one as decent a movie as possible each year. It would have been an old-fashioned strategy but it would have been honourable. We know talented directors, like Sidney Lumet and George Cukor, felt Elvis had acting talent. Elvis could, like Sinatra, have mixed the fake, prestigious movie with the commercial. Such thinking was beyond Parker.

Writing about Parker, though, does provoke an obligation on my part. Elaine Dundy stated that any commentary on Parker had to refer to the original contract between Elvis and Parker. Her book, 'Elvis And Gladys', deserves such admiration that there is no option but to reproduce this scandalous document in the attached lists. As Dundy has already written, the document, full of phoney-legal language, is totally unaware that the tortuous syntax of lawyers is normally used to provide clarity. Here, it merely supports ambiguity. It may be badly written but it is, as my mother used to say, 'soft on the right side'. The document is obsessed with Elvis and what he has to do for Parker who appears to have hardly any responsibilities at all. The contract states that, as a special concession, Elvis and his musicians had to perform 100 concerts for the special rate of $200. The contract does not make clear if this is $200 per concert or $200 for all 100 concerts. Either way, it is unbelievable. Peter Guralnick quotes the contract in his book without mentioning the absurdities. This decision is baffling.

Originally, Elvis and his father thought Parker would only promote and manage his stage appearances but he soon leapfrogged not only that expectation but the subsequent arrangement for Elvis to be jointly managed by Parker and Hank Snow, the Canadian, country singer. In a manner similar to how Stalin seized power from Trotsky, Parker finessed Snow out of the deal by asking Snow to pledge his royalties to purchase the contract from Sam Phillips. When Snow predictably said no, Parker rushed to buy the contract that weekend. This has to be regretted because

Snow would have insisted upon a strategy and some standards. Anybody who can make a record as witty as 'Rhumba Boogie' would never have settled for being a witness to the destruction caused by Parker. Elvis, of course, did settle for what Snow would have rejected. In his book, 'Elvis', Albert Goldman argues that Parker was 'the kind of overbearing ruinous huckster who needed a donkey on a carrot.' Alanna Nash is convinced that, as the twin-less twin, Elvis needed a controlling figure, he needed to be the donkey that Parker required. Perhaps the tolerance in Elvis rested on several elements - apathy, a lack of sophistication that contained the belief Parker was the mojo who had brought him the luck to become successful and, as Nash argues, fatal, Freudian dependency.

Elvis paid a price for this tolerance. He made movies he hated, recorded songs he did not like and was obliged to perform in Vegas long after he realised it was damaging his career and him. Ronnie Tutt, his drummer from 1969, said that Parker did not understand the needs of the creative temperament but knew how to exploit its weakness, the desire for recognition and the fear of oblivion.

'Do not listen to others, only me,' said Parker.

Not the normal blueprint to inspire creativity.

If the existence of Hollywood, Bienstock and Parker, does not excuse Elvis, his failings do not excuse them. They had decent incomes, only, because of his talent. They had obligations. To quote out of context the play, 'Hamlet', 'Madness in great ones must not unwatched go.' Their failure and blindness were immense. Bienstock and Parker are the main characters that helped destroy the career of Elvis. Hollywood was also destructive but the movies exist as a self-contained period. Bienstock and Parker were malign influences until the end. Chet Atkins and Felton Jarvis may have not been what Elvis needed but they did try to be professional. Bienstock and Parker are different from others because they were relentless and did more damage.

The only compensation for Elvis fans is that the next time they listen to an Elvis classic they can do so with the knowledge that its pleasures, like many others that involve the appreciation of something other than the self, were never available for the obsessive, self-centred Parker. And neither should they have been.

In the great film noir, 'Gilda', the repellent villain, Balin Mundsen, warns his protégé, Johnny. 'Hate is the only thing that ever warmed me.'

Reading the above on Parker, some may be surprised by the vicious tone, the extent of the animosity he inspires. So, perhaps, in this saga, Parker is as important as Elvis because, to stay loyal, we need more than heroes. Without Parker, the curiosity in Elvis would be like that we have for the others, a few CDs on the shelf that are listened to when it is their turn. Maybe it is Parker, the villain, who makes Elvis, the man, interesting and, maybe, this is what Parker always told himself.

The others, whom Elvis leaned upon, influenced him for good and bad. His mother who encouraged the neurotic yearnings that led him towards, but, ultimately, away from music, the indolent but tolerant father who encouraged his free spirit but may have helped Elvis justify those long periods when he managed only partial commitment, the dead twin who left him with grand ambition but also the cynicism of the incomplete yet triumphant survivor and the many women who convinced him that they should dominate his life and music. He had many girlfriends and we really would have suffered if they had all each inspired a too sweet ballad. These are the shadows in the action but just as interesting as the shadows are the ghosts who haunted him behind the shadows. Throughout his life, he was attracted to the voices and performers who stalked the airwaves around Mississippi and Memphis, the bluesmen, gospel singers, opera divas and country performers. Elvis always sought nurture. The Creature had the same imagination, wanted to meet people other than the brutal few he encountered, people like the characters in his books, characters that inspired his dreams while he read in his hovel in the forest. The voices from the radio are the ghosts in the life of Elvis. Of course, the best ghost stories are always those in which it is not clear if the ghost exists, where the mystery is as compelling as the apparition. There may be an example.

The woman in white

Before it re-invented itself as something earnest, the music paper, 'New Musical Express', had a back page written by an anonymous, gossip writer. His column consisted of one line snippets that may or may not have been true. Some of it was mere opinion but the journalist also anticipated future events and gave brief, background information to what had already happened. If what he wrote was not always reliable, it was readable. Its news occasionally offered hope and it was a pleasant alternative to PR interviews with musicians.

In the early seventies, one item referred to Elvis having a new interest, the music of the English singer, Dorothy Squires. Dorothy was famous for marrying Roger Moore when he was young and before he became James Bond. She sued him for divorce. He was much younger than his wife and she became less appealing to the still young husband as she aged and sagged. She alleged she had conjugal rights that he failed to fulfil. The scandal was embarrassing for Moore but, with time, it faded.

There is no evidence to suggest that Elvis knew about the incident that caused the uproar. Neither have the heavily researched biographies on Elvis confirmed his interest in the music of Squires. It could have been a bored, gossip writer having a joke at the expense of Elvis fans. Dorothy Squires was a very limited singer, a tuneless Shirley Bassey. But, according to the columnist, Elvis had collected all her albums and was listening to them attentively in Graceland. Whatever his limitations as a critic, Elvis knew a bad note and Dorothy ploughed into them fearlessly. Despite her awful voice, Squires had a strong collection of devoted fans. Her record sales were modest but she always packed the London Palladium and she did have one big seller album which was a recording of one of her concerts at the Palladium. She wore extravagant costumes - white gowns and huge feather boas - and included obvious show stoppers like 'My Way', 'The Impossible Dream' and 'What Now My Love'. Anybody with any sense would dismiss the assertion by the man from the 'New Musical Express', except, soon after the brief entry appeared in the column Elvis changed his act. In 1972, his concert repertoire altered dramatically and, to the surprise of everyone, it included the crowd pleasers favoured by Squires. He added jewels and a cape to his costume. The clothes, like the music, were suddenly about honour and rank, a celebration of past glory which is all that is left to the old and the weakening as Squires who, after her sexual rejections, may have understood.

It could be mere coincidence because the appeal of Squires was limited to Britain. There is, though, enough in the coincidence to disturb. Elvis knew English people, so, perhaps, when he complained of the weakening of his voice or that Vegas and his 'medication' were wrecking his sinuses, somebody, maybe Tom Jones, said, 'You should hear Dorothy Squires. She can't sing for toffee but she packs them in.'

It may be that the gossip writer was given real information. An insecure, reduced Elvis had decided he would borrow the tricks from a singer who he knew was old and hopeless. He listened to the albums not to hear Squires but to understand how an audience could be inspired by a drama outside the music. Is this a tale we can believe?

The story has never been mentioned anywhere else and, now, nobody can even remember who wrote the column but those who really know should not tell. It is best this particular tale remains a ghost story. No, make that horror.

Alternative nurture - The Lost Episode Of The Cosmic Medic

'This is bad, man, and it ain't been good for a while,' says Lamar Fike.

Jerry Schilling and Sonny West nod but continue to stare at the unkempt figure lying flat on the floor. The patterned shirt has come loose from the waistband of the white trousers and the trousers are heavily creased behind the knees.

On the streets of downtown Vegas it is 117 degrees centigrade. The room on the top floor of the hotel is artificial cold.

'He's breathing,' says Schilling.

West bends down and puts his hand to the puffy face. The slow but urgent breaths create small ripples in the excess, facial flesh.

'This can't go on,' says Fike. 'This guy needs a break. He needs to be in a hospital.'

The room is a large bedroom and it has a huge bed and luxury furniture surrounded by carpeted space as ostentatious as the furniture. Another figure sits close to the door at the other end of the room. On the table next to him are cold snacks, coffee and an unfinished game of cards. He wears a wide brimmed hat and smokes a cigar.

Parker, the man smoking the cigar, adjusts his hat and shouts, 'Get him off the damned floor. Your job is to get him on that damned stage. We have a contract and he won't have me breaking my promises. All my hard work is not going to be for nothing. RCA are on my back all the time asking when he might record. I've had to put up with this crap for years.' He turns over a playing card. 'Shit,' he says.

Fike breathes deeply and grinds his teeth. West shrugs his impressive shoulders and Schilling, who looks the saddest of the three men, shakes his well groomed head.

'I said get him off the damned floor,' shouts Parker. 'All that I do and he flops on the floor like a pathetic baby.'

Sonny West opens his mouth to argue but Schilling puts his hand on the arm of West. 'Don't say anything, Sonny. He doesn't get it.'

Without any enthusiasm, the three men bend over to lift the swollen figure.

They hesitate because another man emerges from the bathroom and steps over the figure on the floor. He is wearing odd clothes, a bow tie and a coloured waistcoat. His dark hair is thick and wild and he has wide-open eyes.

'Son of a bitch,' says Fike.

'How the hell he did he get in here?' says West

'He came out of the bathroom,' says Schilling.

'How did he get in the damned bathroom?' shouts Parker. He has a cane which he holds upright between his enormous thighs. He stamps the cane on the floor. 'Call security right now.' He stops to think. 'Look, get Elvis off the damned floor.'

'Hello, I suspect you are surprised by me,' says the man in the coloured waistcoat. 'Yes? People usually are but they are always interested which helps if you know what I mean.'

'Who the hell are you?' says Fike.

'He's been hiding there,' says West. 'He must be an English fan. They are all crazy.'

'No. As it happens, I have just arrived. Not the most glamorous of arrivals, a bathroom in Las Vegas. But I specialise in unpredictable appearances. This weather is rather hot, do you not think?'

'Jesus Christ,' says Fike. 'The son of a bitch is crazy.'

'He's English,' says West.

'Will somebody lift Elvis off the damned floor?' shouts Parker but he is ignored.

'But how did you get in the bathroom?' says Schilling.

'Not especially tricky although incredibly difficult to explain. Look all the way down there,' says the intruder.

West, Schilling and Fike walk towards the window. The wiry figure points his thin arm at the secluded car park way below. His jacket sleeve hangs loose around the bony wrist. 'See the contraption that you may not know. See the big, square box. Just there it is, on top of that strange, golden, sports car.'

'You dumb mother,' says West. 'You could have flattened Elvis' Mercedes.'

'What the hell is that?' says Fike. He points at the square box below.

'Will somebody get him off the damned floor?' shouts Parker.

'In one moment, sir,' says the thin figure. 'No matter the urgency, remember planning is as always important as action. Although we all know that has never been your virtue. I can tell you, I have been in more urgent situations than this. The subject of our concern is breathing and quiet.' The strange figure grins and points at the big box again. 'That is my traveller. It enables me to negotiate worlds and without separate worlds we do not have real distance.' The thin figure frowns and sighs. 'I am very good at journeys but poor at destinations which, no doubt, is why I am here.'

'What the hell is he talking about?' says West. 'Throw the damned mother out of here.'

'Let him talk,' says Schilling. 'I want to know how he got in the bathroom.'

'Ah, good,' says the owner of the big, square box on top of the Mercedes. 'We have a curious man and that always helps. It is a matter of moments. I pick a moment in one sequence that is independent of the sequential moments I wish to enter and, then, make the transference from one sequence to another at the shortest distance between the two points. It makes me appear as out of nowhere whereas I have been there for some time which, of course, always disappears as if it never existed. The some time which I refer to is, as you have no doubt guessed, the real distance in my journey. The first occasion I did it I was quite impressed but now the mechanics all appear very obvious. We are at our weakest when we are impressed by our accomplishments.'

The three men look at Parker and the unkempt figure on the floor and sigh.

'Will somebody get him off the damned floor?' shouts Parker. 'Sonny, throw this crazy weirdo out.'

'Are you telling us you are a time traveller?' says Schilling.

'It is more complicated than that but, yes, it serves as an explanation. I should introduce myself. I am the Cosmic Medic.'

'Cosmic?' says West. 'Are you from New York?'

'You have never heard of me?' says Medic. 'Well, I am indeed pleased to meet you all. The Cosmic Medic is what I am called.'

'Son of a bitch,' says Fike. 'Don't wake Elvis for Christ sake. This could get out of hand.'

'Then, you are not English?' says Schilling.

'No, I'm afraid not, although England after my many adventures does feel like a second home.'

'He must be Australian,' says West. 'Maybe he knocked a hole through the wall.'

'Will somebody get Elvis off the damned floor?' shouts Parker.

The Cosmic Medic looks at the figure on the floor. 'That is probably a good idea. But, first, I need to make him comfortable.'

'Heh, you stay away from him,' shouts Parker.

They do not understand why but Fike, West and Schilling have faith in the man and they make no protest. The Cosmic Medic acts very quickly and points at Elvis a large pen that has a powerful, glowing light and makes a strange noise. The light from the pen changes the colour of the room immediately and the quiet is punctuated by several staccato shrieks.

'This man has real problems,' says Medic. 'His brain is cloudy with emotional confusion and he is already arthritic. The eyes are deteriorating. There are many poisons in his system. His stomach is particularly problematical.'

'Elvis needs to lose weight,' says Schilling. 'He hates Vegas.'

'What the hell are you guys whispering about?' says Parker.

'It is inside the stomach where the problems are,' says Medic. 'He can be made healthy but it will not last more than a few days unless he becomes a different man, unless he eats and lives differently. But we can remove the poisons and arrest his nervous systems so there are no damaging side effects. I can work on the neck and spine and, because they are important, they will improve his state of being. There are parts of his body that are in conflict and I can resolve that as well.'

'How long will all that take?' says Schilling.

'We need him on that stage tonight,' shouts Parker. He bangs his cane on the carpet.

'Take? I have already done it,' says Medic. He lifts his pen for the three men to see. 'If I say so, myself, it is an impressive device. Not my first attempt, of course.'

On the floor, Elvis opens his eyes. Without raising his head, he grins. The three men move to lift him.

The Cosmic Medic waves them away. 'He can stand up. He is okay for the moment.'

Elvis hears the words stand up and decides to do just that. The three men move aside and the Cosmic Medic nods and smiles. He looks pleased to see Elvis awake. Elvis looks around the room as if he is seeing his hotel suite for the first time. He smiles at his three friends and looks quizzically at the Cosmic Medic. Elvis spots Parker in the corner and he frowns.

He looks at the Cosmic Medic again. 'Who the hell are you?' he says.

'He is the Cosmic Medic,' says Schilling.

'Have you examined me?' says Elvis.

'I certainly have,' says Medic.

'The son of a bitch came out the toilet,' says Fike.

'Are you alright, Elvis?' says Sonny West.

'Man, I feel great,' says Elvis.

'Good,' shouts Parker. 'You have two shows tonight.'

'I hate Vegas,' says Elvis.

His face darkens and his friends worry as they watch him once again retreat into his own thoughts. Elvis walks over to a large, comfortable chair and sits down.

'Heh, the Cosmic Medic fixed you,' says Schilling.

'For the moment,' says Medic.

He walks over to the large, comfortable chair where Elvis sits tapping his fingers to an old, boogie woogie tune that has suddenly popped into his head.

'Man,' says Elvis, 'you done fixed me good. I haven't felt this good in years.'

'It will have been worthless if you do not change the way you live.'

'Man, I need you on the payroll. Lamar, fix this guy up with a contract. Cosmic, this is where you get a raise.'

'It's not that simple, Elvis. You need to be different. You need to make some big choices. The body needs to restore what it has lost.'

'Shut this guy up,' shouts Parker. 'He didn't do anything. He's a damned nobody.'

Schilling looks at Parker with contempt and faces Elvis. 'The Cosmic Medic is a time traveller.'

Elvis grins and laughs. 'What? He is a what?'

'I do travel significant distances between dimensions although I am not entirely comfortable with the word distance and the notion of time only adds to the confusion.' The Cosmic Medic points outside to the land below. 'That is the machine I travel in. It is the big box on top of the gold automobile.'

Elvis looks out of the window. 'Man, you could have wrecked my Mercedes. Quaint looking thing, isn't it? It's cute. I like weird things.'

'Elvis, if I said to you I could put you in that box without you moving, would you say yes? I could take you to a life where you will make the choices and perhaps have the strength to live well. And, for a short time, you could be my travelling companion. I am in between companions. What do you say?'

'Elvis, you have two shows tonight,' shouts Parker.

'All you have to do is say yes. You have to do nothing else. Nobody will drag you out of the door. But, if you say yes, you will in an instant join me in the box. I promise you, your life will change, so think carefully.'

Elvis looks at Schilling, West and Fike and waits.

'He came out of nowhere,' says Schilling. 'It was like he just clicked his fingers.'

'I will not pretend there will not be consequences,' says the Cosmic Medic. 'The words yes and no are simple but the decision is important and, whatever you do, you will make a decision. Deferment is the biggest decision of all. I learnt that a very, very long time ago in circumstances quite different.'

The Cosmic Medic remembers and grins.

'Aw, I have two shows tonight,' says Elvis. 'These guys are depending on me. Man, this is weird. You're a time traveller, right?'

'I can always return you to this moment later if you need to return. They won't miss you. All you have to do is say yes.'

'I sure feel good,' says Elvis. He looks around the room and sighs when his eyes meet the stare of Parker.

'I will return you. I always do.'

'One click of the fingers and we are inside the box?'

'It shouldn't take that long.'

Elvis grins and Lamar Fike thinks about laughing but resists.

'For so long, I've put off everything I could,' says Elvis. He looks at Parker for an instant. 'He let me because it was what he wanted. You're right, man. I was making decisions and didn't even know it.'

Elvis stops speaking and looks around the Vegas suite again and grins.
'Yes or no,' says Medic.

'Why not?' says Elvis. 'You'd better believe it. Yes.'

Parker stamps his cane on the floor but, before he can say anything, the Cosmic Medic and Elvis disappear from the room. Fike, Schilling and West dash to the window. They watch the big box disappear in the same way as Elvis and the Cosmic Medic left the room, lost in the briefest and palest of shadows.

'He'll be back,' shouts Parker. 'You watch. He'll be here for the first show at eight.'

'He may well be,' says Schilling who, like Fike and West, is still staring at the empty space on top of the golden Mercedes. 'But I do hope not.'

'You won't say that when the women run out,' says West.

'Son of a bitch,' says Fike. 'Wait till we tell Esposito.'

'I don't understand it,' says West.

'The Cosmic Medic was a time traveller,' says Schilling.

'I understand that shit,' says West. 'I don't understand why Elvis didn't take a wardrobe.'

The three men laugh and soon they are giggling uncontrollably.

In the corner, Parker turns over a playing card. He will wait until eight o'clock to see if Elvis returns. If not, he will make some telephone calls.

The failure to nurture the memory

The accusers

The accusers merit scrutiny. In the novel, 'Frankenstein', the Creature through observing the De Lacey family was able to become articulate and literate. He read and enjoyed 'Paradise Lost' by John Milton. For all his skills, the Creature never understood properly how others sustained themselves with importance or how they relied on carefully observed proprieties. He assumed mistakenly that his knowledge and understanding were important to others. He did not realise they were inadequate substitutes for mutual grooming when dealing with people. Elvis was not as literate as the Creature but he also failed to understand the proprieties. He described professional music in two ways. When he was being serious he used the word 'business'. When he was being cynical or wanted to shock he would use the word 'racket'. The orthodox or the cool were offended by this. They found him uncouth because he did not understand their values and beliefs. They called him an imposter and, to prohibit more uncouth characters appearing, the orthodox began to use words like 'poetry', 'genius' and 'artist' to identify the acceptable. They were determined to establish modern proprieties that would be more attuned to grooming than understanding.

After the sixties, some of the groomed felt obliged to justify the appeal of the simple music that began with the neglected poor of the American South. This justification required the belief that the singers and strummers they enjoyed were artists and that their finer moments had poetical significance. They forgot that recorded music had changed how we listen to music and that prior to the invention of the gramophone record their artists and poets could be found earning their living half cut in the local bar. They frequently quoted the lyrics and they identified one-line diamonds but they ignored the depressing statistic that few of the songs qualified as sustained poetry.

Undoubtedly, some will consider this fanciful, so I should explain. The notion that the music Elvis produced is art is misleading, it both flatters and diminishes. American popular music, or at least the American music which provided the inspiration for Elvis, was produced by performers who were part of their community. The achievement of their lives was how they connected with their community and entertained them at the same time. Greil Marcus, in his book 'Mystery Train', was wrong to condemn Elvis for not providing the emphatic 'no' to his society that he initially promised and that Marcus wanted. It is not required. Elvis is a performer. The notion of saying 'no' comes from 'Bartleby', the classic story by Herman Melville, which is about a character that 'prefers not to'. To connect this with performers who expect payment, and who know that sustained payment will not be forthcoming unless they inspire applause from strangers, is odd. Unfortunately, it is at the heart of the inconsistent way we talk about popular music. There is an irony here because the refusal by Elvis to deliver an emphatic 'no' may itself have been a form of 'no'. His 'no' occurred in the divided United States of the seventies when many of those saying 'no' were actually picking a side.

American music, the music which has been utilised and plagiarised worldwide, is best understood as a regional cuisine. The great performers of this music were like great chefs. Chefs deliver what people want, a special meal with a bottle of wine, but, somehow, the great chefs make it seem fresh and distinct. This is achieved by avoiding blandness, by doing something different but not too different and by achieving a standard not previously experienced. We like the food by the great chefs but the cuisine also has to include more standard fare, the steak and chips they invariably include in the menu. This metaphor clearly has its limitations but it makes more sense than critics desperately searching for troubadour poets in the past.

Interestingly, it helps explain why we are more conservative about music than painting, why music, which does not belong to the cuisine we know or adopt, can irritate us so much. David Stubbs has suggested in his book, 'Fear Of Music', that music is different to the visual arts because most of us resist the aural avant-garde. In music, we expect order and pleasantness, harmony. He is talking about classical music but his argument does support the notion of American, regional music as a cuisine.

It certainly supports my own relationship with music.

What is odd is how modern, rock music has moved away from the regional cuisine and has actually facilitated the advance of the avant-garde, how it has progressed from virtuosity to the conceptual in a way similar to the visual arts. It produces fresh genres every other year. The music of Elvis and his peers is not completely devoid of artistic moments. Art happens in the oddest places for the strangest reasons but its spasmodic existence in the American music of the South is within a social context more significant. This is why well executed clichés within blues and country music can be as exciting as originality. The odd moments that can be confused with art should not oblige us to wander around believing we have found a musical form that is only vital when it challenges the cliché. Elvis and his peers were men and women who engaged with a way of life and complemented it with their music. Usually, these musicians were people who could provide comfort for ordinary people to lead fuller lives but, themselves, often led an alternative existence. This sense of isolation gave them their identity but it did not prevent them from offering emotional understanding of the struggles of their audience.

The arguments against the notion that American music is a cuisine are, of course, numerous and quite persuasive. For example, music because it is dependent on a mix of rhythm and melody is inevitably poetical, too much music is driven by the choices of the musicians themselves for their artistic authority to be ignored and some of it inevitably carries both political and artistic messages. The supporters of these arguments are powerful and are usually individuals without any self-doubt. We all have different interests but my own beliefs or prejudices are enforced when I read the record reviews written by these advocates. The Estuary squeak of David Bowie was described by Graeme Thompson, in the New Statesman, as a voice that is 'rich basso profundo, imperious'. I am obliged to ask if this is the price of inappropriate pretensions. Nobody has ears any more.

So, art happens occasionally anywhere and, admittedly, music has changed from what appeals to me and which is relevant to an appreciation of Elvis. But much of what we call art in rock music is mere baggage, a side dish insisted upon by overbearing diners. Admittedly, modern, rock music facilitates the avant-garde but I lose interest when the tuneless Paul

Weller insists in 'The Guardian' without any sense of irony that he is an artist and he has the rights of an artist.

Popular music for the vast majority of people is tribal. Often they restrict themselves to a genre. The genres are numerous - soul, country, rap, hip hop, disco, technic, easy listening, jazz, blues, rhythm and blues, vintage rock and roll, indie and the rest. The genres often have fashions or modes of dress, language and, even, recreational drugs to signal the musical loyalty of the fan. I am somewhat tribal myself. I defend my narrowness by arguing that I am interested in a specific period in a particular society but it is only self-justification.

This is very different to how we watch movies. Most of us dip into the different genres and, in our more serious, patient moments, watch slow moving, character studies on grainy film that transcend narrative. We accept that genres, although enjoyable, can compromise quality. We neither condemn whole movie genres nor insist one has to dominate. There are a small number of people who devote themselves to only one kind of movie but these people usually have other issues and require help.

Popular music is about identity and often that identity accommodates rebellion or feeling different at least. Because it provides company with others, the need to belong is crucial. No wonder Elvis was popular in the fifties, a man who was very different but who never really had the pure instincts or the despair of the angry rebel.

The inventions in popular music focus on movements and groups and these are important for adolescents as they distance themselves from their parents and form more meaningful relationships with other people like them. These tribes, though, are not simply about making distances from parents. They are about status.

A letter writer in 'The Guardian' one day past expressed his astonishment that somebody could spend a lifetime listening to music as repetitive as that offered by Bruce Springsteen. The person, who wrote the letter, believed in the superiority of classical music. He was right. Fans, and I include myself, organise their lives around music with a range remarkably limited. The explanation for Springsteen is, of course, straightforward. Bruce provides, apart from his music, an identity for his tribe of adoring fans and semi-detached rebels who think he is hip, cool and on the right side. As this is a privilege not afforded Elvis fans, I envy them.

The tribes do not just provide identity. They also allow their members to believe in their superiority and sneer at those outside the tribe. The members believe they have exclusive information and understanding, that it is not an accident they happen to be in a tribe with these benefits. They have found company for a reason. They are like their heroes. Hip, cool and on the right side.

Self–congratulation and sneering at others has been an activity very popular with human beings for some time and popular music facilitates it remarkably well. These tribal instincts encourage both narrowness and radicalism and fans are obliged to adopt an aesthetic that some 'Guardian' letter writers will consider bewilderingly restricted. Critics in popular music are sometimes mere tribal members who rely on above average commitment to their narrow aesthetic. They are able to claim fame because they have better information about the history of that aesthetic. These people are the know alls. Other critics, though, think they offer more. They attempt to identify what makes which musicians special and they select moments that they claim are either transcendental or historic. These are the sensitive types. These critics, whilst reminding their readers that the group conformity must still be endorsed, nominate within the genre those performers whom they believe are capable of independent creativity and thought. They seek out those whom they claim are capable of the personal. Their heroes are both loyal to the aesthetic of the group which ultimately makes them all hip and cool but they are also exceptional because of their individual vision. Such auteurs are superior to the rest who merely reproduce the approved forms. Anybody who has faith in objective judgement in these circumstances needs to use the internet carefully or, as Kurt Vonnegut once said, 'So it goes.'

Modern tastes depend on specific tenets - the belief that popular music requires authors and artists, the faith in the merit of the subversive, the need for lyrical significance, the importance of appearance and being cool and a faith in the purity of negritude and black culture. These arguments often determine position and identity, so my dependency on Elvis could be as much about how I clash with those who oppose him rather than his inspiration.

None of the above means that all the people who dislike Elvis are narrow minded, pretentious bigots. We all have our different needs,

the world has to change and some people really do like music I find
unlistenable. There are many who find Elvis distasteful and think his
music irrelevant to them. They are entitled to do so and many will have
good reasons. But is he given a fair hearing? I doubt it.

Of course, I may be being unreasonable. I have not outgrown the child
who has to insist he really did see someone fabulous by the lake. Perhaps
my motives are not pure but, before rock and roll became dominant,
music used to be categorised into folk music, light entertainment and
classical. The latter was where you had to go to for art. No doubt this
stratification was the work of snobs but now they appear sensible, people
who possessed perspective. Wagner said that classical music expresses
thoughts whereas the popular alternative is about sensation and feeling.
These feelings can be complex but in themselves do not qualify as art.
Lyrics, although important to many modern listeners, do not constitute
music. Earnest lyrics are added to pop records because there is always
someone to insist upon the cerebral, the vegetables in the cuisine.

The Creature was always impatient with what the villagers demanded
for themselves. He knew that their aspirations created hostility to
what made a talented but not groomed creature unique and it was their
response, as much as his deformities, that scarred him. Elvis became
famous but those who assume he had universal approval are mistaken.
Elvis fans belong to a cult, albeit a large one. What makes his fans
different to those outside the cult is that they for various reasons, but
mainly because of addiction, permit their creature from rock and roll
history to be flawed and uncouth. The village exists and, for all his
popularity and earning power, Elvis will always be outside it.

The accusations

There is always a minority opinion and those, who have it, are blessed
with knowing that it exists to make life tolerable for another lonely soul
somewhere else. Briefly, I will be contrary.

The novel, 'Frankenstein', is a critique of two wilful, ambitious men
whose destiny is linked. Indeed, the book has a terrifying vision of
masculinity. Shelley imagines fathers who reject babies because of their

imperfection and potential independence and sons who respond with violent revenge. Although she regards shared domesticity as a virtue, there is no scope for women in the life of the Creature. After Elvis met Parker, there was no constructive role for women in the life of Elvis. His obsession with his female lovers, people excluded from his destiny by fate, was defiant but he misunderstood what his life was meant to resolve. I believe that his desire to create 'the living spirit of love' was trivial. His persistence with this naive expectancy helps explain why he dealt so inadequately with Parker. At least, the Creature realised he had to prevail over Frankenstein but, of course, it was his similar obsession with female companionship which led to the destructive war with his creator. Shelley would have insisted that Elvis was entitled to both a career and domesticity but maybe this should be challenged. Both Elvis and the Creature wanted their female companions but did they misunderstand what was appropriate for them? If they had denied themselves properly and focussed on their exceptional but narrow potential, there would have been no tragedy, only romance. Elvis and the Creature failed to understand a fundamental truth, that all romance is based on sacrifice; solitary purpose, monogamous love, ascetic purity in the countryside or glorious death.

Mary Shelley rejected Romanticism as too narrow but she was a homemaker. The preface to the 1818 edition states that her novel is committed 'to the exhibition of domestic affection and the excellence of universal virtue'. Clearly, she would have scorned my suggestions above and some of my other opinions that now follow. She would have concluded my nature is unduly argumentative. As I am convinced by her conviction about the importance of nurture, I must be. I only hope I can console other odd, lonely souls.

In the 'Let It Rock' magazine in the early 1970s, a reader or accuser mentioned how time revised judgements. He quoted an example to illustrate his reasonable point. 'Surely Elvis Presley must be the biggest dork of all time.' After expressing this opinion, he no doubt returned to the village to listen to his 'rock' albums and ponder the lyrics. This is the debate. Some people think Elvis is brilliant whilst his accusers insist he is talentless. These are the accusations.

He did not write his own songs

'Johnny Cash fakes it,' Elvis said to his audience on one occasion.

It is odd how the cult of the singer-songwriter has become entrenched. Admittedly, there are marvellous exceptions but the individual who does both well is unusual. Usually, one is faked. Elvis was aware of this.

Songwriters, like Johnny Cash for instance, often write material that mitigates the limitations of their voices while modern technology, both in the recording studio and on stage, can produce an alternative version of the actual voice. Often, fans will accept the limitations of the vocals of their favourite singer-songwriters or assume that their favourite croaks and squeals reveal character and intelligence and, to be fair, sometimes they may. Again, Johnny Cash is an example.

We are now so used to hearing people who cannot sing, we no longer expect it. Something similar happened to blank verse in theatrical drama. Indeed, it is not too difficult to imagine a future where nobody sings properly. If Elvis is lucky he could, like Shakespeare, be the sole survivor of his type. In the future, we could have people blissfully unaware of the other great singers of his day, listeners obliged to stare into their iPod equivalents and wonder how he could do that.

But, if singing in the modern age is often faked, how can that dreadful responsibility of producing the cherished masterpiece from that intimidating piece of blank paper be avoided? Simple, you get help. Not all but many songs are actually the product of collaboration. This can be done either with someone else who is independent from the performance or within the context of the band. Elton John and Bernie Taupin are an example of the former and The Beatles belong to the latter. It has been asked what would have happened had Elvis been born later in a modern market where he would have been obliged to write his own songs. He would have had three choices. He could have formed a band that included songwriters and, while they wrote their songs about their inner conflict and angst, watched football on television, he could have written songs with other members of the band or he could have become a jazz singer and sang old standards and played the piano which is how those who do not write songs these days are often marketed. I suspect he would have taken the second option, drawn inspiration and, sometimes, assistance from others. We have to remember that Elvis did arrive at Sun studio with his own songs. No doubt, they would have been unacceptable but, in the modern world surrounded by band members equally obliged to produce songs, he would have improved. How much would he contribute to these songs? Who knows and it would not matter because he would, at least, have his name on the songs and the critics would be reassured. Let us assume the first option; he watched television whilst the more cerebral and anguished within the group produced the songs. Presumably, in this instance, Elvis would have been the least important performer in the band. Oh, yeah, I doubt it.

Oddly, Scotty Moore, Bill Black and DJ Fontana, the musicians who played with Elvis in the fifties, were never criticised for not writing songs. But they are musicians and, as what they do involves practice, it is considered difficult. Singing is easy and, just like playing football, anybody can do it. There is, though, a difference between how spectators play football and what they watch inside a stadium. The Premier League stars have talent and are exceptional. Virtually every young man plays football but the existence of all this competition makes it more, not less, difficult to become professional. All we have to do is count the rejected multitude. The same applies to singing. Some people have flexible brains and can write songs, some people have flexible fingers and can play instruments and some people have flexible tonsils and can sing.

As the music professor said to Susan Alexander, the distraught wife of Charles Foster Kane, in the famous movie, 'Some people can sing. Some cannot. You cannot. Impossible!'

Those who can sing very well are exceptional. Those who think it easy should try it for themselves or, more sensibly, listen to an Elvis impersonator. Considering that Elvis made such a modest contribution to his records, it is odd how nobody has ever been able to produce an exact copy of what he did. So far, it has proved easier to reproduce a masterpiece by Rembrandt or Renoir. Apart from the cloth-eared, nobody has ever mistaken an Elvis imitator or copy for the real thing.

Neither is the song the fundamental element in the record that is automatically assumed. We all have our favourite records but they are not always our favourites because of the songs themselves. Nobody noticed the song, 'Suspicious Minds', until it was sung by Elvis. The original release by Mark James failed. Although the song is now hailed as a soul classic, it could be arranged differently to suit the Beach Boys. No? Listen again. I remember once challenging a Stevie Wonder fan about the record, 'Superstition', which, to me, always sounds like a riff pretending to be a song.

'Yeah, but the production is perfect,' said the fan.

Ah, so that is why it is a great record. It has tasteful engineering and technology. I am a big admirer of Stevie Wonder and it is possible that in this instance the engineering contributed little to the song. But anybody who thinks record producers are of little significance compared to songwriters should note what they are paid. We are talking about popular music, three minute ditties and, despite earnest, rap composers who are desperate to be the next Samuel Taylor Coleridge, lyrics of limited quality. Technology does play a part. This is why people will buy albums of remakes by artists inferior to the originals. They want to hear stereo or a louder bass and, without these technical additions, the original songs to some people will be unlistenable.

Much of the material in popular music can be changed radically by interpretation. This is not the case with classical music. Nobody so far has produced a gently understated, Bossa Nova version of 'The Ride Of The Valkyries'. Whatever one thinks of Wagner, it is clear that he wrote his music to ensure it would have only one interpretation. I remember many years ago browsing in a bookshop and reading a critic who argued that this was why classical music was superior to pop music. The performer could not alter the intent of the composer. The writer may have used a phrase about the exclusive integrity of the content. If he is right, it implies that popular music is rubbish or what stops it being rubbish is the quality of the performances or how the record producer can fake those performances. This view may be extreme but it cannot be dismissed as easily as some think.

Once, I had a conversation with a classical music devotee who was astonished at my affection for the blues.

'Blues music is simple,' I said, 'but what makes it special is the feeling. Not the formula. Sometimes, it is what you don't hear.'

'Well, they always said the blacks could play the cracks in the piano.'

He was right but, in classical music, the composers control the cracks themselves. Listen to an accomplished pianist play the familiar, Debussy composition, 'Clair Du Lune'. The talented musician will play it slowly and with composure. Nothing is rushed and the music and the spaces between complement one another perfectly. The cracks define the melody and they can only be heard with the help of an accomplished musician but it is Debussy who put the cracks there.

Popular music is defined by the performance whether virtuous or faked. People buy records and not music sheets. Strangely, movie criticism has tilted in the other direction and almost ignores the scriptwriter who is the equivalent in film production of the songwriter. This is because, just as popular music is dominated by performers, movies are determined by what happens around the camera. Sam Peckinpah once acknowledged that 'Dirty Harry' was a fine film.

'The script, though,' Sam said, 'was a terrible piece of trash.'

Popular music, like the movies, will always be dominated by form. That is how they make it popular. But rock critics, who have nurtured the singer-songwriter cult, constantly promote content at the expense of form. This is not surprising because very few of them are musical. Paul Morley, a famous rock critic, decided after he read 'The Rest Is Noise' by Alex Ross that he should enrol in the Royal Academy of Music. He realised he did not know the difference between minor and major chords. Odd, that it only took him twenty years to notice. These critics have to analyse song lyrics as if they have significance. Many are not qualified to do anything else.

But, at least, what the songwriter does is original. The songwriter only has the blank piece of paper. The performers have the infrastructure. But nobody starts with nothing. Mary Shelley did not dream Frankenstein as is often claimed; she may not have even dreamt the name. The novel was inspired by the Prometheus myth which she acknowledged in the full title of her novel, 'Frankenstein or The Modern Prometheus'. Songs are often based on others, either consciously or unconsciously. All the musical talents - composing, playing an instrument or singing - only emerge after the absorption of ideas and practice. After time, it can become automatic such as Dylan hearing songs pop into his head or Elvis simply singing the song the way he feels. But it requires study. Elvis did not form his unique, singing style walking along an empty beach, like James Joyce, listening to the waves hiss. He listened to other singers. Memories not only aid development but determine execution when what occurs is often a variation on what was previously heard. This can be Dylan altering slightly an Irish, folk song, BB King bending his guitar notes after hearing T Bone Walker or Elvis copying the Ink Spots to create rock and roll ballads.

Literature and movie scripts are also composed and, considering the number of words involved in these creations, the effort required must be considerable. These people must be really talented. But no one assumes that any book or script is a complete work of originality. 'The Wild Bunch' by Sam Peckinpah steals scenes from 'The Treasure Of The Sierra Madre' and Ernest Hemingway was heavily influenced by the Russian writer, Ivan Turgenev. Both, though, are given deserved credit for being special and original talents. In literature and movies, the influence of others exists to the highest degree in genres - thrillers, westerns, spies, romance and so on. This is because narrative is so important and plots have to be recycled with only minor variations. The word genre should be familiar because genres dominate in popular music. Oh, dear.

We still need the songwriters to write songs to sustain the genres. Possibly, but Jerry Wexler once said that soul music was country music with horns. He meant it was the vocal styles and arrangements that defined the genre. When the record producer, Chips Moman, was preparing for the Memphis session with Elvis in 1969 he asked for country material. The tracks on the album, when it was released, were described as soul music.

The talent of the songwriter in popular music should not be dismissed but all the talents are important and essential. The obsession with the songwriter has become wearisome. And, why do we settle for performances that are a compromise? No one assumes Beethoven sat at his piano and imagined his Fifth Symphony being played by anybody other than excellent musicians. Their rare talent is essential to his vision. Unlike Beethoven, our critics need to believe in songwriters as self-contained poets (their word not mine). If the notion of the all rounder has its own romantic attraction, it has led unfortunately to bands that are no more than pub entertainers being hailed as world class performers. People will argue that the singer-songwriter tradition is consistent with the folk tradition of the wandering performer singing his own songs. This tradition, though, had disappeared before the sixties. Whilst the return of the singer-songwriter may have been a return to those more authentic traditions, the likelihood is it was inspired more by the change in the music business. When songwriters were becoming rich from music sheet sales they preferred, like Beethoven, to have their songs performed by the gifted. After the money disappeared, after the public started spending their money on records, the songwriters responded, as Karl Marx would have predicted, by muscling in on the economic action. This is why we have had to settle for these musical compromises.

I have a friend who still watches his favourite, soul singers whenever they appear on stage. He wears earplugs so he can hear the vocals properly. So, that is why they play the music so loudly in concerts.

His music is badly undermined by sentimentality

In the opening section of 'Last Train To Memphis', the first volume of the Elvis biography by Peter Guralnick, the author not only describes Elvis as a great blues singer but admits that he hoped Elvis conceived of himself in the same way. He considers his more sentimental music inexplicable.

This is interesting in two respects. First, it reveals that Elvis was to Guralnick at one stage a person whom he thought or hoped would share his opinions, someone who might want to be what Guralnick wanted him to be. This is not unusual amongst critics or fans. The performer makes music that has an impact on their well being, helps them achieve what Guralnick describes in his excellent review of 'From Elvis In Memphis' as 'the obliteration of self.' We assume that the person who has touched us in this way must be a kindred spirit, a double. Critics sneer at Elvis fans who talk about loving him. But all they are mocking is the clumsiness of these fans with words. Instead, the fans should be given credit for identifying what is a real phenomenon. Not just Elvis fans have this reaction. When William Godwin read 'A Short Residence' by Mary Wollenstoncraft he wrote, 'if there was a book calculated to make a man fall in love with its author this appears to me to be the book.' Later, he married Wollenstoncraft and fathered Mary Shelley. He made the same assumption that we all make, that the performer, writer, actor, movie director who inspires us and offers relief is a sympathetic figure. The problem for Elvis is that he was odd from day one.

He was a genuine outsider who, in fifties Memphis, grew his hair long, wore make up and dressed as if he was black. Inevitably, he disappointed those in search of a double, those who wanted his taste in music to be like their own. Elvis never was like other people. For many, including me at certain moments, this has been a real disappointment.

The second point of interest is that Peter Guralnick describes the sentimental numbers as inexplicable. The obvious question is why. Does he mean inexplicable because it challenges the kindred spirit he imagined the first time he heard Elvis sing the blues in a way no white man had ever managed or has managed since? Presumably, he thinks it inconceivable that any person of real, musical talent could like such material.

Elvis came from a culture that approves of sentimental material, poor people who found it comforting rather than embarrassing. W J Cash, in 'The Mind Of The South', described American Southerners as the most sentimental people in history and identified the combination of romance and hedonism as a fundamental characteristic of the Southerner. Elvis was not an aristocrat groomed on intrigue and cynicism. Although his diversity is impressive, it can be safely concluded that Restoration comedies are beyond him. His innocence is either appealing or embarrassing. It is a matter of taste. It is not, though, evidence of a lack of merit. 'Old Shep' warrants another mention. This is a tale of someone who has to shoot the dog that he loves. It ends with Elvis concluding that, if dogs do have a heaven, he knows Old Shep will have a wonderful home. Actually, it could be argued that the version is quite tasteful. For instance, we do not hear the sound of the shotgun exploding, the anguished cries of the poor dog dying a painful death nor the uncontrollable sobs of the man who has pulled the trigger.

Elvis recorded 'Old Shep' for his album, 'Rock And Roll No 2'. He had sung it in a competition as a child and it had memories for him. He may have thought he would balance out the up-tempo material with a song with which he was familiar. If we progress through his career in the fifties, we discover sessions where the sentimental ballads are used to vary the material. Two exceptions are the Christmas albums which have different commercial ambitions and the ballads and sentimentality are over represented. Two of Elvis' toughest blues, 'Santa Claus Is Back In Town' and 'Merry Xmas Baby', were recorded in sessions of Christmas material. Here the balancing is done in reverse and the blues songs are used as antidotes. Much needed antidotes as it happens.

In the sixties, ballads increase but this is for two reasons. First, there is an attempt to change the style to widen the appeal but, outside the middle period of 1961 to 1963 where the ballads dominate dreadfully, there is always an attempt to balance material. The studio catalogues for 1960 and 1964 to 1968 are more than acceptable. Nor can we ignore that many of the ballads sung in 1961 to 1963 are marvellous. Second, the situation after 1960 was made much worse by the material provided for the movies. This is material over which he had no control. Since his death, most of this has slowly been removed from his catalogue although God knows what will happen when the copyright is removed. Unfortunately, they endure in the memory and many who refer to Elvis as being sentimental are remembering the nightmares within these celluloid disasters.

Nothing, though, in this fifteen year period from 1954 to 1969 is inexplicable.

In the comeback period of 1969 to 1971, the music is not sentimental. There are the occasional errors. I would include 'Mama Liked The Roses' and 'Don't Cry Daddy' but these exist because he asked for two songs that he could dedicate to his parents. These individual choices are not inexplicable. If anything, they indicate an admirable loyalty to his roots.

After 1971, during the period of his decline, the ballads dominate again but he still covers a wide range of material. The general opinion is that this choice reflected his morose mood. Optimism and faith had long disappeared and Elvis was obliged to explore his incomprehension of his emotional state. He had a need, like the Creature, to surrender to sadness, 'A gush of tears somewhat soothed me.' Elvis adopted the ambition of the Creature, 'I am miserable and they shall share my wretchedness.'

What was happening inside his head, he may have found inexplicable but his choice of material is easily explained by his state of mind. His curiosity also obliged him to seek alternative, musical forms and the deterioration in his voice also affected the material he attempted. This later music is actually darker than his rock and roll. The ballads are about dependency and betrayal and their existence as permanent companions. The sentimentality is therefore explicable. All it requires is sympathy.

I will tell a tale that may embarrass. I am ten years old and I travel with my grandmother to visit an aunt who has older children than me. They are teenagers and working. With their money, they can afford records unavailable to me. My own musical meal is a nightly battle with the temperamental, radio signal of Radio Luxembourg. When I arrive I pounce on the record collection. I play the other side of 'All Shook Up'. A few bars into the song, my grandmother asks, 'Who is this?'

'It's Elvis,' I say.

'Elvis, is that him? He has a nice voice,' she says.

The song is 'That's When Your Heartaches Begin.' It is a melodramatic, Ink Spots ballad with a spoken monologue in the middle. She listens to the voice and I am too busy listening to a previously unheard record to notice her reaction. At the end of the song, I look across the living room of my aunt to ask my grandmother if she is impressed with her introduction to the scandalous Elvis. I realise that tears are pouring down her face.

Consider the tale itself. Is that sentimental? Is it tasteless or mawkish to reveal it here or does it say something important about the unmitigated heartbreak that the innocent and the poor know they have to endure? But is that what my grandmother was remembering as she sat there or did she simply have sentimental taste? Tears, though, are real emotion whereas sentiment is often smug and self-congratulating. Tears are important. They reduce the right of others to feel superior. Elvis cried after he recorded 'Mama Liked The Roses.' I do not like the song although there is one phrase in particular where his singing is marvellous. A strong record producer or company should have said, 'Sorry, Elvis, we know why the song is important to you but this record will alienate too many.' They did not and the record exists to embarrass me further. But the tears cannot be ignored, neither those of Elvis nor those of my grandmother.

The unmitigated heartbreak that the innocent and the poor know they have to endure. The phrase is worth remembering because Elvis in the best of his sentimental music remembered. The tears of my grandmother meant that the record clearly moved her.

The capacity to enjoy and draw feeling from an artifact implies sophistication or, at least, critical capacity. In the magazine, 'Prospect', Mark Cousins once described a scene from the Russian movie, 'Mother and Son'. It is when the son carries his ageing and ill mother into the sunshine to provide her with a little pleasure and relief before she dies. The scene left Cousins in tears. 'Mother and Son' is an extremely slow moving, art movie and poetry without plot is not to the taste of the average movie goer. The tears of Mark Cousins were a consequence of his sophistication, his understanding and open mind.

What was important to my grandmother was the emotion the performance contained and the memories it inspired. She had no need of self-conscious virtuosity. Something similar must have happened to Elvis when he heard his record of 'Mama Liked The Roses.'

I had a friend who hated the Elvis ballad, 'Always On My Mind', because he thought it was sentimental. He is now divorced and, fortunately for him, recovered. 'Always On My Mind' is now one of his favourite records. Some sentimentality is within our range but other examples are not. That is not always the fault of the music. It is often best to ignore what we find difficult and merely admire what appeals. Admittedly, CDs filled with songs not relevant to the purchaser can be expensive but, presumably, that is why they invented itunes. If you require music that is cynical, hip or, if not danceable, loaded with clever word play, virtually all the ballads will be tedious. Such preferences, though valid, do dismiss the tastes of whole generations and continents.

The song that made Elvis weep, 'Mama Liked The Roses', was included in a retrospective compilation of the 1969 Memphis Sessions called 'Memphis Record'. Peter Guralnick wrote the liner notes, again excellent, and, I assume, he approved the selection of material. Guralnick says nothing to indicate he thinks 'Roses' is inexplicably sentimental or unacceptable. It is close to the roots of Elvis and falls within the range of authentic country and is presumably palatable to Guralnick He may feel the same about 'That's When Your Heartaches Begin.' There will be other sentimental examples that, as an American, he will like because he can identify with its roots. Many of us, of course, are not directly linked to the continent and culture that produced this taste for melodramatic sentiment and find it somewhat odd. We all, though, have unpredictable boundaries; include records others think are corny. Whilst taboo themes emerge, dead dogs and dead people, for example, we all include the surprising exception, the guilty pleasure. There are people who balance the material against the performance and there are people who are interested only in the performance. I had a friend who was a folk purist and merciless with what she regarded as the sweet side of Elvis. She loved, though, 'The Wonder Of You' which I often avoid. Others relish the gospel song, 'If That Isn't Love', but the title itself makes me paranoid and I have a real problem with the line about the little sparrows that cannot fly. Quality, or what we regard as quality, still exists within sentimentality but it is very subjective. When Elvis is at his strongest and performing well the instances of sentimentality are less obvious. This supports the notion of good and bad sentimentality.

Old Shep' was not an original story. Apart from the folk song, 'Bellum', a similar tale was twice made into a film. 'The Yearling' and 'Old Yeller' were very different movies but both involved the loss of an animal important to a family. 'The Yearling', directed by Clarence Brown, is regarded as a tasteful classic and 'Old Yeller', which was made for children, has been condemned as Disney ham. Both are sentimental but the talented Clarence Brown uses his material to evoke a simpler world with strong, human values. His film is complex because, as admirable as they are, those values fail to protect humans from pain and unfairness. Most movie fans today would acknowledge the merit of the film. It proves there is good sentimentality. We are, though, talking about film and the effort movie fans make to appreciate different styles. Elvis does have his sweet side but sweetness is not without merit when it evokes a way of life or if it stresses how we need the support of others in our struggles. The folk purist liked 'The Wonder Of You' because, for her, its karaoke style embraced community and faith. No surprise, she was a folk purist. I like 'Can't Help Falling In Love' because it suggests powerlessness and the absence of choice, the weight of fate. In these songs, and many others, Elvis does what was recognised as an achievement by Clarence Brown. He adds something. If the listener is alert or just sympathetic, like the divorced friend or the folk purist, he or she will be more than capable of ignoring the sentimentality and will even accept it is fundamental to the aspects that appeal. Not all of the sentimental Elvis achieves this. Much of the movie material is often worthless because the songs are frequently poor and Elvis makes no effort to rescue the material. His performances in the seventies are also uneven and some of the music, which could have been redeemed by a performer at his peak, perishes in treacle. If he is poorly motivated or ill, he can descend to Disney ham but there are plenty of instances when he ascends rather than descends.

Much of his sentimental material becomes even more rewarding after listening to recent box sets that reveal early outtakes of what were originally thought to be cringe worthy songs. Listened to in this way before RCA either added strings or altered the mix to reduce the contribution of the musicians, the material is often more heartfelt than sweet. Whilst it does not always transform these records into classics, it is worthwhile to hear Elvis working with musicians to add poignancy to the material, to hear them find the cracks in the piano. Cracks that RCA philistines were too often determined to fill.

So, the sentimentality does exist but there are extenuating circumstances, these are his background, the movies, his personal problems at the end of his career and a second rate, interfering record company. There were also romantic compulsions in his nature that would have benefited from curtailment through creative support. Aretha Franklin had Jerry Wexler. Elvis only had accountants.

Nevertheless, his own lapses into very questionable material are actually not extreme by the standards of some white, Southern singers of his generation. In a normal career, his errors could have been forgiven but, added to what happened in the movies and his moves away from rock and roll, they exist for some as the ultimate proof of worthlessness. This view, though, neglects the many brilliant, moving examples that exist within his gentler side. These would not have existed without his sentimentality. Mark Kermode, the film critic, horror buff and rockabilly musician, has for some time argued correctly about the dark sub-text of the movie, 'Mary Poppins'. The same bleak realisation about existence exists in 'Hawaiian Wedding Song' or, at least, it does in the version by Elvis.

Without the rubbish, he would not have been as great.

He did not develop and grow

Paul Gambaccini, a DJ and media presenter, has an uncomplicated view which he expressed on a BBC, radio programme. In the nineteen fifties, when his music offered for his generation a release from conformity and repression, Elvis had been great. Unfortunately, according to Paul, Elvis spent two years in the Army and returned to find that his audience had left him behind. They were now more hip than Elvis had ever been. Elvis was simply too unsophisticated to make the music demanded by these hip, rebellious and unleashed human beings. Unlike The Beatles and others, he did not become more ambitious as he became older. He failed to embrace the superior tastes and the innovations that were emerging in the second half of the century.

Inevitably, there are half truths in this but some clarity is required. The music scene did not become more 'hip' in 1960. In the mid-fifties, the majority of rock and roll, rhythm and blues and rockabilly records had been created by small, independent record labels. This musical revolution was relatively short lived and, by 1960, the major labels were back in control. Rock and roll had become integrated into mainstream pop. Charlie Gillet records all this in his worthwhile rock and roll and rhythm and blues history, 'The Sound Of The City.'

The music scene did, though, change dramatically in the mid-60s with the arrival of The Beatles and Bob Dylan and, just as important, the contraceptive pill, political unrest and fashionable drugs. Elvis was never entirely disconnected from this scene. He had fans within this generation who had been exposed to his music when young and his personality already embraced some of the freedoms that were being espoused. When, in 1961, Elvis performed at the Ellis Auditorium in Memphis the local paper reported, 'he combined Negro cotton field harmony, camp meeting fervour, Hollywood showmanship, beatnik nonchalance and some manipulation of mass psychology.' The reference to 'beatnik nonchalance' is important because it reveals Elvis was complex and, for a working class Southerner, always ahead of his time. But the teenagers of the mid-sixties were still a different generation and they were unimpressed by his complexity which they interpreted as a disappointingly partial commitment to their values.

THE FAILURE TO NURTURE

The musical movement of the mid-sixties which, at times, preached violent, socialist revolution was unbelievably facilitated by the major labels. These were the same cynical capitalists that had crowded out the independent labels that produced fifties rock and roll. In the sixties, the images of Karl Marx, Fidel Castro and Che Guevara became fashion accessories. Of course, there was very little socialism. Social democracy actually retreated in America and Britain. This was the generation that assumed moral scorn, smoked marijuana and later voted for Ronald Reagan and Margaret Thatcher.

The social changes, which were real, happened when Elvis was trapped in movie contracts and his efforts to record different material in the studios were being hampered. He only truly engaged with this new scene after his 'TV Special' of 1968. The comeback helped him improve his records but a different generation wanted performers who were more like them and whom they felt were taking steps beyond Elvis. These performers included Dylan, Hendrix and others. Elvis did attract new fans but not many. I was at University at the time and I did interest friends in the Elvis classics. Indeed, they would often talk more eloquently than me about how much they enjoyed his music. But it was only me who actually bought his records. This is not me merely being self-pitying. Years later, it is understandable why Elvis ignored the wishes of the more hip critics. They did not pay for his records. These critics and their readers had other heroes. Elvis, though, was more aware and appreciative of these hip critics than is realised.

Jon Landau was a music writer for 'Rolling Stone' magazine. More than today, the magazine combined music journalism with radical politics. Landau was an Elvis fan but very much committed to the radical revolution, ignore the irony for now. Later, he became a record producer for Bruce Springsteen. In Boston in 1971, Landau saw Elvis perform and he wrote a review that was highly appreciative but unflinching in describing the horrors that had happened to Elvis in the sixties. Landau still admired Elvis as the great, American performer, someone capable of spine melting, musical moments, and he complemented this understanding with a left-wing and rebellious perspective. I would have liked Elvis to have read the review and to have understood the potential that fans of my generation believed he had. To read something that would motivate him to seek proper nurture and free himself from the oppressive forces of his buck hungry management. Unfortunately, the physical decline had already started and, in the years that followed, Elvis realised less of his potential, not more.

Years later, soon after he died when his estate was being tidied and organised, someone, searching amongst the many items that remained in Graceland, found a plastic wallet. Inside, protected by the wallet and in pristine condition was the review by hip radical, Jon Landau. Elvis had read the review and he had been impressed and moved. Had someone found the Rosebud of Elvis?

The tale itself should not be too surprising. The conventional view is that Elvis was a traditional, Southern conservative only comfortable with Southern conformists. Whilst Elvis was close to his roots, he did, though, form surprising relationships. His closeness to New York songwriters, Leiber and Stoller, and his alliance with Steve Binder, the producer of the 'TV Special', are obvious examples. Although never comfortable in conversation with the educated, they did sometimes inspire him and make him optimistic.

The tale of the review by Jon Landau which is recalled in the mammoth diary, 'Elvis Day By Day', makes me think of Paul Gambaccini. His claims in the BBC, radio programme depended on the belief that modern music represents a period equivalent to the enlightenment. For a few brief moments, Elvis, not unlike Isaac Newton, bridged the gap between the dark ages and the very different era that followed but he did no more than that. This may be a pretentious example but there is a historical parallel which will be explored later. Paul Gambaccini has his allegiance and Elvis is simply on the wrong side.

Although his career was disappointing and tragic, Elvis did grow. He constantly re-defined his material and broadened his range to give himself different, vocal challenges. This route was complicated by movie contracts and his physical and emotional decline, so the journey collected too much unfortunate baggage but the journey is still impressive. True, he drifted away from many fans and critics and those who often stayed with him often did so because they were simply unable to resist the voice and, in some instances, the man. But, as Landau said in his review of that Boston concert, Elvis did not need to apologise to anyone.

He recorded material that recognised the present and sometimes anticipated the future but, like Newton again, he always acknowledged the past. He always reminded himself of both his own roots and the different. Although he needed change, he was not prepared to settle for what was merely modern. He was always interested in what had gone before. He was a mix of the traditional and the radical.

Albert Goldman, who wrote the book, 'Elvis', deserves to be condemned for his errors and bigotry against the poor but he has a point when he argues that rock and roll was not modern. Elvis took American music back to where it had been before jazz stylists had remade the blues. It took somebody radical and original to do it but the move itself was reactionary. To pull off this trick, he had to 'goose it up a little', to use the words of Elvis. What happened was that everybody was so entranced with the goosing they failed to notice his intent and direction. Does this actually prove the point made by Gambaccini? No because pop music is still dominated by the rock and roll form. In the main, the inventions of jazz have been ignored and we are still back in the past where Elvis always intended us to be. Critics forget that the middle of the road performers with their tuxedos and cocktails were not traditionalists. In the fifties and sixties, they were committed to the modern and to progress just as much as rock musicians thought they were later. This is why Frank Sinatra and Bing Crosby hated Elvis so much when he appeared. They disliked him because he was taking music backwards and rejecting sophisticated affluence, polish and taste, not because he was introducing the modern. Listen to his version of 'Guitar Man' and, although the record always sounds fresh, it is not difficult to imagine people at the beginning of the last century tapping their feet to the music. There is an alternative history to Gambaccini.

When Elvis appeared in the fifties he challenged the prejudices of the time which insisted upon material being smooth and restrained. Elvis and many others helped demolish these prejudices. After the Beatles, Elvis realises the music world is different from what he expected. The open minded world he thought he had helped usher in does not exist. Instead, there are fresh prejudices that insist on only what is considered modern. The beat in rock and roll now has to prevail over everything. The dark ages still exist but the taboos have changed. Elvis does what he did in the fifties. He records music to challenge these new prejudices, insisting, as he always did, on an open mind. He is obstructed by the demands of his management and makes some bad decisions himself but his intentions can be heard on any Elvis CD.

Like the Gambaccini version, this is not historically accurate either. These half truths understate his human weakness and carelessness but they are just as valid as those of Gambaccini. If anything, the paragraph more accurately describes the career of Ray Charles who, benefiting from more personal strength and supportive management, actually realised his ambitions. Elvis followed a similar path to Ray Charles but his intentions were obscured by weaknesses in himself and an inept management team and record company. Of course, Ray Charles was also condemned for abandoning his roots but, with time, more people have realised his achievement and now accept that he successfully united different aspects of American music to define both himself and his culture.

Although Elvis attempted this as well, it is not as obvious because the appalling efforts in the movies and the much weakened individual of the seventies lead to easy and false conclusions. Faced with this material, critics, like Gambaccini, identify the existence of the good Elvis and the rubbish Elvis. But the rubbish Elvis consists of two elements. First, there actually is the rubbish Elvis, the singer who treats himself and his material with contempt. This person can be heard on most of the movie material and too often in the seventies. But, whilst this is happening, there is also the different Elvis and, although this Elvis is not the rock and roll champion Gambaccini insists upon, this third Elvis is not rubbish. This Elvis can be heard extending his range into simple, trusting Americana in the sixties and wary, folk music and romantic fatalism in the seventies. In the fifties and the 'TV Special', one Elvis dominates. This Elvis is what people describe as the great Elvis, ready to rock and committed to his talent. Outside these periods, though, Elvis was always two performers that existed side by side, one performer not unlike the independent Ray Charles and the other a weary ham servicing the bids of his masters. It does make understanding complicated and it has led many to assume that, outside the fifties and the brief period of his late sixties comeback, Elvis only slumbered. Well, the mid-sixties and the seventies were not his best times but he never abandoned what was important to him, the need to add to his legacy and to extend his range.

Undoubtedly, he could have been more diligent and responsible. There are, though, apart from the rock and roll, two distinct groups of material, one worthy and the other not. Their separate existences imply a responsibility on our part to distinguish between these two groups. Some people will still only like the rock and roll Elvis but, unfortunately, many who make this claim have never attempted to make this distinction.

To repeat, there are three Elvis characters just like there are three Creatures, the two within the novel and the dope in the movies. We have the enthusiastic fifties and comeback Elvis, the cynical Elvis fulfilling contracts and, finally, the obscured Elvis, the independent oracle always filled with remorse like the Creature but constantly trying to define and extend his identity with a broader range of material. This third Elvis wants to 'escape the bitter gall of envy within me' and to be something other than what Parker created, the Satan that 'is an emblem of my condition'. Two of these three characters have merit; one exists before the fall and one after. If this point has been laboured, it is justified. It has been ignored for fifty years.

He became a middle of the road entertainer

What is middle of the road music? Some years ago, on a day like any other, I was obliged to move the coat of my daughter. The weight in the pocket was unusually heavy and I looked. I discovered that my daughter had a dark side. This does not make me unique amongst parents. Our children have secrets and parents think they need to know them, even if knowing is painful. I found an Andy Williams CD.

We talked about it. Quite quickly, she turned the argument into her favour, making me feel guilty about how she had felt compelled to hide the CD. My daughter liked soul music and Elvis but she did belong to her generation and she also liked the indie bands of the day. Nothing as extreme as this, though.

I felt responsible as parents always will when faced with an unexpected revelation.

'Are you shocked?' said my daughter.

'I am but I think we have to go forward,' I said.

'What do you mean?' she said.

'Maybe some jazz,' I said.

I made a Mel Torme CD for her.

It appeared that this middle of the road music was quite fashionable amongst her age group. Apparently, when not listening to music that makes them stare blank eyed at the walls and shake their heads with rage, they like crooners with decent voices singing melodic material. Since the post modernist breakthrough of the generation of my daughter, it has become possible to visit record shops and actually see young people, often of odd appearance, curiously flicking through these CDs. Middle of the road is now called easy listening. The young listen to it as an alternative form, music that they think is pleasant and which offers restrained instrumentation to support decent voices. To them, the music is fresh and clean. The more knowledgeable of these young people claim that there exists within this genre both good and bad music, strong and weak entertainers.

Easy listening is assumed to be flawed because it is unable to deliver the adrenaline fix available through rock and roll. It ignores the roots of American music and lacks soul. I am not an easy listening fan but that does not mean I am resistant to its triumphs when they occur. The Elvis record, 'I Need Somebody To Lean On', with its cocktail style can be described as middle of the road material. It also happens to be fabulous, the record and performance is compulsive from beginning to end. The genre can be a retreat for the mediocre but so can all the genres. This is why country music has countrypolitan and soul music produced Syreeta and Lionel Ritchie. Soul music has never had Val Doonican but easy listening does contain Sinatra whose effort required him to swim underwater to improve his breath control and Peggy Lee who is inspirational. The best of it is closer to jazz than is often realised which is why my daughter enjoyed the Mel Torme CD. My tastes, as I stated above, are American and I prefer its roots because I find the therapy it provides heartening. But that is me. I have never drunk a cocktail and I am not sophisticated. To condemn music, though, for being middle of the road is not adequate. It is no more than the tribal cry of people trapped in adolescent bigotry.

What is odd, though, is that Elvis never really became middle of the road. His stage show was always based on a solid, rock band and there was always a respect for rock and roll. The rock numbers always began the show. When his health really suffered he would take a break on stage and use his band members to provide instrumental solos. None of these were ever melodic or lyrical because his show had to have a certain level of energy. If he could no longer provide or sustain it, his musicians had to substitute. Before his death, Elvis never released an album that was exclusively ballads. Although doped and weary at the end, he managed the odd, rock number. There are the ballads that offend but they are usually country tunes and far removed from the tuxedo world of easy listening. He does very occasionally wander into the middle of the road material but that is Elvis. He wanders into everything, eventually. The stereotype has emerged because of several factors.

Key singles like 'It's Now Or Never' and 'Are You Lonesome Tonight', the material used in the movies, the way he continually extended his material and his final weakening as a performer have all been identified as evidence of middle of the road drift. Although their musical merit is obvious, the big hits 'Never' and 'Lonesome Tonight' were a betrayal of sorts. But they were not typical of the record session that produced them, a session that included the marvellous 'Reconsider Baby', his toughest, darkest and richest blues ever.

At the end of the 1960s, Jerry Lee Lewis released an excellent, country album called 'Another Place, Another Time'. The liner notes referred to Elvis as a retired rock and roller who only crooned for the movies. The writer was convinced Elvis did nothing else. A problem with the movies was that the material was poor. Songs like 'The Meanest Girl In Town' and 'I've Got To Find My Baby' from the film. 'Girl Happy' may have been terrible, lifeless rock and roll but, on these records, he is definitely not crooning. Elvis lacked commitment but to say this was not enough. If Elvis was bad, it could only be because he was no longer rock and roll and one of us.

Elvis was never the ultimate, rock and roll hero but he should not be criticized for this. Rock and roll was part of his armoury but a man with a voice that could produce top As at will had to have other ambitions. These ambitions were best realised in his American Sound sessions in Memphis where rock material was included but slow numbers actually dominated. The derided ballads that followed in the seventies differ from the acclaimed performances of Memphis in 1969 because Elvis had deteriorated. If he had kept his health, he would have controlled better his material and performances.

Elvis did not become middle of the road but he did in 1971, suddenly and without warning, become prematurely old and this happened after his best years had been wasted on movie pap. The decline in his health and the events which led to that deterioration did tilt his material, commitment and approach but he usually offered a balance of music. His heart was no longer engaged with what he was doing and this was confirmed when he destroyed himself quite quickly after the catalytic events of 1971. Self-destruction is not an act normally associated with middle of the road performers. The belief that he abandoned the rock and roll myth and embraced the sentimental myth is erroneous and ignores the drug sodden corpse. To say Elvis became middle of the road is not only inaccurate but insensitive and even callous. What happened to Elvis was much darker and much more tragic and a huge distance from the secure conformity of the tuxedoed. It involved an escape into an icy waste inside his head and concluded with a funeral that burned brightly for television, one that had white limousines instead of snow.

He is crass and the white suits are embarrassing

There was probably never a time when it was simple to decide what were the strengths and weaknesses of popular music. Critical opinion has always embraced faith in the sophisticated and the progressive whilst defending what it regarded as the uncomplicated and the naive. This has often been done without any hint that these positions might be contradictory. Heroes are segregated and different standards are applied depending on the banner being carried. Modern, rock stars will be expected to be uncompromised, free spirited individuals, men and women who can lead their followers into the future, whereas figures from the poor, rural past can be excused from these demands. Black culture and history complicates it even further because this is often viewed as standing apart. Blues singers were automatically assumed to be men who could also face the required future, unhindered spirits whose intolerance of hard work and appreciation of good whisky and big legged women were to be applauded. This view, which prevailed throughout most of my life, is clearly racist but it was never regarded as such. Many people thought they were being sympathetic to an oppressed people.

Sometimes, country singers have also been honoured as antagonistic alternatives to conformity, Hank Williams, for example, but nobody really believes country musicians existed completely outside the values of their unfashionable community. Their belief in God and country was usually avoided rather than denied.

We remain intolerant of the supposedly naive when they embrace another culture. The sophisticated can borrow culture and they assume it is to their credit because it involves no aspiration for them but they are quick to disapprove when the opposite happens with people they regard as less informed. Their nominated working class heroes have to avoid those values that challenge what is important to the sophisticated. The naive should not be sentimental or adopt the materialistic aspirations that the sophisticated who, because they are affluent, can regard as unimportant. The situation is complicated. The inconsistencies, double standards and self-serving judgements are numerous and infect us all when we are deciding what merit exists in others.

Elvis was unusual and often bewildering but he had the responsibility of carrying a career well beyond his background. There was a distance between him and his critics. Praise was not always withheld but he was invariably judged according to their values and not his. The easiest option for the critics, and me, was to deny him his career, keep him within his roots. This happens to many musicians. Elvis suffered particularly because, in his case, the personal distance between him and the critics was huge. The problem was magnified when this distance increased with his success. Unfortunately, he had no creative support to help him manage that distance.

Elvis is not the only naive, poorly nurtured victim in popular music. He merely happens to be the most famous. Many of the other victims, in particular, blues singers, finished their working lives as janitors or pumping gas. It does not mean, either, that Elvis did not have will power or made regrettable decisions. Personal responsibility is not incompatible with victimhood. It is not difficult to imagine a talented, blues guitarist cleaning out the school toilet and wishing he had done another take of his one record release. The absence of that extra take does not mean he is not a victim. Without able, experienced mentors, most of us can be quite dumb. Even if Guralnick is right and there are no villains in the story of Elvis Presley, he has to acknowledge that after Sam Phillips there is a real absence of supportive people.

Most of us have seen the movie, 'Amadeus', and now know that Mozart was a scatological adolescent with hardly a sensitive bone in his body. This book is supposed to be about the talent of Elvis and not his personality. If others dismiss him simply because they think he was thick and fat, it is not important. The only charge in this particular criticism is that, like Mozart, Elvis was a bit of an idiot.

Except, rock and roll writing in my generation was dependent on a faith which asserted that rock and roll stars were enlightened heroes, people who could carry the banner of the moment. The rock establishment demanded and believed in people who, according to Greil Marcus, said no. Most of us should now realise that rock and roll never did produce heroes and what we regarded as enlightenment is proving to be something quite different. Dylan, who has paraded his non-conformist edge as blatantly as anyone, was a man of his age. Do we think Hendrix, like Elvis, unable to control either his appetites or paranoia was a hero? Many vintage rock and rollers claim that Jerry Lee Lewis, rather than Elvis, is the more admirable rock and roll figure but they soon look at the floor when you mention the dead wife in his bedroom with her head blown off by his hand gun. These people were musicians, people who needed the approval of an audience. I may be small minded but I cannot imagine Shane being a credible hero if the saved family had clapped him at the end of the film. True heroes do not invite applause.

The musical giants were able in their performances, though, to appear to be capable of this, to look like heroic warriors, talents who could make us adore rather than patronise. This was done through a mixture of novelty, fashion, attitude, daring and a hunger for complete attention. In this respect, Elvis was as capable as others but we are talking about a stage show, a performance. John Wayne was not a Western hero, he was an actor. Their tricks spill over into identity but we are still only engaged with appearance. Elvis revealed similar leakage in a press conference in Houston when a journalist asked him about his elaborate outfit.

'If you see the stage show it makes sense,' he said.

The journalist never said what should have been obvious to all. 'But Elvis you are not on stage now.'

Elvis may have failed himself but, as a musician, he left us with 'heroic' moments and, as the records of his later concerts reveal, these moments did not disappear entirely. During a celebration of Queen Elizabeth 2, I cannot remember which, many rock stars participated in a musical tribute and they all appeared on stage in the finale to sing Happy Birthday. Brian Wilson was lost in the crowd looking fragile and damaged and Paul McCartney at the front led the sing along.

McCartney made a smug bow at the end and said, 'Thank you, Ma'am.'

The pliancy of these rebels was as depressing as the visit of Elvis to Richard Nixon to claim his police badge. Aretha Franklin had been invited to participate in the show and had seriously considered being involved. Elvis was dead and not willing to attend but it was possible to imagine him there and somehow alive and well. In his life, the political views of Elvis might have been all too accommodating of the unworthy. His personal flaws also deny him admiration. It would, though, have been a different evening if he had participated. The show and its monarchist message would have been unable to contain him in the way it did McCartney and the others. Without him wanting to challenge, it would have taken no more than a grin or gesture from him to expose the limitations of this particular elite. Something similar would have happened if Aretha had attended. The Royal Family would have been much diminished from being exposed to the talent and the democratic pomp of Aretha or Elvis. Neither Elvis nor Aretha sustained that pomp throughout their careers but we held our breath when they did. As David Thomson said of Orson Welles, 'He inhaled legend and changed the air we breathe.' So he did. So did Aretha. So did Elvis. They produced moments of liberation that only the truly gifted can share with their audiences. Much of it is illusion but nobody minds because the deceit is dipped in the magic of their talent.

This is what we need to remember. Not the disappointing moments and failures when they weaken and make inevitable mistakes. Others may be more consistent. When there is no need for transcendence, though, the achievement of consistency becomes less difficult. This is why the bright flames of the fabulous can burn out so quickly and the modestly gifted often improve over time. We need to remember only the moments that made the greats fabulous, not indulge prejudices that lead us to falsely expect kindred spirits or heroes. Elvis delivered these moments.

Unfortunately, Elvis became fat and he wore the white suit. The weight we now know to be a consequence of an eating disorder that was a consequence of depression, drugs and a lethal Southern diet. The irony is that Elvis was a poor eater as a child as was the Creature who, in his brief life, had to survive on berries and vegetables. It may have been no more than faddishness but, possibly, food was valued so highly in the impoverished, Presley family that Elvis felt obliged to eat sparingly. Aretha avoided the drugs because she watched soap operas, instead, but she also suffered from the same diet. Despite her weight problem, she still remains the only woman on the planet whose good name I used my fists to defend but that is another story and it did involve alcohol and a short temper.

The white suit deserves special attention. The irony is that Elvis did not like to wear white on stage but preferred black. In his first shows in Vegas, he wore a black suit as he did in the 'TV Special'. Some damned, lighting technician suggested that white would make it easier for him to light Elvis on stage. As W H Auden nearly said, power and influence never reside where you expect.

The image of the suit has become seriously dated but it was not considered that outlandish in the seventies. Elvis was the first to wear a jump suit and many followed. These included major, rock stars such as Mick Jagger and David Bowie and many black performers like Bobby Womack, Wilson Pickett and Earth, Wind And Fire. In fact, the only rock performer I remember avoiding similar attire back then was Bob Dylan. Elvis, though, persisted with the jump suit longer than most and he did become fat. It has become an unpleasant memory but, when he appeared in the 1970 documentary, 'That's The Way It Is', it was greeted at the time as a magnificent image.

I remember sitting in the now closed Pelican restaurant in London with a friend. He had just had his second book published and it had been nominated for a 'Guardian' literary award for that year. Predictably, the book and the friend dominated the conversation but, equally predictably, I sneaked Elvis into our chat.

'I admit that he made classic records but I am not sure the substantial criticism is undeserved,' he said. 'Elvis was a dumb boy, I reckon. I am no fan of the white suits and the show business.'

Scotty Moore, when interviewed after the death of Elvis, admitted he did not care for Elvis in the seventies. 'That was show business,' he said.

It is only a suit but it is clear to many that it indicated not only a change in direction but a major flaw in the man. When my friend in the restaurant made the link between the suits, show business and stupidity the remark was left to stand unchallenged. I may have been weak but writers who have just had a book nominated for a major award adopt a certain tone in conversation that soon convinces you argument is futile. Old, retired rock stars speak in similar fashion. What did Scotty Moore mean when he said that Elvis was showbusiness in the seventies?

Elvis always thought he had a career in show business. If he was being cynical, he would refer to the music industry as a racket. When he appeared on stage in the fifties the object was to entertain the crowd and this was done with a mixture of music, flirtation, energy and effect. The approach in the seventies may have been different but the elements were the same. The remark by Scotty Moore implies that he is the serious musician who avoided show business but this neglects him indolently hanging up his guitar in the early seventies. At least, Elvis kept working and entertaining.

In the early eighties, BBC 2 ran an all night tribute to the blues. It consisted of what the BBC had in its vaults. The clips and shows were linked by a presenter with a superior tone, posh Midlands. BB King was always keen to promote the blues and, with his famous guitar, Lucille, he generously appeared between clips to discuss the music. One of the items was an edited version of a BB King concert. After the show finished, the programme returned to the studio.

The presenter looked at BB King and said, 'That, of course, is the blues as entertainment.'

BB King is not only a gentleman but is devoted to his guitars, otherwise, we might have seen a BBC presenter with a six string Gibson rammed down his throat. The arrogance and the rudeness of the remark may be astonishing but it contains no surprises. BB King would have argued the same as Elvis and that nothing had changed. He is paid to put on a show for the folks and what you pretentious, city idiots do with it is your business. The remark by the BBC presenter implied that blues musicians must not only maintain the content of back home but also ensure they demonstrate that it and they have integrity. Back home has its special merits and I accept some of the material included in his seventies shows reduced Elvis but, when the argument is levelled at BB King in such an uncharitable way, one has to conclude that this aesthetic has always been charged with snobbery. Either you be like us, which you never will be, or ensure that you exist in your charming, primitive singularity which we can pretend exists without commercial compromises and corny tricks. The telling irony is that the white suit is not show business. It is pure back home.

To understand the white suit, it is necessary to look at the guitar Elvis wears on stage. In between the frets, there are silver letters that spell his name This is back home as well and was first used by country singers before the Second World War. Jimmie Rodgers, the country blues yodeller, is a famous example. Elvis probably spotted it as a child and included it in his shows as a reference to his roots. It is interesting that, at a point in his career when he was expected to master the modern, he would be prepared to delve so far back into the past. But his reactionary, musical impulses have been mentioned earlier. Like his guitar, the white suit refers to the past, to the suits embroidered with rhinestone that country singers wore. Hank Williams used to wear white jackets adorned with large, musical notes. Why not? It is not obligatory to wear a polar neck when sharing existential angst. The fancy clothes had a specific purpose in country music, to let the audience know a big star was in town. What is unusual is how the suits, which Elvis wears, attempt to combine this country tradition of rhinestone and decoration with the freer and bolder outfits worn by black performers. The white suits combine the two back home cultures, white and black, exaggerated by the excesses of the seventies. The number of the black performers who adopted the jump suit supports this view.

The song, 'An American Trilogy', like the white suits, has also been condemned as show business. It is not. It is back home like the white suit and was included to please the people that Elvis thought he understood, his own. When the musicians queried 'An American Trilogy' being included in his show Elvis replied, 'It will go down well with my crowd.'

Elvis knew that the song, 'An American Trilogy', offended his critics but he had other priorities. He also needed it as bombast to replace the rock and roll he could no longer manage. This unrestrained tradition of musicians giving the people what will make them happy is strong in the American South. It exists within the songs of the great but neglected The Sons Of The Pioneers but it is also shared by visionary, Hank Williams, who, despite his gloomy insights, not only charged his audience to watch him marry on stage but also had another audience pay to watch the rehearsal. Two blissful, wedding ceremonies that would be followed by repertoires committed to doom and tragedy. Gospel singer, Sister Rosetta Tharpe, also married on stage and she released an album of the performance that followed the ceremony.

Many of the big, power ballads he delivered on stage in the seventies are best appreciated now on a CD played loudly. This allows the listener to imagine Elvis without global success and somewhere in the American South. I picture him in a large tent, anointing his audience with his flash clothes and top As. Anyone not convinced should listen to his live versions of 'Unchained Melody' or 'How Great Thou Art' or read the Nic Cohn review of an Elvis concert at Long Island in 1975 when he watched and heard Elvis sing 'You'll Never Walk Alone' and felt his spine turn to mush. Elvis celebrates his past and his audience with both his material and his fake, 'showbiz' glamour.

The white suits are embarrassing because he wore them for too long and became fat. Elvis Presley, sentimental and flash, nothing could be worse. The critics are right, he was unsophisticated. But this aspect of his nature he made into a virtue. It enabled him to not only connect with his audience but to value them. Ultimately, his self-destruction meant he failed not only himself but the people he thought he was valuing but time has moved on and they, in the main, have forgiven him and so have I. What we cherish now is his unchanging, democratic faith in ordinary people. What makes him awful also makes him great.

The Creature was not a crude monster but it required special circumstances for this to be recognised, the blindness of the man in the forest and the moment the Creature revealed to Robert Walton his grief over the death of Frankenstein. These were moments when the easy condemnations were challenged. Sloppy thinking will always exist about the Creature. It is only avoided if we read the novel, recognise his potential and understand his response to a world that denied him. Similarly, we have to do more than dismiss Elvis as a fat man in a white suit. The curious listen to the more obscure Elvis records and, by accepting his insistence that his concerns are ackowledged, they recognise his talent.

In his movies he looked like an idiot

In 1969, a music paper, probably 'Disc And Music Echo', claimed it had a full and frank interview with Elvis. The interview was a little thin. Elvis managed about a dozen words and he definitely repeated the words yep and nope. He was asked if he regretted making so many movies of dubious quality. Supposedly, Elvis grinned and answered, 'The movies are for city folks.'

Perhaps Elvis said no more than yep and nope to everything and the desperate journalist took a chance and threw in a wisecrack to beef up his article. I would like it to be true, like to think that maybe Elvis consoled himself with the thought that if he had to suffer so did the sophisticates. What we do know is that he hated his movies. This is apparent from what others have subsequently said and from the interviews he did for the movie, 'Elvis On Tour', when he talked about how they made him feel discouraged and ill.

Inevitably, revisionists have argued that the movies can be watched and appreciated for their sub-text. They have explained that the films often began life as earnest scripts written by talented writers. Unable to be filmed as a serious project, these scripts were then adapted for Elvis. The revisionists have a point. There often is a sub-text and, between songs, Elvis is faced with moral choices that involve choosing between freedom or responsibility, male camaraderie or romance with a potential spouse. Elvis movies also continue the Howard Hawks tradition of movie making, a straightforward narrative of men and women trying to relate to each other against a background of masculine action and ambition. Surprisingly, this has never been properly recognised but the Hawks movie, 'Red Line 7000', is disturbingly like an Elvis film without the songs. The

Elvis movie, 'Spinout', actually used a Howard Hawks scriptwriter. None of this, though, prevents the obvious from being true. The movies were indeed awful. Even the exceptions are only partially successful.

'Jailhouse Rock' is my favourite because it is a good example of what Elvis would have achieved if he had found the company of malcontented Marxists more often. The script was based on a story by blacklisted writer, Ned Young. The scene where Elvis slams his guitar down on the table of a not sufficiently attentive listener is surely a reference to the story in the memoirs of Duke Ellington. Supposedly, Will Marion Cook barged in on a critic who had hailed him as the finest, black violinist. Cook smashed his violin on the desk shouting, 'I am not the world's greatest black violinist. I am the world's greatest violinist.'

Surprisingly, Elvis never made a bad film with a talented director. These were 'King Creole', 'Flaming Star' and 'Viva Las Vegas'. 'Jailhouse Rock' was directed by Richard Thorpe, a limited talent who was fortunate enough to have the film carried by a decent script, some good songs and a star who delivered. 'Follow That Dream', which was also entertaining, was made by the competent journeyman, Gordon Douglas.

In another BBC 2 radio show on Elvis, Peter Guralnick excused Thomas Parker from culpability. He stated that the only mistake Parker made was to underestimate the long term appeal of rock and roll. Parker, though, was the man who refused to read the scripts and insisted he sacrifice any quality control on either the scripts or production values. This meant that Elvis not only had to endure mediocre directors but, on one occasion, was obliged to star in a film directed by a mediocre talent who had actually become blind, Norman Taurog.

Parker was cynical and destructive but, considering his values, it could have been worse. After he had big hits in the sixties, Roy Orbison starred in a film called 'The Fastest Guitar Alive'. No prizes for guessing for whom the film was originally intended. The film, a Western, was an unwatchable disaster. The sets were cheap and lit by a strange, orange light which, somehow, persisted when the film moved outdoors. The main problem was, sad to say, the Big O. His acting ability was so limited that a single line of dialogue to him was as impossible as the role of Lear. This could have been ignored by the charitable but the falsetto that was the source of his musical appeal also meant he had a poor, speaking voice.

Worse than this, the Big O without his dark glasses could barely open his eyes. His humiliation was the consequence of commercial cynicism.

Elvis complained that the films made him feel ill but a bad stomach does not necessarily excuse responsibility. Certainly, all the other rock stars watched what happened to Elvis and, from that point, approached movie contracts warily. The Beatles did two films and one documentary and Dylan limited himself in Hollywood to a cameo in the Sam Peckinpah Western, 'Pat Garrett And Billy The Kid'.

If it is difficult to imagine Dylan or The Beatles agreeing to appear in three films a year, it is impossible to believe that they would sacrifice their right to choose suitable scripts. Just as difficult to conceive are managers treating their headline clients in such a manner. Parker was not a manager, he was an exploiter and he only ever regarded Presley as a property. Clearly, it was a difficult position for Elvis. Parker was not only wilful, he could be persuasive and he did have financial figures to support his arguments. Initially, the musicals made money and the soundtrack albums outsold the studio albums. These were his arguments. His actual intentions, revealed by his willingness to work with schlock, Hollywood producer, Sam Katzman, were much darker. Parker had contempt, aggression and cruelty and all are essential for the galvaniser. Frankenstein not only refused to give life to the female he created for the Creature, he savagely destroyed his female creation, committed a murder where none was needed. Parker insisted upon redundant junk.

It is painful for an audience to endure a screening of 'Harum Scarum' and it must have been even worse for its lead actor. The rest of the cast were no doubt glad to be working, even, if it was only for fifteen days and the lighting on the set was so inadequate nobody in the cinemas would see them. But Elvis was not another actor. He was the most successful rock and roll musician of his generation. 'Harum Scarum' was made after the British invasion led by The Beatles and The Rolling Stones. For another three years, Elvis continued making these films without indicating he knew he should respond to the challenge. Ultimately, he could have mutinied but it would have taken courage to sacrifice fame, fortune and numerous Hollywood women for possible obscurity. Not every actor would have reacted to 'Harum Scarum' by walking away from a million dollars a picture. Elvis, though, cannot be denied some responsibility.

The tragedy is that Elvis understood his moral failure. The protests he makes to the directors of 'Elvis On Tour' in 1972 are not unequivocal admissions of shame but what is obvious is that the despair over what happened has not been dissipated by the success of his recent comeback. Elvis knew he had betrayed his talent and the knowledge within self-betrayal frequently ensures it is repeated before a life is completed. Meanwhile, his inept manager merely observed.

In the beginning, Elvis did try to resist. As early as his first movie, 'Love Me Tender', he made complaints about his movie songs and how they were produced. The four songs from the movie are tolerable but he was right to complain. The Hollywood musicians are competent but they are at ease, well-fed spirits and the records lack the edge of his other fifties material. Few of the record buying public complained, so it is clear that this Elvis, the one that existed in 1956, not only had standards but was willing to communicate those standards. Afterwards, mumbles and complaints were made periodically. When Elvis was obliged to sing 'Old McDonald's Farm' for the film, 'Double Trouble', in 1966 his main protests, though, were to his wife, Priscilla, back at Graceland. Elvis was either a changed or broken man or, maybe, both.

Oddly, his vocal performances of this material can be interpreted as his real protest. Although there are rare exceptions, after 1961 he treats his movie material with contempt. Whether this was a sound strategy is debateable. His desultory efforts probably did contribute to declining sales and profit and this led to the Hollywood contracts not being renewed. Unfortunately, Parker was slow to react. Nothing satisfied the ego of his manager more than persuading the suckers to buy junk. It also meant Elvis wasted much of the decent material that did exist. Those who only blame the songwriters should listen to 'Power Of My Love' and 'Rubberneckin'. The former is written by Giant, Baum and Kaye, names that feature frequently on his soundtrack albums. The latter was actually included in a film. Because Elvis is motivated, and working in Memphis with a talented producer, he adapts material supplied by movie songwriters to create tracks that are now regarded as essential.

Ultimately, one should have some sympathy for Elvis. He did let himself down but he was badly exposed by being the first global, rock and roll star and he was cynically exploited. His human weakness was revealed and that is a price in itself but the damage to his career and his achievements cannot be underestimated. He is still famous and appreciated by some for the fine records that exist within the dross but this was a man who, with care from others, could have shaped and directed American music throughout his life. My view is that the British dominance in the sixties would never have happened without these movies. If Elvis managed by someone else had signed for Atlantic records, he may have actually fulfilled his potential and integrated popular music with jazz. It never happened and that is what I regret. My curiosity remains unsatisfied. If this sounds fanciful, listen to the final verse of his version of 'Such A Night' or all of 'I Need Somebody To Lean On'.

Elvis was weak which ensured he was obliged to pay for normal corruption in a way that the talentless escape. The payment he made certainly includes a long standing underestimation of his worth and talent. His later self-destruction had many causes but, if the exploitation by Hollywood precipitated his self-hatred, premature death has to be included in the final accounting.

It has to be more than coincidence that Hollywood had to insist that both Elvis and the Creature were inarticulate idiots, had to turn away from the souls that made them memorable. Modern society has left me with a bad taste all my life that no growth chart in 'The Economist' ever sweetens. The youth of the sixties assumed foolishly that music would be an escape, an alternative to the worship of money and hierarchy. What happened to Elvis should tell us what is hateful about the modern world.

He was no more than a pretty boy with a voice

The criticism is actually worded in a way that demonstrates progress. For many years, his opponents denied he could even sing, so it is clear that he has always inspired many to minimise his ability. When 'Frankenstein' was published more than one critic insisted there must be an alternative author, such a book could not have been written by a woman. When the person behind the talent is not acceptable we are capable of sidestepping either, the talent or the person. Even from their first records, The Beatles always rated higher approval from the establishment. This is explained by the different nature of their talents, the singer-songwriter compared to the singer. It does not, though, explain the hatred that Elvis always generated. Only later, because of the mismanagement of his career and his self-destruction, was this hatred converted to contempt and scorn. The hatred of Elvis is best understood by reading the Albert Goldman biography, 'Elvis', which has been rightly condemned for its complete absence of human sympathy. The most positive view of Elvis that emerges from this book, but only briefly, is that Elvis could have been a man of soul but his indolence and dirt ignorance ensured he would always be inferior to the superior people who inspired Goldman. The repellent prejudice of Goldman is exposed by this remark. 'A more deracinated race cannot be imagined – just as the hillbillies had no real awareness of the present they had no grasp of the past.' In this version, Elvis, descended from inferior hillbillies, amounts to no more than an uncultured talent in an unlikeable man.

Not only did the hatred of Elvis exist, it prompted the absurd belief that he is not musical. Thinking of him as an untalented idiot has always provided comfort for many. It is true, he could not be bothered placing his fingers on the guitar chords when posing for publicity shots for his movies but it is clear from his 'TV Special' that he can play a guitar. He is limited but has a distinct and very bluesy style and there is a key moment in the show when he swops his acoustic with the electric guitar of Scotty Moore. The inference is clear. The proceedings need extra drive and he can provide it on the electric which, of course, is what he does.

Most fans now know what happened when he recorded the song, 'Baby I Don't Care'. Elvis played bass instead of Bill Black who had stormed out of the studio because of his failure to master the part. Supposedly, Elvis simply picked up the bass and said, 'We can do this. I can manage the bass.' Not only does he manage the part, he adds a flourish at the end of the record that for the times was almost revolutionary. Elvis has also played piano on some of his records. In the eighties, experienced, record producer, Robert Matthew Walker, wrote in his book, 'Heartbreak Hotel', an interesting analysis of all of the records made by Elvis. His account is by someone who has a musical and professional ear and it makes a pleasant change from the usual, unmusical critic. He describes Elvis as a talented pianist. Chet Atkins, his record producer, but no soul mate, once famously said, 'Hell, he was different. He was musical. He could play guitar, piano and drums.'

Gene Smith, a cousin of Elvis, has said something like, 'I remember the first time Elvis played the piano. He taught himself. It took him about half an hour.'

That definitely sounds musical to me.

The split that occurred between Elvis and Scotty Moore, Bill Black and DJ Fontana inevitably featured complaints about money but there were other factors. One was that Elvis had agreed that they could record an instrumental album at the end of the sessions that produced the 'Christmas album' in 1957. Parker refused for the usual reason, it was an event beyond his control and Elvis had agreed without a fee to complete the instrumental group on piano. It is interesting that Scotty, Bill and DJ had no doubts that he would cope as their pianist.

Also interesting is the famous, 'Million Dollar Quartet' session that occurred when Elvis returned to Sun Studios in 1956. Elvis dominates this session and plays the piano while Jerry Lee Lewis merely accompanies vocally. Admittedly, this may not have occurred later when Jerry Lee was more famous but it still happened and Jerry Lee, not a man distinguished by self-effacement, accepted his minor role until Elvis departed. Elvis was always more than a singer which is why he was able to create himself as a singer of such potency.

Jerry Schilling has always insisted that Elvis has always been underrated as a record producer. According to Schilling, this ability is rooted in his exceptional hearing. Others have referred to his extraordinary memory. But can his dominance be narrowed to such specifics? More likely, his musical gift facilitates advantages like similar gifts do for linguists or mathematicians who remember languages and multiplication tables quicker than the rest of us. Music is easier and clearer to him than others and this is obvious from the many outtakes that now exist. The outtake, 'One Night Of Sin', is an important example of Elvis waiting patiently for his musicians to acquire his mastery of the material. Released on the 'Follow That Dream' label is a two CD version of his 1956 album, 'Elvis Presley'. Take after take, he delivers astonishing and flawless performances.

Later, it was different and Elvis strung out on dope became less of a musician. Goldman makes the point that Elvis had problems with his hearing in the last phase of his life. As a child, he had chronic ear trouble and had urine poured into his ears as a possible cure. It may have been the subsequent difficulties with his once superior hearing that contributed to his unwillingness in the seventies to visit the studio. In this phase, the last six years, Elvis relied much more on the arrangements in the demos. From 1971, he became more like the creature described by his critics. There is a famous story about P J Proby. P J is at a music festival in Europe and has to rehearse a ballad with an Italian orchestra. At the end of the rehearsal, the maestro puts down his baton and says, 'Mr Proby, how do you do it?'

'I don't do,' says P J. 'I am.'

In the seventies, Elvis often was no more than that. But it was enough. Although the music in this period was uneven, he usually gave a song a different feel. There are periods, though, when he was much more. These occurred most in the fifties but, in the period following the comeback and before the decline, there are many examples that can only be described as Elvis creations. 'I'll Hold You In My Heart', 'Stranger In My Own Home Town' and 'After Loving You' are not the records the producer, Chips Moman, would have made willingly. At the time, he must have listened to them with gritted teeth but, I suspect, he now acknowledges them as highlights of these sessions. Only the hard of hearing can listen to the early takes of the plodding arrangement of 'True Love Travels On A Gravel Road' and not appreciate how Elvis uses his sixties, musical memories to transform the song into something to be cherished. There are similar moments in the Nashville sessions of 1970 and many of these are featured on the 'Elvis Country' album. Often, within his catalogue, there are examples that would have been used to define the careers of lesser performers, individual records that almost constitute a genre within themselves. The really weird and now sadly neglected 'Is It So Strange' has no precedent. This record can only be described as Gothic Doo Wop and why it has never featured on the soundtrack of a vampire movie is beyond me. More influential is the rockabilly defining 'Baby Let's Play House'.

Elvis was, though, uncouth to some and, because this made him repellent, his fluency, like that of the Creature, was unheard by them. They found the temptation to dismiss him as a pretty boy impossible to resist. He was a hell of a singer and he was, like all the true greats, a unique creative force capable of creating music that did not exist within the imagination of others. In his final, weaker moments, he relied more on his presence to lift a song but there are still examples of alternative approaches. His version of 'Blue Eyes Crying In The Rain' suffers because his voice is wrecked but, not quite capable and stoned, he still manages a bluesy arrangement that is both novel and inspiring.

His music is embarrassingly simple

Tolstoy at the beginning of 'War And Peace' claims simplicity, goodness and truth as the three great virtues, so it depends on your perspective whether you think simple is a strength or a weakness. Simple that works for the audience is difficult but worthwhile because it ensures that the quality that exists is more than clever sophistication. These uncomplicated triumphs that move others remain unaffected and undiminished by time because something not obvious resides in the memory of the listener or viewer, a quality worth more than applied creativity. The simple that succeeds is easily appreciated. There are, of course, many who claim their work is not difficult and open to all if only we will let ourselves respond emotionally. What they forget to say is that their creations are so simple they usually induce boredom.

The Elvis version of 'Tomorrow Is A Long Time' is a note for note steal from the singer Odetta. This should diminish his achievement but it does not. Odetta sings the same arrangement but she needs to add the odd inflection to sustain interest. A talented and interesting performer she may be but she is unable to rely on only the quality of her voice in the same way Elvis can. If he had not appeared, her version would have been appreciated for being an interesting arrangement of a good song. She would have been credited with sustaining a heartfelt performance and it would have been noted that her singing had been enhanced by moments of astute, vocal shading. Indeed, all this is meritorious but, after Elvis, it merely feels like trickery. We can acknowledge Odetta for creating the arrangement but the Elvis version is what we want to hear. Life is not fair. What he has done is horrible because, in this instance, Odetta has been vanquished by a rogue and a thief.

His version has suspense and tension but the source of the suspense cannot be heard or identified because it is completely achieved without effect. It exists like an invisible presence in a great photograph. We are obliged to experience rather than listen.

Dylan picked the version by Elvis as his favourite recording by another singer of one of his songs. 'It's so simple,' he said.

Of course, it has been argued that this is what happens when Elvis records subtle and mature material and, too often, his material is anything but this. I am not convinced. It is not the lyrics of 'Tomorrow Is A Long Time' that holds the attention but his performance. Elvis fills it with anguish and consequence. He does something similar with many other songs. He makes the normally unappealing 'Hawaiian Wedding Song' echo not only with the joy of commitment but the bleak uncertainty that will follow.

The simplicity in the music of Elvis is essential. If we are obliged to be critical, it is a consequence of his great weakness, his self-obsession and vanity. This means that his music is mainly about him and needs space so he can dominate. But Elvis is such a strong and complex personality, it does not feel like a weakness to me. His rock and roll needs, and is enriched by, his innocent ambition and appetites. His ballads give vent to his persistent doubt and it is always apparent that the doubt is a challenge to himself and his faith. The best of them remind me of the Southern characters in the novels of Flannery O'Connor. Fallen and tawdry, useless human beings in a hopeless world, they still retain their belief in God and the only possible consolation He can provide but they know that this consolation, because it is a dependency, will take them further away from redemption. If the music of Elvis was not simple, it would not be possible to imagine these overtones.

Stephen Sondheim insisted that simple is difficult to achieve. Simple is important but not merely because it allows for complex and meaningful emotional resonance. I was eight years old when I first heard Elvis. Now, I am not as sophisticated or as understanding as I would like to be but the eight year old child was a much cruder creature. The simplicity of his music welcomed me and the glorious moments that were enjoyed, rather than appreciated, not only confirmed me as a fan, they provided me with an odd faith in myself and a taste for growth. They inspired a curiosity, yearning and interest. Not just in Elvis but other American music, books and movies. Simple is important because it changes lives.

The lyrics to his songs are banal and embarrassing

Virtually all of the songs recorded by Elvis are in the first person and are concerned with romance. This is never explored in a meaningful way and the songs either say the world is wonderful because his love is reciprocated or appalling because his love is rejected. There is little to indicate why the women whom he thinks are wonderful should be considered as such or why the end of the relationship may be inevitable. In many of his big hits, there are remarkably few words. He does not pick songs for the appeal of their word play and they are short of humour and irony.

There are exceptions but not enough of them to invalidate the argument. The argument, though, is not entirely relevant. The great Elvis records exist despite the lack of lyrical quality. The corny failures which do exist are not a consequence of Elvis selecting inappropriate lyrics but because he has misjudged the arrangement or because Elvis is too sincere in his approach. For example, the critics of 'It's Now Or Never' dislike the operatic ambition and regard it as a betrayal of rock and roll. The lyrics are actually quite risqué and were widely condemned at the time. The harmonica player, Larry Adler, appeared on TV and said the song was vulgar and about sex. He meant it as a criticism. These days, the same arguments are used to defend the record. The point is a simple one. It is the arrangement and the delivery that matters more than the lyrics when deciding if material is embarrassing.

Popular culture needs irony and it is his lack of irony with the sweeter material that weakens Elvis but it is a flaw he shares with many other country musicians of his generation. Elvis has a sense of humour and is more than capable of a sneer but, unlike Jerry Lee Lewis, it is not permanent. This makes him more interesting and more ambitious than Jerry Lee but many rock and roll fans prefer Jerry Lee because his sneer is everlasting. He is the great exception amongst white, Southern singers and, for this reason, is acceptable to English taste in American music. They like their music to contain only the contempt and anger, devotion and dependency are taboo. This explains why many are exclusively loyal to rock and roll and the blues. It is also why the song, 'Suspicious Minds', is so popular amongst non-Elvis fans, why this song more than others is deemed acceptable. The devotion and dependency are recognised as both ruinous and fundamental and this keeps everyone happy, the romantics and the cynics. There is also a hint of anger in the performance.

If Elvis is in the mood, he can transform most material which is what he did in his three golden periods, 1954-1958, 1960-1961 and 1968-1970. The absence of meaningful, lyrical content may be a handicap but he overcomes it when in form. We listen to Elvis for his performances, the musicality within them and the emotion behind those performances. He corrupted me a long time ago. I notice the odd line but I now find it impossible to quote any song in full. We do not listen to his records for word play although there are the odd songs with amusing moments.

But we should not assume that meaningful lyrics are widely prevalent in the material of other performers. Clearly, some songwriters are better than others but even the lyrics of the best songs usually need a tune to support them. These songs contain brilliant lines but that is often what they are, lines only, and their achievements usually consist of wit or a memory that is poignant and accurate. When sung such lines can appear profound but few would tempt Seamus Heaney to plagiarise.

Perhaps it is inevitable. A genuine poem put to music would not leave enough room for the performers to provide the musical contribution we need and like to remember. Peggy Lee does a marvellous version of 'The Folks Who Live On The Hill'. Her brilliance is that she is able to reveal horror whilst supposedly communicating her heartfelt belief that what disturbs the listener will only provide her with happiness. Despite our knowledge, we travel willingly and pleasantly with her to existential defeat. If the lyrics themselves had provided that horror, the record would be neither powerful nor seductive. So, perhaps, the modest contributions of lyrics to a song are evidence that these lyricists are cleverer than we think. Elvis was a great performer and he always had enough willpower to want to make his own contribution. It is his contributions that we value and not the lyrics.

He recorded too much rubbish

This argument has been effectively argued by David Bowie. 'There is just too much rubbish,' he once said.

So there is but, as I type this, I am listening to an Elvis CD of

up-tempo, catchy material I recently made for a very young relative. I will
pick the first five songs on the CD. They are:

'Mystery Train'
'His Latest Flame'
'I Got Stung'
'I Need Your Love Tonight'
'A Mess Of Blues'

These are all great records and I would classify 'His Latest Flame',
'Mystery Train' and 'A Mess Of Blues' as sublime achievements. All
five, though, make the David Bowie hit, 'Jean Genie', sound inadequate,
nothing more than crude sing along posing as rock and roll.

The sublime is important and we are frequently too willing to
confuse the clever and the original with the transcendent. Bowie and
many other performers are responsible for this. There is a price for their
sophistication and intelligence. Once the sublime has been outlawed
by seriousness and pretension, Elvis can be quickly ignored and his
pretenders and other conceptualists can claim undeserved importance.

His fans may be addicts but this does not make them uncritical.
Anyone can develop critical skills quite quickly when exposed to
brilliance. Spend an evening with 'Elvis Golden Records Volume 2',
as I did as an eleven year old, nicely rounded off with repeated plays of
'Jailhouse Rock', and, believe me, you become alert.

The film critic, David Thomson, said of Orson Welles, 'We still
remember and worship Orson Welles because at his best he was more
brilliant than anyone else.'

He could have added that, because of that best, we are also able to
endure the problems in his later, unsuccessful films. Because of the
peerless brilliance of 'Citizen Kane', we will search through the cheap
and reduced trash of 'Mr Arkadin' for mere reminders of his talent and, as
awful as 'Mr Arkadin' might be, the reminders inevitably exist. The same
is true of Elvis.

People who are not Elvis fans usually fall into two categories. First,
there are those who are intolerant of his mistakes and are able to resist
everything. Second, there are those who only have curiosity for the
iconic exceptions. Fans, though, listen to Elvis in the same way David
Thomson watches the films of Orson Welles. We like to be reminded

of his brilliance but we are also fascinated at how it has been reduced by circumstances, himself and others. More than this, there is a belief that the truly gifted, whatever their inconsistencies, always manage a splendour denied to others. The brilliant always fail more impressively than the rest.

Of course, since Elvis has died, we are prohibited from demanding he delivers his best and much of what was once regarded as rubbish is now seen as weaker but acceptable examples of his talent. We listen gratefully. This also occurs in literature and painting. For example, since John Updike died, his readers are now unable to demand work equal to his famous 'Rabbit' trilogy. Instead, they revisit books they once dismissed as lightweight. They will settle for this because, for them, there is always the elegant prose. In the same way, art experts become excited about an attic full of Cezanne rejects. The content may not be inspired but they still demonstrate a master at work. Something similar has happened with Elvis fans and his weaker material. Produced by an Elvis struggling with his health, the inadequate material or his circumstances, these cannot equal what he did at his best but, in the same way Cezanne can draw a line, Elvis can still sing in tune. Not all but much of this material exists as a reminder that he was unique and had a talent beyond others.

The fifties records need no excuses and are gloriously consistent. Between 1961 and 1966, there is in his studio material too much emphasis on appealing to a wider audience but these records are not rubbish. Too much is reduced by Chet Atkins but some of the performances are quite fabulous and no one can deny Elvis is growing as a performer as he reveals the wonder and capability of his voice. The growth may not be welcome to all but it is present, nevertheless. The truly awful records made by Elvis have two specific sources. They are the movie material and his decline in the seventies. In the movies, Elvis refuses to commit himself wholeheartedly to this material. This is not necessarily to his credit because fans paid money for these soundtrack albums. Elvis would have earned more respect, and prevented me from wasting money, if he had refused to participate. The weaknesses in his behaviour, though, have been considered elsewhere. In the seventies, his health and the voice declined. Elvis still managed to transform decent material into good records but they were rarely sublime. Unfortunately, the quality of the material was not always decent and it is often unacceptable. The publishing deals arranged by his manager, Parker, and the increasingly slack selection by Freddie Bienstock created this situation. In this period, Elvis often only chose a song in desperation and he would abandon it in a couple of takes. Later, the record company, desperate for material, would release the substandard recording. So, there is rubbish but there are reasons.

In fact, in the seventies, the situation for Elvis in the recording studios is not unlike what Orson Welles must have experienced working on his later films. Two exceptional, American talents were obliged to forfeit control and opportunities whilst others less gifted were facilitated and supported. It should be odd but it is not. Both men were unable to master accountants. Able to persuade many easily, both lacked the confidence to outwit alien, narrow men whose only strength was cynical greed. The very men capable of inspiring devotion and admiration are invariably a catalyst for destructive envy in others. Elvis had his music re-mastered without his permission and Welles had his films edited contrary to his wishes.

There is an added complication that also weighs against Elvis. He is a man who makes heart music. It carries no intellectual messages and virtuosity for its own sake is eschewed. This means that his records either work or do not. The more serious performers may have wider ambitions but within that ambition exists insurance. The same applies to art house movies. They can be dull but interesting. Commercial music and popular cinema have no alternative but to deliver. Oddly, this means that the challenge of consistency is greater than that which exists for supposed serious musicians. When the responsibility that exists is to produce a record that works emotionally or rhythmically you have to be inspired. Nobody will give you credit for cleverness because it has been ignored in favour of popular appeal. The same problem existed for filmmakers like Howard Hawks and Alfred Hitchcock. The critics may now crawl over their movies for sub-text and meaning but their successful movies are like great records. These directors needed to find a groove and to sustain it. Their best movies do which is why they are enjoyed by millions. When the soufflé fails in a Hitchcock or a Hawks movie the millions who enjoyed previous films are mystified and disappointed but there is no mystery. A soufflé sometimes does fail. The trick takes nerve, skill and luck.

Elvis at his best, and in control, appeared to achieve consistency easily. Critics have argued that this is simply an issue of material. In those periods when he was popular and dominant, he had great songs available to him. The acclaimed albums, 'Elvis Is Back' and 'From Elvis In Memphis', exist to contradict the argument. There are great songs on both albums but fourteen of the twenty four songs are covers of records by other people. The original songs on the albums are okay but nobody would argue that they are classics. These were not great albums because of the material.

On form, Elvis was exceptional and, although there is always a mix of the sublime and the predictable, he was actually capable of a consistency beyond others. He was not, though, capable of demonstrating that consistency throughout his career. This is because his career included phases when he was not in control. This lack of control was a consequence of the interference of others and his self-destruction which appeared to range from slumber to self-obliteration. This is more than mere irony. If the self-destruction was a response to the indifference of his management, the people who thought they had created him, it was a hell of a tragedy. No wonder, the Creature had so much grief when he saw the dead Frankenstein below deck. He realised his life was doomed to ultimate failure because, now, he never would overcome the indifference of his creator to his potential and worth. Parker did not die but Elvis realised long before his own death that he never would persuade his substitute father that he had talent. Read the final scene in the novel by Shelley and it is not too fanciful to believe that it was this perpetual indifference by Parker that broke the heart and spirit of Elvis, to think this is why so many of the bad records exist.

He did not invent rock and roll and he copied from black musicians

Some years ago, 'The Guardian' printed an article on who was responsible for the creation of rock and roll. The piece was hidden in its review section but the front page ran a trailer above the name of the newspaper. It had a small photograph of Elvis; taken from one of his movies, he looked groomed in plastic. Next to the photograph was written, 'Who invented rock and roll? Well, it wasn't him.'

The malice and glee were obvious which was surprising because his career was a tragedy. Not the only dark episode in American music but the most famous. An exceptional talent waylaid by crass moneymen and his own flaws. The result may not have been poverty as in the case of less famous musicians but the avoidable ridicule and waste is still heartbreaking.

Like most musical genres, rock and roll emerged and was not invented. This phenomenon is normal for American, popular music. Independent, regional strands appear and often merge and, within these strands, individual stylists create their own distinct contribution. In the twentieth century, American, popular music had various sources and these included jazz, blues, gospel and country. Black musicians created the first two categories, dominated the third and influenced country music more than is understood, so the importance of black musicians cannot be over-stated. The music of black and white was probably closest in the twenties and thirties when bluegrass was not too dissimilar from rural blues. The gap widened with the introduction of the electric guitar. Later, Chicago blues and soul music gave popular, black music a fresh identity. These were genuine developments but the gap between the music of black and white musicians has often been deliberately exaggerated and cultivated to suit a music industry determined to define and retain separate markets. These distinctions required blues to have a harder edge and country music to be more sentimental. Musicians played their part, bluesman Charlie Patton produced a sharp, tough style that was clearly influential, but it should not be forgotten that it suited the businessmen to keep the races apart and keep their markets intact.

Two statements have to be made about American music that may at first appear contradictory. Black performers dominate American music; blues, jazz, soul and rhythm and blues are all categories of black music. Social class is the biggest divider in American music and not race. This truth has been distorted by business and racism. Or, at least, it used to be true; the recent past is beyond me I am afraid. But, in the middle of the last century, the white, working class, American in the South had more in common musically with his black counterpart than with his white, middle class neighbour.

This is partly why Millie Jackson will aim a Merle Haggard, country song at the soul charts and why Merle has no inhibitions about including New Orleans horns on one of his country albums. These innovations also occur because the musicians are both keen to reflect their influences and because they have curiosity. When it happens it often incurs the objections of the record label owners. Listen to the great, soul singer, Bobby Womack, slam the demands of record labels before he launches into his cover of 'They Long To Be Close To You' by the Carpenters. His message is clear. If he wants to sing pretty tunes by white people, he will. Apart from innovations by forceful musicians, the regional variations within these categories also reflect different roots. The country music of the South East is based on gospel vocals whilst the alternative in the West is lighter and reflects its Mexican and cowboy traditions. The relaxed, New Orleans culture produces music that lacks the hard blues edge of the music produced in Memphis. Within these generalisations, there are always exceptions because American music is a product of a web of communities and these are usually influenced by local non-conformists and eccentrics.

It is complicated. Mary Shelley wrote 'Frankenstein' but it required four people telling horror tales to each other to draw the commitment. Her husband added the odd touches to her prose. Rock and roll was a fractured result of rhythm and blues which, in itself, was a combination of blues and jazz. Rhythm and blues contained within it various other fractures - jump blues, piano boogie woogie, commercial jazz and so on.

Nobody invented rock and roll. It emerged but only because of the key contributions of original stylists and, despite the fuss, it was not that different from what had previously existed in rhythm and blues. If rock and roll was sourced by the roots music of the American South, it is essential to recognise how the phenomenon of the big, swing bands of the forties had also previously facilitated the escapism of hedonistic youth. Fifties rock and rollers jived just like their parents. The more it changes the more it stays the same. But something was in the air and Elvis, Chuck Berry, Jerry Lee Lewis, LaVern Baker, Larry Williams, Bo Diddley, Chuck Willis, Ike Turner, the Everly Brothers and many other original stylists gave their generation a fresh identity. The independent labels also played their part. They may have narrowed the contributions of their performers but they helped the music of the fifties blossom into different, recognisable styles. Speciality gave New Orleans rhythm and blues a faster tempo, Sun produced rockabilly and Atlantic encouraged its blues performers to swing their way to fame. Other labels, desperate to be included, promoted wild amateurs who helped it anticipate punk.

Rock and roll exists as a misleading, marketing term and has different meanings in the USA and Britain. The Americans use it to refer to rock music whilst the British use it to define fifties rock and roll. Sensibly, the Americans split fifties rock and roll into rhythm and blues and rockabilly. When they talk about Elvis inventing rock and roll they mean rockabilly and white rock music. In the fifties, rock and roll music (as defined by the British) contained fifties pop, sentimental doo-wop, rockabilly, commercial jazz with a soft blues beat, blues, western swing, hillbilly boogie, New Orleans rhythm and blues like Fats Domino and rhythm and blues from everywhere else. Elvis did not invent all of this. Nobody did.

It emerged despite the American, music industry wanting to inhibit those musicians who were willing to fracture the different genres. Today, the commercial, record producers have the opposite strategy. To appeal to everyone on the planet, they use their multiple track synthesisers to include rhythms from virtually everywhere. The result is usually a globalised mess. The rock and roll era was important because the industry for a few years lost control. Major labels lost their power. Influence shifted to the independent labels and neglected regions within America. Even today, musical movements are usually launched from independent labels. The difference nowadays is that the commercial world is quicker to respond and exploit.

After soul music emerged as a force, the contribution of black music and the importance of its musicians were at last properly recognised but we should not think that fifties rock and roll was exclusively white with black musicians completely ignored. The whites had more representation than their ability warranted but, even then, the charts were multi-racial. Similarly, black music was recognised by cultural establishments in both America and Britain. Although Miles Davis and others would make further breakthroughs, jazz was already in the fifties considered to be a complex, art form. Jazz records did not sell in big numbers but it did have critical approval. The fifties rock and roll revolution was about class as much as race. It exposed the world to the music of hillbillies and the urban, black poor. As Jerry Wexler said, 'the music represents social class five and the best of it has grit between its toes.'

Elvis may not have invented rock and roll but he still did enough to qualify as great and, after him, people were obliged to take seriously those who had, to remember Wexler, grit between their toes. Elvis was able to embrace a huge amount of American music and simultaneously reflect its variety and define his singularity. Like others, he contributed a unique style, except, there were many styles that were unique to him. At least, two of his contributions inspired genres that continue, these are rockabilly and rock. His rockabilly music combined not just country and blues but hardcore elements within those genres. It is this music that refutes the charge that he simply copied black musicians. His rockabilly legacy, and the impact it had on both black and white musicians, mark him out as something other than an imitator.

His double-sided single, 'Hound Dog' and 'Don't Be Cruel', which he recorded later at RCA, was also important because it set out the parameters for mainstream, commercial rock for a young, rebellious audience. His version of 'Hound Dog' does not deserve to be challenged by revisionists claiming it is an inferior blues to the original by Mama Thornton. They are missing the point. Elvis created something different, the ultimate, nihilistic anthem. Elvis is also supposed to have copied the arrangement by the modestly talented Freddie And The Bell Boys. This is not true. The arrangement by Freddie is traditional, jump rhythm and blues. If Hound Dog' is not truly revolutionary, it is not because of Big Mama Thornton or Freddie And The Bell Boys but because Little Richard had produced raucous rock and roll similar to 'Hound Dog' as early as 1954. This is what inspired Elvis. After 'Hound Dog', it was important to be loud, aggressive and crude and, suddenly, Little Richard was acceptable. In the fifties, there were several great performers that staked a new future. Elvis was one of them and he had more impact than anyone because he was so popular. Did the extent of that impact depend on him being white? Undoubtedly, but his influence would not have happened without his exceptional, musical ability and willingness to experiment.

His three singles, 'Heartbreak Hotel', 'Hound Dog' and 'All Shook Up', were fortuitous because they all had strange titles. In different ways, they suggested a new, remote and powerful generation. None of them invented rock and roll but it is these singles, rather than his superior, rockabilly records, that launched the revolution. Rock critics write about these singles as if they were a benevolent influence but they too easily assume we have existed in a period of enlightenment since the sixties. Elvis saw it differently and some have suggested he eventually became disillusioned with what followed him. Rhythm and blues had its golden period before Elvis. In the fifties, jazz still appeared in the charts and popular music was dominated by great singers like Peggy Lee, Ella Fitzgerald, Nat 'King' Cole and Frank Sinatra. The most depressing development in popular music after the fifties was how something as narrow as modern rock and roll came to dominate. Of course, this achievement required American boys much more assertive than the poor of the South. They also had their friends the British who, in any fight for dominance, can always be relied on to add their imperial arrogance.

If the influence of Elvis was destructive, he remains an important performer. The fifties material from RCA alone compares favourably with his peers because of its sustained quality, invention, diversity and the subtlety of its effects. Anyone who doubts the use of the word subtle to describe rock and roll should try dancing to one of his classics. 'Jailhouse Rock' is a good example. Is it rock music or actually swing? His sense of rhythm is marvellous and mysterious. When his RCA, fifties music is complemented with the breakthrough that he achieved at Sun he has the edge over other rock and roll musicians in this period. Elvis did not reinvent himself as a white Negro as is claimed. Negritude did inform his identity but so did androgeny, narcissism, populism and romantic swashbuckling. Critics have insisted that black musicians have not just a talent but a birthright denied to white people, an uncorrupted primitivism sustained by being excluded from white society. Perhaps this is true but a great talent will not respect it and many of us are unable to resist the great talent, no matter what he poaches.

It is true he was well paid and achieved fame denied some important, black musicians. This was the consequence of a racist society and distorted economic rewards. It is impossible to know what career he would have had in a non-racist America although I hazarded a not entirely serious guess earlier in this book that he would have still been important. I suggested that in a world of paradoxes his personality may have suited a lower profile. He could have avoided the mistakes that ultimately undermined him and achieved the critical respect made available to Ray Charles and Aretha Franklin. Many black critics feel that after slavery, economic domination, physical abuse and social discrimination Elvis was the final insult. The grievance demands sympathy but what happened in music is the least of the crimes of a white race prone to careless genocide. The musicians of America were like lovers. Not all the musicians cohabited with each other but those in heat were impossible to keep apart. In the novel, 'Frankenstein', sensationalism, romance and radical opinion clash memorably. The emphasis on horror in the movie versions is admired by genre loyalists but we all respond to the distinctive mix of Gothic horror and radical philosophy offered by Shelley, a woman whose efforts were first considered more appropriate for a man.

His rock and roll music is inferior to the more authentic and tougher rhythm and blues music that he imitated

What is odd about this argument is that it only developed after his records moved away from rock and roll and rhythm and blues. When he was making music that exploited the traditions of black culture only a few complained in this way. It is as if everybody wanted the cool Elvis to sing black music. But, once he lost his rebellious identity, the idea of him singing music clearly influenced by black culture became completely unacceptable. It is comparable to the relationship the Creature had with the De Lacey family whom he observed in the forest. Elvis in Tupelo watched and learnt from the neighbouring, black community and also benefited from their support because he worked for a local, black businessman. His early records were appreciated. Little Richard and Chuck Berry claimed Elvis provided opportunities for black music to be heard. Once, though, Elvis was compromised by success, after he was whitened again, the family saw a monster, the exploiter the community warned against. From then, he was reviled and barred from the community, chased away by those, like Felix in the novel, who were convinced acceptance would undermine the family. The young man who attended the WDIA concert in Memphis and posed for photographs alongside black musicians was no longer welcome.

Although there is doubt about the accuracy of the music charts in the fifties, Elvis achieved hit after hit on the black charts with his early rock and roll records. Bobby Womack said Elvis had the impact of an earthquake on his neighbourhood. Bobby has obviously read Mary Shelley, 'an earthquake had changed the scene.' His white critics also applauded the efforts of Elvis in this period. Elvis did cover black originals but, amazingly, his versions often, but not always, surpass the originals for energy and feeling. The examples are numerous, his Sun classics such as 'Mystery Train,' 'That's All Right' and 'Good Rockin' Tonight', the RCA highlights 'Reconsider Baby', 'So Glad You're Mine', 'Stranger In My Own Home Town', 'Merry Xmas Baby', 'Lawdy Miss Clawdy' and many others. It cannot be said he was careful to only pick modest achievements or songs he considered within his range. His rhythm and blues repertoire is actually wider than any other rhythm and blues performer, black or white. This is unbelievable but true, just look at the attached List 7 that refers to his rhythm and blues records. The range is extraordinary. This is what he achieves within one genre but, of course, he is not confined to one genre.

Unfortunately, what happens is that Elvis is compared to all of black music. Inevitably, he cannot equal the efforts of all the black performers but no individual can match all the other performers when their efforts are aggregated. There is no doubt that black music is easily the most important element within popular music. The music of black America is rich, original and has complex, independent roots and rhythms but, apart from that, it draws on its gospel tradition of using music to seek religious ecstasy. Although white, gospel music is lively, this tradition is not matched in white, American music. The strident and passionately vibrant gospel and soul music of the more raucous performers cannot be equalled by any white alternatives. This includes Elvis but there is a rehearsal of 'Oh Happy Day' where Elvis actually delivers this intense, religious style. Here, though, we have to compare his achievement and not his potential.

The existence of the ecstatic element within black music persuades many blues and soul fans to draw a line around a single culture. This attitude of soul fans denies the euphoria and lyricism that exist in other music and it also simplifies and underestimates black culture. Not every black performer should be obliged to deliver the ecstatically intense in every performance and not every one does. Black music incorporates many styles and what is obvious is that Elvis has mastered more than a few and dabbled with most.

For many soul fans clichés are important and Elvis, whose clichés are specific to him, will never be authentic enough. The fetish of stereotyped authenticity in popular music is explored brilliantly by Hugh Barker and Yuval Taylor in their book, 'Faking It'. They expose the hypocrisies and absurdities that exist in music criticism and how performers can be misunderstood because of the importance of their social identity. They quote the example of Mississippi John Hurt who, because he was black, was promoted and accepted as a rebellious bluesman but who was actually a lyrical, folk ballad singer. I remember seeing Bobby Bland in Colne in Lancashire. One member of the audience attended so he could savour his ecstatic, soul show release. Throughout the show, the young man danced hysterically and shook his head to the slow ballads of Bland.

At one point, Bobby stopped, looked down at the young man gripped in fervour and said, 'that guy needs help.'

Not help, Bobby, just taste.

To estimate how Elvis compares to the best of black music, he has to be compared to individual performers. This was done in the section on his rivals, so the comparisons will not be laboured here. There are many black performers capable of music beyond Elvis but he is also capable of music beyond them. Unfortunately, too many people now see the process as one way and only recognise the inability of Elvis to be Bobby Bland or James Brown. Elvis has made some great, blues records but neither he nor anyone else can match Muddy Waters and Howling Wolf for aggression and power. Inevitably, there will be people who are impressed more by Bobby Bland or Muddy Waters, for example, than Elvis but this does not automatically make Elvis inferior, especially, as no one can match Elvis for diversity. Their different strengths are what make all of them important musicians. All of the great performers do what they do better than anyone else and they developed different styles because they had ability unique to them. Music depends on many talents.

Recently, the rapper Chuck D intervened in the argument. In one of his songs he said, 'They called him the King but he don't mean shit to me.'

Later, Chuck D appeared on an Elvis documentary and was placatory.

He acknowledged that Elvis had a special gift but reminded the viewers that there were other fine talents. American music is not just about one man. If that is what he intended to say with the words 'he don't mean shit to me', he needs to take lessons. Although his remark was about someone who became the most famous individual in rock and roll, it was also about a man who was obliged to endure undeserved ridicule and who paid for his mistakes and the callousness of others with his life.

James Brown, Bobby Womack, Mohammed Ali, Albert King, Isaac Hayes, Jackie Wilson, BB King and LaVern Baker were all Elvis fans. None of them could be described as Uncle Tom. Compared to them, Chuck D don't mean much to me.

The above accusations are specific to Elvis and rock and roll but they can be summarised and expressed very differently. His hostile critics allege Elvis was uncouth, inauthentic, had weak moments that they definitely did not like, was irritatingly excitable and an offensive spirit to the times. These were the main charges against the Creature, all underwritten by a conviction that he lacked the dimension that made humans more sophisticated and aware. His critics confused grooming with worth. The same conviction and confusion applies to Elvis. The Creature had a gift for reasoning and an appreciation of literature and art. The villagers assumed he was only a monster and, fearful of curiosity, they avoided objective enquiry. His gifts, like the musical talent of Elvis, were deemed impossible. In both cases, the scorn and sneers united the hostile. Both the Creature and Elvis were chased away from the village.

———————

THE MISUNDERSTOOD
– ELVIS PRESLEY

When we look at the frontispiece of the 1831 edition for the novel, 'Frankenstein', we see a Creature that is far from horrifying. Indeed, he has hair and a six pack that most males dream about. His most disturbing aspects are the alien confusion in his eyes and his size. The Creature was eight feet tall because Frankenstein needed him to have large limbs to make his work easier. This challenging innocence and superior strength are the aspects that may have convinced Victor Frankenstein that his creation had not given him control but denied it. The initial flight by Frankenstein reminds the reader how easily we can misunderstand not only events but one another. This is why Shelley insists brilliantly on a Creature that is both hero and monster. What she demands from her readers is an acknowledgment of capricious circumstance and the complex contradictions of character. The career of Elvis insists upon the same.

Frankenstein reacts with terror when he witnesses life in a Creature whose inert form has shared his flat, his womb, for the last six months. Critics, aware of how Mary Wollenstonecraft died of an illness caused by giving birth to her daughter, Mary, have suggested the scene in 'Frankenstein' is inspired by the legacy of her birth. Arguably, Mary Shelley was hinting at an alternative reaction of parents to the first sight of their children, life in less than perfectly formed beings, and was suggesting that the look in the eyes of babies, like their existence, is as challenging as it is enchanting. The novel, 'Frankenstein', is unsentimental about childbirth, paternity, inheritance, fate and destiny. The violence is modest. The real horror in this book is the absence of comforting sentimentality.

Alanna Nash explains Elvis by putting a similar, unsentimental emphasis on character and childbirth. She believes his tragedy was permanent entrapment in frustration, the result of his complicated childhood and the loss of his twin. Undoubtedly, he was unable to outgrow adolescence. When Michael Jackson was found dead at the age of fifty, and discovered to be a victim of prescription drugs, it revealed strength in the daughter of Elvis, Lisa Marie, not previously recognised. Flawed though her taste in men may have been, she knew how to pick a father substitute. Elvis and Michael Jackson were two men whose adolescence clashed with fame and the sub-conscious of Lisa Marie was not fooled by any difference in race and generation. She knew what made them similar.

Whilst Nash has correctly identified appropriate elements, I disagree with her interpretation. His psychological issues are not his tragedy. They are his burden. Their existence may not even be an explanation of the tragedy. The tragedy is what she dismisses as the unfortunate consequences, his early death and the absence of creative projects to inspire him. Admittedly, the psychological burden is significant. Linda Thompson, his girlfriend, recalls him dreaming of being born and only surviving because the twin suffocated. Elvis told Linda that she was the twin in the dream. The trauma cannot be disputed and, if we accept the Freudian analysis, it weakened him and this weakness may have dissipated his aspiration and integrity. But it is a dangerous assumption. Freud may or may not explain the participant but he definitely should not be trusted with history. Call me an old-fashioned, European dialectical-materialist but events and others have to play a part.

Personal weakness and physical and emotional decline contributed but, as the other bearded one, Karl Marx, said, and Mary Shelley understood, 'Men make their own history but never in circumstances of their choosing.'

Circumstance and others inspire or frustrate which is why it was necessary to look at key figures such as Parker and Chet Atkins and describe briefly how Elvis progressed through a changing world that without warning erected barriers against him. Without attempting to exonerate, we can never underestimate the impact of Hollywood and Vegas. The examination of his rivals was intended to show that he may not have been the only towering figure in American music but he did have comparable gifts. Characters in different fields were also included to demonstrate he is not the first inexplicable figure in history. (There is also one more who needs to be mentioned.)

In 'Careless Love', Peter Guralnick does refer to the career as a tragedy and it is because, as great as he was, Elvis could have been much more. Imagine what would have happened if he had signed for Atlantic records or if Leiber and Stoller had been allowed to welcome him back from the Army or if he had been allowed to establish creative relationships with genuine talents rather than be obliged to support the lackeys acceptable to Parker. With only a little help, he could have avoided some of the disasters that besmirch his memory and legacy. True, he had the freedom to create his own shows on stage but the inhibiting context of an inconclusive, career strategy allowed him to waste the final years of his life. This self-destruction was not solely precipitated by his divorce from Priscilla. 'Baby Let's Play House' by Alanna Nash reveals more about the man than any other book but, as it recounts the decline, there is nothing in the odd behaviour being monitored that indicates the breakup of the couple precipitated a sudden change in character. Elvis changed after his stint in the Army and the death of his mother. After he returned, his attitude to himself and his career was different. He was capable of responding to the occasional challenge but unable to create an identity that could maximise his renewed career or himself.

The influences of his management team and, as Alanna Nash rightly insists, his family are important. We must not, though, forget the impact of two years in the Army, working in an institution that is second to none in creating docile obedience. Additionally, his army duty may have contributed to his hostility to the performers who emerged in the sixties. Although he was reluctant to join the Army, he, according to Alanna Nash, actually enjoyed his service. He liked the routine and the camaraderie. His musical rivals were capable of irritating because they were rivals but was his ire exaggerated by the knowledge that he had served two years in the Army for no more than meagre pay? As time passed, he may have concluded it made him more of a man than his peers or successors.

To ascribe his failure to childhood trauma and the divorce from Priscilla is to ignore what Elvis must have realised in the early sixties, that he would never define his career as intended. If this realisation and the weight of missed opportunities did not perish his soul, it played a substantial part. Guralnick is correct to use the word tragedy but it is ultimately inadequate. This particular tragedy contains real madness. Indeed, it was an essential requirement. The tragedy of the Creature needed the irrational behaviour of Frankenstein when he observed the independent life in his impressive but less than perfect creation. The destruction of Elvis, or his destiny as the first doomed, romantic hero in rock and roll, required an insanity rooted in the mystery that is the personality of Elvis, the coarse, self-serving excesses of American capitalism and, if that were not enough, the perverse wilfulness of Parker.

These two men never understood each other and, inevitably, never determined adequately their responsibilities to the other. No wonder they finished on their own icy waste, locked into each other and incomprehensible to the witnesses who were obliged to be curious. As Frankenstein said, 'My tale is not one to announce publicly; its outstanding horror would be looked upon as madness by the vulgar.'

His early rock and roll was not the unadulterated nihillism some feared. This can be heard on the 'Million Dollar Quartet' CD that captured him playing music for fun with Jerry Lee Lewis and Carl Perkins at Sun records. This rock and roller was an innocent always keen to steer Lewis and Perkins to one of his gospel favourites. When he became pampered and privileged his music changed into something sweeter again. In 1974, a debauched Elvis recorded the sentimental, country tune, 'Green Green Grass Of Home'. In 1966, still relatively innocent, he had rejected it. After the Army, Elvis no longer wanted innocent freedom, he wanted escape. The complicity and abuse of his management complemented his flight from responsibility and unwittingly ensured that this escape would amount to no more than ineffectual fantasy and, finally, dark retreat.

The explanation of my writer friend still leaves me with rancour. It is too easy for the well-educated to dismiss him as a dumb boy. Equally, all of us should be careful about accepting the comments of arranger, Billy Goldenberg, who said, 'So incredibly different from all the people around him. He had class. I mean underneath all that stuff ...' Perhaps Elvis did or he may have just had power and status and he was, apart from his talent, no better than the rest of us. More persuasive is the remark by author, Sherwood Anderson, quoted in 'Images And Fancies', a collection of essays on Elvis. 'If there is any good in the man he will never get over being a boy,' or as Mary Shelley observed in 'The Last Man', 'The companions of our childhood always possess a certain power over our minds which hardly any later friend can obtain'.

This applies and it can be heard in his music and recognised in the commitments he made to friends and family. The loyalty to his childhood and his efforts to reconcile his over remunerated success with the experience of his impoverished childhood do not deserve contempt. Elvis may not have been an intellectual but he was not shallow because he was a person with a sensitive heart. Despite his self-indulgent weaknesses, he understood the importance of warmth between human beings. Indeed, we have testimonies from his girlfriends that insist he did. When he could no longer achieve this warmth from others he used his music as a substitute and it is this search for a replacement for missing tenderness that dominates his music of the seventies and ultimately makes this flawed part of his career worthwhile.

If Nash and Freud are correct, his boyhood did more than haunt. It played a part and it gave him nightmares but the self-destruction was more likely the result of what happened to him after he became one of the most famous men on the planet. He realised he could make millions by grinning stupidly at a movie camera and adoring fans but he also had to accept that he would always be obliged to disgust as many as those who adored. There have always been ascetics who self-destruct because they are too obsessed with spiritual purity to think about earning a living. Before technology, they would waste away in caves. Elvis was no ascetic. His self-destruction required self-hatred, temptation and opportunity, all were dipped in decadence. His career facilitated all these factors.

Sometimes the simplest and briefest explanations are the most accurate, stuff such as Priscilla saying, 'he was a very human being.' Tragedy, though, entitles us to be more curious. Much has been written about his spiritual ambition and his faith was important to him but this was not a religious man in any meaningful sense of the word. There did come a point in his life when he wanted to discover the transcendental and spiritual that he believed resided in him and other human beings. Such ambition, though, never sits easily with men who need the physical intimacy of constant company. Albert Goldman expressed surprise at the violence that occurred in the games between Elvis and the Memphis Mafia. But sex and violence are both aspects of the need for intimacy in males. One relates to the need for intimacy with women and the other between men. The more we read about Elvis, the more we understand that what he always wanted was cuddles, sex and violence. All acknowledge a desire for intimacy with others. The Creature read his books and understood why he was obliged to have yearnings for company. When we listen to the records of Elvis we realise cuddles, sex and violence were what defined his music. Expressed this way, Elvis appears to be quite normal. (This does not mean his life defined his music. He was too much of a performer for that but his life is in there. Greil Marcus has quoted Walt Whitman when discussing Elvis and, as the American poet once said, 'this is no book, who touches this touches a man.')

In my opinion, his spiritual curiosity was driven by the masculine ambition for control and potency, to master rather than enjoy the mystery. His will to power was obvious and manifested itself in lackeys, karate and physical omnipotence. This was complemented with technical armoury that included guns, cars and motorbikes. Like all egoists, he did not idolise his God, he battled with him. Guralnick concluded in a BBC, radio programme that at the end Elvis had real emptiness. Elvis realised 'he had betrayed himself, his talent and his God.' This assumes only self-hatred but Elvis may have thought himself more as a victim and what he really wanted from God was an explanation. If God was willing to free Elvis from obscurity and poverty, if he was sympathetic, why did he exact the terrible price of widespread ridicule and personal emptiness? The reaction from Elvis to the death of his mother was to become promiscuous; he acted like a vengeful husband who had been humiliated by the adultery of his wife. So, it is possible that his sub-conscious felt the death of his mother as a betrayal. If his promiscuity was a response to the betrayal of his mother, his self-destruction may have been a reaction to what he perceived as the betrayal of him by his God. The Creature expressed similar resentment with violence, 'Oh, my creator make me happy; let me feel gratitude towards you for one benefit.'

A willingness by Elvis to assert his will against his interests was a perverse result of his will to power, a wilfulness that existed despite his superstitious compliance with Parker. His need for control and power is why his religious curiosity was combined with an interest in law enforcement.

This did not make Elvis stupid because Isaac Newton had the same weaknesses and Isaac was definitely not thick. These flaws are not restricted to the stupid. Now Newton has been mentioned again, there is an obligation to point out other similarities. Obviously, many will consider this a ridiculous comparison and, even, I suspect this is absurd which is why Isaac was not included in the talented rivals. Although his talent and versatility are unique, particularly, when we understand the historical context, there is no way Newton could have equalled records like 'Mystery Train' or 'A Mess Of Blues'.

I am teasing. Newton is only like Elvis because his memory has the same propensity to baffle. He lived from 1643 to 1727. He was born in Grantham in Lincolnshire which is the town also responsible for Margaret Thatcher. I was actually in Grantham on the day of a recent eclipse which I thought was quite neat. In his early years, Newton was singular and independent and he complimented his immense, intellectual talent with dedication and will. Unlike Elvis or The Beatles, Newton does qualify as a genius. In 1687, he published 'Philosophiae Naturalis Principia Mathematica'. This is to the history of science what 'That's All Right' is to rock and roll and more. He explained universal gravitation and discovered something called 'The Three Laws Of Motion'. He also later explained light and optics and, in his spare time, invented a prism reflecting telescope. Admittedly, there was no football or television to distract him. There is much more but this is not a book about Isaac Newton. Although his theories have needed to be redefined because of subsequent discoveries, scientists acknowledge that the modern world is indebted to Newton and it may have actually begun with him.

Nobody could be more unlike Elvis, except there are two strange parallels. Newton helped to introduce another age, rationalism. But Newton was not like his followers who adopted the rationalism wholeheartedly. Newton never abandoned his mystical faith in God and he stayed loyal to the alchemists and their search for the magic that would produce gold. Those who succeeded Newton felt that his logic had made the alchemists redundant. Newton said that he had stood on the shoulders of giants to make his discoveries but, where he remembered giants, his descendants and followers, instead, now only saw these predecessors as deluded pygmies. It is what happens with revolutionaries, men who stand between different eras. The people who succeed the revolution neither have the potential of the revolutionary for change nor the capacity to understand the world the revolutionary experienced and enjoyed. After Elvis, many rock and roll fans were not willing to indulge the music that had preceded Elvis, the sentimental ballads or pretty tunes that had been recorded by talented performers before him. Elvis was not prepared to abandon music made by musicians whom he still saw as important.

Newton had God and gold makers and Elvis had the Ink Spots. Rock and roll loyalists were mystified by the sentimental attachments of Elvis. Scientists, since the death of Newton, have been bemused by his loyalty to the bogus practice of alchemy.

The second paralled is how Newton changed direction in his life. The solitary intellectual, who eccentrically had poked a needle in his eye to aid his research into optical principles, spent most of his early life avoiding other people. Later, he became a high powered Civil Servant which, in the seventeenth century, meant being recruited to the court of the King. In 1696, a mere nine years after he had published his groundbreaking work on gravitation and motion, he took responsibility for the Royal Mint. Counterfeiting was a problem at the time and Newton pursued counterfeiters. He was zealous and, as counterfeiting was classified as treason, he was responsible for the hanging of twenty six criminals. The most notorious and skilful was someone called William Challoner. This second career for Isaac meant that he died a rich man and the well-fed administrator must have been unrecognisable from the ascetic puncturing his eyeball in search for intellectual truth.

Of course, Newton may have considered his contrasting ambitions anything but contradictory. If intellectual truth tempted the younger man, it is not inexplicable that status and fame seduced his older equivalent. After modelling the universe, he was faced with a declining curve in intellectual achievement and the genius was tempted by an alternative career that offered both progress and success. Presumably, this is how it looks on the inside for an iconoclastic revolutionary. For those embarrassed by the infamous photograph of Elvis and Nixon when Elvis offered to work for the FBI as an undercover investigator, think of Newton and the twenty six counterfeiters he ordered to be hanged. (Jerry Schilling has argued that the gesture by Elvis was more liberal than realised. Elvis wanted to help people avoid drug dependency, not punish them. This explanation has convinced few but it is possible the motives of Elvis were more complex than his clumsy letter to Hoover indicates.)

Apart from making decisions based on financial gain, there are other similarities between Elvis and Newton. Both men produced their best work in short bursts of creativity and both inspired the wordy. Wordsworth described Newton as 'voyaging through strange seas of thought alone' and Alexander Pope, anticipating Dylan fans, said, 'God said, 'Let Newton be', and all was light'. Much later, rock critic, Dave Marsh, referred to Elvis as 'an explorer of reality and illusion – a maker of maps.' Like Elvis, Newton also inspired malice in others. Elvis has David Bowie as a critic but Newton had to suffer the indignation of Blake and Byron. Graceland in Memphis was stacked with a huge library of spiritualist teachings and Newton had a large collection of alchemist writing. There is more. The famous economist, John Maynard Keynes described Newton as the last great magician and Elvis has been explained as the last great, primitive shaman. Newton believed that the Universe had an active spirit and nothing contained this as much as light. Elvis believed in the human heart as an inexhaustible source of mystery. The reluctance of Elvis to visit the studio at the end of his career is echoed by Newton resisting the encouragement of John Locke to teach at Charterhouse. 'The competition is hazardous and I am loathe to sing a new song.'

I know, I am getting carried away. The point is a simple one. Both men created cracks in history. Obviously, Newton created something more permanent and deeper. Nevertheless, those cracks later became vices for the two men. The same happened to Orson Welles and others. Their response is only properly understood by those caught in the vice, those obliged to be criticised by the more modest innovators that follow.

Newton moved into law enforcement whilst Elvis fantasised and dressed up in police uniforms. The desire for control that Elvis shared with Newton implies he either felt he was being treated like a puppet or was unable to realise himself because of personal flaws. He did have flaws but other people did have control over him. The support they provided was inadequate. An unsophisticated and insecure individual like Elvis needed creative nourishment. This substance was not entirely absent as the presence of Sam Phillips, Leiber and Stoller, Steve Binder and Chips Moman confirm but their presence was temporary and fleeting. It did not qualify as the nurture Mary Shelley insisted was important.

Moman, denying any great credit for the success of his Memphis sessions, has said, 'only a fool could not succeed with Elvis'. Moman is analytically correct. The too powerful fools certainly existed and they dominated Elvis because, as Jonathan Swift believed, a confederacy of dunces prevails over everything. The career of Elvis was defined by three institutions and two individuals. These were Hollywood, RCA, Vegas and Bienstock and Parker. Rather than provide nurture and nourishment, they fed from him and all were obsessed with quantity rather than quality. They assumed that they were dealing with product best suited for a section of the population that could safely be regarded as inferior and malleable.

Parker has been discussed elsewhere but, in the context of providing creative nourishment, he appears more ridiculous than ever. He made a lot of money from a phenomenon he never properly recognised and, like Frankenstein, misunderstood the metaphysical meaning of galvanisation. He assumed he had created rather than discovered life. This allowed him to believe that the life was only entitled to be subject to his control and wishes. The difference between Parker and Frankenstein was that Parker had more confidence and believed galvanisation was a trick that could be repeated without cost. He was not tempted to run away. Instead of developing the talent within his charge, he treated it as a freak which he isolated from reality and around which he created his own self-indulgent circus. Unable to nurture the talent, he nourished instead the appetites and ego of his client because that was all the grubby money-maker had to offer. Albert Goldman, who thinks the self-loathing by Elvis began in 1964, defines it quite well. 'The good Elvis was starved and the bad Elvis glutted.'

If Peter Gurlanick is right, villainy was never really in the heart of Parker. Possibly, Parker suffered more than anyone and it was he who had his confused head turned by Hollywood and Vegas. Like a football manager, he did have good and bad periods. We should not, though, be prepared to give Parker the benefit of the doubt. He lived a long, affluent life and disapproval is now without consequence but this is one tab he has to collect. In the introduction to the 1931 movie, the mad scientist, Frankenstein, is condemned for not reckoning with God. When I think of Parker it sounds fair. There is enough in the tawdry detail of his chiselling existence for him to be viewed as low life with unwarranted ambition. It is significant that the posthumous Elvis has become a more formidable presence in our culture since the tone deaf phoney has died.

Elvis needed creative inspiration and, like the Creature, the hope of renewal. Parker required a dedicated professional whom he could use to achieve commercial domination. Neither delivered what the other wanted. There is a paradox. Elvis was a victim but he was also blessed with privilege and this not only offered excessive reward but facilitated mistakes by Elvis. If his fame brought the baggage of compromise and errors, an odd gem always emerged to add to his achievements. A good example of how the story of Elvis always involved abuse and indulgence is what happened in 1976. In a desperate attempt to persuade Elvis to make records, RCA took their recording equipment to Graceland and recorded him singing in the Jungle Room basement. At this stage, any other performer would have been abandoned but Elvis had a name that shifted product. Because he was indulged, we now have decent records like 'He'll Have To Go' and 'Pledging My Love' but we also have disasters like 'The Last Farewell' and 'Solitaire'. Elvis was restricted by song writing deals and money obsessed, long-term contracts but he was also afforded a degree of trust not available to others. Sometimes, he stumbled because he was allowed to, in circumstances that only the privileged attain. The talent of Elvis was diverse but he had fame and he could express his talent even when weak.

There is a contradiction within the statement by F. Scott Fitzgerald, 'There are no second acts in American life.' There are because the belief in money will sustain the successful beyond the point it should, even, if the disproportionate influence of money and profit mean the second acts soon become disappointing and confusing. But, with the gifted, they are never less than interesting. Elvis was allowed to be embarrassing and he took advantage. Elvis was not without responsibility and, though Parker needs to be condemned, we have to accept that Elvis would never have stayed true to his rock and roll roots. His romantic dependencies and his voice constantly reminded him he had priorities outside rock and roll. He was always destined to drift out of reach of the village.

Drift, though, is not the same as self-destruction. Making popular music is not like writing books or assembling films. It may require inspiration but there is nowhere near the same amount of effort. The real tragedy of Elvis is it could have been so easy. The 'Elvis Country' album exists as proof. For a couple of nights, he threw away the script and sang songs that he liked and remembered from his youth. His talent allowed his instinct to immediately take the songs in a different direction and to another level. He did not fail because, in these circumstances, his brilliance would always ensure he inspired himself and his musicians.

Chips Moman was right to say 'only a fool could not succeed with Elvis' but Elvis had to be a fool not to succeed with Elvis. If the silly sod had just made the music he liked and, if the other management mediocrities had only realised that was all he had to do and they were best doing nothing, this book would have no purpose. This is the madness at the centre of this tragedy and it is heartbreaking.

The movie, 'Barton Fink', by the Coen Brothers explores the difficulties an idealistic writer encounters in Hollywood. What emerges from the movie is how a creative talent spends his life either being described as a genius or an inconsequential insect. The conversations are not difficult to imagine. 'This is a marvellous work full of real feeling.' This is the genius part. 'What makes you think the public will have any interest in what you say? Perhaps, if we market it differently it might appeal to the Saturday night crowd. It will require a lot of changes. I have a lot of projects on my desk.' This is the inconsequential insect revelation.

The problem with these contradictory messages that a creative talent receives is that the recipient may not have the skills to balance the contradictions. Some individuals will remember nothing other than being told they are a genius but others will forget they had any talent and dwell only on the sudden realisation that they are an inconsequential insect. For many, their feelings will change from day to day or they will have periods within their career where one aspect dominates at the expense of the other. The irritating truth is we will never know where Elvis stood exactly in all this, only that the equation applied to him as it does to all performers who use their talent to make a living. There is, though, enough in his career and his brief revelations of how his success had left him feeling empty for us to assume that he felt the sharpness of the distinction as much as anyone. This emptiness helped undermine and destroy him. Somewhere in all the confusion, he lost faith in himself and his original ambition. Elvis was lucky because, not only did he have a talent, he was well rewarded, was given plenty of exposure and superb facilities to practise his talent. But the luck was always double edged. Hollywood demanded a terrible price from him because he was denied both the recording studio and the stage when he was in his prime. His good looks were also a curse because they obliged him to often use his music to enhance an image.

There are always buts with Elvis.

He was directed to blandness by the bureaucracy that controlled him and he excused them with his own excesses. Nevertheless, he did make attempts to nourish his talent and he ensured it was expressed on a significant number of occasions. He had a will and his wayward ambition reminds us of the Creature stubbornly driving his sledge across the ice to nowhere simply because it is just that. The efforts of Elvis may be bewildering but it is never easy to understand the purposes of others. This is why Shelley allows the Creature to talk at length at the end of the book. He explains his strange violence and why he thinks he has no alternative but to build his funeral pyre at the point furthest from man. His speech covers four uninterrupted pages. Elvis Presley was always reluctant to be so candid.

Despite what the loyalists say, the actions of Elvis were not heroic. No man is a hero to his valet and Elvis had plenty and all have talked. If he is badly flawed, there are, besides their myopic revelations, the many musical achievements which ensure he is not worth contempt either. Albert Goldman states he lacked the commitment of a Charlie Parker who, though self-destructive, never took his talent less than seriously. No doubt, there is some truth in this but both men struggled to equate the talent with the inconsequential insect. Both men oscillated between self-belief and self-hatred. In this struggle, the outcomes are far from predictable and the easy judgements and contempt of Goldman only repel. The relationship Elvis had with Parker was peculiarly strange. He was often critical of the man but, also, remarkably loyal. Elvis probably enjoyed his company and, for a while, thought he had found a supportive, alternative, working class hero who could keep the big shots in their place. It is clear, though, that Elvis soon had doubts about his manager but was too superstitious and too lacking in confidence to abandon him. If he kept him as manager because of a fear that he may lose the key element in his exceptional success, he soon realised the consequences or the price. Full of self-hatred, he had no alternative but to betray Parker and himself. This destruction was accelerated because the two men, like Frankenstein and the Creature, became a double for the other. Frankenstein and the Creature were both culpable in the death of Justine. The Creature acted vindictively and Frankenstein was too timid to reveal the truth. Elvis imitated Parker and became a glutton and, like his creator, asserted a need for control over friends and women. Meanwhile, Parker imitated his creation and became self-destructive and used ridiculous amounts of money to gamble. He needed to stimulate inconsequential adrenalin and claim attention. The galvaniser and the galvanised, addicted to artificial stimulus, finished their lives dependent on repeated galvanisation.

The icebergs Elvis battled with were inside his own head where Parker unwittingly forced him to travel. The instincts of Parker told him that, if he had to pursue his creature across unknown land, his creature would destroy both of them. Instead, Parker indulged Elvis and allowed him a relaxed and comfortable life and, because he thought he was managing a freak, never made any qualitative demands of the talent. Unfortunately, the emphasis on short term gratification tempted Elvis. Parker and, sometimes, Elvis saw it as a healthy alternative to 'fancy ideas'. This desensitised the performer and soon produced alienation. The word alienation, though, is too weak. As Miranda Seymour, the biographer of Shelley, states, 'fame drained the life fluid.' Elvis became a semi-corpse dependent on galvanisation rather than life because that was what others had arranged with his complicity. This is the curse of galvanisation; it refuses to acknowledge independent life and, surviving on the substitutes that galvanisation provides, the famous watch themselves disappear from their own view. Mary Shelley, though, had other concerns beside celebrity. She foresaw a modern world dominated by transcendent technology and materialism. Admittedly, she missed the benefits but she understood how it would delude more than the famous into thinking the highs of galvanisation could be a substitute for life. The irony for Elvis is that he wanted to make the 'domestic connection' with others that Shelley believed in.

If the life of Elvis was a warning against galvanisation, his music proved that he had a considerable talent and, okay, he did not change the world on his own but he did have the glory for a while of making it look like he did. He may not have invented rock and roll but, because he was so famous, he, more than anyone, tilted the world to the inspired primitivism of his homeland, the music that proclaimed, like Shelley, 'if our impulses were confined to hunger, thirst and desire we might nearly be free.' Sir Arthur Conan Doyle wrote that there are three elements to a human being - character, intelligence and soul. None of us, he realised, were consistent in all three. Mary Shelley also understood this, 'such is human nature that beauty and deformity are often closely linked.' Elvis became a musical figurehead. The three elements in that creation were the talent, the work and the man. Like the human beings whose flaws bemused Conan Doyle, Elvis was inconsistent in his three elements and the work and the man, because of cruel circumstance and his own flaws, became less impressive than the talent.

I propose that at the core of this interesting and complex human being there was always a philistine having to cope in a world operated by sophisticates. Inevitably, he was obliged to embarrass and fail because philistines or the uncouth always will offend and threaten. As DJ Fontana once said to a disconsolate Elvis, 'You just got too big.' If Elvis was always the philistine that the critics condemn, it only confirms his talent as extraordinary because nobody has ever made such a seductive case for philistinism. His rivals claimed authenticity and, later, the rock and roll heroes had to insist they were sophisticated. This was the only way they could prevail. Sublime philistinism is indeed his extraordinary talent. For all his timidity, he was obliged and willing to confront the world with his simple passions and unrefined taste. All he had as armour was his marvellous voice, innate rhythm, heart, good looks and invention. He was not a great artist because he was instead a marvellous alternative to art and its baggage. His innocent challenge would not have been possible without American capitalism and democracy but it was business and supposed superiors that ensured he would never win. They assumed that he was a freak rather than a talent. He also lost heart for the fight. But for a while, and at his best, it looked as if he could win. What tantalises is the possibility that with just a tilt in circumstances, and one or two different characters in the screenplay, it could have been a different movie with the grand philistine as a conqueror for all time.

I sometimes imagine Elvis in heaven where he is, no doubt, demanding more attention from God than anyone else and possibly scheming stupidly to relocate Parker from hell. When God has managed to avoid him Elvis will look down at the world and watch emaciated youths with guitars wail their way through weighty lyrics and extend their instrumental solos. He will smile at their insistence on sophistication and consequence. On his better days, he will laugh at how his special brand of reactionary philistinism and simple tunes persist as an inelegant form that still corrupts the artistic ambitions of the earnest sophisticates that followed.

He was a contradiction and, as he was considered odd by the world that produced him, it is probably no surprise he is still considered odd by the worlds that follow. He was a singer who could make a tune memorable and we appreciate his best records, sometimes, without noticing that his singing is brilliant. This led many to believe that values and conceptualism were all important. Although he was more than a singer, he was also more than the conceptualist and hero whom so many insisted he had to be. He did, though, provide the link between these two different approaches to pop music but he was supported in providing the link by many others who came from the American South. Elvis may not have changed the world and he may have been only a facilitator of what was inevitable. But the world to change requires some people to not only behave differently but be remarkably persuasive. Whoever they are, he belonged with them.

What makes his fans so loyal? Why do we want him to prevail? For me, it is because I know his legacy has been obscured by an odd conspiracy of his own inferior ambitions and the prejudice of others. The novel, 'Frankenstein', and the Elvis record catalogue are ignored by too many and such neglect will always leave some of us obsessed. We know what Elvis said to his nurse a couple of months before he died. He confessed he would go to his grave with the knowledge that he would never be remembered and had never made anything that would last. He confided something similar to Kathy Westmoreland, his backup singer, 'How will they remember me. They're not going to remember me. I've never done anything lasting. I've never done a classic film.' He knew he had something that could be remembered but he also had the silly dream of being an actor and thought that was his only route to respect. The tragedy continues because he now rests unaware that, whilst the numbers may be declining, fans who need his music as part of their lives are still being recruited. Not quite Van Gogh who went to his grave without any acclamation at all but similarly sad.

Some years ago, probably as many as twenty five, I read about an artist who had an exhibition in London that included Elvis montages. I forget her name now. She explained her obsession with Elvis with words something like, 'You think you have him understood and then you find another detail or hear another song and you are as mystified as ever. It is endless.'

I began this book with the same frustration but over a year and a hundred and thirty thousand words later I am not quite so mystified. The mysteries may endure but they appear more complicated than they are, only, because there is more than one. Considered individually, all are possible of an explanation.

He was active when the inspiration or support of others made him enthusiastic and indolent when the demands of others left him bored. The plot of 'Frankenstein' requires The Creature to go to sleep at key points and the narrative prescribed by Parker required the same of Elvis.

He had a taste for revolution because he was different to others but was conservative because he was loyal to his parents. The same contradiction existed in his music because he liked what he heard as a child but his creativity and singularity obliged him to innovate. His hedonism was pursued with such determination that it became to the establishment disturbing nihilism. It terrified them and possibly him. Elvis belonged to a generation that wanted to redefine itself; a mere ten years later The Beatles and Bob Dylan had to represent a generation that wanted to re-define itself and the world. This is why he did not understand them and they were baffled by him. His music was a mix of the sentimental and hedonistic because that was the Southern identity which shaped him. If his energetic hedonism led him towards nihilism, his passionate sentimentality led him to obsessive romance. He was extreme because it suited his nature and because he could be. His major weakness was an inability to say no to the insurance of money, 'the vagabond pursuit.' Because of the people around him, this led to bizarre compromises that distorted the already uneasy balance in his music between his hedonism and sentimentality.

But all the great talents and innovators have baggage. The Creature was violent but receptive. Elvis was talented but defensive. They break through not because of crystal clear consistency but because their talent has a wide reach. Dickens savaged the bourgeois for their callous utilitarianism but, as George Orwell noted, he found it impossible to imagine for his wounded heroes any resolution other than the ideal, middle class family. Charlotte Bronte gave a voice to the neglected female but romanticised the brutal male and Hitchcock in his masterpiece, 'Vertigo', made a film about his masculine, sexist fantasies that later inspired feminists. As Dave Marsh once wrote about Elvis, special talents always give us more than we want.

What made Elvis 'awful' also helped make him great. It not only made him unique but ensured he was always willing to affirm others who were also considered vulgar. But, despite his complexity, he was still obliged to give us more than he would have wanted, the rubbish insisted upon by 'the vagabond pursuit' of money. It meant that fans, like me, had to imitate Frankenstein and pursue the maligned creature at the heart of the contradictions. Only after this attempt to explain him, do I now feel able to abide in a settled world.

Elvis destroyed himself because he was allowed to and because he went crazy. This craziness was a consequence of personal flaws, disappointments, being indulged, being betrayed and the burden of fame. His response was to retreat into himself. Once, when discussing yoga, Elvis pleaded he wanted to be free of the conditions of cause and effect. He was a complex man but too much of a show off to be capable of successful, inner escape. The Creature shared similar torment. 'I was the slave, not the master, of an impulse which I detested, yet could not disobey.'

Fate chose him for a puzzling destiny but it was only interested because he had exceptional talent. Fate ensured Elvis would have flaws and allowed Parker and others to do real damage because fate is like that. It has no mercy and, as Orson Welles insisted, its cynicism is beyond us all. And when it is not, there will always be men with misguided wills and too much faith in the future, men prepared and willing to destroy talented innocents like the Creature and Elvis and even themselves. These men, and now women, overrate ambition. They ignore the importance of human connection or propriety and are the galvanisers Mary Shelley sought to resist. When I suggested earlier that the Creature and Elvis should have abandoned hopes of domesticity I was not arguing for ambition. What they needed was resignation.

But why listen to me? I am, like his many other fans, the biggest mystery of all. I belong to the addicts who failed to abandon him after he abandoned himself. My mystery is my emotional dependency on his music and story. I used to think it was simply because he was brilliant and because he had infected the dreams of an eight year old. Whilst the explanation contains some truth, I think I am clearer on that now.

A couple of years ago, probably more, I heard a programme on Radio 4 about madness. Various psychiatrists explained how madness could actually be photographed by a machine as a blob on the brain. According to these psychiatrists, we all have these blobs and the blobs on the normal are no smaller than the blobs on the schizophrenics. The normal people are lucky because they have harmless blobs. What was also apparent from the programme was how lucid the schizophrenics were after successful treatment. One woman described how her madness was to her now inexplicable. Equally mysterious was how easily she could attract converts when she thought she was the Messiah. She regularly picked up disciples in supermarkets. The woman who told this tale was rational and charming. Elvis is part of my madness but it is bigger than him because it includes American music and all my other loyalties and prejudices. It also includes my more serious aspirations, which because they are thought serious, go unnoticed. The madness is not without consequence but it does not require medication, fortunately, only CD and DVD collections, books and a season ticket for Liverpool Football Club. It is as Waylon Jennings, the country singer, once said, 'I've always been crazy, it stopped me from going insane.'

The curiosity will continue and, if I think I understand Elvis now, it will never fail to respond to another revealing book or re-mastered album. The blob is still there bubbling away under my skull, its switch set to galvanised standby.

At the beginning of this book, I mentioned how Elvis made me think about myself and my social class differently. Ultimately, I suppose that is what is important to me. I may have other interests but I still need his defiant and seductive philistinism, his open innocence and heart, otherwise too much of my life and myself would have to be dismissed. Maybe it is nothing to do with class but simply an allegiance to youthful optimism and faith. Elvis may be an authentic, working class hero but his music does not celebrate working class life. He remembers his musical roots but, finally, he celebrates only his curiosity and himself. His critics might argue that this is why he was obliged to lose interest.

Forget the world, he changed me and that is why I still attend his virtual concerts even though the songs do not always suit what I think of as his finer self. The moment when the world is revealed as having more potential than you thought possible cannot be repeated but its potency is addictive. This, rather than pure craziness, is, I hope, why I find his music an irresistible form. If that initial moment of discovery, when remembered again, is never quite so pure then it, and its potential, can still be remembered and Elvis reminds me continually and brilliantly. No doubt rock and roll purists will argue that I have overestimated the man because of my blob but I ask those to ignore my madness and refer to the collection in the attached List 7. Much of his other material I admire, respect and enjoy but the records on this list of his R&B material are the source of my narcotic addiction. They fertilised the blob and they, alone, in my opinion, mean that he should be accorded respect by anyone interested in American music. He is, of course, much more than his R&B records.

It is unfortunate that Elvis is a man more famous than the music he made. This did not happen because he has no music that deserves fame. Unfortunately, there is baggage that holds him to ridicule. This baggage was often insisted upon by others but, like the Creature, he was often taunted and he sometimes responded badly. Elvis has not lasted because he established his worth as a human being or because some confuse his charisma with heroism. He made music that singled him out from others, complex and contradictory it is unique to him and, for many people, it has become essential.

His fans say there will never be another Elvis. His personality contained ambition, animalism, compliance, curiosity, cynicism, dependency, hedonism, independence, innocence, loyalty, lyricism, rebellion, romance, self-destruction, sentimentality and violence. Of course, the simultaneous existence of these qualities may only make him typical. Idealism, debate and analysis, though, are not on the list. Their absence meant he suffered but his music embraced all the other human contradictions and their expression in his music make him, well, work it out for yourselves.

But we must not forget the Creature who was not only complex and had many of the qualities in the previous paragraph but who was also capable of debate and analysis. Both he and Elvis should be acknowledged as special and unique, even, if both were capable of destruction when faced with hatred or contempt. Without a flawed Frankenstein or Parker, they would not have had to rely so much on gesture to confirm their presence. Resistant to persuasion and lacking curiosity, the majority too quickly assumed the two figures were no more than their flaws or appearance. The Creature and Elvis reacted to a world that they knew would never understand them. Mary Shelley insisted upon the complexity within all, the normal and the odd. This is why Lionel Verney, the narrator of 'The Last Man' and the fictional character she based on herself, is 'committed to history and the biographies of those misunderstood and underestimated.' She understood that too many of us have to insist the odd and rare are either heroes or villains but argued this is superficial. The responsibility to understand means we must not be deterred nor surprised when those who are different refuse to follow predicable paths. More chilling than that, she demonstrated how their paths are always a response to our ignorance. The flaws that led to the doom of the Creature and Elvis resided not just within the created but their creators and, more important than anyone, because of our numbers and because we continue to ignore our responsibilities, the witnesses.

———————

THE LISTS - THE CURSE OF THE NEGLECTED LEGACY

The list of the lists

The lists

List 1.   The classic albums
List 2.   One man jukebox
List 3.   The gospel music
List 4.   The live music
List 5.   The movies in the sixties
List 6.   The 'Hitstory' collection
List 7.   The rhythm and blues collection
List 8.   The best 50
List 9.   The missing tracks from 'Walk A Mile In My Shoes'
List 10. The albums that were never released
List 11. The albums that should have been released in the 1960s
List 12. The albums that should have been released in the 1970s
List 13. The 'Chips Moman Memphis selection'
List 14. The 'missing folk album'
List 15. The neglected legacy summarised

The ratings

a) Lists 1, 6, 9, 10, 11 and 12 have ratings. These lists refer to the missing tracks from 'Walk A Mile In My Shoes' and the albums that were either released or should have been.

b) Lists 4, 5, 7, 8, 13 and 14 have not been rated. These refer to selections that are either personal or fanciful. The merit of individual tracks is not as important as it is in the other lists.

c) Lists 2, 3, and 15 consist of text only

Although tempting to give the truly sublime moments 5 points, the idea was rejected because it implies in very good records a failure that does not exist. Instead, I have included List 8 which consists of what I regard as his best 50 records. This will have to serve as his sublime moments. No doubt, many will disagree with individual markings in these lists but, whoever marks these records fairly, will aggregate a similar number of points. The points are awarded as follows: 4 – Very good, 3 – Has merit, more than listenable, 2 – Listenable but either seriously flawed or dull and 1 - How could he?

———————

List 1 - The Classic Albums

Album	Rating
How Great Thou Art	
How Great Thou Art	★★★★
In The Garden	★★★★
Somebody Bigger Than You And I	★★★★
Farther Along	★★★★
Stand By Me	★★★★
Without Him	★★★★
So High	★★★★
Where Could I Go But To The Lord	★★★★
By And By	★★★☆
If The Lord Wasn't Walking By My Side	★★★☆
Run On	★★★★
Where No One Stands Alone	★★★★
Bonus track	
Crying In The Chapel	★★★★
From Elvis In Memphis	
Wearing That Loved On Look	★★★★
Only The Strong Survive	★★★★
I'll Hold You In My Heart	★★★★
Long Black Limousine	★★★★
It Keeps Right On A'Hurtin'	★★★☆
I'm Movin' On	★★★★
Power Of My Love	★★★★
Gentle On My Mind	★★★★
After Loving You	★★★★
True Love Travels On A Gravel Road	★★★★
Any Day Now	★★★★
In The Ghetto	★★★☆

Album	Rating

Elvis Presley

Blue Suede Shoes	★★★☆
I'm Counting On You	★★★☆
I Got A Woman	★★★☆
One Sided Love Affair	★★★★
I Love You Because	★★★☆
Just Because	★★★☆
Tutti Frutti	★★★☆
Trying To Get To You	★★★★
I'm Gonna Sit Right Down And Cry Over You	★★★★
I'll Never Let You Go	★★★★
Blue Moon	★★★★
Money Honey	★★★★

Elvis Is Back

Make Me Know It	★★★☆
Fever	★★★★
The Girl Of My Best Friend	★★★☆
I Will Be Home Again	★★★★
Dirty Dirty Feeling	★★★★
Thrill Of Your Love	★★★★
Soldier Boy	★★★★
Such A Night	★★★★
It Feels So Right	★★★★
Girl Next Door Went A'Walkin'	★★★★
Like A Baby	★★★★
Reconsider Baby	★★★★

Elvis Rock And Roll No. 2

Rip It Up	★★★☆
Love Me	★★★☆
When My Blue Moon Turns To Gold	★★★★
Long Tall Sally	★★★☆
First In Line	★★★☆

Paralysed	★★★☆
So Glad You're Mine	★★★★
Old Shep	★★★★
Ready Teddy	★★★★
Any Place Is Paradise	★★★★
How's The World Treating You	★★★★
How Do You Think I Feel	★★★★

Elvis Country

Snowbird	★☆☆☆
Tomorrow Never Comes	★★★★
Little Cabin On The Hill	★★★☆
Whole Lotta Shakin' Goin' On	★★★★
Funny How Time Slips Away	★★★★
I Really Don't Want To Know	★★★★
There Goes My Everything	★★★★
It's Your Baby You Rock It	★★★★
The Fool	★★★★
Faded Love	★★★★
I Washed My Hands In Muddy Water	★★★★
Make The World Go Away	★★★☆

His Hand In Mine

His Hand In Mine	★★★★
I'm Gonna Walk Dem Golden Stairs	★★★☆
In My Father's House	★★★☆
Milky White Way	★★★★
Known Only To Him	★★★★
I Believe In The Man In The Sky	★★★★
Joshua Fit The Battle	★★★☆
He Knows Just What I Need	★★★★
Swing Low Sweet Chariot	★★★☆
Mansion Over The Hilltop	★★★★
If We Never Meet Again	★★★☆
Working On The Building	★★★★

Album	Rating

Elvis TV Special
    Trouble/Guitar Man.
    Lawdy Miss Clawdy/Baby What You Want Me To Do.
    Heartbreak Hotel/Hound Dog/All Shook Up/Can't Help Falling In Love/
    Jailhouse Rock/Don't Be Cruel/Blue Suede Shoes/Love Me Tender.
    Where Could I Go But To The Lord/Up Above My Head/Saved.
    Baby What You Want Me To Do/That's All Right/Blue Christmas/
    One Night/Tiger Man/Trying To Get To You.
    Memories.
    Nothingville/Big Boss Man/Let Yourself Go/It Hurts Me/Guitar Man/
    Little Egypt/Trouble/Guitar Man.
    If I Can Dream.

Note - ratings for individual tracks on this album are not included. This performance includes medleys which make it difficult but it is best enjoyed as a complete performance. To award ratings would miss the point. This is the 76 minute CD version of the TV show. The extra tracks are too good not to be included.

King Creole

Track	Rating
King Creole	★★★★
As Long As I Have You	★★★★
Hard Headed Woman	★★★★
Trouble	★★★☆
Dixieland Rock	★★★★
Don't Ask Me Why	★★★☆
Lover Doll	★★★☆
Young Dreams	★★★☆
Crawfish	★★★★
Steadfast Loyal And True	★★☆☆
New Orleans	★★★★

List 2 – One Man Jukebox – a guide to the box sets for each decade

The seventeenth century, English poet, John Dryden, said, 'To be sure there is a joyness in madness which that but only madmen know.' There are fifteen CDs contained in the three box sets that cover the fifties, sixties and seventies. The music they contain is the joy in my madness. Not the complete joy because they refer only briefly to his live performances and they omit his two classic, gospel albums.

This section will concentrate on songs not previously mentioned. The box set for the fifties, 'Elvis Presley - The King of Rock 'N' Roll' is the best of the three but inadequate as a statement of his glory because the triumphs elsewhere are also important. What was said earlier needs to be repeated. *Despite his decline, Elvis Presley still managed in each of the three decades to deliver music he was incapable of in the other decades.* The fifties had rock and roll and daring, the sixties had a glorious voice and the seventies revealed emotional wounds and curiosity.

The fifties –'The King Of Rock 'N' Roll' - although the box set reveals a weakening after the movie contracts have been signed, this is the collection that has the most consistent performances. The early compromises, movies and Christmas fodder are all exposed but Elvis is mainly magnificent. It is impossible to skip any of the one hundred and forty tracks when listening to these CDs. This cannot be said of the other box sets. Because it has everything from the fifties, 'The King Of Rock 'N' Roll' includes the classic albums and the hit singles from that period. It also includes all the Sun singles and these alone are worth the cost of the package. In addition to what has already been discussed in other sections, there are many highlights, too many to be given the attention they deserve.

The first CD is dominated by his music from Sun and the very first Sun single is great and interesting because Elvis launched himself immediately with an immortal, double A sided record. *'That's All Right'* never sounds anything less than fresh, no matter how many times it is played. In his obituary in 'The New Yorker', this was described as 'a significant song by a significant man'. After it was released in Memphis, the local youngsters used the title as a greeting. Those two achievements alone were probably beyond his dreams. 'That's All Right' was coupled with *'Blue Moon Of Kentucky'* which is so good it inspired Bill Monroe, a bluegrass purist, to record the song again. *'Good Rockin' Tonight'* strikes musical independence and leaves previous genres in its wake. It is a warning that the talented youth will listen to everyone and then ignore them all. Neither rhythm and blues nor country boogie woogie will be sufficient for his ambition. Like the best of his records, it has a pictorial strength. I can see the barn where all the fun will happen. Later, I was pleased when it came to life under a jet black sky in the classic movie, 'Night Of The Hunter', the unique, noir tribute to the Deep South that was directed by Charles Laughton, the English actor, who, with unrestrained glee, first introduced Elvis on the Ed Sullivan Show. These coincidences have to have meaning.

More glories follow quickly. *'Baby Let's Play House'* ploughs the same, independent field and defines rockabilly for those who are talented but are obliged to follow and imitate. Raw and sly, it combines defiance with irony but is important, simply, because it bounces like nothing before. Never to be forgotten is the beautifully pure *'You're A Heartbreaker'* because, despite the broken heart, the innocence remains inspiringly intact. The ordinary, country song called *'I Forgot To Remember To Forget'* is brought to vibrant life by a heartfelt vocal and inspired production by Sam Phillips and the spine chilling *'Milk Cow Blues Boogie'* has Elvis digging deep into the roots of rural America. He celebrates it as well as anyone but the deliberately false start still reminds us he has his own independent voice. *'Just Because'* and *'I Don't Care If The Sun Don't Shine'* are done as standard rockabilly which makes them suddenly worthy. The former has two guitar solos that occupy 40% of its running time which gives it an added virtue. *'I'm Left, You're Right, She's Gone'* has a groove which is impalpably exquisite, the end of every line becomes a delicious hook. It is one of many examples that make Elvis stand apart from other rockabilly performers. Best of all the Sun singles is *'Mystery Train'* which is as good as any other rock and roll record by him or anyone and has Elvis sweeping along into a drama way beyond the song, an American landscape dotted with lost souls whose questions it refuses to answer.

Like Elvis, the box set moves on to RCA. Compared to Ray Charles, the version by Elvis of *'I Got A Woman'* is basic. The version by Charles swings and is blessed with a controlled vocal and a jazzy, saxophone break. Elvis wails primitively and his band stomps but, of course, this is what makes much of rockabilly appealing. It is unashamedly crude but, because it rocks, the crudeness becomes disturbing rebellion. The big hit, *'Heartbreak Hotel'*, has lost some of its power in the last five decades but it does not take much imagination to understand its spectacular triumph. The songwriters in 'Writing For The King' usually identified dull ideas for their inspirations. 'Heartbreak Hotel' is the glorious exception because it was inspired by a suicide. The weird sound, the jazzy piano and the vocal by Elvis that merges a punk styled Billy Eckstein with his intense Sun treble, all make it unique. *'I'm Counting On You'* is a Don Robertson song but sounds unlike the Don Robertson material Elvis recorded in the sixties which is an indication that the moods of Elvis determined the sound of his music as much as anything. *'One Sided Love Affair'* helps to extend the rockabilly format so it merges with boogie woogie. Elvis is lively and frantic rather than passionate but he does enough to ensure the beat is complemented with both charm and grit. His version of *'Tutti Frutti'* is lighter than the version by Little Richard but it exists on its own terms as knowing rockabilly and it moves along adequately with Elvis in full control and able to indulge in enough tricks to keep the attention. *'I'm Gonna Sit Right Down And Cry'* has Elvis in playful mood, alternating devotion with an implied threat. Despite the implications of the title, Elvis makes it clear that the relationship will be on his terms. His version of *'Blue Suede Shoes'* was subsequently condemned by Sam Phillips for being too fast. He may be right but many of us grew up on the Elvis alternative and, compared to his full on assault, the version by Carl Perkins sounds like safety first rockabilly. Elvis pushes it to the limit and his wild, daredevil irresponsibility actually suits the manic obsession in the song. *'Lawdy Miss Clawdy'* is intense, great rock and roll. With anybody else, the record would be driven by the piano but, although the piano is marvellous, it is the urgent vocal that makes it come alive. It exists as an urban alternative to 'Good

Rockin' Tonight' because it repeats the potent challenge he offered to the previously all conquering world of rhythm and blues. *'My Baby Left Me'* is an Arthur Crudup song and, thanks to a guitar contribution that echoes 'Mystery Train', it is breathlessly dynamic and equal to what Elvis recorded at Sun although it has its own iconic identity. George Harrison thought this was the best record made by Elvis and his statement demonstrates how profusely the monuments are scattered. *'Shake Rattle And Roll'* is not in the same class but it is a driving, rock alternative to the swing of Joe Turner and, because it has two guitar solos, is probably beyond criticism. The Bill Haley type chorus is a little strange but it works because it complements the hard edge in the main vocal. Leiber and Stoller wrote *'Love Me'* as a send up. Elvis invests the song with real heart and ignores the irony. The song was originally recorded by Georgia Gibbs. She was not a straight country singer and she had on more than one occasion covered the hits of LaVern Baker. There is the famous tale of LaVern taking out life insurance before a flight. 'This is for Georgia,' she quipped, 'because if it crashes she's out of business.' It exists not as rhythm and blues or even doo wop but as an example of the commercial, white rhythm and blues that was popular in the fifties. When sung by young men it soon became identified with rock and roll. The example by Elvis is superior to the others. It is enjoyable because it defines an age and because Elvis is so much better than his rivals. Elvis sings *'First In Line'* with a pure, vulnerable sincerity as if he is, like the dog killer in 'Old Shep', an innocent obliged to endure a tragedy. His voice reaches beyond mere misery towards seductive gloom. The emphasis is where it should be in all his ballads - Elvis, the bass and the piano. It is difficult to believe that Elvis is only twenty one years old because this is extremely confident singing. *'How Do You Think I Feel'* has the purity and clarity of 'You're A Heartbreaker' but is closer to Western Swing than rock n roll. Ernst Jorgenson makes the point that Bill Black struggled with the bass part but the vocal by Elvis is so accurate with all the shaded emphasis in the right spots that he carries the day and the shortcomings by the band appear to be no more than rockabilly eccentricity. Apart from looking like a Hollywood film star capable of melting any private eye, Cindy Walker wrote and sung *'When My Blue Moon Turns To Gold'*. Surely, she never anticipated the version by Elvis and its jubilee gospel style. It manages to be both tuneful and to have an urgent rhythm and is proof of how radical Elvis can be when he is in the mood. *'Paralysed'* is basically 'Don't Be Cruel' revisited but it is more than sufficient.

More exceptional, are the three ballads, *'Don't', 'Is It So Strange'* and *'Anyway You Want Me'*, which, despite conventional lyrics, Elvis transforms into dark material. 'Don't' has a pleasant melody but it carries a sinister threat similar to 'Reconsider Baby' whilst 'Strange' is a plea from a damaged soul lost in self-sustaining, Gothic illusions. 'Anyway You Want Me' is another, great original and I had my proof that Elvis was unique when I heard it for the first time on my 'Elvis Golden Records Volume One' album. The performance, like the arrangement, is unrestrained drama and emotion. Loaded unashamedly with crude hooks, it is all delivered with a defiance and assertive scorn that renders accusations of bad taste meaningless. His covers of the Little Richard hits, *'Long Tall Sally', 'Rip It Up'* and *'Ready Teddy'*, are less powerful than the originals but Elvis converts them all into frantic rockabilly and this gives them purpose. The rapport between Elvis and the musicians is pure pleasure.

The sureness of touch and claim to independence is persistent throughout the set, so a song as ordinary as *'Doncha Think It's Time'* becomes essential for its subtle beat and gentle throb as does *'I Beg Of You'* which has a perfect, insistent groove that has been shamefully ignored by critics. Even the 'Christmas album' and the 'Loving You' soundtrack have their moments. The 'Christmas album' includes a great, gospel number, *'Peace In The Valley'*, full of drama and anticipation that Elvis delivers in a strong, brooding baritone and *'Santa Claus Is Back In Town'*, a raucous blues as wild as Muddy Waters. *'Blue Christmas'* is a weird mix of everything that is both catchy and original. The rumour is that Elvis made it as tasteless as possible so it would not be released as a single but this does not convince because the same ideas already exist in 'Any Way You Want Me'. The throwaway *'Santa Bring My Baby Back To Me'* is lighter material but delivered with the confident panache that also makes *'Treat Me Nice'* and *'Baby I Don't Care'* from the 'Jailhouse Rock' soundtrack such exceptional records. The same, sure touch is also present in the other tracks from 'Jailhouse Rock'. The simple ballad, *'Young And Beautiful'*, is achingly sincere and the morose faith irresistible whilst

'*Don't Leave Me Now*' is Elvis and Leiber and Stoller at their subtle best. The blues influence is no thicker than thin lace but that, and the swing in the vocal, helps it to work perfectly. His version of '*Take My Hand Precious Lord*' is surpassed by others, including a peerless rendition by Aretha, but it is still soulful and it makes a decent companion for 'Peace In The Valley'. The songs from 'Love Me Tender' are weak but better than what happened in the sixties movies. Nobody, though, has matched his version of '*Mean Woman Blues*' from the film, 'Loving You', when he delivered a growl that squeezed out its own rhythm between the beat. This is far more than what Jerry Lee Lewis and Roy Orbison manage in their cover versions. His versions of '*Party*' and '*Got A Lot A Livin' To Do*' are not authentic rockabilly but they are loaded with energy and drive and can be enjoyed for what they are which is Hollywood rock and roll delivered by a fabulous singer.

The Ivory Joe Hunter song, '*I Need You So*', is a worthy example of fifties rhythm and blues because of the wailing vocal. The heavy drum backbeat is unusual for an Elvis ballad and my opinion regarding it varies. Some days, I endure it yet others I think it works. Even in my endurance moods, the ambitious vocal makes the record worthwhile.

The last CD of studio material contains the previously discussed 'King Creole' album and a clutch of wild rockers that he recorded as a final, violent gesture before the Army consumed him. Recorded just after he had been enlisted, '*I Need Your Love Tonight*' combines urgent eroticism and masculine arrogance and, today, it perhaps offers an insight on how Elvis felt he was entitled to use sex as a compensation for his compromises. All the great tracks from these sessions were used as singles and all deserved to be. '*A Fool Such As I*' is an extravagant, beat version of what was originally a very appealing, plaintive, country ballad. Here rock and roll conquers and there is no time for regret. '*I Got Stung*' is breathtaking and with exquisite timing Elvis warns the listener to expect both ecstasy and danger. The roots of his later self-destructiveness are being exposed but, inevitably, such dark motives make great rock and roll. The band responds magnificently to suggest they realise they are recording something special; loud, amplified music which will anticipate and galvanise the future. '*A Big Hunk Of Love*' is full tilt rock. Only, when heard as it was originally released with added reverberation is it possible to understand why this record was for a long while considered the ultimate in wild rock and roll. *'Wear My Ring Around Your Neck'*, which was actually recorded before the final triumphant session, is weaker but the jazzy piano still moves. From the 'King Creole' soundtrack, there are gems not included in the album review earlier. The title track, *'King Creole'*, ignites immediately because of a simple but dramatic guitar introduction. The edgy, bass vocal from Elvis that follows soon makes way for a soaring treble on the chorus. The performance combines melodrama with throw away teasing and that makes it special. *'New Orleans'* is dodgy material and more Hollywood than 'Crawfish' but Elvis is at his licentious best. At times, his admissions of lust and his references to women are so raw that the listener feels a little sympathy for the female victim. Again, his singing is full of invention and he pronounces 'Orleans' in a way that is probably not replicable. He also makes 'looisee – oosee –ooosiana' redolent with insolence and testosterone. Not in the best of taste, perhaps, but loaded with impact.

The fifth CD contains rare performances not previously available. Whilst valuable and appreciated, they do not qualify as a part of this legacy which, in the main, concentrates on what was intentionally recorded for release. They are of interest and aimed at curious fans. The early take of 'I Beg Of You' is especially revealing because it confirms how Elvis could re-invent a song when needed.

His other periods have triumphs and appeal but it is this music from the fifties that represents Elvis at his peak. Here, he still honours his roots but, because he blesses them with his own importance and individuality, he is making music that will not conform to what others expect. If this review races through this collection, it is because it is probably worth a book in itself.

The sixties – 'From Nashville To Memphis' - the content on the sixties box set is not the unmitigated triumph of the fifties collection but there is enough material to justify a decade. The set avoids all the movie and gospel material from this period. These are collected on other CDs and box sets which will be mentioned later.

The first CD is dominated by the 'Elvis Is Back' sessions so it makes a marvellous opening. Within the album there are tracks not previously mentioned. *'Soldier Boy'* was originally recorded by the black, vocal group, The Four Fellows. The version by Elvis is more fluid and cohesive. The original is connected with various vocal effects whereas with Elvis it all flows effortlessly into what comes next. *'It Feels So Right'* is a pastiche blues that presumably came out of the Brill Building in New York. Fortunately, Elvis gives a magnificent, sensual performance that transforms second rate material completely. The most obvious pop song is *'The Girl Of My Best Friend'*. Not only does Elvis sing it brilliantly, a deliciously slurred vocal with the oddest pronunciation that squeezes the tension out of every line, he actually adds characterisation. The song is about a man who is betraying his friend by having an affair with the girl of the friend. Elvis sings it with effete self-pity and we soon realise that the narrator is both doomed and repellent. The experiment with added characterisation is extended by his performance of *'Dirty, Dirty Feeling'*. For once, Elvis responds to the humour of Leiber and Stoller but not to the extent that the song no longer rocks. This is a fine record with a tough, guitar solo and Elvis, as the naïve, indignant enthusiast, is perfect. He is like the hick cowboy played by Don Murray in the Marilyn Monroe movie, 'Bus Stop'. A simple, blind soul but an unstoppable force of nature and half the fun is imagining how he will eventually recover the equally innocent lady who misguidedly thinks she has left him.

His version of *'Fever'* is not as bluesy as those by Little Willie John and Bobby Bland and, for that reason, many not unreasonably will prefer their attempts. Elvis is more restrained but, within the formality, the blues can still be heard and he manages to distance himself from Peggy Lee but pay his tribute at the same time. It has an independent identity and is memorable. *'Girl Next Door Went A' Walkin'* is obviously filler material but Elvis is inspired and he makes it all simmer. He is full of energy and sparks it into life by picking out odd words to startle the listener. It shares the same conviction as 'Such A Night', that promiscuity should be the chosen life but this comes more from Elvis than the song. His contempt for the girl looking for a monogamous relationship is obvious. It is easy to picture Elvis strutting down the street, the Jordanaires behind their leader and the whole gang sneering at the premature couples around them. *'I Will Be Home Again'* was originally recorded by The Golden Gate Quartet but as a secular song on an album. It is traditional and sentimental material but this is its strength. The sentiment is undercut by a quite tough, acoustic guitar which sounds like it is played by Elvis. Although Floyd Cramer tinkles away on the treble end of the piano, his frills are quite bluesy. This is not simple pop. Another gospel styled tune is *'Thrill Of Your Love'*. Elvis sings seductively and the Jordanaires add to the gospel feel and are on this occasion a positive addition. The chorus has a beat but the whole record hums with feeling. Elvis faces different challenges in the song but he manages them all with ease. Apart from the great album, the first CD has *'A Mess Of Blues'* and *'Fame And Fortune'*. The former is a rocker and this remark alone is a marvellous complement because the record is actually too slow for dancing. At this tempo, any other singer would simply swing but Elvis makes it do much more than that. It is performed in a style unique to Elvis and unusual for him. His voice grinds against the backing and it is this friction plus his complete control and power that makes the record brilliant. The second is a moody ballad full of irony. It has a very effective and simple introduction but, again, his vocal dominates the music and pushes the band. *'I Gotta Know'* is pop rock and roll but delivered with such finesse and suppressed power to be irresistible. Previously ignored, *'It's Now Or Never'* and *'Are You Lonesome Tonight'* are inspiring performances and the records resonate which is why they became such huge hits. *'Stuck On You'* was also a hit and, though another pop tune, Elvis includes distinctive moments. Interestingly, this is the first track from the sessions and the band is not so impressive.

The 'Something For Everybody' sessions straddle the first and second CD of the set and this album also contains worthwhile material. Not a classic album, perhaps, but worth a brief review which is what will happen now. *'There's Always Me'* is a great ballad but damaged by a lunatic, operatic ending for which Elvis and everybody else in the studio has to take responsibility. Because of the ending of 'Always Me', the honour of best ballad goes to *'Starting Today'*. This simple song, full of atmosphere and expectancy, has a fine balance between Elvis and Floyd Cramer on piano. *'I Want You With Me'* is more pastiche rhythm and blues but Elvis sings it with passion and energy and there are moments in his performance that delight. *'Give Me The Right'* is a smooth, blues effort that, maybe, should have been bluesier but, if accepted as different material to the blues on 'Elvis Is Back', it can be enjoyed on its own soulful terms. *'Judy'* is decent pop but some think it a classic. *'It's A Sin'* is a little sweet but has a recognisable country feel and an interesting conclusion on guitar that makes it appealing. The best track, which was not included on the original album, is his version of *'I Feel So Bad'*. Subsequently, this has been surpassed by the version by Little Milton but it still has plenty of merit. The Elvis record rocks more than the original by Chuck Willis which has a more pronounced Caribbean feel and both versions are superior to the attempt by Ray Charles who, surprisingly for once, does not master this song. *'I'm Coming Home'* is updated rockabilly but the added smoothness detracts from the final result and it suffers in comparison to 'His Latest Flame'. Despite that, it is a fine record and, because Elvis captures the rhythm and tempo perfectly, would have made a good single. At the end, the band slows down like a train and this is very effective and done perfectly *'Sentimental Me'* is a good ballad with a beat and *'Put The Blame On Me'* is a good, rhythm and blues pastiche with interesting use of a harpsichord.

The second CD in the set contains only one great rocker, *'Little Sister'*, which is already perfect in the verses but becomes unmatchable in the choruses. At this higher level, the rock and roll aggression becomes ecstatic surprise and self-enhancing revelation. It inspired an inferior tribute from LaVern Baker but she is a great performer and her gesture is much appreciated. Whilst *'His Latest Flame'* is equally great, it is also evidence of the search for perfect, popular music. But, it is magical. The final tracks from the 'Something For Everybody' album lift the second CD a little. Overall, though, the CD lacks life. The ballads become wearisome simply because of the quantity. Apart from the great, double A sided single, 'Little Sister / His Latest Flame', the other classic tracks are all ballads, usually, but not always, inspired by the talented songwriter, Don Robertson. The ballads include a magnificent trio from the 'Pot Luck' album. *'I'm Yours'* is beautiful and benefits from Elvis double tracking his vocal on the chorus in a way that is marvellously restrained and lyrical. The spoken section is very brief and does not mar what is a great record. As great as it is, it equals neither *'Just For Old Time's Sake'* nor *'That's Someone You Never Forget'*. The title alone makes the intentions of 'Old Times Sake' clear. Elvis teases with various tricks and, like a great chef, adds the tiniest pinch of blues to a line in the final verse. 'Someone' is not entirely perfect because the melodramatic, middle eight bars are not of the standard of what has preceded them but the verses are truly fabulous. The record shimmers but Elvis keeps his vocal simple and tense with a hint of Bobby Bland so the record captures perfectly the impact, mystery and legacy of a close relationship. *'Anything That's Part Of You'* is a fine song by Don Roberston and it echoes 'How's The World Treating You' which Elvis recorded in 1956. His voice is pure. Unfortunately, the weak line, 'no reason left for me to live', exaggerates the effect of dependency but, of course, we now know in the case of Elvis that the dependency this song describes was all too accurate. *'Something Blue'* is also a fine ballad that has Elvis, again in chef mood, adding subtle adjustments. These are perfectly complemented by the briefest of codas on saxophone by Boots Randolph. *'I Met Her Today'* is another strong performance and Elvis sings the ambiguous lyrics perfectly. Again, his singing is so evocative it is easy to imagine the man being left alone in the street, his fate darkened by an absence of what he will always need. *'Witchcraft'* is decent rhythm and blues but awfully light. The outtake with heavier percussion is better. Nevertheless, he succeeded in his intentions which may or may not have been honourable. *'Devil In Disguise'* has improved with age but this and the other rockers, *'Night Rider'* and *'Gonna Get Back Home Somehow'* would have benefited if Elvis had insisted on his original idea of heavy drums and bass. Parker and Atkins prevailed and the rockers lack spark. This is a major problem with this CD. The tracks have been relentlessly sweetened by Chet Atkins. (The outtakes from these sessions confirm his destructive presence.) *'What Now, What Next, Where To'*, *'Suspicion'* and *'Such An Easy Question'* are clever pop songs delivered by a master but, today, they require a tolerant listener. All the pop tracks are listenable except the mediocre *'Kiss Me Quick'* which is particularly challenging but none of them are classics. This probably sums up the second CD, short of classics apart from one great rocker, one magical pop record and some memorable ballads.

This music cannot be dismissed because, in this brief period after 'Elvis Is Back', his voice proclaims a newly discovered purity and control. A few more rockers, though, would have been appreciated. Even the glory of his voice diminishes as the CD progresses because it includes some of the final, recording session between Elvis and Chet Atkins when their relationship was no longer productive. Overall, the CD is an enjoyable listen but the relentless ballads need to be interrupted with a cup of tea.

The third CD contains the remainder of the last sessions recorded by Chet Atkins and the initial material produced by Felton Jarvis. After Atkins leaves, there is a sense of freedom previously lacking which makes the recordings at the end of the CD superior to those at the beginning. But quality material is becoming difficult to obtain and a small number of songs are weak, two ballads are, in particular. *'Suppose'* and *'Mine'* have hooks that would have tempted Elvis but both are turgid. The rockers, though, are great. *'Down In The Alley'* is raucous and raw and a reminder that simple rock and roll is an essential part of Elvis. *'Come What May'* and *'Fools Fall In Love'* are lighter rhythm and blues but both are loaded with charm and the former has an inspired ending. These are complemented by the tracks Elvis made with Jerry Reed on guitar. *'Guitar Man'* is so great that it overshadows the other fine rockers and, like 'That's All Right', it never loses its magic no matter how many times you listen to the record. His version of *'Too Much Monkey Business'* is a radical take on a Chuck Berry song. It has an irresistible, independent groove and benefits from the guitar of Reed and an inspired, slurred hiccup by Elvis. *'US Male'* is politically incorrect but, like the sexist 'Mannish Boy' by Muddy Waters, it is funny. It is best appreciated by awfully understanding females or by males who are listening alone. *'Big Boss Man'* and *'High Heel Sneakers'* have both been recorded many times but Elvis provides distinct versions. The rapport between Elvis and the musicians is exceptional and, in both instances, Elvis deliberately adjusts his voice. He lowers the volume on 'Big Boss Man' so the band is allowed to shine. On the record, 'Sneakers', he makes his voice husky so it complements perfectly a modern arrangement that has echoes of British blues. The version on the CD is nearly five minutes and, without ever repeating himself, he growls and scats his way to the end. *'Just Call Me Lonesome'* is a traditional, country tune that complements the blues and, as soon as the steel guitar is heard, it is clear that, again, nothing will be done to compromise its roots. All of this is enough but there are also great ballads. I am not a big fan of *'Ask Me'* but it is produced and performed with care and my reservations put me in a small minority. *'I'll Remember You'* and *'It Hurts Me'* are pure class. 'I'll Remember You' is American, romantic fatalism at its very best and is the tune Orson Welles should have been listening to as he walked away from the dead Rita Hayworth at the end of 'Lady From Shanghai'. The arrangement is okay although the backing vocals are too loud on modern re-masters. It does not matter. The mood is contained brilliantly within his vocal which captures not just the sadness but the glory of failure, an exquisite persistence that promises possible infinity. 'It Hurts Me' throbs with incomprehension, self-pity and resentment but it is also a marvellous mix of blues and country and is one of his very best efforts. It makes a perfect, companion piece to the equally great 'Long Black Limousine' and it is easy to believe the two narrators are the one man in the same claustrophobic, small town. In 'It Hurts Me', his femme fatale is still around to taunt him with other lovers. In 'Limousine', the inevitable has happened and she has left for glory and met one lover too many. When listened to together we not only have the extra appeal of knowing more about the narrator but are given a history of the woman that has irked him all his life. To really appreciate their quality, listen while reading a Jim Thompson novel. 'It Hurts Me' is also important for me because it was the Elvis record my mother liked best. Finally, there are the inspired but subtle versions of *'Love Letters'* and the Bob Dylan song, *'Tomorrow Is A Long Time'*. The original version by Ketty Lester of 'Love Letters' is fabulous but Elvis rises to the challenge and, with perfect fluency, manages a sensitivity beyond Lester. Elvis is so inspired on 'Love Letters', the drummer never catches the subtle feel of the vocal. Fortunately, he uses a snare drum but his contribution needs to be minimised in future re-mastering. 'Tomorrow Is A Long Time' has been mentioned before but it is a marvellous example of Elvis doing, to quote Stephen Sondheim again, the very difficult, the simple. Despite the repetition, it is never dull.

Properly managed, all this material from this third CD would have constituted a magnificent Elvis comeback before the 'TV Special' but Parker wasted his chance. Most of these songs were used as bonus tracks on soundtrack albums. This third CD also includes *'Long Lonely Highway (It's A)'* from the last Chet Atkins session, pop, perhaps, but infectious and Elvis is in total control. He drives it along with just enough grit to make it endure, squeezing the rhythm through his teeth when needed.

The remaining two CDs contain all that was recorded in the famous, Chips Moman produced sessions in Memphis in 1969 and these are complemented by some valuable outtakes. The classic album, 'From Elvis In Memphis', is a fitting testament but the CDs contain many more gems. The fourth CD also has some duds because the problem with studio material that began in 1966 persists but the peaks are sufficient and, again, the glory is the voice. It is a very different voice from the pure tenor that distinguished the second CD. The voice is more passionate and fuller and, at times, is gospel drenched. An example of his willingness to lean on his roots is *'This Is The Story'* which is a mediocre, English song but Elvis gives it a gospel treatment. He makes it not only appealing but meaningful. *'You'll Think Of Me'* is a catchy tune that swings along in mid-tempo but the lyrics and the quite brilliant vocal make it poignant and atmospheric. Consequently, it has significance and Elvis is convincing as someone who has to follow a destiny beyond responsibility. The lyrics of *'Gentle On My Mind'* are pretentious but, fortunately, the band and Elvis are inspired. The bass and guitar players add plenty of fine moments. Elvis pushes the song as hard as he can without being melodramatic and his vocal tricks communicate anger and a restlessness that has only left him with memories. It makes what should have been awful a pleasure. Elvis returns to his roots for *'I'm Moving On'*. Because the arrangement is placed somewhere between the original by Hank Snow and the radical revision by Ray Charles, it allows for an extended contribution by the house band. As his version of *'After Loving You'* is bluesier than Dinah Washington, Elvis takes the song further away from its country roots. He is tough and confident and uses this and 'Moving On' to confirm his identity and strengths. The arrangement on *'In The Ghetto'* is not perfect but, only, because of the too obvious girl singers at the end. The horns and strings are very musical and are atmospheric as is the slurred, bass voice of Elvis which cleverly evokes the cold wind of Chicago. It is his singing rather than the song that ensures the story is never less than important. *'True Love Travels On A Gravel Road'* is a standard, country song that Elvis sings brilliantly and his phrasing on 'we'll stay together' is inspired, superior Solomon Burke. Subsequent outtakes have revealed that the song was re-defined in the studio. Elvis uses his own memory of his sixties hits to add a pop sensibility that lifts the verses and helps what had previously been an unexceptional tune. *'It Keeps Right On A Hurtin''* is sweet and not ambitious but it has its own integrity. The piano is perfect as is Elvis. It invokes memories of broken innocence which suits well the idea of persistent hurt. The unequivocal rocker, *'Power Of My Love'*, is much different. What was probably intended to be a movie song, Elvis attacks with a ferocity never heard in his movies and he delivers an erotic charge echoed splendidly by the female vocalists. The band adds a powerful beat and the production by Moman is excellent. Best of all is the fabulous *'Stranger In My Own Home Town'*. This is an old Percy Mayfield blues and Elvis turns it into a celebration that has nothing to do with the song or the brilliant but gloomy Mayfield. It is exhilarating and timeless. It is no more than Elvis and the musicians sparking together between more formal efforts. But what sparks and what invention by Elvis who reveals the various ways the word 'own' can be pronounced. *'Without Love'* is also based on old, rhythm and blues material, in this instance a hit by Clyde McPhatter. The version by Elvis is smoother but as soulful and is underpinned more by a gospel piano and a measured beat. It mixes perfectly the strength of the American roots that Elvis admires and the contemporary polish of Chips Moman.

The last CD contains more classics from the 'Elvis In Memphis' sessions and is concluded with outtakes, some from the Memphis sessions but others from earlier sixties recordings. The hit single, *'Kentucky Rain'*, is a flawed song but a favourite of many, probably, because Elvis sings with such intensity. Oddly, it has improved with age. One of the outtakes, in particular, is worth a mention. This is his first version of *'Memphis Tennessee'*. The intact master is revealing because it shows how the tepid rockers of the 'Pot Luck' album would have been improved if Elvis had been allowed to record them in the way he would have liked.

Peter Guralnick defined the 'From Nashville To Memphis' box set rather well in his liner notes. It has its dips but it begins and ends magnificently and, even in the dips, there are fabulous moments. Despite the problems of the decade, Elvis justifies himself.

The seventies –'Walk A Mile In My Shoes' - the third box set is the music of an altered man and, because of this, it is more problematical than the others. The set exists as a separate, flawed entity which is sufficient in scope to reveal his carelessness, his drive to self-pitying material and his self-destructiveness. It does not contain all his studio tracks from the decade. These could have been included if the fifth CD had been utilised but that is devoted to a selection of his live performances. The tracks that are excluded not only contain the worst horrors of the seventies but a couple of efforts that fans regard as classics and some that are no worse than the more dodgy moments in the existing collection.

Much of the material is quite poor because it includes too many British songs acquired cheaply by Freddie Bienstock, the Viennese meddler who, surely, could have been found a part in 'The Third Man' and sacrificed instead of Orson Welles. Elvis at his best would have rescued much of his seventies material as, indeed, he does in 1970 when he is still functioning normally. 'Just Pretend' and 'This Is The Story' are good examples of how, earlier, he took poor British material and gave them gospel life.

Elvis, though, is not often at his best which means the collection raises problems for those sensitive to self-destruction and waste although for some it enhances its appeal. Julian Lloyd Webber, the classical cellist, once described for 'The Guardian' his admiration of Elvis but he baulked at the seventies material. There is always a qualification with Elvis or put more simply there is always a but. No doubt, the box set exists as a record of a fallen giant stumbling around in territories unsuited to him but the stumbles of a giant are different to those of other men. He drips blood but, like a champion boxer, it only reminds us of his magnificence. Consequently, and paradoxically, the box set exists as another confirmation of his talent. Many think the music is terrible and it probably is if you want the polished work of a calculating craftsman but this music is terrible in a way a flat, Hitchcock movie or a plodding, later novel by Norman Mailer are terrible. Awful work, perhaps, but they still exist as achievements. Glutted with self-absorption and an indifference to his talent, his efforts are a reminder of when there was so much more but the same indifference allows the talent to scorn fashion and its audience and explore. Like others and, like Hitchcock and Mailer in their weak moments, Elvis in his self-destruction became someone willing to expose his disturbing singularity.

But, of the three box sets, this inspires the least enthusiasm. Obviously, all fans are aware of the decline and have bitter memories of his seventies albums, bizarre, string swamped collections that appeared to have the intent of minimising his achievements and magnifying his errors. The box set is a superior alternative to his seventies albums and, at the end after listening to the live concert, the listener is aware of something more positive and worthwhile than mere waste. He was no longer an inspired record maker and he finished his career as a man too keen to complete tracks quickly but he could in this phase still deliver emotion. Time has helped his seventies music to develop from being barely tolerable to essential although the too many absurdities where the despair tilts into self-pitying and self-important melodrama are no less embarrassing. Nevertheless, it stands as a unique collection of music, best appreciated if listened to on his terms rather than those of the listener. In describing this box set, more tracks will be mentioned than in the other box sets. As this box set includes the material for only one classic album, 'Elvis Country', it means that most of these songs have never been mentioned before.

The first two CDs collect the singles from the seventies and the last consists of live material arranged to imitate a 'best of' show. In between these three CDs, we have highlights from the Nashville sessions in 1970, easily the best CD in the collection and, on the other CD, the highlights from 1971 to 1976. His decreasing effectiveness is the reason for the chronological imbalance between these two middle CDs. The imbalance is redressed a little by the two CDs of singles. Here, the songs are in chronological order and are spread across the whole period of his decline.

Inevitably, the selections in the box set have been challenged by individual fans but any selection, like mine in these lists, will offend others. It gives a fair representation of what happened in the final period, the simultaneous decline and growth that occurred which has confused critics since his death. This makes it an essential purchase unless, of course, you happen to be sensitive and play the cello. Still, there are thirty four tracks not included, so it fails to be a complete picture. The missing thirty four tracks are listed and rated in List 9. About a dozen could have been incorporated in the main collection without a drop in standard and the rest put on a bonus CD called something like The Dross Of The Dark Side with a warning sign that it may offend.

My taste should not necessarily prevail but some of the choices are definitely odd, considering the box set omits 'Early Morning Rain',

'There's A Honky Tonk Angel', 'She Wears My Ring' and 'Bitter They Are The Harder They Fall', all fine records. The omission of 'Honky Tonk' is inexplicable because it is a recognised classic. The odd selections also exist in the live show on the final CD. This includes his versions of 'Let It Be Me', 'Something' and, even worse, 'It's Impossible', all of which are uninspired. Similarly, his versions of 'I'll Take You Home Again, Kathleen' and 'Danny Boy' blot the CD containing the highlights of 1971-1976. Admittedly, they are sung sensitively, especially, the latter but these songs have become hackneyed to many listeners.

The first two CDs should be the best because they contain the singles but, because this is RCA and Parker, normal rules do not apply. They improve when listened to again and after the box set has been heard in full. Listening to them for the first time, without the knowledge that the set will improve, can be dispiriting. Of these two CDs, the first is less disheartening because, unlike the second, it does not demonstrate in brutal, chronological fashion his corrosion. Both CDs have their moments and both have their mistakes but, because Elvis is weakening, the stronger songs provide the moments. This was not the case when he was younger and more capable.

'Patch It Up' is a decent rocker but, by his standards, it sounds a little mechanical. His voice, though, is in good condition and he catches the song well. The drumming drives it along but to no real destination. It makes a decent, rock track for an album which was probably what was intended. 'I've Lost You' is too melodramatic but it is a powerhouse performance and is always impressive, if dubious. He gives 'You Don't Have To Say You Love Me' a different interpretation to Dusty and it is sung very well but the arrangement is overdone and, like most of these seventies hits, is no golden moment. The hits on this CD likely to persist are 'I'm Leaving', 'An American Trilogy', 'I Just Can't Help Believing' and 'Burning Love'. The best of the three is the precious 'I'm Leaving' which he sings perfectly. His performance suggests a fumbling man surrounded by swirling confusion and it involves the listener completely. It is an unusual song and the support from the band is perfect. Their instrumentation is tight and independent. Detached but participating, they ensure that the record is more than self-pity. 'I'm Leaving' does not leave the listener with a grin but this is an introspective journey that thrills, even if it suggests emotional collapse. Elvis communicates perfectly his stubborn compulsion to gloom and his performance is anticipated by Mary Shelley in 'The Last Man'. Surely, the romantic but wilful Perdita, a woman who is implacable against the attempts of others 'to soothe and soften her mind' is his female, soul mate. Perdita could easily be Elvis when she says, 'lost as I am I have no thought to spare from my own wretched engrossing self.' 'An American Trilogy' is a classic performance and the climax suits his operatic voice perfectly. The song is no simple piece of patriotism. Elvis adds a climatic reprise which makes people think it might be but this addition is more personal than political. The faith he shares is his faith in himself and ordinary people which is why it always drew an appreciative response from his audiences. 'I Just Can't Help Believing' is a fine, modern ballad with an interesting structure but the best version is on the 'Live In Las Vegas' box set. 'Burning Love' reveals that his voice is beginning to fray but it is a top-notch song and the band is excellent. Elvis just about survives in the middle of a musical triumph by all. *'I Really Don't Want To Know'* has already been mentioned earlier and is great and so, most people say, is *'The Wonder Of You'* but the melody is plodding. The song, *'There Goes My Everything'*, is hardcore country and belongs to the type of nakedly heartfelt material that British listeners normally find easy to resist. It is, though, in this instance almost hip. 'Everything' is played at a stately pace. In his response to the departure of the girlfriend, Elvis captures perfectly the now comprehended gloom. He avoids the self-pitying wail that the song encourages so it becomes a mature, controlled meditation and, contained within his vocal, is a measured, anticipatory breath weighed heavy with wariness. The added strings are excellent. The astute Carl Perkins recognised its merit and said it was his favourite Elvis record.

Besides these, the other moments amongst the singles are interesting rather than fabulous. *'Rags To Riches'* is eccentrically retrospective which is why it appeals to me. *'How The Web Was Woven'* is a plain song but Elvis sings it well, similarly *'It's A Matter Of Time'*. His sincerity is obvious on *'Until It's Time For You To Go'* which is occasionally hammy but still inspiring. This is complemented quite well by *'Separate Ways'* which has a very similar feel. These two desolate ballads improve with listening but you have to be sympathetic to Elvis using the opportunity to feel sorry for himself.

Although more disturbing, the second CD is oddly more interesting because Elvis is less concerned with being contemporary, so we have reminders of what preoccupies him. These include a live, bizarre version of the blues satire by James Taylor, *'Steamroller Blues'*. Elvis appears to abandon the satire and humour completely although it is likely that the words would have appealed to his Monty Python sense of humour. Again, this is not the best version. That was recorded as late as 1974 in Memphis. Here, the band lets him down badly and Elvis never catches the groove. *'Always On My Mind'* is the most famous track on the second CD and deserves to be. Although his voice is harsh in places, he carries the tune perfectly and the feeling of desolate incomprehension, once heard, is never forgotten. The two Tony Joe White songs, *'For Ol' Times Sake'* and *'I've Got A Thing About You Baby'*, are not that different from the originals but he adds something so they improve on the earlier versions which is to his credit because his voice is no longer the blessing it used to be. If the singing is fragile, 'Ol Times Sake' is sung by a vocalist who has developed his technique so he is now a fine actor. In the performance, there is a still centre and it is around this that the music revolves. 'Thing About You Baby' is modest and he sings it out the side of his mouth but it is a foot tapper and the gentle, self-effacing insistence behind the beat suits the lyrics and adds to its charm. Younger fans and critics have hailed his version of *'Promised Land'* as a classic. I am not convinced but re-mastering has made it sound clearer and it can now be listened to more sympathetically. It compares reasonably well with the original by Chuck Berry but it is no match for the Cajun masterpiece by Johnny Allen. *'T-R-O-U-B-L-E'* starts off badly and should have been re-recorded but it finishes strongly and cannot be ignored. The later version by Travis Tritt is an improvement and it exists as a reminder that the perfectionist Elvis who would do twenty nine takes to make a record right had long disappeared. *'If You Talk In Your Sleep'* is a decent song and, in his youth, Elvis would have made it a winner. This result does not deserve that status but it is listenable. I am listening to it now as I type and it is definitely okay. If these rock efforts are acceptable but require qualifications, none are needed for *'Loving Arms'*. Elvis does not do anything original with the song and I am not convinced from listening to the outtakes that he made much effort. He can, though, switch on the emotion and, here, he does it perfectly.

Although Elvis fans like his seventies material, they do not agree wholeheartedly on what constitutes its classics. Over time, certain songs have emerged as favourites but, apart from consensual triumphs like 'Always On My Mind', we all find individual nuggets that have personal appeal. There are critics who attach themselves to 'My Boy' which I can listen to but think was a mistake. We all have guilty pleasures. Amongst mine is *'Bringing It Back'*. His voice is not too great and neither is the song but there is something about the lilting rhythm and the way his voice complements the backing singers on the chorus that hooks me every time. He also appears to like the sound of the lyrics and I really enjoy the way he caresses the rhymes. It is not a classic but he brings it to life. The same happens with *'Thinking About You'*. The accompaniment is much simpler than the melody that Elvis has to carry. Compared to the band, he sounds as if he is improvising like a jazz musician, wandering freely and independently. *'Pledging My Love'* is a copy of a fine, revisionist arrangement by Delbert McClinton except Elvis is more restrained and tender than Delbert which makes it pitch back towards the original by Johnny Ace. The chorus, he sings in a semi-operatic voice and that, and the country playing of James Burton on guitar, lifts Elvis who, without really trying, creates an original version. Not bad, considering he was wrecked at the time. *'It's Midnight'* and *'Pieces Of My Life'* are far from perfect but they cannot be ignored. Like the box set, they inspire and irritate. The song, 'It's Midnight', is compelling but melodramatic. The strings are also overpowering and Felton Jarvis makes a suitable scapegoat so we can blame him. Elvis, though, catches perfectly the groove behind what is awkward material. I know, I am beginning to sound like the critics who rate 'My Boy'. This is the problem with his seventies music. Weak songs, a reduced performer but, once that is understood, the talent then emerges to confirm his glory. 'Pieces' is overall a good song but the lyrics have too many damned 'pieces' and Elvis foolishly emphasises the word instead of minimising its impact. There is an alternative version where the word is not repeated melodramatically at the end and this improves the performance significantly.

The third CD was recorded in 1970 and this is much better than the first two CDs. Elvis is still relatively healthy. Its core is the 'Elvis Country' album less the single from that album which is on the first CD. Apart from the album, there are other highlights and, within these, there is a wide range of material. The blues are represented by a quickly recorded but quite brilliant version of *'Got My Mojo Working'* which is cleverly segued with another blues classic, the much lighter *'Keep Your Hands Off Of It'*. He invests both with energy and power and, by integrating them, makes them both different to what they were. In 'The Complete Recording Sessions', Ernst Jorgenson recalls the conversation that occurred after the recording was finished. Resisting the praise of his fellow musicians, Elvis said, 'We grew up on this mediocre shit, man. It's the type of material that's not good or bad – it's just mediocre shit, you know.' What did Elvis mean? Was he teasing the musicians and what was his attitude to the blues now he was older? The musicians have never clarified the conversation and neither does Jorgenson. It is tempting to compare what happened to the scene in the movie, 'Good Will Hunting', where, after demonstrating his skills with a few quick formulas, the mathematical genius says something like, 'You don't understand. This is easy for me. It's boring.' Perhaps, that was what happened with Elvis. What many of us find the most thrilling, his blues and rock music, is what he not surprisingly found the easiest and the least rewarding. This is maybe why he was willing to indulge dirge-like material so often. To quote Miles Davis in a context Miles would not like, 'you have to play what you don't know how to play.'

The songs, *'Just Pretend'* and *'Stranger In The Crowd'*, fall maybe into this category but Elvis responds to the challenge they offer and he makes them valid. Through sheer gospel feeling, he adds tension and rhythm to ensure 'Just Pretend' is a compelling ballad. The appeal in the chorus is his achievement alone and the repeated climax provides a real thrill. 'Stranger In The Crowd' is close to sing along pop but his gutsy vocal pulls it towards respectable material like that recorded by The Drifters. The drumming enhances its appeal but the guitar solo is a little weak. Despite that, it all moves along well. Authentic country is apparent in *'It Ain't No Big Thing'* and this justifies its existence. The lyrics are a bit obvious but not out of place with what the song represents. Elvis sings in a deeper baritone than normal but he never loses the feel of the song which is its strength and he purrs through to a satisfying conclusion. In his book, 'Heartbreak Hotel', Robert Matthew Walker thinks Elvis sounds uninterested on *'Make The World Go Away'*. This does not prevent him giving it a soulful edge and a powerful, gospel-style chorus. The bluesy Dobro from James Burton re-defines the song significantly. Perhaps it is not the most promising material for this treatment which is why there are rough edges and notes where the delivery by Elvis is not entirely convincing. What it lacks in perfection is more than compensated with intensity. Not too long after this, as he deteriorated, Elvis fans would become desperate for this kind of performance and commitment. The bluegrass song, *'Little Cabin On The Hill'*, would have benefited from a couple of more takes or, perhaps, somebody telling Elvis to put down his acoustic guitar. The roughness is okay because it has a pleasant, back porch mood that vibrates with affection and warmth. Elvis sings it well and captures the bluegrass feel without straining. He keeps enough of his own identity to avoid it being an imitation or simple nostalgia. *'It's Your Baby, You Rock It'* is a marvellous example of what can be done with undistinguished material. Elvis and his band are great and they give the song a bite. Norbert Putnam is prominent and excellent throughout on bass and he duets with James Burton on Dobro in the instrumental break. That would have been enough but Charlie McCoy also provides great harmonica. What could have been dreary becomes a little gem. *'Whole Lotta Shakin' Going On'*, which was recorded at the later, unsuccessful, September session, is not as good as the original by Jerry Lee but it is different, fierce and exciting. At this session, Elvis had a bad temper and was in a foul mood. Here, though, the anger produces energy rather than indifference. This is modern Elvis singing rock and roll with a first class band and is to be cherished. *'Funny How Time Slips Away'* is even better. This is an exceptional song by Willie Nelson and it draws singers like a magnet. There are many fine versions but Elvis is a match for anyone. The moments when he repeats 'ain't it surprising' and opens his voice on 'I'll remember' take an already brilliant song to another level. The band is particularly inspired and everyone catches perfectly the complex mood of rumination and hostile blues.

Younger fans like *'20 Days And 20 Nights'*. It is similar material to 'Just Pretend' except there is not the same scope for a dramatic chorus. The record is a little boring but I have the same opinion of some of the songs on the 'Dusty In Memphis' album which it resembles. The efforts by Dusty Springfield have received critical praise and it is the equal of them. His singing is marvellous and perfect. His voice trails away at the end of the lines but, cleverly, the volume never fades. This enhances his confused state without weakening the melody. But, for all that, the song is not great and it commits the cardinal sin of taking itself too seriously. This flaw is not mitigated by the arrangement. Many of the people who rave over '20 Days' condemn *'Cindy, Cindy'* but to my crude ears it sounds okay. He takes a sing along hit from the movie, 'Rio Bravo', and transforms it into a rocker. Not one of his greatest, perhaps, but it has plenty of aggression and the nursery rhyme lyrics suddenly become risqué, full of erotic threat. The folk tune, *'That's What You Get For Loving Me'*, is anything but sensitive unless it contains an irony that I have missed but it skips along lightly and Elvis and the musicians master the material totally. His version of *'I Was Born 10,000 Years Ago'* is a casual, one-take effort. Elvis has produced classics in such circumstances before but it does not happen on this occasion. The tape should have been edited and the first thirty seconds, when the musicians work out what they are actually playing, removed. Listened to from that point, it is much more engaging but it is nowhere near the equal of the original by The Golden Gate Quartet. Unlike 'Joshua Fit The Battle' and 'Swing Low Sweet Chariot', which Elvis also performed as a tribute to his favourite black, gospel group, this version is very different from the original, so it is interesting as a reminder of his taste and his ability to reinvent a song. *'Lady Madonna'* is okay but again no more than a snatch of Elvis having fun with the musicians, a pity because the results are promising. The final track of interest is *'Mary In The Morning'*. The song is a little sweet but the melody is appealing, or pretty as Elvis described it. The arrangement is overdone but it does contain interesting elements.

The fourth and final CD devoted to studio recordings contains highlights from the final six years of his career. As indicated above, the choice is puzzling and it would have been improved if the chosen material had been closer to his roots and avoided Irish sludge. *'He'll Have To Go'* was recorded in Graceland and is famous because, that night, Elvis only recorded one song and tormented his musicians by wanting to do anything but sing. Consequently, many have assumed the recording is poor. This is not true. Elvis sings it slow and bluesy and hits a decent low note at the end. We are in a very different world to the marital failure described by Jim Reeves. The relationship in this version contains two doomed characters with clear failings whose lives echo with chaos. The insistence that the friend has 'to go' is no mere attempt at resurrection but a disturbing reminder of anarchy. James Burton is excellent on guitar. The song, *'Are You Sincere'*, is sweet pop but Elvis transforms it into decent Doo Wop full of feeling. It is not perfect but still fine and the bluesy undertone is subtle and effortless. *'I Got A Feeling In My Body'* is a modern, gospel song which Elvis infuses with a not entirely misplaced eroticism. The result is a very unusual and effective record. The version on this box set is marvellous which is fortunate because, on the original 'Good Times' album, it had been previously re-mastered disastrously with exaggerated echo. But this is fine and, though his powers have weakened, the performance of Elvis still swings. Even without the chorus, it would have been great but the girl singers are excellent. His version of *'Don't Think Twice It's Alright'* by Bob Dylan is equally compelling. Again, the voice shows wear and tear but his sly insolence is exactly what the song needs and, no matter he recorded it in just one take, the groove is established quickly and everybody springs into life. He lets his musicians have plenty of space and the song switches imperceptibly between their different contributions. It is very different from the version by Dylan. When Elvis sings of the lonesome road the possibilities feel endless. The actual take lasted twelve minutes and, if this would have probably been tedious on record, one can imagine what the experience would have been like in the studio for the musicians. He also sings the Dylan song, *'I Shall Be Released'*, albeit briefly. The extract is haunting but the limited length causes frustration. Two efforts originally recorded by Ivory Joe Hunter are included. *'It's Still Here'* and *'I Will Be True'* are rhythm and blues songs. They are performed slowly and deliberately with unadorned accompaniment from Elvis on the piano. This sacrifices their commercial appeal but, somehow, they are both given spiritual gravitas. The Jerry Reed song, *'Talk About The Good Times'*, is the country equivalent of the gospel 'Feeling In My Body', revivalism without the religion. I have always found this recording resistable which is odd because everyone is excellent and Elvis does everything he should. Ultimately, I am not convinced by Elvis as the backward-looking nostalgic that the song requires. Technically, though, it is perfect and even inspired. It is probably me. Much more convincing is the morose *'Good Time Charlie's Got The Blues'*. The singing by Elvis is not ambitious but he captures the mood perfectly and, this time, there are no doubts about the sad character in the song. The band is excellent and the two guitars that complement one another extremely effectively are deservedly prominent. The CD also contains an alternative version of *'Tiger Man'*. This is less raucous than the version in the 'TV Special' but it has its own distinct and appealing groove. It offers good evidence of how Elvis can redefine a song by adjusting the rhythm to inflections in his voice. The process sounds simple but it is beyond many.

Four songs are taken from the sessions that produced the 'Today' album. It is now clear from the outtakes that Elvis was not at his most inspired at this event. But the songs included are adequate efforts because, even when he is betraying his capabilities, he is still a competent talent with a fine voice. The sessions are famous for the argument between Elvis and RCA. After years of them sabotaging his records, he finally had had enough and insisted on the album being re-mixed with a new bass player to replace Duke Bardwell. The argument must have had an effect on producer, Felton Jarvis, because, for once, he actually uses the recording studio to flatter the efforts of his singer. The revised recordings have a crispness that adds to their impact. *'Shake A Hand'* is great material, an old, rhythm and blues hit based on an even older, gospel tune. A doped Elvis cannot match the power of the great Faye Adams but he finds a seductive groove and his less passionate version has plenty of appeal. Felton has actually added very effective, New Orleans style horns. The songs, *'You Asked Me To'* and *'Susan When She Tried'*, are typical of seventies country, light rather than intense. Elvis brings little of himself to this material but he is at ease and his safety first policy ensures no errors if no startling surprises. They are listenable and, because they are not normal for him, they complement his achievements. The final song from the session, *'I Can Help'*, has been condemned by some critics because Elvis raises the tempo and drama. This is taking the song, which is no more than light rockabilly fare, a little too seriously. It works reasonably well without being a classic and the old-fashioned ending is a tempting treat. Finally, amongst the highlights of the highlights, we have the diamond, *'Merry Xmas Baby'*. Without apparently making too much effort, he re-works the old, Charles Brown hit into something quite special and very different from the original. As with 'He'll Have To Go', he makes the material darker and sleazier. In the original, the song begins under the mistletoe. In his version, Elvis sounds as if he might be experiencing post-coital bliss. The track nearly lasts six minutes and it is undisciplined at times but, mostly, it is magnificent. If he is badly flat on one note just after the three minute mark, he compensates brilliantly in the final minute. Throughout the record, he evokes an atmosphere of a poor couple celebrating Xmas day. They may not have much money but there is good music on the radio and they can have sex. Every time I listen to the record, I imagine a small, transistor radio close to a cheap curtain flapping inadequately against the corner of a window in a tenement block. Of all his blues records, it is this one where he demonstrates his empathy with the oppressed.

The final CD is the live 'concert'. It would not have been my selection but it stands as an example of what made him great on stage. This CD includes his treatment of the bleak, Hank Williams song, *'I'm So Lonesome I Could Cry'*, which is one of the finer moments of the 'Aloha From Hawaii' concert. It also has his version of *'Unchained Melody'* which, though wrecked, he invests with power and mystery. The showstoppers, *'Polk Salad Annie'*, *'Suspicious Minds'* and *'You've Lost That Loving Feeling'*, are all included and each of these, alone, would have been worth the price of the admission. They demand to be seen and heard. It also features other fine performances like *'Heartbreak Hotel'*, *'See See Rider'*, *'You Gave Me A Mountain'*, *'A Big Hunk Of Love'* and *'It's Over'*.

If more words have been devoted to this box set than the others, the reasons are simple. The other box sets contained more classic albums. Fewer tracks from the seventies have already been mentioned. As the songs invoke his tragic history, this also creeps into the account. Ultimately, these performances have emotion and, as flawed as sometimes they are, they leave their mark. His classics can be enjoyed for their obvious triumph. These seventies recordings are more complicated. Within their appeal is something that disturbs and makes us wonder.

The three box sets do not include the 'TV Special' or any gospel material apart from the four track 'Peace In The Valley' EP which is on the fifties 'King Of Rock 'N' Roll' box set and one gospel outtake which is on the seventies 'Walk A Mile In My Shoes' collection. Songs from the movies that he made after he returned from the Army are also ignored, thankfully, and one CD at the end of the seventies box set cannot represent his live material adequately. We need to dig some more.

List 3 - The Gospel Music

His gospel material is best presented on the 'Amazing Grace' double CD collection and this can still be obtained on Amazon, usually, quite cheaply. The most recent, four CD box set, 'I Believe', is too expansive; it contains movie junk and the abomination that is the alternative version of 'I Got A Feeling In My Body'. The two classic, gospel albums from the sixties are both on 'Amazing Grace' but Elvis also recorded a gospel album in the seventies and the odd, gospel tune in various sessions. After the glories of 'How Great Thou Art', the original, seventies, gospel album was a disappointment but it still had its moments. If we visit the 'Amazing Grace' collection, it is relatively easy to create an improved third album of gospel material. Not the equal of previous efforts but fine. List 12 contains what I think would have made a sensible choice for RCA to release as a third gospel album.

This improved album is created by including the best of the 'He Touched Me' album from 1972 and a couple of tracks left over from earlier sessions. Included, is his version of *'You'll Never Walk Alone'*. This is very simple and features Elvis on the piano. His singing is marvellous and, justifiably, it received a Grammy award for best, gospel performance. He captures perfectly the terror and inspiration that faith creates. The outtake with heavier drumming is more aggressive and makes the terror more obvious. *'Only Believe'* is very traditional material that has been adopted often by both black and white gospel performers. The version by Elvis leans more to the style of black performers but he makes it much less ornate than normal. This has the odd effect of ensuring it has a more powerful hook but it is perhaps not so interesting although it is difficult to assess because the seventies strings, which are persistent, are a real handicap and detract from his soulful performance. This problem is avoided in the very good *'Lead Me, Guide Me'* which has a sparse, instrumental backing dominated by organ and piano. The main thrust comes from Elvis and the quartet and he locates the performance, as he does so often, right in the centre between white and black gospel.

The seventies album also included unusual material in an attempt to be contemporary and to avoid repeating his previous gospel efforts. In the context of a successful selection, which, not surprisingly, I imagine mine to be, the oddities are much more enjoyable and justifiable. *'A Thing Called Love'* becomes a charming, modern eccentricity with a deliberate performance from Elvis that is gently lyrical and effective because his bass lead is musical and understated. *'There Is No God But God'* is more traditional but unusual for Elvis because it captures the world of simple faith and trust. It avoids the emotional complexity that features in most of his other, gospel material, making it easy to imagine this being sung by a staid congregation, all middle aged and all with a smile on their face. *'I've Got Confidence'* is also unusual material but the complete opposite of 'No God But God'. It works well for those who like contemporary, gospel music. Elvis is particularly good on the chorus but, to be a classic, it needs a more modern, urban setting than either Elvis or James Burton can provide. But, once its limitations are accepted, its appeal surprisingly grows. More traditional are *'An Evening Prayer'* and *'Reach Out To Jesus'*. Both are intense and compelling and they have plenty of inspiring moments. The contributions of the musicians are highlighted more than on his sixties recordings and this is a bonus. Elvis, though, dominates and, because he understands the material, he ensures it grips as he intends. 'Reach Out' could have been a classic except the climax is flawed but, up till then, it brilliantly tugs at the listener. *'He Touched Me'* is also very fine and Elvis sings with sustained power throughout and, as he moves between tenderness and drama, with plenty of shading. The alternative take of *'Amazing Grace'* on the seventies box set is too good to be ignored which is why it is mentioned here although I included the original version on this gospel album in the Lists. In the alternative version, James Burton adds bottleneck guitar and David Briggs is brilliant and aggressive on piano. Elvis leads it with a passionate vocal but it is clear that any salvation will involve struggle and disappointments. He loads with ambiguity, the phrase, 'now I see', which dominates the song. Consequently, we are not sure if what he is seeing is that pleasant. The final track on this album is *'Bosom Of Abraham'*. It is a mere one minute and thirty seven seconds. An unimaginative interpretation performed by people of talent, it makes an effective but modest introduction to the improved set. Much better is his version of *'I, John'*. Although he avoids testing himself, this is a more careful recording. The song has an interesting narrative and Elvis makes it swing in the way the sermon demands.

As the 'Amazing Grace' box set also includes the two classic, gospel albums, it contains additional, fabulous tracks not previously mentioned. If his weakest vocal on 'How Great Thou Art' is on *'If The Lord Wasn't Walking By My Side'*, the record is still important. The result of Elvis being modest is that Jake Hess is allowed to dominate and reveal his talent and there is a dramatic moment when Elvis suddenly pretends he is a bass singer and the whole group move to another level. *'By And By'* and *'So High'* also have Elvis singing more like a bass singer, in a style not dissimilar to Jimmy Jones. Both songs are used as opportunities for Elvis to harmonise and encourage his fellow singers. They exist as examples of mutual respect and communal strength. *'Farther Along'* and *'Where Could I Go But To The Lord'* are achingly slow and soulful, slower than the originals. The weird mix of defeat and optimism which forms the emotional pulse of the songs is drenched with humility, ensuring they complement one another beautifully. The touch on both is masterful. *'Without Him'* and *'Where No One Stands Alone'* are sung with restraint but passion and the endings, although climatic, avoid the barnstorming top As of his seventies concerts. He sings as if his music is trapped within an ascetic spirit determined to prevail but willing to suffer. *'In The Garden'* is the track that Jake Hess acknowledged as supreme and perfect. The faith it has in sublime, all-conquering spirituality is actually rare in the gospel music of Elvis but he is able to communicate a mature acceptance and a joy that exists beyond relief or diversion. This is pious ecstasy and, no wonder, it inspired Jake Hess and others.

Similar riches are contributed by the *'His Hand In Mine'* album. The title track has Elvis harmonising with Charlie Hodge for most of the verses. Halfway through the song, Elvis changes his voice to take the bass part and this has the odd effect of him stepping forward from his own performance. It is quite eerie, suggesting he walks ahead of his friends to take the hand of God. Floyd Cramer on piano is excellent, he is restrained but he contributes a couple of patterns to make us listen. The version of *'Milky White Way'* by Elvis is slightly faster than the original by The Trumpeteers. Although Elvis copies the 'well, well' asides, his vocal is different and he neither emphasises the beat as closely nor reacts in the same way to the changes in the song. Instead, Elvis is determined to keep the song within the same groove from beginning to end. He exerts a marvellous hold. *'I Believe In The Man In The Sky'* uses the original arrangement from The Statesman Quartet but Boots Randolph contributes a strange, whispery sax which suggests he has just wandered in from a nightclub and he needs redemption. Derivative, the recording may be but the high, piercing voice of Elvis is flawless. *'If We Never Meet Again'* is both beautiful and heartbreaking. Again, Elvis reproduces perfectly the essence of this music, the simple desire for a life uncluttered by the damaging will and appetites of the interfering powerful. *'Known Only To Him'* is sung mainly in a high tenor and hints at something just beyond our fingertips. The 'great hidden secrets' will be revealed later and it is the innocent trust in the celestial parent that Elvis makes sound convincing. *'Joshua Fit The Battle Of Jericho'* and *'Swing Low Sweet Chariot'* are songs that have become a little too familiar over the years. Although there is nothing in his approach to bring them to independent life, his performances do remind us of their original appeal and both hum along pleasantly.

List 4- The Live Music

Songs only ever recorded on stage
See See Rider
Proud Mary (Madison Square Garden version)
Never Been To Spain
My Babe
Let It Be Me
Words
Release Me
I Can't Stop Loving You
The Wonder Of You
Baby What You Want Me To Do
Runaway
Johnny B Goode
Sweet Caroline
Walk A Mile In My Shoes
I'm So Lonesome I Could Cry
You Gave Me A Mountain
Welcome To My World
Steamroller Blues (Memphis '74 version)
It's Over
You've Lost That Lovin' Feeling
You're The Reason I'm Living
Softly As I Leave You
Polk Salad Annie
I Just Can't Help Believing
Unchained Melody
What Now My Love
Let Me Be There
If You Love Me
An American Trilogy
Impossible Dream

Later comments identify the sources for these tracks.

The Live Album – my selection

	Source
See See Rider	On Stage (Legacy edition)
Johnny B Goode	On Stage (Legacy edition)
I Got A Woman	Live In Las Vegas
Long Tall Sally	On Stage (Legacy edition)
One Night	That's The Way It Is (Special edition)
Heartbreak Hotel	That's The Way It Is (Special edition)
Mystery Train/Tiger Man	On Stage (Legacy edition)
Little Sister/Get Back	That's The Way It Is (Special edition)
Proud Mary	An Afternoon In The Garden
Never Been To Spain	Live In Las Vegas
You've Lost That Lovin' Feeling	That's The Way It Is (Special edition)
Baby What You Want Me To Do	Live In Las Vegas
Steamroller Blues	Elvis Recorded Live On Stage In Memphis
Reconsider Baby	On Stage (Legacy edition)
My Babe	On Stage (Legacy edition)
Polk Salad Annie	On Stage (Legacy edition)
How Great Thou Art	Elvis Recorded Live On Stage In Memphis
Trying To Get To You	Elvis Recorded Live On Stage In Memphis
Bridge Over Troubled Water	That's The Way It Is (Special edition)
I Can't Stop Loving You	Live In Las Vegas
Suspicious Minds	On Stage (Legacy edition)
Lawdy Miss Clawdy	Elvis Recorded Live On Stage In Memphis
Can't Help Falling In Love	Elvis Recorded Live On Stage In Memphis
Closing Vamp	Elvis Recorded Live On Stage In Memphis
Bonus track	
Money Honey (Live 56)	A Golden Celebration

His live music has been captured best by the CDs that were released after his death. There are plenty and the Elvis fans that collect all his live performances so they can compare the variations in performance are easily recognised. They live on the street amidst cardboard or they would do if the modern world had economic logic. The live CDs are numerous and fall into three categories. One, those released by the main Elvis record label - BMG, two, the more obscure, stage shows released on the 'Follow That Dream' label - a subsidiary of BMG but aimed specifically at collectors and three, the bootlegs that breed like rabbits. The simplest approach is not to stray from the main label but there is one purchase on the 'Follow That Dream' label which is recommended. The bootlegs mean economic ruin and, although the CD covers mention song selections that often look interesting, remember that Elvis was in decline from 1971. If his stage shows always have odd, marvellous moments, the decline on stage is uninspiring.

The best performances are between 1969 and 1971. The shows on stage in the fifties have historical interest but, unlike his seventies performances, they do not exist as a separate entity from his records.

The first list above refers *to those songs that he only recorded on stage*. There is more than would be needed to fill a CD. No other major rock and roll performer has used his live performances in this way. Jerry Lee Lewis was happy to let the hits of other performers dominate his exciting, live shows but he had usually recorded those songs in the studio. The material on this CD is variable and this reflects his weakening, the definite influence of Vegas, his reaction to his audience and his taste which was becoming unpredictable. The thirty songs identified in this list are not the only songs that qualify but they are sung in full and, apart from one exception, they can be regarded as songs that played a significant part in the development of his shows. *'It's Impossible'* and *'Something'* are ignored. Not only do I hate them, they soon perished after their introduction. If the selections were edited to twenty four, they would make an excellent, old-style double album. The arrangements may be overblown on occasion but the power and drama survive to inspire. It complements what he recorded in the studio and this separate legacy is a reminder that his creativity, although hampered, continued until his death. The performances are mainly available on 'Walk A Mile In My Shoes', the 'Live In Las Vegas' box set and the Legacy addition of the 'On Stage' album. These are essential purchases. The list also includes the Memphis '74 versions of *'Steamroller Blues'* and *'Let Me Be There'* and the Madison Square Garden live performance of *'Proud Mary'*. The extended

'Elvis Recorded Live On Stage In Memphis' album, which includes 'Steamroller Blues', is on the 'Follow That Dream' label. This Memphis performance is a good show despite being from 1974 and it is the one live album that is recommended from the 'Follow That Dream' label. The concert in Madison Square Garden, which is available on BMG, adds little other than the version of 'Proud Mary' and it may be considered a needless purchase for those who think the earlier but very different version of 'Proud Mary', which is available on the 'On Stage' CD, is adequate.

Within this list of thirty songs are some real triumphs already mentioned, like 'You've Lost That Loving Feeling' and 'Polk Salad Annie', and, of course, some big hits like 'The Wonder Of You', 'An American Trilogy' and 'I Just Can't Help Believing'. The rest is less well known. The early, Las Vegas performances contain some exceptional rockers and his version of *'Johnny B Goode'* is as wild as anything I have heard on stage apart from his live version of *'I Got A Woman'* which is not included in this list because it was also recorded in the studio. He also does driving and unusual versions of *'See See Rider'*, *'My Babe'* and *'I Can't Stop Loving You'*. In similar mode, he attempts to transform *'Release Me'* into an urgent, soul record. Unbelievably, Englebert Humperdink is replaced with a gospel growl. There are plenty of big, power ballads and none of them can be ignored, even *'The Impossible Dream'* has a beautiful middle section and a powerful ending. The best of the power ballads are *'It's Over'* and *'You Gave Me A Mountain'*. The first is slightly more lyrical and seduces whereas the second relies on aggression and grabs. The Olivia Newton John songs, *'Let Me Be There'* and *'If You Love Me'*, appear to be an odd choice but the former has a fabulous reprise from Elvis in response to a request from a fan and both songs work well with his audience as, of course, Elvis knew they would. They also suit the Elvis sound on stage and enable his portable choir to belt out the responses. *'Softly As I Leave You'* is a brave choice because it is quiet and bleak. It is fascinating and moving to hear Elvis share his growing preoccupation with death. He attempts contemporary pop with his versions of *'Words'*, *'Sweet Caroline'* and *'Walk A Mile In My Shoes'* and all are fine renditions but I have to be in a good mood to endure 'Sweet Caroline' and, although he improves 'Words' significantly by adding a beat, his version of 'Walk A Mile' is not in the same class as the brilliant original by Joe South. *'Never Been To Spain'* is blessed with great guitar from James Burton and Elvis and James grind out something soulful from what was originally fake rock and roll by Three Dog Night. These thirty songs remind us why the seventies are important and have to be acknowledged, no matter how fastidious our taste might be.

The other selection of live music in the attached lists is no more than my favourite performances from his stage shows in the seventies. The devoted, who have bought all the bootlegs, will argue that I have done no more than scrape the surface. I accept this because I have listened to Elvis for too long. Those bootlegs will have startling surprises for those willing to embrace the decline. The thrills will exist because that is Elvis. Worth mentioning is the famous concert in 1974 when he revamped his show for the third time and which is available on bootleg. It is interesting that between 1969 and 1971 he twice changed his show significantly. In 1970, he moved away from the blues and in 1971 he added more raunch to the show he took on the road. He continued to tinker, usually adding ballads, but he only really revamped it dramatically on one more occasion and, then, he abandoned his changes after only one night. What happened in August 1974 was poignant because it has overtones of the classic story of an individual making a fatal mistake and sacrificing the redemption that was within his grasp. Unfortunately, the 1974 show has been overrated. By then, Elvis was a beaten man and, although the song selection was an improvement, his breath control was in a much reduced state. But, if he was willing to be mediocre in his final phase, there are always interruptions as the second CD demonstrates. The tracks in the second example have been selected because they are great, can be easily purchased and have good sound quality. This makes it easy to adapt the CDs on the PC to produce eighty minutes of sustained excitement. It overlaps with the other live list but is essential for the fabulous and previously mentioned 'I Got A Woman', so powerful it even surpasses his fifties studio recording. Particularly great are his versions of *'Mystery Train'* and *'Tiger Man'* and *'Little Sister'* and *'Get Back'* which he combines into two melodies. It also includes *'Bridge Over Troubled Water'*, *'Suspicious Minds'* and *'How Great Thou Art'* which, all in their own way, remind the listener of his exceptional capabilities and ambition.

The 'TV Special'

There is now a four CD box set devoted to the event. The 'TV Special' has been re-christened the '68 TV Comeback Special' but I prefer to think of it in more simple terms. The collection is excessive but the original CD was poorly recorded and the seventy six minute CD has been superseded by other releases. It makes sense to buy this box set and re-create the unedited, original album and complement it with the alternative, seventy six minute collection that represents the full show. The two TV shows can then be compared which is always rewarding. These collections can be expanded further with whatever bonus tracks that might appeal. Within the box set, there are CDs that focus on different aspects. I prefer to listen to the show as it was intended by Binder but it is also worthwhile listening to the sit down shows in their entirety.

List 5 - The movies in the sixties

Sixties froth
    GI Blues
    Pocketful Of Rainbows
    Frankfurt Special
    Tonight Is So Right For Love
    <u>Doin' The Best I Can</u>
    Shoppin' Around
    Flaming Star
    I Slipped I Stumbled I Fell
    In My Way
    Blue Hawaii
    Rock A Hula Baby
    Hawaiian Sunset
    No More
    <u>Can't Help Falling In Love</u>
    <u>Hawaiian Wedding Song</u>
    <u>Follow That Dream</u>
    What A Wonderful Life
    King Of The Whole Wide World
    <u>Return To Sender</u>
    <u>Bossa Nova Baby</u>
    Marguerita
    I Think I'm Gonna Like It Here
    <u>They Remind Me Too Much Of You</u>
    <u>Viva Las Vegas</u>
    <u>You're The Boss</u>
    C'mon Everybody
    What'd I Say?
    <u>I Need Somebody To Lean On</u>
    Little Egypt
    Big Love Big Heartache

Kissin' Cousins
<u>This Is My Heaven</u>
Spinout
Let Yourself Go
All That I Am
How Can You Lose What You Never Had
All I Needed Was The Rain
Rubberneckin'
<u>Clean Up Your Own Backyard</u>

This list consists of what I think is the more charming or least offensive sixties, movie fodder that he recorded. (The songs from his fifties movies are included in *The King Of Rock 'N' Roll* box set.) The tracks constitute pleasant listening and they can lighten a car journey with children or be valuable late at night when exhausted and an alternative to thought and feeling is needed. Despite me being sniffy about what Parker saw as his life work, there are classic moments. But they are rare. The movies before 1963 are disproportionately represented. This is because Elvis made less effort in each subsequent movie. I have underlined what I consider to be classics.

Elvis made twenty nine films, excluding his documentaries, and most had a soundtrack album. Inevitably, the songs were often questionable and so were the vocal performances by Elvis, especially in the later films. There is a very revealing scene in the movie, 'Frankie And Johnny'. Elvis is obliged to sing a song called 'Look Out Broadway'. He sings this forgettable item with three of the cast. He is the only performer on screen who is not dubbed by someone else. Listening to this group, Elvis and three anonymous, professional singers, it is easy to conclude that the worst vocalist in the group is Elvis. The other three are earning a good living in Hollywood and are diligent and professional. They are not alienated, authentic talents with the capability, as Jerry Leiber described, to 'make fucking history.' People of significant but unexceptional talent, they are happy to take work from people who, again quoting Leiber, 'only wanted to make another nickel.' Elvis had more potential and he knew it.

What we have from Hollywood is a catalogue that consists of songs often conceived as pure, movie filling, sung by a singer who appears to want us to believe that he is actually inept. One of the clichés that supportive friends and musicians offer is that, although the movie songs were usually awful, Elvis always behaved professionally. Anyone with a pair of ears knows this is not true. Unfortunately, by distancing himself from this material, as he may also have done with some of the seventies dross, he made it difficult for people to understand the talent that actually did exist. The best of his movie material, he recorded in the fifties and is collected on the first box set. The other movie material is on odd compilations and soundtrack albums that are now sold quite cheaply. I usually buy them second hand, copy the odd track and, then, try to hide them. The quality in the movie material is very rare, the odd rhythm and blues cover or sensitive ballad that brings him to life. During the sixties, the material splits. In the half dozen films from 'G I Blues' to 'Kid Galahad', he not only sings the occasional classic but elevates the froth into something tolerable for the non-purist. In fact, his Hollywood musical fare in this period is much superior to normal, Hollywood music. After 'Kid Galahad', he treats the froth with contempt and responds inconsistently to the decent songs. This compilation includes the well-performed, early sixties froth and the moments after when there is a flickering of interest in him. But beware. If Elvis fans disagree about his seventies material, they are even more subjective about his sixties, movie songs. My judgement is suspect. Many years ago, I would listen to this collection in the car with my children and we would all sing along. It pleasantly passed the time spent driving. It is not recommended for mature adults but it inevitably has its moments and, amazingly, it is not entirely devoid of classics. Also, since some songs have been re-mastered and we can now hear the instruments properly, and not the way the tone deaf Dutchman preferred, they are much improved. This surprise, though, does not invalidate the previous criticisms. The compilation above actually amounts to a short, double CD but do not let us overestimate its worth.

'Doin' The Best I Can' is the best track on the G I Blues, soundtrack album and Elvis adds real weight to a moody ballad. It is heavily influenced by the Ink Spots but full of enough, original Elvis to make it very different. His vocal is beautifully slurred. This is enhanced with drops of baritone from the bass singer. The record is eccentric but full of

impact, it counts as pure gold. *'Pocketful Of Rainbows'* is another catchy ballad and, though banal, it is brilliantly sung. *'Frankfurt Special'* may be no more than Tin Pan Alley calculation but it is Tin Pan Alley at its least offensive and it is interesting to hear Elvis handle such material. The title track, *'G I Blues'*, is also horribly contrived but Elvis is on top form and the chorus consists of a great, powerful voice squeezing out the high notes on its way through the thrills. The next film, *'Flaming Star'*, only had two songs which, in retrospect, is something of a relief. The title track is pure Hollywood but it is odd where a great talent can land and its sing-along, fake-Western rhythm allows Elvis to show his brilliance. He captures an essence beyond the song. If you want to understand how great he is, listen to the Jordanaires who sing their parts competently but are unable to share that essence. *'I Slipped I Stumbled I Fell'* is an okay rocker from 'Wild In The Country' but both the song and Elvis are imitating previous successes. *'In My Way'* has Elvis singing with only an acoustic guitar for accompaniment and this makes it seductive. *'Blue Hawaii'*, despite its terrible reputation, manages to provide a clutch of songs. The title track is inventive and has sufficient Doo Wop in there to make it listenable. I am not one of those who regard *'Rock A Hula Baby'* as a classic but it is included because it kept the kids happy. *'Can't Help Falling In Love'* is famous and deserves to be because it burns with anxiety. His voice is truly special on *'Hawaiian Wedding Song'* and his baritone can be heard communicating the wary expectation that haunts the performer, the horror and the promise he was always willing to share with the children by the lake. The record exerts real power but he is too indulgent of The Jordanaires who should have been asked to leave. *'Follow That Dream'*, since it has been re-mastered, has emerged as much funkier than previously thought and it may even be worth classic status. What a difference a set of drums and a bass can make. *'King Of The Whole Wide World'* benefits from a strong, bluesy chorus but it is froth, albeit infectious. *'Return To Sender'* is an exceptional song and the performance from Elvis is flawless. He pronounces the word 'sender' oddly and what could have become a boring repetition now becomes an addictive hook. More froth is encountered in the movie, 'Fun In Acapulco', but most are agreed now that *'Bossa Nova Baby'* is a masterpiece, a tightly controlled groove from beginning to end. The movie also includes a decent, catchy,

Don Robertson song *'Marguerita'* and a very light but quite jazzy and pleasant *'I Think I'm Gonna Like It Here'*.

The accomplished movie, *'Viva Las Vegas'*, has the title track which has become very popular. I was never convinced that Elvis had delivered but it is more enjoyable and meritorious since it has been re-mastered with added emphasis on the instruments. *'You're The Boss'* is a duet with Ann-Margret. Sultry and erotic, this is a very respectable effort that apart from being pleasing always brings a sly smile to the face, especially, when Ann-Margret compares Elvis to a horse. This allusion is never properly explained. His version of *'What'd I Say'* is not the equal of the original by Ray Charles but, then, nothing is. It is okay but it suffers from the Hollywood context and, when released, the record made clear that it would take Elvis time to return to his roots and do this kind of material justice again. In the same way, the song, *'C'mon Everybody'*, would have also benefited from an Elvis on top form. Instead, it serves only as a pleasant distraction. No such qualifications are needed for *'I Need Somebody To Lean On'*, a genuine milestone. This is a cocktail, jazz type ballad with a subtle hint of blues. It is Peggy Lee minimalism and Elvis is perfect in this mode, proving, like Peggy insisted, that less is often more. In the film, *'Kissin' Cousins'*, Elvis plays two characters, a smooth American and a hillbilly. The title track has a beat and merits study because he sings it in the two voices of the characters. Neither is authentic but it is clear that after years in Hollywood he is now closer to the smooth American than the hillbilly. It serves as a fascinating study of a man with an identity crisis. *'Little Egypt'* is a good song but it requires a little more raunch than Elvis musters on this occasion. His version in the 'TV Special' is much better but this lighter alternative merits being indulged. *'This Is My Heaven'* is a beautiful ballad with exquisite harmonies, the fragility of his vocal is perfectly judged and he breathes seductively over the less demanding passages before reminding the listener of the vulnerability below the charm. A terrific record whose re-master sounds marvellous on a modern hi-fi system. The ballad, *'All That I Am'*, has a strong melody which is probably why it has subsequently been recorded by Tony Bennett. This is another cocktail effort but without the jazz and blues. It is famous for being the first Elvis record to feature orchestral strings. The music is definitely sweet and not suited to the taste of everyone. It is the type of song that can feature in a relationship before reality sets in.

Eventually, some effort was made to mitigate the deteriorating situation in the movie songs and some half-decent rock and roll material was provided for the film 'Spinout' or 'California Holiday' as it was called in Britain. Elvis was no longer playing and he wasted songs like *'Spinout'* that could have been made special. He responded in the same way to the song, *'Let Yourself Go'*, from 'Speedway'. This was only blessed with genuine effort when it was included in the 'TV Special'.

Most odd of the later movie songs, is *'How Can You Lose What You Never Had'* which is the kind of pop-jazz-blues that white crooners sang in the fifties. Elvis is not entirely comfortable with this material and he is not entirely serious. But it has its moments and it is another of my guilty pleasures. A little better is *'All I Needed Was The Rain'*. This would have benefited from more intensity but, as a light blues, it works and Elvis captures the feel of the song remarkably well. He never convinces the listener that he is fully engaged but it is an example of a great singer in relaxed mood. It also benefits from excellent harp playing. *'Rubberneckin'* is standard, movie material but is improved immeasurably by being recorded with Chips Moman in Memphis. The final song in the collection is a classic which is a relief because they are scarce in this particular list. *'Clean Up Your Own Backyard'* was released in Britain after the number one hit, 'In The Ghetto'. The irony of these two titles being juxtaposed was lost on an insensitive RCA. The record is discussed elsewhere but it does no harm to mention again the brilliant, edgy vocal with its twists and turns and the fabulous Dobro. It is also a fine song with sharp lyrics and stands comparison with 'The Weight' by Aretha Franklin. That puts it firmly in the memorable arena.

List 6 - The 'HITSTORY' collection

Song	Rating
Disc 1	
Heartbreak Hotel	★★★★
Don't Be Cruel	★★★★
Hound Dog	★★★★
Love Me Tender	★★☆☆
Too Much	★★★☆
All Shook Up	★★★★
Teddy Bear	★★★☆
Jailhouse Rock	★★★★
Don't	★★★★
Hard Headed Woman	★★★★
One Night	★★★★
A Fool Such As I	★★★★
A Big Hunk Of Love	★★★★
Stuck On You	★★★☆
It's Now Or Never	★★★★
Are You Lonesome Tonight	★★★★
Wooden Heart	★☆☆☆
Surrender	★★★☆
His Latest Flame	★★★★
Can't Help Falling In Love	★★★★
Good Luck Charm	★★☆☆
She's Not You	★★★☆
Return To Sender	★★★★
Devil In Disguise	★★★☆
Crying In The Chapel	★★★★
In The Ghetto	★★★☆
Suspicious Minds	★★★★
The Wonder Of You	★★★☆

Burning Love	★★★★
Way Down	★★☆☆

Disc 2

That's All Right	★★★★
I Forgot To Remember To Forget	★★★☆
Blue Suede Shoes	★★★★
I Want You I Need You I Love You	★★★☆
Love Me	★★★☆
Mean Woman Blues	★★★★
Loving You	★★★☆
Treat Me Nice	★★★★
Wear My Ring Around Your Neck	★★★☆
King Creole	★★★★
Trouble	★★★☆
I Got Stung	★★★★
I Need Your Love Tonight	★★★★
A Mess Of Blues	★★★★
I Feel So Bad	★★★★
Little Sister	★★★★
Rock A Hula Baby	★★☆☆
Bossa Nova Baby	★★★★
Viva Las Vegas	★★★★
If I Can Dream	★★★★
Memories	★★☆☆
Don't Cry Daddy	★★☆☆
Kentucky Rain	★★★★
You Don't Have To Say You Love Me	★★★☆
An American Trilogy	★★★★
Always On My Mind	★★★★
Promised Land	★★★☆
Moody Blue	★★☆☆
I'm A Roustabout	★★☆☆

Song	Rating
Disc 3	
Blue Moon	★★★★
Mystery Train	★★★★
Rip It Up	★★★☆
Got A Lot Of Livin' To Do	★★★☆
Trying To Get To You	★★★★
Lawdy Miss Clawdy	★★★★
Paralysed	★★★☆
Party	★★★☆
I'm Left You're Right She's Gone	★★★★
The Girl Of My Best Friend	★★★☆
Wild In The Country	★★☆☆
One Broken Heart For Sale	★★★☆
Kiss Me Quick	★★★★
Kissin' Cousins	★★★☆
Such A Night	★★★★
Ain't That Loving You Baby	★★★★
Tell Me Why	★★★☆
Frankie And Johnny	★★☆☆
All That I Am	★★★★
Guitar Man	★★★★
US Male	★★★☆
I've Lost You	★★★☆
There Goes My Everything	★★★★
Rags To Riches	★★★☆
I Just Can't Help Believing	★★★★
Until It's Time For You To Go	★★☆☆
My Boy	★★★☆
Suspicion	★★★☆
My Way	★☆☆☆

It may be considered extravagant to list all the tracks on this BMG collection but it has been done because the list is so impressive. The collection of four stars makes the point. Also underlined are the records that are magnificent and make him especially important. These hit records demonstrate how he confirmed his roots, maintained a presence in the commercial world of the charts and simultaneously destroyed himself.

Apart from half a dozen movie songs, all these singles are included in the three decade box sets but it is worth listening to them in isolation. The first two CDs have been re-mastered for improved clarity and extra bass. There has been considerable debate about whether this actually improves the records. It improves the sixties and seventies records because, by then, RCA and Parker were determined to amplify the vocal at the expense of the musicians. Not everyone is convinced that the fifties re-masters have been so successful. Many older fans prefer the fifties records as they first heard them, amplified by something called 'the big Columbia sound'. This was mentioned earlier. 'Mystery Train' will always be a great record but hear it as it was first heard fifty years ago and it is immediately understandable why it was considered revolutionary. In this format, not only is 'A Big Hunk Of Love' the wildest rock record ever it is easily the wildest.

Ernst Jorgensen, who has abandoned this sound for his re-mastering, defends himself by saying that he has always worked to the original acetate which is what Elvis would have intended. This may well be true and it is possible that the 'Columbia sound' actually flattered Elvis but only to the extent that it compensated for him not being in the room. Nowadays, we are listening to Elvis in a more natural setting but we still do not have him in the room. We are treating the records like folk music when what made them successful was their impact and drama. For quite some time, pop music has relied on technology to re-invent itself and to ignore fifties technological enhancements sells short the innovations. Jorgensen is right when he says there is no right and wrong. It is a matter of taste and the hopeless, like me, resolve it easily. We have both.

For the less ambitious, 'HITSTORY' serves as an excellent summary of his chart career and it does complement the classic albums with many fine tracks. It does not contain every single which is good because, apart from the awful *'Wooden Heart'* and the very sentimental *'Don't Cry Daddy'*, there is little to make one really squirm amongst the ninety tracks. Many young fans have heard these CDs once and been converted. At least twenty two tracks can be identified as classics and less than a handful rate less than three stars. This is especially impressive because the singles collection has to deal with both his physical and emotional decline and the movie songs that found their way on to the charts. Many fans will also feel that my judgements are far too harsh. In the classic twenty two tracks, there is no place for either 'Hound Dog' or 'It's Now Or Never', both of which contain seminal performances. But, no, there is a need for strict judgements. And, if many of the tracks outside the classic twenty two have their own delights, greats such as 'King Creole' and 'Trouble' for example, the twenty two are of such quality that they make one salivate. We should also be aware of the exceptional double 'A' sides such as 'Hound Dog/Don't Be Cruel', 'Jailhouse Rock/Treat Me Nice', 'One Night'/'I Got Stung' and, what has been described by Richard Williams in 'The Guardian' as the greatest single ever, 'His Latest Flame'/'Little Sister'. Some of these are actually included in the twenty two classics but there are many other gems from the singles such as 'Guitar Man' and 'A Mess Of Blues'.

It is impossible to listen to these tracks and imagine Elvis as a singer whose pretty boy looks exaggerated his importance. These tracks are why he became famous. These are what created the icon. The music is daring and Elvis sings like a man removed from the rest, in the distance but still triumphant. But even this glory is an inadequate explanation of his talent. It is not just the best of his singles but the great tracks from the classic albums and the many hidden nuggets that convince Elvis fans he is unique and special. True, he is versatile and this is his ultimate claim to greatness but his very best records also reveal a singular potential. In the same way other great musicians have qualities specific to them, Elvis can make music that is unique to him. Much has already been said about how he promises freedom but his records do more than that. Roger Scruton, in 'The Aesthetics Of Music', refers to the best of pop as having an inner voice and a non-mechanical rhythm. At his best, Elvis delivers this brilliantly and often. It can be 'A Mess Of Blues' that somehow combines a compelling swing with sledgehammer force or 'Return To Sender' which he transforms with sly humour into a celebration of his talent and confidence. Similarly, listen to 'Bossa Nova Baby' and compare it to the inferior original by Tippi And The Clovers. Without any apparent effort, Elvis rides the rhythm brilliantly so we hardly notice how little the beat is emphasised. We respond to the rhythm and him. Listening to 'Bossa Nova Baby' is like facing a glistening iceberg; we are conscious that this is only the tip of his talent which, of course, is confirmed by the rest of the tracks. Later, we are dragged into his gloom and we now have a new inner voice, the lost spirit who knows that apart from uninhibited freedom the innocents have the capacity for inexplicable pain. Songs like 'Can't Help Falling In Love' and 'Always On My Mind' succeed because they offer no understanding. If there was comprehension, the vulnerability would be reduced. All of it defies genres to define his personality and it is this Elvis, a piece of popular, American culture wrapped in his own mystery, which inevitably became the icon. As time passed, this became less obvious and fewer and fewer people have been less beguiled by the mystery but, at the beginning, its impact was immense. He may have been weakened when he recorded 'An American Trilogy' but he is still able to remind us of this unique complexity. The record and so many others are valuable and moving because he lets us know that he understands or feels, at least, the challenge of being human and the democratic connection that needs to embrace us all. Even when he is not at his best, the records of Elvis are often distinguished by the inner life required by Scruton. It may not always be an appealing life but it exists. This existence is even apparent in the drudge he recorded at the end of his career.

If the singles collection demonstrates inevitably his decline and loss of power, it reminds us of how much he achieved in his comeback and the brief periods before and just after he was in the army. It explains why his music has persisted for so long.

———————

List 7 - The rhythm and blues collection

That's All Right
Tomorrow Night
Good Rockin' Tonight
Milkcow Blues Boogie
Baby Let's Play House
Mystery Train
Trying To Get To You
I Got A Woman
Money Honey
My Baby Left Me
So Glad You're Mine
Tutti Frutti
Lawdy Miss Clawdy
Shake Rattle And Roll
Hound Dog
Long Tall Sally
Any Place Is Paradise
Ready Teddy
Rip It Up
Blueberry Hill
Mean Woman Blues
One Night
I Need You So
When It Rains It Really Pours
Jailhouse Rock
Santa Claus Is Back In Town
New Orleans
Ain't That Loving You Baby
Soldier Boy
A Mess Of Blues
It Feels So Right

Fever
Like A Baby
Such A Night
Reconsider Baby
Give Me The Right
I Feel So Bad
I Want You With Me
Put The Blame On Me
Bossa Nova Baby
Witchcraft
What'd I Say
Memphis Tennessee
Little Egypt
Down In The Alley
Come What May
Fools Fall In Love
Big Boss Man
High Heel Sneakers
Too Much Monkey Business
Baby What You Want Me To Do
Tiger Man
Stranger In My Own Home Town
Power Of My Love
Johnny B Goode
My Babe
Got My Mojo Workin'
Merry Xmas Baby
Its Still Here
I Will Be True
Promised Land
Shake A Hand
Pledging My Love

Elvis is more than a rhythm and blues singer. If many of us have become more open to his other music as we have become older, these songs are the source of my dependency. These records contained a promise that

I found unable to resist. What was that promise? I am obliged to quote the usual clichés, freedom and potency. More important than my reaction is how the collection demonstrates his versatility. Even here, when restricted to one genre, he is more versatile than anyone else. This is before we examine all the other genres he attempted. This is difficult to believe but true. Look at the collection and compare it with any other rhythm and blues performer. Not only is it wide ranging, it is peppered with highlights. This list alone guarantees him eminence. Included in the list are a few songs that are pastiche rhythm and blues. This is okay because Elvis performs them well. All the songs are in chronological order but it is better to listen to them jumbled up on 'shuffle'.

List 8 - The best fifty

That's All Right
Blue Moon
Good Rockin' Tonight
Milkcow Blues Boogie
Mystery Train
Trying To Get To You
Baby Let's Play House
My Baby Left Me
So Glad You're Mine
Lawdy Miss Clawdy
Don't Be Cruel
There'll Be Peace In The Valley
Is It So Strange
One Night
Jailhouse Rock
Santa Claus Is Back In Town
Don't
A Big Hunk Of Love
I Got Stung
Fame And Fortune
A Mess Of Blues
Such A Night
Reconsider Baby
Can't Help Falling In Love
That's Someone You Never Forget
His Latest Flame
Little Sister
Return To Sender
I Need Somebody To Lean On
It Hurts Me
Run On

How Great Thou Art
Stand By Me
Tomorrow Is A Long Time
Love Letters
I'll Remember You
Guitar Man
If I Can Dream
Clean Up Your Own Backyard
Long Black Limousine
I'll Hold You In My Heart
Suspicious Minds
Stranger In My Own Home Town
Polk Salad Annie
I Really Don't Want To Know
I Washed My Hands In Muddy Water
Merry Christmas Baby
I'm Leaving
Loving Arms
There's A Honky Tonk Angel

These reflect what I felt, the day I typed the list. My opinions on this subject change frequently but, within the list, there are some constants. I doubt if there is a person on the planet who would agree exactly with the selection. It is included for the worst reason of all. Everybody else does it. The list is for comparison only. What is important is what has been left out. No 'Hound Dog' for example. The standard is very high but only corrupt record companies and the insane think Elvis can be appreciated on a mere fifty recordings.

———————

List 9 - The missing tracks from 'Walk A Mile In My Shoes'

Tracks	Rating
Bridge Over Troubled Water*	★★☆☆
I'll Never Know	★☆☆☆
This Is Our Dance	★☆☆☆
When I'm Over You	★☆☆☆
Love Letters (remake)	★★☆☆
If I Were You	★★★☆
Sylvia	★☆☆☆
Early Morning Rain	★★★☆
Padre	★☆☆☆
Help Me Make It Through The Night	★☆☆☆
It's Only Love	★★☆☆
Love Me Love The Life I Lead	★☆☆☆
My Way	★☆☆☆
Where Do I Go From Here	★☆☆☆
If You Don't Come Back	★★☆☆
Three Corn Patches	★☆☆☆
Find Out What's Happening	★★☆☆
Girl Of Mine	★☆☆☆
Sweet Angeline	★★☆☆
I Miss You	★★☆☆
Love Song Of The Year	★☆☆☆
Your Love's Been A Long Time Coming	★☆☆☆
There's A Honky Tonk Angel	★★★★
If That Isn't Love	★★★☆
Spanish Eyes	★★☆☆
She Wears My Ring	★★★☆
Fairytale	★★☆☆
And I Love You So	★★☆☆
Woman Without Love	★☆☆☆

The Last Farewell	★☆☆☆
Solitaire	★☆☆☆
Never Again	★☆☆☆
Blue Eyes Crying In The Rain	★★★☆
It's Easy For You	★☆☆☆
Never Gonna Fall In Love Again	★★☆☆
Bitter They Are Harder They Fall	★★★☆

This list is dominated by awful songs and misjudged performances which is why so many of the tracks have only been awarded with one star. Without these tracks, the 'Walk A Mile In My Shoes' box set still reveals decline. Add these and the tragedy that Elvis in his final years endured and helped create is fully exposed. This really is the dark side of the dross but the two star tracks that are listenable, the three star efforts and the one four star exception should have been included on the box set. The tracks underlined are those that could have been added to 'Walk A Mile In My Shoes' without weakening the collection.

   * *This studio recording is much inferior to his inspiring live version.*

List 10 - The albums that were never released

Album Rating

Lost album 1

Echoes Of Love	★★☆☆
Please Don't Drag That String Around	★★☆☆
Devil In Disguise	★★★☆
Never Ending	★★☆☆
What Now What Next Where To	★★★☆
Witchcraft	★★★☆
Finders Keepers Losers Weepers	★★☆☆
Love Me Tonight	★★★☆
Long Lonely Highway (It's A)	★★★★
Western Union	★★☆☆
Slowly But Surely	★★★☆
Blue River	★☆☆☆

Note – as can be seen from the ratings this album recorded in 1963 was a weak effort. It is mainly listenable but Blue River completely fails to ignite. The album was, though, an improvement on the soundtrack alternatives for which it provided bonus tracks.

Lost album 2

Down In The Alley	★★★★
Come What May	★★★☆
Tomorrow Is A Long Time	★★★★
I'll Remember You	★★★★
Fools Fall In Love	★★★☆
Memphis Tennessee	★★★★
U.S. Male	★★★☆
Guitar Man	★★★★

Big Boss Man	★★★★
Ask Me	★★★☆
Just Call Me Lonesome	★★★☆
High Heel Sneakers	★★★★
You Don't Know Me	★★★☆
It Hurts Me	★★★★

Note – this album is much stronger than the predecessor and has many classic moments. After Elvis died, a compilation of this period (1964 – 1968) was expanded for CD and was released under the title, 'Tomorrow Is A Long Time'. It is a marvellous CD. Subsequently, the Follow That Dream label has released an album called 'Elvis Sings Guitar Man' that also covers this period. The selection is as misguided as the title.

List 11 – The albums that should have been released in the 1960s

Album	Rating

Something For Everybody - 1961

Album	Rating
In Your Arms	★★★☆
Sentimental Me	★★★☆
There's Always Me	★★★☆
Gently	★★★☆
I'm Coming Home	★★★☆
Starting Today	★★★★
It's A Sin	★★★☆
I Want You With Me	★★★★
Give Me The Right	★★★★
Judy	★★★☆
Put The Blame On Me	★★★★
I Feel So Bad	★★★★

Note – the tracks are ordered similar to 'Elvis Is Back' and the song, 'Feel So Bad,' is included. This version of the album is much more enjoyable and is also more comparable with 'Elvis Is Back'. For those who wonder, why, ultimately, it lacks the magic of 'Elvis Is Back', there is an explanation. This session was conducted on the basis that Elvis could only record twelve tracks. Parker was making it clear to RCA that movies were the priority. It is hardly a surprise that the session does not possess the creative spark that infused the 'Elvis Is Back' sessions. It is, though, in this format, a good album.

Pot Luck - 1962

Album	Rating
Suspicion	★★★☆
Such An Easy Question	★★★☆
She's Not You	★★★☆

I'm Yours	★★★★
Little Sister	★★★★
Just Tell Her Jim Said Hello	★★★☆
That's Someone You Never Forget	★★★★
Anything That's Part Of You	★★★★
Just For Old Time's Sake	★★★★
Something Blue	★★★☆
Night Rider (outtake)	★★★☆
His Latest Flame	★★★★

Note – 'Pot Luck' was not actually recorded as an album. RCA used tracks from various sessions. The same is done here, concentrating on what I think are three and four star tracks. 'Night Rider' sounds much better before Atkins and RCA interfered and the outtake just about makes 3 stars.

Back In Memphis - 1969

From A Jack To A King (remastered)	★★★☆
Suspicious Minds	★★★★
Inherit The Wind	★★★☆
This Is The Story	★★★★
Rubberneckin'	★★★☆
If I'm A Fool (For Loving You)	★★★☆
Do You Know Who I Am	★★★★
You'll Think Of Me	★★★★
Kentucky Rain	★★★★
The Fair Is Moving On	★★☆☆
Without Love	★★★★
Stranger In My Own Home Town	★★★★

Note – this album is not the equal of 'From Elvis In Memphis' but it is very good and a damned sight better than the original 'Back In Memphis'. Some fans will argue I have been unfair by omitting 'And The Grass Won't Pay No Mind'. The song is very well done but the chorus leaves me cold. This collection also takes advantage of the Legacy re-mastered edition of 'From A Jack To A King.'

List 12 - The albums that should have been released in the 1970s

Album Date Rating

Just Pretend - 1970

It Ain't No Big Thing	★★★☆
Twenty Days And Twenty Nights	★★★☆
How The Web Was Woven	★★★☆
If I Were You	★★★☆
Cindy Cindy	★★★☆
Just Pretend	★★★★
I've Lost You	★★★☆
Mary In The Morning	★★★☆
Stranger In The Crowd	★★★☆
Patch It Up	★★★☆
Rags To Riches	★★★☆
Got My Mojo Working	★★★★

Note – this album assumes that the live material would have been kept separate and that the 1970 Nashville sessions would have been used to create two credible, studio albums. This is not as powerful as 'Elvis Country' which was recorded at the same sessions. The material is sometimes dubious but Elvis is in great voice and the three rockers stop it from becoming too stodgy.

He Touched Me - 1971

Bosom Of Abraham	★★☆☆
Amazing Grace (original version)	★★★☆
Lead Me Guide Me	★★★☆
I've Got Confidence	★★★☆
He Touched Me	★★★★
A Thing Called Love	★★★☆

An Evening Prayer	★★★★
Reach Out To Jesus	★★★☆
There Is No God But God	★★★☆
I, John	★★★★
Only Believe	★★★☆
You'll Never Walk Alone	★★★★

Note - although the original 'He Touched Me' was a disappointment, it did receive a Grammy award. This is revamped a little. It dumps the inexcusable 'He Is My Everything' and takes advantage of two earlier, gospel tracks not featured elsewhere in these lists. Listened to like this, the album is quite acceptable but no equal of the supreme 'How Great Thou Art'

Burning Love - 1972

Don't Think Twice It's Alright	★★★★
I Will Be True	★★★★
Always On My Mind	★★★★
Until It's Time For You To Go	★★★☆
Burning Love	★★★★
Early Morning Rain	★★★☆
Separate Ways	★★★☆
That's What You Get For Loving Me	★★★★
For The Good Times	★★☆☆
I'm Leaving	★★★★
Amazing Grace (alternative version)	★★★☆
Merry Christmas Baby	★★★★

Note – these revised albums from 1972 can be accused of using hindsight unfairly but who knows how an intelligent company would have reacted to his decline. Of course, this assumes that with intelligent people around him Elvis would have declined in the same way. In the circumstances, these revised albums do not flatter Elvis and, in these formats, these albums sound much better than people might expect. What is surprising about the above selection is the quality of the songs. The alternative version of 'Amazing Grace' can be regarded as a bonus track.

Album	Rating

Promised Land - 1973

I've Got A Thing About You Baby	★★★☆
Thinking About You	★★★☆
It's Midnight	★★★☆
For Ol' Times Sake	★★★☆
Just A Little Bit	★★★☆
Are You Sincere	★★★★
It's Still Here	★★★☆
Promised Land	★★★☆
Help Me	★★★☆
Good Time Charlie's Got The Blues	★★★☆
If You Talk In Your Sleep	★★★☆
I Got A Feeling In My Body	★★★★

Note – nothing to say other than far better than the original

1974 - *Note – insufficient, acceptable studio material would have been available for an album but RCA had plenty of live material that could have been used this year.*

Loving Arms - 1975

Bringing It Back	★★★☆
There's A Honky Tonk Angel	★★★★
Talk About The Good Times	★★★☆
She Wears My Ring (not dubbed)	★★★☆
T-R-O-U-B-L-E	★★★☆
Loving Arms	★★★★
If That Isn't Love (not dubbed)	★★★☆
Susan When She Tried	★★★☆
Tiger Man	★★★☆
I Can Help	★★★☆

You Asked Me To ★★★☆
Shake A Hand ★★★☆

Note - this is material derived from two sessions in different years and it would have required somebody at RCA to admit they had problems to have kept material in hand to supplement a future session. 'If That Isn't Love' is far less cloying without the dubbing and it does feature a good, Elvis vocal. Similarly, once the dubbing is removed from 'She Wears My Ring', it is transformed from sentimental corn to borderland mystery.

Elvis In Graceland - 1976
Moody Blue ★★☆☆
Bitter They Are The Harder They Fall ★★★☆
I'll Never Fall In Love Again ★★☆☆
Hurt ★★★☆
Way Down ★★☆☆
Unchained Melody ★★★★
Danny Boy ★★★☆
Blue Eyes Crying In The Rain ★★★☆
He'll Have To Go ★★★★
She Thinks I Still Care (alternative version) ★★★☆
Pledging My Love ★★★☆
For The Heart ★★☆☆

Note – the paucity of stars reflects the physical and emotional state of Elvis. This is a record by a dying man. It is not without merit but the voice is often ragged. Despite that, he manages a couple of four stars. It does, though, require tolerance. The alternative version of 'She Thinks I Still Care' is used to mitigate the gloom that exists on other tracks.

List 13 – The 'Chips Moman Memphis album'

Alternative 'From Elvis In Memphis'
Only The Strong Survive
Inherit The Wind
And The Grass Won't Pay No Mind
Long Black Limousine
Do You Know Who I Am
Any Day Now
Wearing That Loved On Look
Gentle On My Mind
True Love Travels On A Gravel Road
You'll Think Of Me
Mama Liked The Roses
I'm Moving On

The singles
Suspicious Minds c/w The Fair Is Moving On
In The Ghetto c/w This Is The Story
Kentucky Rain c/w Don't Cry Daddy

This is the album and the three singles that I think Chips Moman would have selected from the Memphis sessions that he produced if he had been trusted with that decision. This collection would have been closer to his vision and a little closer to the acclaimed album, 'Dusty In Memphis' by Dusty Springfield. Clearly, I am being presumptuous. So, in case Chips ever reads this and disagrees violently, I will apologise in advance. This different playlist does, though, make an interesting, if inferior, alternative.

———

List 14 - The 'missing folk album'

'Don't Think Twice'
Early Morning Rain
Steamroller Blues
<u>Gentle On My Mind</u>
Good Time Charlie's Got The Blues
<u>I Washed My Hands In Muddy Water</u>
Until It's Time For You To Go
Don't Think Twice It's All Right
For The Good Times
Bridge Over Troubled Water
I'm Leaving
That's What You Get For Loving Me
<u>Tomorrow Is A Long Time</u>

This 'missing' album consists of the best twelve tracks from the attempts by Elvis to perform folk music. His endeavours were thwarted by his physical decline but, although it reveals deterioration, this represents meaningful effort. If all these had been recorded before his decline, he would have produced something historic. The evidence for this consists of tracks 3, 5 and 12 (underlined) which were all recorded before 1971 and are great, innovative and genre busting. As it is, this imaginary album still contains four exceptional performances. (Track 10 is the other.) Some would argue it includes more. Not everybody will agree that 'I'm Leaving' is folk music but, I think, it suits the selection.

List 15 - The neglected legacy summarised

The heart of the legacy is the three box sets devoted to the fifties, sixties and seventies decades. Within them are nine classic albums plus many more fabulous treasures and neglected masterpieces. We can also compile from the 'Amazing Grace' CD collection a three album, mainly superb, gospel collection. Finally, from various CDs, I compiled two impressive CD collections of his live material and a CD of movie songs that never should have been made but offer pleasure in peculiar moments. There also exists a three CD collection of hot singles that ranges from the fabulous to the listenable.

Having identified the quantity of material that can be enjoyed and appreciated, it may baffle some as to why his critical reputation struggles. The worthwhile selections from the box sets dedicated to the decades would amount to nearly twelve hours of studio recorded material. To this, we can add nearly two hours of gospel music and over two hours of live performances. There are few performers who can match this. If critics were exposed to this music and nothing else, their reaction would be different. Remember the response of Dave Gelly, the jazz critic, when he was obliged to listen to the album, 'Moody Blue', or the hostile Kenneth Moore who was exposed to the single, 'Such A Night.' What existed and what they thought existed were very different. This has always been a major difficulty but there are other reasons why Elvis fails to persuade so many. What we cannot discount is the impact of the dross. Some rubbish exists on the sixties and seventies box sets but there are also the thirty four tracks that were not included on the latter and, if half a dozen deserve to be heard, the rest are too often awful, performances from an alienated and confused performer that should never have been released. There is also a Christmas album from the seventies which, here, has been conveniently overlooked. But, as damaging as his mistakes were in the studio, they are nothing compared to what happened in the movies. The Creature was never forgiven after he murdered William, Clerval and Elizabeth. The mistakes of Elvis, many have found inexcusable.

Is the rubbish important or can it be safely ignored? Elvis has to be judged by his achievements and, as they are impressive, this has to be acknowledged. The achievements exist as an explanation of why so many think he is great and are still loyal and curious. The dross reminds us that he was flawed and badly managed and that his career had disastrous elements.

But the many hours of his worthwhile music above tells us only the final achievement. To understand rather than appreciate is important and, as you listen more, you realise that it is a thin dividing line between the two. Those who want to understand and appreciate his talent, feel obliged to also listen to the outtakes that are available on additional box sets and the expanded album collections that are now available on the specialist, 'Follow That Dream' label which has been specifically designed for curious addicts like me. There are also the many bootleg albums devoted to his live concerts.

The box set, 'A Golden Celebration', is informative because it not only has the live performances from the fifties which make it worthwhile but other fine moments such as a home recording of the Doo Wop classic, *'Earth Angel'*. His live version of *'Money Honey'* from 1956 is powerful and defining which is why it is included as a bonus track on the live, seventies selection. An excited and gleeful Charles Laughton, introducing Elvis on the Ed Sullivan Show, is also a delightful surprise. The box sets 'Close Up' and 'Today Tomorrow And Forever' give a revealing perspective on his performances and confirm the vandalism of RCA, Atkins and Parker. And that, and the records that have been mentioned earlier in the book before the lists, is his music or, at least, his music that stayed inside my head. But mere words cannot do it justice. For that you need ears and, probably, tolerance and faith.

MORE LISTS

More lists

1A. Recommended purchases and how to save money

2A. Talented rivals – recommended purchases and how to save money

3A. Recommended viewing

4A. Recommended reading

5A. Important black performers in blues, rhythm and blues and soul

6A. The original contract between Elvis Presley and Thomas Parker.

List 1A - Recommended purchases and how to save money

The last time I looked, the recommended albums/box sets below were available on the internet. The prices vary, so some days you can find a real bargain. The decade box sets have now been re-issued in a reduced format but with the same liner notes and photographs. These can be bought on Amazon for less than £13 each. This is fabulous value and, like the 'Amazing Grace' box set below, the sets are refutations of the theory that the price mechanism efficiently distributes resources.

The fifties box set – 'The King Of Rock 'N' Roll'
The sixties box set – 'From Nashville To Memphis'
The seventies box set – 'Walk A Mile In My Shoes'
The gospel set – 'Amazing Grace' - this includes the two classic albums and the material for the rearranged seventies gospel album in List 12. If that was not enough, it includes an unbelievably good, live version of 'How Great Thou Art'.
The live box set – 'Elvis Live In Las Vegas'
The movies – best of luck but there is or was a decent compilation called 'Elvis In Hollywood'.
The rest are for devotees rather than those who simply aspire to be aficionados. As yet, they are not available on the NHS.
'On Stage Legacy Edition' – it duplicates 'Live In Las Vegas' but, based on his live comeback in 1969, it is a fabulous collection.
'The Deluxe Edition Of 'That's The Way It Is' - contains a classic concert.
'Close Up' box set - contains interesting outtakes.
'Today Tomorrow And Forever' - contains interesting outtakes.
'A Golden Celebration' - live performances from the fifties and private recordings.
'The Million Dollar Quartet' – the famous, informal session with Elvis, Carl Perkins and Jerry Lee Lewis. This is marvellous, not only is the music enthralling but the relaxed setting gives us a glimpse of people from another age.

The 'Follow That Dream' Label does expanded, double CD collections of his albums with outtakes. Recommended as highlights from the Follow That Dream series are the 'Elvis Recorded Live On Stage In Memphis' album and the expanded editions of 'How Great Thou Art' and 'Elvis Is Back'.

The Legacy Editions offer better value than the Follow That Dream label but duplicate what is contained in the box sets above.

The mean spirited or broke who know they will never buy more than three CDs of anyone should buy 'Artist Of The Century' or perhaps the four CD set 'Elvis 75 Good Rockin' Tonight'. Both of these give a good overview but the fifties box set really is the place to start.

List 2A - Talented rivals - Recommended purchases and how to save money

The purpose of this section is to mention important CD collections that can make a difference to a life. It is not an attempt at a discography. These musicians have been covered in depth in other books. Regard the information below as useful hints. The experts can skip this basic information. Some of the CDs below have been deleted by the record companies but they usually can be obtained from the main internet suppliers. Of course, today, music can be downloaded but this often puts the emphasis on individual records rather than performers. Quoting CDs is my way of showing respect.

Ray Charles

Stay away from single and double CD compilations as you should with Elvis because they are inadequate. His original albums can be bought quite cheaply and always contain something of real merit. 'Pure Genius - The Complete Atlantic Recordings (1952-1959)' box set has the most elaborate and charming packaging ever. This eight CD collection is essential for devotees but not entirely successful because the mix of studio and live recordings prevents his music from taking off in the way it should. But, if you have money, it should be bought and organised to suit personal taste. The three CD package, 'The Birth Of Soul', is a cheaper alternative for his Atlantic music. It does not demonstrate, like the complete set, how interesting he was at Atlantic but it is a fabulous monument to his early rhythm and blues. The box set, 'The Genius Of Soul', is a full career perspective. This duplicates some of the Atlantic material and it is far from complete but it offers some obscure gems. A cheaper alternative is 'The Classic Ray Charles' on Castle. These three CDs ignore the Atlantic period and concentrate on his music for ABC. This box set and 'The Birth Of Soul' are much more than an introduction to Ray Charles and these two together for some may be sufficient.

Aretha Franklin

'The Queen Of Soul' collects her best music on Atlantic and is unusual amongst box sets because there is not one weak track. It consists of four CDs and ranges from the seminal to the merely fabulous. It will not be enough for addicts but it can soon be complemented with individual albums quite cheaply. Those who want more than the four CD set should start at the beginning of her career at Atlantic with the sensational 'I Never Loved A Man' album. The 'Amazing Grace' double, gospel album is exceptionally powerful and essential. Spiritually rich, it includes rousing, traditional gospel and remarkable re-inventions of numbers like 'You'll Never Walk Alone' and 'Wholly Holy'. Atlantic has now released cheaply priced, five-album packs of both Aretha and Ray. These are excellent value.

Jerry Lee Lewis

His catalogue is in a mess or it would be if it was not for the obsessive people at Bear Family Records. They have produced three marvellous box sets of his Mercury and Sun recordings. Usually, though, they are very expensive. The two Bear family box sets devoted to his Mercury recordings and the cheaper, Charly, four CD compilation of his time at Sun cover his career until the less interesting, final years. The other CDs are inadequate, single CD compilations that underestimate him dreadfully but they are usually cheap. If you cannot afford the Bear Family and the Charly box sets, you will have to work your way through the individual CD sets at your local HMV. Start with the Sun material but also look out for anything that mentions Smash and Jerry Kennedy.

BB King

He has a four CD box set called 'The King Of The Blues'. A decent collection but, like 'The Genius Of Soul' for Ray Charles, it frustrates because there are too many omissions. Nevertheless, it should be bought. I obtained mine cheaply after the packaging had been damaged by an IRA bomb blast in Manchester. I assume and hope that you will not be able to take advantage of such opportunities in the future. The box set can be complemented quite well with a collection of his early rhythm and blues. These are numerous and can be bought quite inexpensively. ACE records do a better than most collection. This is called 'The Best Of The

Hit Singles 1951 – 1971'. Indeed, the ACE catalogue is a good place to research rhythm and blues and build a collection. His marvellous album, 'Blues And Jazz', has been deleted and I have found it impossible to obtain on CD. This is a tragedy that needs to be amended. Since the first edition has been printed Mike Faherty in Belfast has copied 'Blues and Jazz' on to a CD for me. Many thanks.

Bobby Bland

The essential album is 'Two Steps From The Blues'. All the tracks are impressive but 'Lead Me On' and 'I'll Take Care Of You' are supreme, soul ballads equal to anything by anyone. Elvis bought 'I'll Take Care Of You' for Priscilla, so he must have loved her once. This is the best, soul album ever. There are also two good compilations. 'The Voice' covers the records he made with Joe Scott for Duke Records. This is a superior collection to 'Greatest Hits Volume 1' which also covers the same period. The collection called 'Greatest Hits Volume 2' on MCA covers some of his great performances for the ABC and Malaco labels. Again, there are stand out tracks such as 'I Wouldn't Treat A Dog' and 'As Soon As The Weather Breaks' but this collection is not comprehensive and real fans buy the individual albums on CDs. Often, these can be obtained cheaply. I bought the album, 'Sweet Vibrations', for one penny.

Bobby Womack

No major box sets. At the moment, there are CDs that contain double albums. These can be obtained for under £10 and are good value. There is also a retrospective of the sessions that produced his 'Poet' albums. Despite the title, these were fine albums and the collection called 'The Best Of The Poet Trilogy' makes a marvellous CD. On the back cover, Bobby wears a very cool trilby. For those who do not like to commit beyond one album, the Music Club label, true to its traditions, has issued a praiseworthy, twenty track retrospective called 'The Very Best Of Bobby Womack'. It is not sufficient but can fit into those odd, music collections which usually include a dozen CD summary of soul music. (You know the type.)

Roy Hamilton and Jackie Wilson

There is no need to buy box sets and obtaining the Jackie Wilson box set may actually be difficult. Jackie Wilson has alternative compilations. There is more than one decent double-CD that covers his full career. Any collection that does not contain at least 'Lonely Teardrops' and 'I Get The Sweetest Feeling' is not serious and should not be considered. Roy Hamilton has various compilations. Like Jackie, his career has two different phases, rhythm and blues in the fifties and soul in the sixties. These are not combined in one collection, as they have been with Jackie Wilson, so two purchases are required. They can be made quite cheaply. The best are 'Anthology' and 'Warm Soul'.

Muddy Waters

There are plenty of Muddy Waters CDs available and it is easy to buy a CD that reveals his talent. Chess, some time ago, released a three CD box set that is both comprehensive and a delight. It is simply called 'Muddy Waters'. The packaging is grey and distinctive and the paper looks as if it may have come from a re-cycled package. In his later years, Muddy calmed a little to become a keen gardener, so, perhaps, he would have approved. This is worth the search on Amazon and eBay.

The others

Virtually, all the blues and soul performers mentioned in list 5A have compilations available that are constantly being updated. Without too much difficulty, it is possible to buy for each musician a CD of their music that enables an appreciation of the talent. For great records made by people who had too brief careers, it is necessary to look at mixed collections. 'The Rhythm And Blues Hits' collections from 1948 to 1955 on the Indigo and Castle labels are consistent in their approach despite the alternative labels. I am biased but this is as good as anything in American popular music. This and Elvis is what I would take to the desert island. TV presenter Mark Lamarr and others have also sponsored or created good, CD compilations of black rock and roll which is basically rhythm and blues with more energy.

Unlike rhythm and blues and soul, the marginal figures in the hardcore blues tradition are less likely to create isolated nuggets but there are exceptions. The record by Robert Wilkins, 'No Way To Get Along', ranks with the best by the famous. The three CD selection, 'Country Blues And Hard Hitters', is a good introduction to the blues as a culture and the label is based on Merseyside so, as my grandmother used to say, 'good luck to it.'. For Soul, the single CD, 'Deep Down South', on Charly is highly recommended. This should be complemented by the three CD series, 'Heart Of Southern Soul', which really does focus on the talented but obscure. I could recommend more black music but I am conscious of the threat of bankruptcy and that we all build CDs and playlists in different ways. The famous, soul singers are well known and are still played on the radio. It should be relatively easy to select interesting perfomers. He has not been mentioned before because he is not really a rival to Elvis but Joe Tex is a fabulous singer who constitutes essential listening. In my opinion, gospel music, unlike Doo Wop which has plenty, does not have box sets that adequately define its history. Instead, there are many double CDs that exist as a decent introduction. The Mahalia Jackson CD on Music Club, which contains her best performances on the Apollo label, is packed with memorable records but a full, three CD collection of her Apollo recordings exists on the West Side label and this is well worth the money. Despite the seminal albums of Stevie Wonder and Marvin Gaye, the double CD collections that exist for both of them, capture their strengths. I would still buy the seminal albums, though. Compared to the Jerry Lee Lewis box sets, this is not big money.

It has been a long time since I listened to The Beatles but I do like the Dylan albums 'Blonde On Blonde' and 'Highway 61 Revisited'. Those interested in either Dylan or The Beatles, though, will not need advice from an Elvis fan. The Sons Of The Pioneers are not easily found but, again, the Bear Family in Germany has produced two marvellous box sets. They are expensive but anyone who enjoys the soundtrack to the John Ford classic, 'Wagonmaster', may find a set a worthwhile purchase.

I have avoided country music because I feel that what made Elvis important was the people he moved towards and because black music is where he led me. But country music was a key element in his identity and the ridiculously cheap box sets by Proper Records that collect Western Swing are essential and inspiring. 'Take Me Back To Tulsa', the set by its leading exponent Bob Wills is highly recommended. So are 'Doughnut Cowboys', which highlights his Western Swing rivals, and 'Hillbilly Boogie' which captures the enthusiasm of the boogie-woogie successors.

List 3A - Recommended Viewing

The movies did real damage to Elvis and, in the main, are awful. Any Elvis movie not included in the list below has to be avoided.

Cinema

'That's The Way It Is – Revised edition'.
This documents his Las Vegas performances in August 1970. The original movie was re-edited by Rick Schmidlin. He also re-edited the Orson Welles film noir, 'Touch Of Evil', and restored the silent masterpiece, 'Greed', by Erich Von Stroheim. (What a job!) This edition avoids the cloying interviews with fans that were included in the original, insisted upon by Parker.

'Elvis On Tour'
Elvis is in serious decline but this is a good documentary and it captures a country and a star on the cusp of change.

'Citizen Kane'
The best Orson Welles movie and a good explanation of how people with everything have nothing. Little Richard said, 'Elvis got what he wanted and lost what he had.' The movie, 'Citizen Kane', explains how this happens.

'The Killer Of Sheep'
This low budget movie by C R Burnett is an authentic look at black American, working class culture. It has a fabulous, music soundtrack. The movie avoids romance and is a chilling rebuke to white fantasists whose CD collections help them confuse escapism and heartbreak with fulfilment and who think that racism and oppression somehow help its victims to find self-realisation.

'The Curse Of Frankenstein' and *'The Bride Of Frankenstein'*
Both directed by James Whale, these two films defined the Creature as an inarticulate and lumbering monster for modern audiences. Despite that, they are great movies and are sympathetic to our hero.

'Frankenstein, The Creature'
This TV movie is the version closest to the novel. It is not inspired but, for those who have not read the book, a revelation and it is much superior to the over-excited version by Kenneth Branagh. Interestingly, in this TV version, the Creature is played by an ex-pop star, Luke Goss of Bros. Anyone who has doubts about the thesis that supports this book should watch the movie. Elvis would have been perfect and he could have indulged himself by growing his hair to his shoulders and wearing cloaks with high collars.

TV

'Elvis TV Special'
Thrilling and persuasive, it usually leaves Elvis haters open mouthed.

'Aloha From Hawaii'
Plenty of songs and it has its moments but it does not confirm his talent.

Elvis Movies

'Loving You'
Dodgy soundtrack but good script and the raw 'Mean Woman Blues' makes it essential.

'Jailhouse Rock'
Good piece of punk protest, it is based on a script by a blacklisted writer.

'King Creole'

This is an old-fashioned melodrama but very professional with a thoughtful script.

'Flaming Star'

Decent Western brought to critical acclaim by 'Cahiers Du Cinema' when they discovered Don Siegel was an auteur.

'Viva Las Vegas'

Good fun but very light despite the mature sub-text mentioned later.

'Follow That Dream'

Quite good comedy directed by journeyman, but competent, Gordon Douglas. It benefits from being filmed entirely on location in Florida. This alone makes it unique amongst Elvis movies.

List 4A - Recommended reading

There are thousands of books on Elvis and almost as many on Mary Shelley and Frankenstein. John Stuart Mill said, 'On all great subjects there is always something more to be said.' No doubt, thousands more will be written. The books in the list below are all essential and are recommended.

'The Rough Guide To Elvis' - Paul Simpson.
Easily the best book on Elvis. It captures the breadth of Elvis and the achievements.

'Elvis Presley: A Life In Music The Complete Recording Sessions'
- Ernst Jorgensen.
This has track by track analysis. Not as revealing as hoped but better than anything else about his music and a credit to Ernst.

'All The Kings Men' - Alanna Nash.
Pure narrative, she simply lets three of the Memphis Mafia speak. The story holds together and there is a strong sense of Elvis becoming a darker human whilst serving in the Army.

'The Colonel' - Alanna Nash.
Unimpressed, she exposes the phoney for what he is. It is packed with information and I am indebted to it.

'Baby Let's Play House' - Alanna Nash.
This is the Freudian explanation and a rewarding interpretation. It is remarkable for the candour of the ex-lovers.

'Last Train To Memphis' and 'Careless Love' - Peter Guralnick.
These are essential volumes and both have a smooth and consistent narrative. Although too forgiving of Parker and too critical of Elvis, they are still quite romantic. Peter Guralnick, as always, writes well about the music.

'Mystery Train' - Greil Marcus.

This contains the excellent essay, 'Presliad'. Marcus uses Elvis to explain the contradictions and tensions within American society. He concludes that Elvis is the only performer talented and ambitious enough to contain those contradictions. The book was important because, at the time, it revealed an Elvis fan could have brains.

'Writing For The King, The Stories Of The Songwriters' - Ken Sharp.

In the main text, this is reviewed in detail. It makes a fabulous gift, either to give or suggest.

'Heartbreak Hotel' – Robert Matthew Walker.

This is a revised and expanded edition of an earlier book that reviewed every song. The extra material does not help the book but the author has a professional and impartial ear and his comments on the individual performances are interesting.

'Elvis And The Cinema' - Douglas Brode.

Elvis, the movie auteur, is put under the analytical microscope of structuralism. Apart from his four Westerns, all the films of Elvis are concerned with a young hero who needs to make personal growth and who will ultimately acknowledge the need to respect women and make a commitment. Supreme amongst these is 'Viva Las Vegas' because, in this movie, the woman is an equal rival and the growth required by the hero is more substantial. The subtexts do exist but the movies are still poor which Brode does recognise. He deserves to be praised for acknowledging the connection with the action movies of Howard Hawks. Fabulous and irresistible, a marvellous read.

'Bigger Elvis' - P.K.Kluger.

A fine novel that manages to be both supportive of Elvis and critical of American imperialism. No easy feat.

'Elvis' - Albert Goldman.

Hatchet job but credit should be given to Goldman for what he or his journalists discovered.

'Images And Fancies'- edited by Jac L Thorpe.

A collection of essays from fans and academics. The essay, 'Images of Elvis, the South and America', makes it important.

'Elvis After Elvis' - Gilbert B Rodman.

This attempts to explain the phenomenon amongst fans by deliberately excluding the possibility of Elvis having talent as an explanation. Although I think the talent of Elvis plays a part, the assumption is a valid starting point and it does identify other factors.

'Race, Rock And Elvis' - Michael T Bertrand.

This is more about racial attitudes in the American South. It is worthwhile because it explains how Elvis was part of a generation of Southerners more racially tolerant than those that preceded and followed.

'The Sound Of The City' - Charlie Gillett.

This must be nearly fifty years old but it is an excellent history of Rhythm and Blues and the rock and roll that followed. Now, its assumptions about black and white music appear racist because they stereotype both races but he meant well and the detail is sufficient reward.

'Faking It, The quest for authenticity in popular music'
- Hugh Barker and Yuval Taylor.

The title explains the book which shows how critics became obsessed with narrow definitions of what was acceptable. It has a fine section on Elvis.

'Frankenstein or The Modern Prometheus' - Mary Shelley.

Available in Wordsworth Press, this reprints the revised 1831 version but uses the original preface. Not acceptable to purists but it is cheap. The original version, though, is superior and worth buying as well. Both versions are an essential read for everyone.

'The Last Man' - Mary Shelley.

This is uneven; especially the section devoted to the ambitions of Raymond but it all builds to a fabulous climax. A scene, where a girl is found in an abandoned house, alone, except for a large Newfoundland dog, may interest those who rate 'Blade Runner'. The girl amuses herself with dance and music while she ponders the waiting apocalypse. More important, the moment when the wounded dog lies down to die with Raymond may have inspired 'Old Shep' but, if it did, Red Foley has never given any indication. The best scene, where Adrian halts the two armies from fighting each other and has them soon weeping over those already dead, makes the book essential. It anticipates much Science Fiction that followed, in particular, the books of Armageddon addict, Olaf Stapledon.

'Mary Shelley' - Miranda Seymour.

Well researched, sympathetic and revealing biography. After finishing the book, readers can decide which of the other novels by Shelley should be read. Without being masterpieces, all have merit but they cannot be recommended in the context of Elvis and the Creature. There is a complete Kindle edition of the work of Mary Shelley available from Amazon. The last time I looked, it was under £2. The novella, 'Mathilda', is poignant and has historical importance.

'Frankenstein's Monster' - Susan Heybour O'Keefe.

Audacious and daring sequel to the original novel. It makes an assumption about the ship captain, Robert Walton, that is dubious and the title is at odds with the novel but it is a compelling read and highly recommended. More important than any of this, there were moments it dried my throat. The less inhibited will cry.

'Tender Is The Night' – F. Scott Fitzgerald.

The best novel on how the price of compromise is only properly understood after the event. It shows how the fading power of talent turns sour the lives of the gifted.

———————

List 5A - Important black performers in blues, rhythm and blues and soul

This list ignores the rich tradition of jazz for two reasons. The list would go on forever and those musicians are a stage too far removed from Elvis to be relevant although Duke Ellington and Louis Armstrong by themselves would give this list another dimension. These people below all made music while Elvis was alive and it is music that Elvis experienced. They made the music that Elvis moved towards. If he never rejected white music, he did retreat from it into something that acknowledged those listed. 'I am not straight country. I always dug the blues,' he said in Houston in 1970.

These musicians are evidence of the richness and superiority of black music in popular culture. His music could not have embraced all the music that was made by the people below. He was obliged to acknowledge some of these people and also many elements not present within this rich tradition. The list is restricted to those I like and regard as significant. Arthur 'Big Boy' Crudup is the exception. I am not a fan but his influence on Elvis has to be acknowledged. Despite being marvellous, Doo Wop is ignored. Few of the groups exceeded their sporadic hits. Apart from the very well known, the names below also exclude gospel music. Although connected to rock and roll, it exists as a specialist strand. Even without all that, these numbers indicate why it is pointless to debate Elvis as an icon in opposition to them. He exists alone and they are numerous. Black American music had all this below and more. Elvis is still great and this becomes apparent when he is compared with other individuals. This is not an attempt to define black American music. The list below merely highlights a fundamental source of popular culture. There are also many people not included who had brief careers before they returned to normal work. The obscure do not always merit full CDs but, despite having limited opportunities, they managed the occasional nugget. It takes usually no longer than a lifetime to know the people below, locate the obscure, discover gospel and Doo Woop and appreciate the jazz giants.

Johnny Adams
LaVern Baker
Chuck Berry
Bobby Bland
Blind Boys Of Alabama
Big Bill Broonzy
Charles Brown
Clarence Gatemouth Brown
James Brown
Maxine Brown
Solomon Burke
Jerry Butler
Wynona Carr
Clarence Carter
Ray Charles
Otis Clay
Willie Clayton
The Clovers
The Coasters
Sam Cooke
Arthur 'Big Boy' Crudup
Tyrone Davis
Bo Diddley
Dixie Hummingbirds
Fats Domino
Aretha Franklin
Marvin Gaye
Al Green
Roy Hamilton
Slim Harpo
John Lee Hooker
Lightning Hopkins
Ivory Joe Hunter
Elmore James
Etta James

Mahalia Jackson
Little Willie John
Lonnie Johnson
Robert Johnson
Louis Jordan
Albert King
BB King
Denise La Salle
Leadbelly
Professor Longhair
Bobby McClure
Clyde McPhatter
Blind Willie McTell
Willie Mabon
Curtis Mayfield
Percy Mayfield
Amos Milburn
Little Milton
McKinley Mitchell
Willie Mitchell
Jelly Roll Morton
The Neville Brothers
Charlie Patton
Ann Peebles
Otis Redding
Little Richard
Fenton Robinson
Smokey Robinson
David Ruffin
Otis Rush
Nina Simone
Memphis Slim
The Staple Singers
Candi Staton
Booker T
Johnny Taylor

Joe Tex

Sister Rosetta Tharpe

Irma Thomas

Big Joe Turner

Ike Turner (without Tina)

Junior Walker

T Bone Walker

Little Walter

Muddy Waters

Johnny Guitar Watson

Larry Williams

Sonny Boy Williamson

Chuck Willis

Jackie Wilson

Howling Wolf

Bobby Womack

Stevie Wonder

O V Wright

———————

List 6A - The original contract between Parker and Elvis

AGREEMENT

SPECIAL AGREEMENT between Elvis Presley, known as artist, his guardians, Mr and/or Mrs Presley, and his manager, Mr BOB NEAL, of Memphis Tennessee, hereinafter referred to as the party of the First Part, and COL. Thomas A. PARKER and/or HANK SNOW ATTRACTIONS of Madison, Tennessee, hereinafter known as the Party of the Second part, this date, August 15, 1955.

COL. PARKER is to act as special advisor to ELVIS PRESLEY and BOB NEAL for the period of one year and two one-year options for the sum of two thousand, five hundred dollars ($2,500) per year, payable in five instalments of five hundred dollars ($500) each, to negotiate and assist in any way possible the build-up of ELVIS PRESLEY as an artist. Col Parker will be reimbursed for any out of pocket expenses for travelling, promotion, advertising as approved by ELVIS PRESLEY and his manager.

As a special concession to Col Parker, ELVIS PRESLEY is to play 100 personal appearances within one year for the special sum of $200.00 (Two hundred dollars) including his musicians.

In the event that negotiations come to a complete standstill and ELVIS PRESLEY and his manager and associates decide to freelance, it is understood that Col. Parker will be reimbursed for the time and expenses involved in trying to negotiate the association of these parties and that he will have first call on a number of cities, as follows, at the special rate of one hundred, seventy five dollars ($175.00) per day for the first appearance and two hundred, fifty dollars ($250.00) for the second appearance and three hundred, fifty dollars ($350.00). San Antonio, El Paso, Phoenix, Tuscon (sic), Albuquerque, Oklahoma City, Denver, Wichita Falls, Wichita, New Orleans, Mobile, Jacksonville, Pensacola, Tampa, Miami, Orlando, Charleston, Greenville, Spartanburg, Asheville, Knoxville, Roanoke, Richmond, Norfolk, Washington D.C., Philadelphia, Newark, New York, Pittsburg (sic), Chicago, Omaha, Milwaukee, Minneapolis, St Paul, Des Moines, Los Angeles, Amarilla (sic), Lubbock, Houston, Galveston, Corpus Christi, Las Vegas, Reno, Cleveland, Dayton, Akron, and Columbus.

Col. Parker is to negotiate all renewals on existing contracts.

Acknowledgements - revised

Special thanks to Angela for the support, advice, corrections and proof reading of the various drafts. Also, thanks to Amy and Barbara for wading through a very inadequate first draft. If mistakes, errors of opinion or unsubstantiated judgements exist in the text, they are, though, my responsibility. Any reader who identifies an error can notify the website. I will acknowledge their help in future editions. Thanks to Les Moorcroft for spotting a couple of typos in the first edition and thanks to John 'Mr Memory Man' Raftery who spotted a couple of typos and a couple of factual errors. I remembered Channel 4 being launched earlier than it happened. I also made a mistake regarding the age of Michael Jackson when he died. The patience of family and friends is always much appreciated. This book has recently dominated gatherings probably more than it should have and Elvis has featured in conversations for even longer. Indeed, as my father said, when Elvis died. 'Our Howard is a big fan. Elvis was part of the family.'

My daughter, Amy Jackson, designed the website mentioned on the back cover, www.howard-jackson.net. Amy also illustrates the weekly blog, The Elvis Presley Challenge. I am extremely grateful for her efforts and am fortunate she is blessed with stamina.

Robin Castle designed the cover and I appreciate very much both the cover and his fine art work inside the book. Chris Payne at Anchorprint has been anything but a pain and he offered encouragement from the beginning.

Paul Simpson, author of 'The Rough Guide To Elvis' spotted a major error about the song 'Could I Fall In Love' and the reference to Malcolm Dodd. This has been corrected. He also suggested that Roy Orbison be included in the section on talented rivals. I am too much of an admirer of his classic 'The Rough Guide To Elvis' to resist. This has been done.

As was said at the opening of this book, this is not a work of journalism. The views and opinions needed facts to support them. These are only available because of others. Usually, I have sourced any facts or quotes within the main text but, sometimes, for the sake of the narrative, I have cheated. The book is, as I hope the main text makes clear, heavily dependent on the investigative work and impressive tomes of Alanna Nash, Peter Guralnick, Ernst Jorgenson and Elaine Dundy. Their information has been complemented with my own memories and internet enquiries. Although I have challenged Nash and Guralnick on certain opinions, I, like others, value their work highly and regard their books as indispensable. They are mentioned in the previous lists but they require a special tribute. Their efforts and achievements are mind boggling and an inspiration.

The quotes within apostrophes that are not referenced to anyone belong to Mary Shelley.

Index

Song, book and movie titles are italicised. Titles that begin with T are indexed under T. eg The Fastest Guitar Alive. Groups that have 'the' in the title are indexed under the name with 'the' after the name. eg Beatles, The. From the lists, the descriptive text is indexed. Items in the actual lists, eg song titles in the classic albums, are not indexed.